MARRIAGE, FAMILY AND THE CHURCH

MARRIAGE, FAMILY AND THE CHURCH

A Boat with New Nets

Pia Matthews

Foreword by Bishop Peter Doyle

Gracewing

First published in England in 2022
by
Gracewing
2 Southern Avenue
Leominster
Herefordshire HR6 0QF
United Kingdom
www.gracewing.co.uk

No part of this publication may be reproduced, stored in a retrieval system, or transmitted in any form or by any means, electronic, mechanical, photocopying, recording or otherwise, without the written permission of the publisher.

The right of Pia Matthews to be identified as the author of this work has been asserted in accordance with the Copyright, Designs and Patents Act 1988.

© 2022 Pia Matthews

ISBN 978 085244 947 5

Typeset by Gracewing

Cover design by Bernardita Peña Hurtado
Cover image: Jacob Jordaens, *The Holy Family with Various Persons and Animals in a Boat* (1652)

CONTENTS

CONTENTS..v

ACKNOWLEDGEMENTS...xi

FOREWORD..xiii

PREFACE...xv

1 A BOAT WITH NEW NETS.....................................1
    Saving marriage: why a theology of marriage matters ...4
    Beginning at the beginning..................................10

2 IN SCRIPTURE AND ANCIENT TIMES..................21
    Marriage in God's plan..22
    Marriage process in the ancient Near East............26
    Marriage process in the Old Testament...............28
    The Old Testament: blessing and covenant..........33
    Love in marriage...36
    The goods of marriage..37
    Marriage and friendship......................................38
    So, from the beginning..39
    Jesus: developments from the Old Testament and later rabbinical debate..40
    Celibacy..46
    Was Jesus married?...47
    Jesus on family life..49
    Jesus 'the bridegroom' and the wedding feasts......51
    So, from Jesus..55
    To St Paul 55

St Paul and the Corinthians..56
St Paul, household codes, the Colossians and the Ephesians..62
Marriage in the ancient Greek world...............................65
Marriage in the ancient Roman world.............................67
Summary...70

3 'IN THE WORLD' WITH THE CHURCH FATHERS........83
Christians in the world..84
Responding to the culture of the time.............................87
The rise of Manichaeism..94
Marriage and celibacy...96
Jovinian and Jerome..102
Responding to Jerome...104
St Augustine: On the Excellence of Marriage and On Holy Virginity...107
Roman Law to the Theodosian Code.............................113
The domestic church..115
Summary..117

4 MARRIAGE RULES: AFTER THE EARLY CHURCH FATHERS TO THE COUNCIL OF TRENT...................125
Marriage and a rule book?..126
Cultural practices..130
Questions to the popes..132
Grace and the path to holiness......................................135
St Aelred: marriage as spiritual friendship 139
What makes marriage?..141
Marriage: a sacrament..144
St Thomas Aquinas: happiness, virtues and the passions.....149
Theological method: changes and challenges...............153

| Contents | vii |

    Martin Luther and the Council of Trent..................156
    Summary..................160

5 POST TRENT TO THE 1917 CODE OF CANON LAW...171
    Catechism and practical spirituality..................173
    Developments in the Natural Law tradition..................178
    Developments in moral theology..................188
    State and Church tensions..................193
    Modernity and Pope Leo XIII..................195
    Canon Law..................197
    Summary..................199

6 GETTING PERSONAL IN THE TWENTIETH CENTURY...205
    The eugenic context..................207
    Casti connubii..................210
    Contract to personalism?..................218
    The contributions of Dietrich von Hildebrand and Herbert Doms..................221
    Holy Office statement of 1944..................225
    Marriage and scientific progress..................227
    The Second Vatican Council..................231
    Pope St Paul VI: marriage and reserved business..........237
    Covenant to the Code of Canon Law 1983..................241
    Summary..................244

7 GETTING TOGETHER: THE 1980 SYNOD AND FAMILIARIS CONSORTIO..................251
    Synods and synodality..................251
    1980 Fifth General Synod of Bishops: the role of the Christian family in today's world..................254
    Familiaris Consortio: On the role of the Christian family in the modern world..................257

And called to holiness...275
Summary...276

8 THEOLOGY OF THE BODY.................................283
Introduction to the Theology of the Body...................285
Identifying the main problems...................................287
Ephesians 5 and Redemption 290
From the beginning..291
Redemption..298
The sacramentality of marriage.................................303
Language of the Body...308
Reflections on *Humanae vitae*.................................312
The Family as Domestic Church?..............................317
Summary...321

9 LIVING THE LARGER LIFE OF THE GOSPEL...........329
Heart speaks to heart...329
Mercy, truth and justice...331
God does not command the impossible? 333
Development of tradition and redefining marriage?....336
Conscience..341
Divorce and attempted remarriage 343
Eastern Orthodox tradition of *oikonomia* and *epikeia*...348
Ratzinger's response..353
Kasper and Ratzinger: On the Church.......................356
Pope Benedict XVI...358
Pope Francis: evangelization and the family.............361
Leading up to Amoris Laetitia...................................364

10 *AMORIS LAETITIA* AND 'DANCING TOWARDS THE FUTURE WITH IMMENSE HOPE'. 373

Contents

A synod experience..374
Amoris Laetitia, The Joy of Love.........................378
And the aftermath...423
Summary...425

11 CONCLUDING REFLECTIONS..................................431

BIBLIOGRAPHY...439

INDEX..443

ACKNOWLEDGEMENTS

I HAVE MANY FRIENDS, both married and not, to thank. To Elizabeth for her constant prayers, Sayuri and Barbara for their Friday friendship. Sarah, Gloria, Sandra and Liz, the 'book group' who put up with me rarely reading the chosen books (to be fair, I do not expect them to read my books) but who share their wit and wisdom on the eccentricities of family life. To Chris and Nick, Sarah and Michael, companions on the way as we have watched our families grow up together; and Sarah and Michael with whom we shared many a family celebration and who also now rejoice in grandchildren shepherding. To Trevor, and Matt, Ashley and the academic family at St Mary's University Twickenham, who help to keep theory and practice together. To the seminary family at Wonersh, and now at Allen Hall, whose depth of friendship I cherish, never mind the seminarians who have had patiently to endure my lectures.

Special thanks to Bishop Peter for his kind words, and to Father Paul at Gracewing for his insightful comments, tactful contributions, and advice.

Of course, this would not be complete without thanks to our children Antony, Tia, Peter, Clare, Paula, Stephen, Richard and Joe. Each in their own way have helped to bring us up as parents and I hope they rate this as a successful enterprise, at least so far. Some of them have introduced new people to our growing family, Frances, Dave, Claire, Christina. Some of them now bring their own little families and we are blessed to see our children's children: Lydia, Dominic, Sebastian, Isla, Elliot and Samuel, not forgetting Agnes who is already in the arms of Jesus. And George, what to say.

Ironically, for the title of the book, I get seasick, I do not care for boats, no underlying message here—and the book talks about no marriage in heaven. Thank you for tender care, fierce friendship, love like good wine, and being together in Christmas, Gethsemane, and Resurrection moments.

Pia
Christmas 2021

FOREWORD

I AM DELIGHTED TO commend this book on marriage and the family by Dr Pia Matthews. Both of us had the privilege of taking part in the Synod on the vocation and mission of the family in the Church and in the contemporary world convoked by Pope Francis in October 2015. Docile to what the Holy Spirit asks us, the Synod tried to be close to today's families in their diversity. Knowing that 'Christ, the new Adam (…) fully reveals a person to him/herself' (*Gaudium et Spes*, 22), we were sensitive to the many challenges which impact on people today, in their emotional life and life as a family. The Church is called to discern the signs of the times, interpreting them in the light of the Gospel. Thus, in language intelligible to each generation, she can respond to the perennial questions which people ask about this present life and the life to come, and about the relationship of the one to the other. Following the Synod, Pope Francis produced his Apostolic Exhortation, *Amoris Laetitia*, on the joy of marriage, which is the subject of the final chapter of this book.

Pia Matthews has traced a detailed picture of the ongoing tradition of the Church in the East and the West in regard to marriage and the family, and this comprehensive body of knowledge will surely be a ready guide for students and for those engaged in pastoral ministry in support of marriage. This text takes into account recent developments in a desire to represent the Church as a field hospital serving Christ, the Divine Physician, who came to call 'not the virtuous but sinners to repentance' (Luke 5:32).

I wish this book the success which it deserves, enriching marriage and the family in today's world.

☩ Peter Doyle
Bishop Emeritus of Northampton
10 December 2021, Our Lady of Loreto

PREFACE

In 2015 I was appointed an expert to the synod on the family by Pope Francis. This gave me the opportunity to participate in a significant event in the story of marriage and the family. The synod brought together clergy and lay people from around the world, all with the common aim of engaging in deeper reflection on marriage and family in the Church. The experience of the synod highlighted the universal nature of the Church, the importance of listening, of dialogue, of responding both with humility and with *parrhesia*. *Parrhesia*, a term favoured by Pope Francis, carries the sense of speaking candidly, with an open heart and mind. It calls for direct and honest speech rather than speech coloured by rhetoric. Rather than seeking to convince or persuade by argument, *parrhesia* encourages the person to say what they truly think and believe.[1] Pope Francis calls *parrhesia* a 'gift of the Holy Spirit' that gives people courage to preach the truth with consistency.[2] For Pope Francis *parrhesia*, and listening 'with humility and welcome, and with an open heart' are the marks of synodality.[3]

As part of the synod process each participant was assigned to a small discussion group. At the first session of my group, I made space for an elderly cleric who had arrived at the last moment. He introduced himself as Father Nicolás. Although originally from Spain, Father Nicolás spoke impeccable English. He and I spoke about his love of Asia, especially of Japan where he had spent much of his ministry, my coming to the synod as an expert, and he noted with approval that I was married. Father Nicolás further observed that we needed an account of the history of marriage and the family. At a later stage I discovered that my new acquaintance was the then head of the Jesuits worldwide, Father Adolfo Nicolás Pachón, the 'Black Pope'. Later still in an interview Father Nicolás reiterated the need for an historical account of marriage. On Church teaching on marriage in general, he added that if we make mistakes, and we will, then we should make them on the side of mercy rather than law.[4]

The year 2021 saw the fifth anniversary of Pope Francis's exhortation on the joy of marriage and the family, *Amoris Laetitia*, the fruit of the 2015 synod. At the end of 2020, a year when the whole world was ravaged by the scourge of Covid–19, Pope Francis announced a 'year of reflection' on *Amoris Laetitia* from 19 March 2021, the date of the promulgation of the exhortation, until 22 June 2022.[5] This was not to detract from the effects of the pandemic, rather it was to emphasize the importance of marriage and the family for society and the Church. Notably the pandemic has had huge ramifications for families and family life, and it has highlighted the significance of the family for building up community ties. For Pope Francis what is needed now, more than ever, is that 'families throughout the world be increasingly fascinated by the evangelical ideal of the Holy Family, so as to become leaven of a new humanity and of a concrete and universal solidarity.'[6]

This book is an attempt to trace the story of marriage, the family and the Church with a focus specifically on the leaven. It is a putting out into the deep waters of the history of marriage, acknowledging at the same time that only God has the complete story and the last word.

Notes

[1] See M. Foucault, *Discourse and Truth and Parrēsia* [1983] (Chicago: University of Chicago Press, 2019).
[2] Pope Francis, *Homily* (18 April 2020).
[3] Pope Francis, *To the Synod Fathers during the First General Congregation of the Third Extraordinary General Assembly of the Synod of Bishops* (6 October 2014).
[4] Interview with Father Adolfo Nicholás Pachón (15 October 2015).
[5] Pope Francis, *Angelus* (27 December 2020).
[6] *Ibid*.

1 A BOAT WITH NEW NETS

When Jesus calls St Peter to follow him, Jesus says that he will make St Peter 'a fisher of men.'[1] As Pope Francis points out, 'for this reason a new type of net is needed.' According to Pope Francis, 'today families are one of the most important nets for the mission of Peter and of the Church.' He adds:

> this is not a net that takes one prisoner! On the contrary, it frees people from the cruel waters of abandonment and indifference, which drown many human beings in the sea of loneliness and indifference. Families know well the feeling of dignity conferred by being sons and daughters and not slaves, nor strangers, not just a number on an identity card.[2]

Both Pope St John Paul II and Pope Francis have used the image of fishing with nets that is relevant for marriage. For Pope St John Paul, 'putting out into the deep' is about taking a risk. It is asking us to pray and discern our vocation, especially in an era that favours non-commitment. It is about trust in Jesus even in moments of apparent failure, 'when tireless effort seems useless.' In opening our hearts to Jesus, we can come to understand our own particular vocation, we grow in holiness, and we become 'increasingly capable of loving in the way that Christ loved.'[3] We become more able to persevere, and able to put ourselves at the service of evangelization, to bring the news of God's love to others.[4] For Pope St John Paul 'put out into the deep' invites us 'to remember the past with gratitude, to live the present with enthusiasm and to look forward to the future with confidence.'[5]

The story of marriage, the family and the Church is bound up in vocation, holiness, evangelization and love. Of course, the

Church is concerned with each and every person as individuals. This is one reason why marriage is seen as a vocation to not only personal fulfilment but also holiness. After all, in the gospel accounts Jesus calls his disciples by name. In St John's account of the call of Simon Peter, Simon's brother St Andrew tells his brother 'we have found the Messiah.' When St Andrew brings his brother to Jesus, Jesus looks hard at him, and gives him the name 'Cephas, Rock.'[6] St Peter's initial reaction may have been to protest that he is undeserving. Nevertheless, as the gospels of Matthew, Mark and Luke demonstrate, calling to discipleship is a calling to mission, even for people who are afraid or are overwhelmed by their unworthiness.[7]

In the unfolding story of marriage and the family, in every chapter of this book, we shall see that the Church has always seen marriage as a 'net for the mission': in the early years of Christianity both St Peter and St Paul observe that a Christian spouse can help in the sanctification of the unbelieving spouse.[8] Whole households are baptized.[9] For the early Church father St John Chrysostom, the family is a 'little church' where its members grow in holiness.[10] Parents care for their own little flock as the bishop cares for his,[11] and the fruit of marriage is 'fellow citizens with the saints' for the worship of God.[12] Married people are called to be 'leaven' in their households and in the world.[13]

In the twelfth century St Aelred Abbot of Rievaulx says 'like a boat is marriage contracted in faith in Jesus Christ. But this boat is flimsy and rickety and ships great quantities of water in its hold; and unless it is bailed out all the time it quickly sinks.'[14] As both Pope St John Paul and Pope Francis found as they reflected on the role, vocation and mission of the family, marriage and the family have their 'bright spots and shadows.'[15] Couples and families need accompaniment and evangelization so that they can be 'leaven' in the world.[16] When Pope Francis speaks of 'a new type of net' he may also be thinking of a new net for the Church, a new evangelization. Due to a variety of reasons the number of couples marrying in the Catholic Church has decreased. Younger couples may be at a stage when they are already distanced from the Church or are reviewing their relationship with the faith in which they were brought up. In other cases, people may simply not be active in the Church or one of the couple may have already been married and not have received a decree of nullity. Some people fear commitment because they fear failure. Some people think that the only measure is their own account of their situation and so resist Church teaching. Some people do not think that a sacramental marriage makes any difference to their relationship.

Intriguingly, the idea that a stable family relationship does not need the Church or that Church teaching is not relevant to a life in Christ in a way parallels the idea that many people have not lost a sense of God or faith in Jesus, but they have lost faith in the Church. However, as Pope St John Paul points out,

> it is necessary to keep these two truths together, namely, the real possibility of salvation in Christ for all mankind and the necessity of the Church for salvation. Both these truths help us to understand the *one mystery of salvation*, so that we can come to know God's mercy and our own responsibility. Salvation, which always remains a gift of the Holy Spirit, requires man's co-operation both to save himself and to save others. This is God's will, and this is why he established the Church and made her a part of his plan of salvation.[17]

For Pope St John Paul 'the kingdom cannot be detached either from Christ or from the Church': we cannot be 'silent about Christ' nor can we undervalue the Church which has a God-given 'specific and necessary role.' Pope St John Paul explains that 'the kingdom demands the promotion of human values' and this promotion is 'at the heart of the Church', but at the same time this must not be detached from other fundamental tasks, such as 'proclaiming Christ and his Gospel, and establishing and building up communities which make present and active within mankind the living image of the kingdom.'[18] The idea that family life does not need the church ignores the close link between marriage of husband and wife and Christ and the Church, a link that is not new: we find it in St Paul's letter to the Ephesians, and it is one of the foundations for marriage as a sacrament. This has always been the delicate balance in the natural good of marriage and personal relationships and marriage in the Church. In the story of marriage and the family, evangelists, church fathers, theologians, popes, canon lawyers, lay writers, priests, married people and families, all the faithful, have the task of promoting the great good of marriage in the kingdom here and now, and in its journey towards the eschatological kingdom. All of this is accomplished under the direction of the Holy Spirit who makes the whole Church missionary.[19] There are difficulties, not least lack of fervour, indifference, and above all lack of joy and hope.[20] But if it is God's work it will not be in vain.[21]

Both Pope St John Paul and Pope Francis think that if people have the right conditions they can grow in faith: as a young priest Pope St John Paul gathered informal small groups of young people to learn together and to be together. He called the group *środowisko*, a growing environment; Pope Francis is well known for encouraging accompanying, walking with people. In all situations Francis begins from the fact that God 'scatters the seeds of his presence in our world, for 'love consists in this, not that we have loved God but that *he loved us* first.'[22]

Saving marriage: why a theology of marriage matters

What difference does Jesus make? This question may seem an unusual starting point for a book on marriage and the family. But in fact, it is *the* question to ask. If we do not begin with Jesus, follow Jesus, and end with Jesus, the story of marriage and family life risks being simply a chronological account of contrasting theological trends or a sociological analysis through time. In the Christian account of marriage and family life theologians who were saturated in their faith in Jesus try and make sense of marriage and family life precisely informed by their theological context. The Christian understanding of marriage is bigger than an account of the partnership of two people through the ages. Marriage matters because it says something significant about us as human beings, about us as Christians in the world, and about us in relationship with God and his Church.

One of the interesting things about marriage is that, despite all the difficulties that surround it, it is a recognizable good in itself. The good of marriage is raised to the dignity of a sacrament by Christ. The fathers of the Second Vatican Council say much the same thing about the human person: human beings are capable of the best and the worst, and that is why we are beset by 'doubt and anxiety'. Each human being is made in the image of God, but we are not meant to be solitary creatures. We are meant for communion. Yet, our relationships with ourselves, others and the world are disrupted, we often refuse to acknowledge our dependence on God, and we find ourselves 'split' within.[23] Jesus came to heal this great split. Jesus reveals the mystery of the Father's steadfast love and in doing so reveals human beings to themselves: beings called to love. Just as Jesus shines a light on the mystery of what it is to be human,[24] so too does belief in Jesus and his Church shine a light on marriage. In order to show that Jesus was truly man as well as truly God the early church fathers had a saying: 'what is not assumed is not healed'.[25] Jesus loves 'with a human heart',[26] Jesus has healed and redeemed human love.

Living by the heart makes you vulnerable. Scripture recognizes this, because Jesus

> who, being in the form of God, did not count equality with God something to be grasped. But he emptied himself, taking the form of a slave, becoming as human beings are; and being in every way like a human being, he was humbler yet, even to accepting death, death on a cross.[27]

Love is a gift of the self, a gift that risks rejection. St Paul asks us all to look to the good of the other rather than our own good, and to make our own 'the mind of Christ Jesus.'[28] The thread running throughout the Church's teaching on marriage holds that love between two people involves vulnerability on many different levels. Perhaps it is helpful to note three particular areas of vulnerability. First, in early centuries women were especially vulnerable to abuse, neglect and powerlessness, and so one of the earliest Church pronouncements to husbands was 'love your wives.'[29] This love is a deep and faithful love, like the love Christ has for the Church, the love Christ demands from his disciples, 'love one another as I have loved you.'[30] Moreover, to give greater protection the Church came to emphasize that consent makes marriage, and that marriage must be publicly witnessed so that no one could break a promise or simply abandon another.

However, a second level of vulnerability is one that comes out of the very nature of love itself. Love is allowing the self to be open to another, to entrust oneself to another. Church teaching from the earliest fathers onwards understands that love and marriage was a part of God's plan from the beginning. Love is a natural desire that God has implanted in human beings. The naturalness of this union is a great good that goes back to Genesis and it is shown in the way husband and wife walk together, looking in the same direction.[31] But as a result of the Fall human beings still have a tendency to love, yet a love tinged with all the spiritual sins of pride, dominance, lust, greed—the kind of sins that do not put the beloved person first. In terms of married love perhaps, we no longer look in the same direction but look only to our own individual pleasure and this makes the beloved vulnerable to another's dominance or selfishness. As St Augustine points out, no life is free from passing and trivial sins. However, he also says that everyday prayer, especially reciting the Our Father blots out these daily, everyday sins.[32] Forgiveness is always available. Unlike sins of the spirit like malice and pride, God is perhaps more ready to forgive sins of love because they come from God given desires and passion,[33] and for St Augustine everything comes back to love. The standard of love is that of proper love of God and neighbour under the grace of the Spirit.[34]

This standard leads to the third vulnerability: certainly, the power of human love is a path to love of God. However human love is so great that there is a tendency to substitute this for love of God. God should be the centre of the life of every Christian. Yet a mistaken understanding of human love may set up this love in competition and the other person becomes the centre of my life. In response the Church reminds married people through the complementary gift of celibacy that our true home and our fulfilment are not here on earth. The call to holiness permeates throughout Church teaching. And married people are called to holiness through marriage. As Pope St John Paul II explains:

> true holiness does not mean a flight from the world; rather, it lies in the effort to incarnate the Gospel in everyday life, in the family, at school and at work, and in social and political involvement. Holiness is the fulness of life which Christ offers: he has come that we "may have life, and have it abundantly".[35]

Indeed, seeing the family as a 'domestic church' is a reminder that holiness is in everyday living. The 'root reason' for human dignity lies in our call to holiness, a 'call to communion with God.'[36] A hope related to the end of time does not diminish the importance of what we are called to do here and now. In fact, this hope gives special motivation.[37] And this raises the issue of being in the world.

Christianity has made a distinction between the things that are Caesar's and the things that are God's. The history of marriage follows the history of the Church's engagement with the world: being in the world though not of the world, having a revealed tradition, having insights that the world needs, but also being at times a sign of contradiction. There are things that are revealed such as moral rules, but this does not make philosophical reasoning superfluous. Recognizing "being in the world", in this book in each chapter the civil development is placed alongside the theological. However, in Mark 12:13-17 when Jesus is asked whether it is permissible to pay taxes to Caesar, the figure head of the Roman occupation, Jesus points to the coin, the denarius, with which the tax was paid. His reply is highly significant: the coin bears the image of Caesar, and Jesus says, 'Give back to Caesar what belongs to Caesar—and to God what belongs to God.' Human beings bear the image of God, so anything that concerns human beings concerns God. And that includes marriage.

Thinking about marriage involves thinking about what is good, our values, the part marriage plays in society and bringing up the next generation, what we should and should not do, and so marriage falls under the umbrella of moral theology and moral philosophy. It is important to note the development in moral theology as this has an impact on thinking about marriage. Different theological and philosophical developments explain why there are particular definitions of marriage and indeed why some people say that marriage can or cannot be redefined, why some think it is a public or a purely private matter, whether it is simply contractual between the two parties, and why marriage matters in the first place. The blessings and goods of marriage slowly unfold with the development of theology. These goods have always been there, they are not simply responses to the times. Certainly, in different eras the focus may fall on one good rather than another, but this does not mean that the other goods were abandoned. Nor is development of the tradition like getting more and more pieces of a jigsaw. Rather it indicates the unfolding of theology. As Pope Benedict XVI explained referring to the beginnings of the Second Vatican Council in 1962, doctrine is not frozen in time but we accept 'the faith professed over the centuries, and cannot sever the roots from which the tree draws its life.'[38] We begin from Jesus, but we see in the tradition different emphases at different times, and this is to be expected since the tradition is "incarnate", and we are in the world. Being in the world but not of it is not a question of a turf war, who has authority over marriage—Church or state. Rather it is a question of being Christian in the world, especially being a married Christian. And pastoral concern for married Christians is not simply about personal growth in holiness or even growth together as a family. It is also about being leaven in the world.

People live complicated lives. Lives are undoubtedly both enriched and frequently enraged by other people. Relationships, marriage, family are complex because people are complex. For many people, the thought of marriage actually makes things more complicated, especially the notion that marriage is for life. Moreover, marriage takes two to make it work, it does not simply depend on the virtuous behaviour or conversion of just one person. Having said that, as Pope Francis shows in *Amoris Laetitia*, and as many theologians in this book point out, loving kindness goes a long way to help change in the other person. And with grace anything is possible. This book looks at marriage from a Catholic perspective in order to explore why the theology of marriage and family matters. Certainly the Catholic perspective carries with it some assumptions: that marriage is a part of God's plan for human beings; that all marriages, natural and sacramental, share in this divine plan; that the great good of marriage holds the goods of faithfulness, children and indissolubility as integral to marriage itself; that our final goal is not simply an earthly reality however wonderful that reality may seem. Nevertheless, some of the reflections from a Catholic perspective also have relevance to other perspectives and can be understood in other traditions.

In Christian thinking, and in Catholicism in particular, marriage is a sacrament. Christ acts through the sacraments and communicates his grace. The sacraments therefore continue his saving work. The words of blessing in the sacrament are life-giving and the blessings given to the couple enable them to glorify God by their lives. One of the special blessings given to a woman and man is the gift of children. As the family responds to these great blessings in thanksgiving to God, so too does the Church offer back to God these blessings so that they will give glory to God. Marriage is a real sign of the power of the Holy Spirit, a tangible making present of the Paschal mystery of Christ that draws everything towards life. Moreover, as Jesus himself says, marriage is a foretaste of that heavenly wedding feast when we reach our proper home with God.[39] Marriage then is about salvation.

It is precisely because marriage is a saving sacrament that we need to think about saving marriage. Marriage and the family matter because they are particular gifts from God that enable people to grow in holiness. People start off good and they grow in holiness: it is an ongoing process, and however difficult are the beginnings or the circumstances, however messy life seems to be, there is no need to give up hope. Although we cooperate, holiness is God's work so it will not be in vain. Going beyond the members of the family, marriage and family matter because they witness to some crucial human truths. We all need other people to help us grow as persons. We all need places of belonging and places of forgiveness. Society needs good models of care, and families who care for each other, especially where they welcome children with disabilities and frail elderly people, can be essential witnesses to a hospitality that is about affirming the dignity of every human being however weak or small. And marriage is evangelization in action because living out married life tells us something about love, and the steadfast merciful love of God who is love.

Beginning at the beginning

Every sacrament begins from the saving work of Jesus Christ. The sacrament of marriage too begins with Christ. However, Christ points backwards to the Old Testament and forwards to the end times. We begin the story of marriage in Chapter 2 by questioning the suggestion that Jesus had a negative attitude to marriage, or at best was indifferent. In fact, we go on to see that Jesus often talks about marriage and family life, not least in the way in which he associates love in families with the love of God for his children, and his attitude reflects the Old Testament vision of marriage and family life where marriage is a blessing and part of God's plan for humanity. Ancient creation myth is set alongside God's creation to show that God's creation of man and woman as sexual beings called to communion is a personal and covenantal creation. Marriage traditions in scripture are set alongside other traditions in the ancient world because one feature of this book is the relationship of the people of God to the world. These traditions include writings on divorce, and this sets the context for the teaching of Jesus on marriage in response to the questions asked by the Pharisees. However, the teaching of Jesus on marriage is not limited to the question of divorce and the chapter looks at Jesus's commendation of celibacy for the Kingdom in relation to marriage, the significance he places on love and family life, his reference to himself as the 'bridegroom', and the way in which marriage is seen in relation to eternal life. Moving onto the writings of St Paul, especially to the Corinthians, we look at some of the urgent problems facing the new converts who had been called to conform their lives and their attitudes to Christ. The chapter also looks at household codes, often the source of concern for modern readers, and the letter to the Ephesians that becomes highly significant for a theology of marriage. The chapter ends with an exploration of marriage in ancient Greek and Roman traditions to demonstrate the public significance of marriage and to set the scene for the next chapter.

The writings of St Paul have greatly influenced the tradition as have those of St Augustine, so in Chapter 3 we explore not only Augustine but the other early theologians, such as St Clement of Alexandria, Tertullian, Origen, Lactantius, St Gregory of Nazianzus and St Basil who have rich pastoral insights to share not only on marriage but also on divorce, adultery and remarriage. In order to understand more fully what they say and why, it is important to have a good sense of the context in which they were writing, and this applies to all the other chapters. The early church fathers respond to thinkers who completely disparage marriage and especially human procreation, and to those who elevate human love beyond its natural reliance on God. Questions also are raised on the relationship of virginity and marriage notably by St Jerome, Carterius and Helvidius in connection with the true marriage between Mary and St Joseph and the perpetual virginity of Mary. The relationship of virginity and marriage comes to a head in the dispute between Jovinian and St Jerome. St Augustine's own dispute with St Jerome and Augustine's real concerns with Pelagianism and the workings of grace, set the scene for Augustine's exposition of the three goods of marriage. By placing Augustine's highly influential thinking on marriage in context we can come better to appreciate its richness. In their pastoral concern for helping people live holy married lives, the fathers frequently present ideas that are counter cultural and the chapter also looks at the Roman Law of marriage. Finally, the chapter explores the idea of the family as 'domestic church.'

In Chapter 4 we trace the thread of the tradition through medieval times to the turbulent times of reform and counter-reform, and the Council of Trent. This chapter looks at the beginnings of church and canonical rules, and at cultural practices that led to various papal interventions. Questions of consent and consummation help to determine what makes marriage. The chapter explores marriage in sacramental theology and the graces the sacrament confers, with reference to the work of Hugh of St Victor, Peter Lombard and St Thomas Aquinas. Aquinas also considers the place of passion and the virtues in marriage. Although this is a time of crystallization of rules, often overlooked is the strong element of pastoral concern and the spirituality of marriage. As a clear indication that theologians were deeply interested in the lives of married people Pope St Gregory I and St Isidore of Seville show particular pastoral concern for the faithful who have a specific place in the Church. Moreover, Jonas of Orleans and Alcuin offer pastoral guidance and moral instruction for married life. St Aelred presents a particularly personal account of spirituality, love and friendship in the partnership of marriage. This chapter also charts the changes in theological method from scholasticism, through humanism to nominalism that eventually lead to a more legalistic understanding of marriage. Questions of grace, and that God does not command the impossible, surface in the discussion of marriage, Martin Luther and the Council of Trent.

Chapter 5 explores the growing regularization of marriage and theories of contract and covenanted love. The context here is of developments in moral theology where a morality of legalism, what is licit and illicit, love of the law for the sake of the law, all jostle with love of the law for human flourishing. Developments in natural law also show a trend towards a naturalistic and physicalistic account of marriage. The context of probabilism through the view of Tomás Sánchez on marriage and the opposing problems of laxity and Jansenism frame the discussion on St Alphonsus Liguori's approach to marriage and grace. The chapter includes the Roman Catechism and the writings of St Ignatius of Loyola, St Robert Bellarmine, and St Francis de Sales on the practical living out of marriage as a Christian vocation. The catechisms and the saints offer not simply directions about what to do but concrete practical ways in which married people can grow in holiness. With the rise of secularism and secularism's stress on marriage as purely a human construct, this chapter also examines the first papal encyclical on marriage, Pope Leo XIII's *Arcanum Divinae* 1880, and the 1917 Code of Canon Law which sets out the ends of marriage.

The twentieth century saw significant advances in technology and the once latent mentality of eugenics becomes more explicit. In Chapter 6 Pope Pius XI's encyclical on marriage, *Casti connubii* 1930 is set in this eugenic context and in response to the 1930 Lambeth Conference, the first time a Christian community had officially accepted contraception. Additionally, in the twentieth century there is an important philosophical turn to the person and the chapter explores the personalistic philosophies that highlight even more the interpersonal nature of marriage, notably the contributions of Dietrich von Hildebrand and Herbert Doms to marriage, and the response and clarifications given by the Sacred Roman Rota in 1944. Turning specifically to the Church in the world, the chapter looks at the calling of the Second Vatican Council with its focus on holiness and marriage as a partnership for life. The chapter includes the dispute that led to Pope St Paul VI's encyclical *Humanae vitae,* and the changes in the new Code of Canon Law 1983. Significantly, marriage and family life are seen as crucial in forming a culture of solidarity and love that can evangelize the world.

In 1980 Pope St John Paul II tasked the Fifth General Synod of Bishops with exploring the role of the Christian family in today's world. Chapter 7 looks at synodality and the workings of the synod. It is important to grasp an idea of the purpose of the synod not least because there is a difference between expectations of synods in the media, and the reality of synod proceedings. This difference has caused some confusion and false expectations for the 1980, 2014 and 2015 synods. The chapter also looks at the meaning and role of the *sensus fidei,* insights that are particularly relevant when it comes to developments in the teaching of marriage and family life. The chapter then makes a close analysis of *Familiaris Consortio* 1981 and Pope St John Paul's invitation for people to deepen their understanding of marriage and the family. For Pope St John Paul, the call of the Christian life is a call to holiness, and the chapter reflects on Pope St John Paul's exhortation *Christifideles Laici* and the vital role had by married couples and the family in the formation of culture and evangelization.

As part of the endeavour to form the faithful through catechetical instruction, Pope St John Paul's writing on the *Theology of the Body* is an invaluable resource. Chapter 8 introduces Pope St John Paul's theology of marriage found in his play *The Jeweller's Shop* with its practical application of attentive kindness. The chapter then explores the *Theology of the Body,* identifying the main challenges of modern dualism, philosophies of consciousness, a distrust of the body and a demeaning of the body reducing it to raw material. Pope St John Paul notes that these modern challenges make the body into the 'problem', rather than lust that has settled in the observer's heart. The chapter explores one of the central texts for Pope St John Paul's theology of marriage, Ephesians 5, and explores key themes of human love 'in the beginning', redemption, the sacramentality of marriage, the language of the body, and Pope St John Paul's reflections on *Humanae vitae*. The chapter ends by explaining how the family as 'domestic church' came to hold a significant place in Pope St John Paul's theology of marriage and family.

Chapter 9 identifies some of the questions that have come through this exploration of the story of marriage and family life so far, since these questions become relevant to interpreting *Amoris Laetitia*. The chapter summarizes the issues surrounding the question God does not command the impossible? It then moves to the question of development of tradition and suggestions to redefine marriage in the light of Pope St John XXIII's bringing the Church 'up to date', and his understanding that the Church has great treasure to offer the world, notably through marriage and living a Christian life. It also explores Pope St Paul VI's understanding of dialogue with the world in *Ecclesiam suam*. The chapter then turns to teaching on conscience in *Dignitatis humanae*, *Gaudium et spes* and *Veritatis splendor* since conscience takes on a particular role in some solutions to the question of remarriage after divorce. The question of attempted remarriage after divorce follows, with an examination of suggestions to find solutions in the 'internal forum' or apply the Orthodox approach to remarriage. The chapter specifically focusses on the 1993 proposal from the German prelates Archbishop Saier, Bishop Lehmann, and Bishop Kasper since this proposal resurfaces at the synods leading up to *Amoris Laetitia*. The chapter gives the reaction of G. Grisez, J. Finnis and W. May and the response in 1994 from the Congregation for the Doctrine of the Faith, noting the difficulties around the notion of objective grave sinfulness, and the meanings of pastoral accompaniment. In order to help with an evaluation of various solutions the chapter outlines the Eastern Orthodox tradition of *oikonomia* and *epikeia*, as well as J. Ratzinger's response to these solutions. Often overlooked in the story of marriage is the highly significant ramifications of different attitudes to divorce and remarriage for understanding the relationship of local churches to the Church and decentralization, attitudes that surface during the 2015 synod. The chapter looks at the exchange between Kasper and Ratzinger on this. Pope Benedict XVI's contribution to marriage reiterates the problem of inadequate catechesis and makes the point that people are not simply the objects of pastoral action. The chapter explains how the 2007 CELAM conference and its Aparecida document contain major themes for Pope Francis on evangelization, the family and the seeds of *Amoris Laetitia*. Finally, the chapter looks at the 2014 synod and Kasper's speech leading up to the 2015 synod.

Chapter 10 begins with the author's own experience of being appointed an expert to the 2015 ordinary synod. The chapter then works through *Amoris Laetitia* making connections between it and previous teaching and explaining some of the difficulties and controversies, including some of the more challenging footnotes. The chapter also looks at the aftermath of the exhortation from the *dubia* published by Cardinals Burke, Caffarra, Brandmuller, and Meisner, to Pope Francis's endorsement of the document from the bishops of Buenos Aires.

The concluding reflections in Chapter 11 take the words of Jesus, 'love one another as I have loved you', and brings together the demands of living a life in Christ in marriage and family life. It includes some thoughts from Pope Francis regarding young people in becoming a community of persons.

Through this adventure we will see that the story of marriage touches on some major theological and practical themes: what is the relationship of the Church to the world? Does marriage really belong in the remit of the Church and why? Does God command the impossible? What about grace? What does marriage say about and to the Church? What does it mean to discern the 'signs of the times' and where does the sense of the faithful for the faith fit in? What is the place of virtue in married life? What do we mean by development of tradition? Can tradition change? What new strategies are required to present marriage more as a dynamic path to personal fulfilment? And what does marriage mean for evangelization?

Reflection on marriage brings out one particular Catholic way of doing theology: using analogy. The Church uses analogy to try and express fundamental realities. Analogy opens up a way of speaking between two extremes: the extreme of apophatic theology which cannot say anything about the eternal and entirely other God, and the extreme of univocal anthropomorphism which reduces everything to the human level. One extreme holds to a vision of God who does not have anything to do with humanity, the other extreme has a God who is so very much involved with humanity that we cannot either think of him or express him other than in terms of human essence and history. The Church uses analogy because human relationships are the best resources we have; however, analogy often points more to radical dissimilarity. As St Augustine points out, the Creator can be partially known by his works, but there are severe limitations and analogies show both great unlikeness and some likeness.[40] This does not make ideas such as the close relationship of Christ and the Church to the relationship of husband and wife, or the family as 'domestic church' merely aspirational. Instead these ideas say something significant about the married relationship.

From the very beginning God's relationship with his people has been described as *hesed*, steadfast love, covenantal love. This love is part of God's plan of salvation: it cannot be disregarded, reduced, or redefined. Marriage has been used to signify this relationship so it cannot be disregarded, reduced, or redefined. Marriage is a concrete experience that manifests albeit 'seeing in a glass darkly' God's love for his people through Christ's love for the Church. This is just one good reason why the Church has special regard for marriage.

Marriage is also a natural reality. Using practical reasoning we can see that it is the building block or first cell for society; that marriage is the worthy context for the flourishing of the dignity and personal nature of human beings; that marriage is prior to and greater than society and is inscribed in human beings. Certainly, we can understand marriage without theology but this risks reducing it to a sociological reality. Moreover, even in relationships that seem the most loving there are difficulties and tensions, simply because we are human. People need accompaniment in difficult times and discernment to see things through. In an interview Pope Francis explains that for St Ignatius of Loyola discernment is 'an instrument of struggle in order to know the Lord and follow him more closely,' it is to 'hear the things of God from God's point of view.' Reflecting on the Constitutions of the Society of Jesus, Pope Francis observes that a Jesuit must 'manifest his conscience,' that is, the person's inner spiritual situation, so that his superior can be more aware and knowledgeable about sending the person on mission. To look deeply into marriage is necessary if we want to know how married people are to be leaven in the world. Pope Francis explains that 'in life, God accompanies persons, and we must accompany them, starting from their situation. It is necessary to accompany them with mercy.' And if we look hard at marriage we realize that we, as well as the 'ministers of the Gospel' must be 'people who can warm the hearts of the people, who walk through the dark night with them, who know how to dialogue and to descend themselves into their people's night, into the darkness, but without getting lost.'[41] To ensure we do not get lost we have to know where we have come from and where we are going.

The Church's moral teaching on marriage has often been characterized as 'cold legalism' and an arbitrary list of what not to do, rescued only in the twentieth century by a more personalistic understanding.[42] This book challenges this characterization and it aims to show that even if 'we', the Church sometimes find it 'difficult to present marriage more as a dynamic path to personal development and fulfilment', instead of a 'life-long burden',[43] when we look deeply into the tradition we will see some

A Boat with New Nets

often surprising and promising areas of reflection, deep wisdom, and a wealth of treasure to bring out for all to see.

The reply to the question, what difference does Christ make, must be: all the difference in the world, and beyond.

Notes

1. Lk 5:10.
2. Pope Francis, *General Audience* (7 October 2015).
3. Lk 5:4; Pope St John Paul II, *Novo millennio ineunte*, 1.
4. Pope St John Paul II, *Message for the 42nd World Day of Prayer for Vocations* (17 April 2005).
5. Pope St John Paul II, *Novo millennio ineunte*, 1.
6. Jn 1:41–42.
7. Mt 4:18–19; Mk 3:13–19; Lk 5:8–11.
8. 1 P 3:1; 1 Co 7:14.
9. Ac 10:47–48; 16:15; 16:33–34; 1 Co 1:16.
10. St John Chrysostom, *Homily 20 On Ephesians*.
11. F. Veronese, 'Jonas of Orleans' in *Great Christian Jurists and Legal Collections in the First Millenium* (Cambridge: Cambridge University Press, 2019), p. 420.
12. Pope Leo XIII, *Arcanum Divinae*, 10.
13. Pope St John Paul II, *Christifideles Laici*, 15, 40; Pope Francis, *Amoris Laetitia*, 289.
14. St Aelred, *Sermon XXII For the Nativity of Mary*, 4.
15. Pope St John Paul II, *Familiaris Consortio*, 4; Pope Francis, *Amoris Laetitia*, 32.
16. Pope Francis, *Amoris Laetitia*, 290, 293.
17. Pope St John Paul II, *Redemptoris Missio*, 9.
18. *Ibid.*, 17–19.
19. *Ibid.*, 26.
20. *Ibid.*, 35–36.
21. 1 Co 15:58.
22. Pope Francis, *Homily Closing Mass of the Eighth World Meeting of Families* (27 September 2015); 1 Jn 4:10.
23. Second Vatican Council, *Gaudium et spes*, 12–13.
24. *Ibid.*, 22.
25. St Gregory of Nazianzus, *Letter 101*.

26 Second Vatican Council, *Gaudium et spes* 22.
27 Ph 2:6–8.
28 Ph 2:5–8.
29 Ep 5:25.
30 Jn 15:12.
31 St Augustine, *The Excellence of Marriage*, 1.
32 St Augustine, *The Enchiridion on Faith, Hope, and Charity*, 70–71.
33 Pope St Gregory I, *The Books of the Morals, An Exposition on the Book of Job* III, XXXIII, ii, 9; xii, 25.
34 *Ibid.*, 121.
35 Pope St John Paul II, *Message to Participants in the Seventh International Meeting of the Catholic Fraternity of Covenant Communities and Fellowships* (9 November 1996), 4.
36 Second Vatican Council, *Gaudium et spes*, 19.
37 *Ibid.*, 21.
38 Pope Benedict XVI, *Letter concerning the remission of the excommunication of the four bishops consecrated by Archbishop Lefebvre* (10 March 2009).
39 See Mt 22:1–14, Mt 25:1–13; Jesus the bridegroom, Mk 2:18–22; Mt 9:14–17; Lk 5:33–39.
40 St Augustine, *The Trinity*, XV, 2–3; XV, 16, 26; 20, 39; 24, 44.
41 A. Spadaro, 'Interview with Pope Francis, A Big Heart Open to God' in *America* (30 September 2013), pp. 15–38.
42 See for instance K. Schemenauer, *Conjugal Love and Procreation: Dietrich von Hildebrand's Superabundant Integration* (Maryland: Lexington, 2011), p. xii.
43 Pope Francis, *Amoris Laetitia*, 37.

2 IN SCRIPTURE AND ANCIENT TIMES

JESUS WAS NOT married. What has he got to say about marriage? M. Satlow, an expert in ancient Judaism argues that Jesus 'had little to say about marriage'; that Jesus 'rejected the value of family and oikos', household; that for Jesus 'the 'family' are those who do his will'; that when Jesus does 'evoke the image of marriage' it is in the context of him as the 'groom' to those who anticipate the kingdom of God. Moreover, for Jesus family and households hindered discipleship and the new social order. Satlow claims that Jesus believed that the kingdom was 'now' and so he saw marriage as 'at best irrelevant', and the early Christians followed this trajectory.[1] Additionally, when Jesus did talk explicitly about marriage it was in the context of divorce.

Satlow's negative interpretation presents a significant challenge for a theology of marriage if we want to relate everything to Christ. However, it is important to remember that Christianity is not simply a set of propositions but rather an encounter with a person, Jesus Christ,[2] and, as we shall see, Satlow's dismissal of Jesus is unwarranted. Many commentators limit what Jesus has to say about marriage to his teaching on divorce and remarriage. But in fact, Jesus often talks about marriage and family life, not least in the way in which he associates love in families with the love of God for his children. Jesus, a Jew, is steeped in the Old Testament vision of marriage and family life where marriage is a blessing and God is love.

In Matthew's gospel some Pharisees come to Jesus to test where Jesus stands on the issue of divorce: does Jesus follow the rabbinic school of Hillel that says that it is legal for a man to divorce his wife for 'any cause' or, following the school of

Shammai must the 'cause' be serious.³ Instead of discussing various interpretations of the law of Moses on divorce, Jesus sends his questioners directly to the theology of marriage found in 'the beginning', in Genesis:

> Have you not read that the one who made them at the beginning 'made them male and female', and said, 'For this reason a man shall leave his father and mother and be joined to his wife, and the two shall become one flesh'? So they are no longer two, but one flesh. Therefore what God has joined together, let no one separate.

As Jesus points out, marriage and family life have their roots in the Old Testament. As the church fathers long recognized the New Testament is hidden in the Old and the Old revealed in the New.[4] However, even though many Christians read the Old Testament in the light of Christ, the Old Testament also has its own intrinsic value. Certainly, in the Old Testament we find marriage as a social reality. However, we also discover that marriage is a part of God's plan for salvation. Marriage is in the order of creation and God is the author of marriage.[5]

Marriage in God's plan

Ancient pagan creation myths of the Near East described the primordial order of things where gods were also subject to the understood world order. The ancient pagan gods belonged to and were subject to nature. They could perish and they could be influenced by their worshippers. Reflecting this often violent world order, in many pagan stories the creation of the world came about as a result of a clash of cosmic forces or some form of sexual coupling. For instance, in the Babylonian creation myths the god Apsu and goddess Tiamat, both associated with water, mingled together to produce male and female gods. Fearing the absolute power of their parents over them, one of these junior gods killed Apsu and a battle ensued between Tiamat, her monsters and the junior gods. One junior god Marduk offered to do battle with

Tiamat on the understanding that should he win he would become the king of the gods. Marduk killed Tiamat and created the world out of her body.[6] In the ancient Mesopotamian Atrahasis epic myth human beings were made from clay mixed with the blood of a god, Illawela. Illawela was sacrificed specifically in order to make human beings to 'bear the load of the gods', that is to do the work of junior gods who had rebelled.[7]

In contrast, the ancient Israelites received their view of the world through God's Revelation. The Pentateuch or Torah, the first five books of the Hebrew scripture, describe in great detail this Revelation: how God broke into the world to claim a people as his own, how he unilaterally chose Israel, how he freed Israel and brought Israel to the Promised Land despite all of Israel's wavering, unfaithfulness, resistance and recalcitrance. Yahweh led his covenantal family. Whereas the pagan gods could be male or female and produced junior gods, Yahweh the God of Israel was one, there was no goddess consort. Moreover, instead of being subject to nature, Yahweh is entirely other.

In ancient Hebrew thinking only God can create and the term *bara*, to create, suggested a cosmic creation out of nothing.[8] The creation stories point to something significant about human beings, known before all the ages: a human being is alone before God, yet also made for a life of communion with others. While marriage and family do not determine this significance, they do give a concrete reality to this significance in history.[9] There are two accounts of the creation of human beings in the Old Testament, reflecting the fact that there are distinctive styles and theological themes in the Torah that the original redactors allowed to stand together.[10] In both accounts human beings are distinguished from the rest of creation and are in a special relationship with God since they are created in God's image and likeness in Genesis 1:27, have both material and immaterial aspects united in a psychophysical unity in Genesis 2:7, and have a preeminent place in relation to the rest of creation in Genesis 1:28 and 2:16–17.

Although positioned before Genesis 2–3, Genesis 1:26 is in fact later, from what is known as the Priestly source. According to Genesis 1 God creates everything through his Word. However, human beings are not simply created from the 'waters on the earth' like plants, fish, birds or other animals. Instead, in Genesis 1:26–31 human beings are created after the other land animals. Human beings are made in the image of God, and they are created male and female together as the pinnacle of God's creation. This indicates that each human person is unique and unrepeatable but also created for community. Sexuality is a part of God's divine plan from the beginning. God blesses the human couple and he calls them to be 'fruitful, multiply, fill the earth and conquer it.' The concept of fruitfulness then is not just a question of biology, rather it involves vocation, co-operating with God's plan.

The earlier Yahwistic source of Genesis 2–3 differs significantly from the Priestly source and this includes the placing of creatures in creation, with man created first, followed by the other animals, and then woman. The first man, *adam*, roughly translates as 'earth creature' and this is seemingly a generic term. Man is formed from the ground, *ha adama*, and as such he is part of the material world. He became a living being, *nephesh*, when God breathed into him. The breath of life, *ruah*, is a gift from God and the source of all being and life; *nephesh* is a being animated by the breath of life. Man is settled in the garden to cultivate and take care of it. Yahweh trusts man to eat the fruit of all the trees in the garden except one, the tree of the knowledge of good and evil. 'To know' is not only intellectual, it is also to do with experience and relationship as indicated by the phrase 'You know when I sit and when I rise' in Psalm 139. This suggests that eating the fruit involves a mastery over life, and so an inappropriate autonomy for an earth creature. There is a limit to autonomy, and the consequence of disobedience is death, being cut off from community with God.

Although all of creation is good, the fact that man is alone is not good. He needs a 'helper', one matching him. The phrase 'bone from my bone' emphasizes the close connection between the two, rather than implying subordination of women to men, and it lays the foundation for the 'one flesh' of marriage and therefore procreation in Genesis 2:24.[11] The helper matches *adam* but is not a replica: in philosophical terms the helper is "an other" who is like but also unlike,[12] introducing perhaps a note of complementarity. A fitting helper, *kenegdo*, is not a servant but one who helps another realize what cannot be realized alone and since woman is not made from the earth but from Adam himself God makes marriage part of creation. Moreover, the creation of woman from man indicates that men are not to be like other animals who mate and then move to another partner: promiscuity is not part of God's plan for human beings. Instead, the two belong exclusively to each other.[13] Marriage and becoming 'one flesh' is more than bodily unity or shared living. The idea that human beings are created social beings does not suggest that their social life is on the same lines as bees in a hive or ants in a colony. The community of human beings is what Pope St John Paul II later will describe as a *communio*, a way of being whereby each person helps the other to become more truly a person.

In their original innocence Adam and Eve are naked and they know no shame with each other. However, the sin of Adam and Eve brings about a very real effect and a change: now there is shame, that universal human experience, and estrangement from God.[14] They are afraid of God, and they blame each other. Notably neither Adam nor Eve are cursed. Yet they do begin to live a diminished existence where subordination and domination rather than equality characterize their relationships. Inequality appears to be the result of sin. Nevertheless, all is not lost for God makes clothes for them as Adam and Eve go out into the world beyond Eden.

The Genesis accounts of the first human beings illustrate the common parentage of humanity: all human beings belong to a kind of being, humankind. In the world beyond Eden the Old Testament follows the history of one particular branch of the human family, the Israelites, and there are certain commonalities in the process of marriage found in the ancient near east and in the Old Testament.

Marriage process in the ancient Near East

Marriage appears to have been the expectation for most people in the ancient Near East. Evidence from ancient texts covering some three thousand years can be found in legal documents, contracts, administrative reports, epic stories, wisdom literature, and even manuals for the use of individual families found in family archives. Given the general reliance on fortune telling and consultation of oracles, it seems likely that recourse would be had to inspection of various parts of an animal sacrifice to see if the gods favoured the match and if the marriage would produce sons. Some texts also point to favourable and unfavourable features to look for in the prospective bride as well as auspicious days for the marriage to take place.[15]

Collating evidence from other academic sources, M. Stol suggests a general outline of marriage practice.[16] The fathers of the bride and groom made an oral agreement for marriage and it was likely that the bride was considerably younger than the groom. The girl received a gift as a dowry from her father and evidence from various written contracts suggests that this became her inheritance and might have been passed down the female line.[17] The couple would then live with the family of the husband for the betrothal period. This could last for months or even years, notably if the girl was particularly young and there appeared to be the possibility of the couple not going through with the marriage in which case there was a fine for the equivalent of a breach of contract.[18] The wedding itself may have included an additional bride-price paid by the girl's father. The wedding ceremony was highly ritualistic and included bathing and possibly anointing of the bride, the ceremonial approach of the groom and his friends to the door of the bride's family home to ask for the bride, feasting, and then escorting the bride and groom to the bed chamber. On the following day there would be another banquet and further celebrations lasting some days.[19]

In these patriarchal societies the relationship between men and women was suffused with inequalities. The husband was free to take a concubine as well as a wife, and if his first wife did not have children, he could then take another wife, the assumption being that the woman rather than the man was infertile. The repudiated first wife would receive back her dowry and the bride-price if one had been paid. Moreover, the husband could lower the status of his wife and raise the status of his concubine. Sons were preferred to daughters, and there is contractual evidence that if a couple only produced daughters the husband could adopt a son who would then marry one of his daughters to preserve the family line.[20] At his father's death the eldest son received a double inheritance.

Adultery, defined as 'consensual sexual intercourse by a married woman with a man other than her husband' was always regarded as a matter of shame.[21] Stol explains that it was conceded that men were always expected to have lustful thoughts about women whereas women were always the instigators of adultery.[22] Stol gives the example of a Hittite law that differentiated some of the circumstances surrounding adultery: if a man took advantage of a woman in the mountains then it was the fault of the man and he was to be killed. This suggests that the woman was in fact the victim of rape. If a man took advantage of a woman in the house, then she was at fault and was to be killed. The idea here is that it was the woman who had seduced the man. If the husband caught his wife and another man in the act of infidelity, then it was assumed that both consented to adultery and so if the husband killed the wife there was 'no problem.'[23]

A husband could divorce his wife for apparently any reason even if she had given him children. Nevertheless, significantly marriage was always regarded as a public affair. Divorce appears also to have been a public event. However, some legal texts suggest that a wife who sought to leave her husband could be subjected to the severe punishment of death from the community whereas a husband simply had to pay a fine. It appears that women could not in fact initiate divorce proceedings so the death penalty may have simply been a threat.[24]

Ancient near east marriage customs also seem to regard the wife as inheritable property. If her husband died the wife still belonged to her husband's family and could be married to his brother, father or even son of another wife.[25]

Marriage process in the Old Testament

In the Old Testament there are no general laws on either marriage or divorce still in existence and the legal fragments available are not sufficient to give a systematic account. Moreover, much of the biblical law on marriage and divorce deal only with special cases.[26] The *Torah* gives little guidance on the marriage process though evidence of the marriage process exists in the narratives in the Old Testament and there are parallels with evidence found in the ancient Near East. A good example of this process is the marriage of Isaac and Rebekah in Genesis 24.

The choice of an appropriate partner was carefully considered, after all, marriage concerned the interests of both families. The father of the groom offered the proposal to the father of the prospective bride, and this might have reflected the practical reality that the girl was not yet fifteen. In some cases, another might be charged to act on behalf of the father of the groom, as Abraham sent his servant to make the relevant inquiries. When agreement had been reached the groom's family gave the bride or the bride's father gifts to demonstrate that the family was serious about the proposal and that the groom could provide for a wife. These gifts, the *mohar*, sealed the betrothal and Abraham's servant gave gifts of silver, gold ornaments and clothes to Rebekah, and additional rich gifts to her brother and mother.[27] The gifts also formed part of the dowry, *nedunyah*, provided by the bride's father that the bride kept as her inheritance in the event either of her husband's death or her divorce.[28] As in other ancient near eastern societies, the marriage was a public affair. The consent of the bride was required under the form 'I take you …', and this consent had social effect. The marriage ceremony then proceeded with prayers blessings and the conducting of the bride by the groom to his house.

On marriage the wife had a specifically legal status and her husband had to undertake to lead a common life with her, to provide her with food, clothing and shelter, and to perform the 'marriage debt', to have sexual intercourse with her, and this applied even if he then took a second wife.[29] Her husband was charged with treating his wife with respect and if he decided to divorce her, he had to give her her dowry. For her part, the wife was to give her husband exclusive sexual rights to her so that he would have absolute security regarding the identity of his children. The husband was referred to as *baal*, a word associated with Lord or a possessor,[30] an 'owner' of the woman.[31] Notably, when the prophet Hosea took back his wayward wife, he said 'You will call me "my husband," no more will you call me "my *baal*".'[32]

As a practical consideration marriage was the way in which the family or clan line continued, and family property remained in the family. Therefore, children were seen to be important. Thus, for instance, a betrothed man was excused from battle in case he died before he had had a chance to have children.[33] Ancient Judaism had access to Greek medical theories since the time of Alexander the Great's conquest of the Middle East in 300 BC, and following ancient Aristotelian biology it was believed that the father was the prime mover in shaping the unborn child, the mother provided nutrition.[34] Often servants were included in the dowry, and female servants could be used as surrogate mothers if the wife could not have children. This may have been a strategy to ensure the husband would not take another wife, and to keep wealth within the family clan. Hence perhaps why Jacob married two sisters, Leah and Rachel, and had children with them and with their servants.[35] If the wife, or rather the marriage, did not produce children then there were three legally accepted courses of action, though to begin with it was assumed that the wife was at fault: she could be divorced; she could continue as her husband's wife and he could take another wife; she could bear children through her servant who acted as a surrogate by becoming her husband's concubine. A husband could have sexual relations with other women, so long as that woman was not married to another man, but the wife remained exclusive to her husband. However, there is a suggestion that polygamy and using servants to produce children of the marriage were judged to be a lack of faith in God's promise to answer prayers.

Although it appears that monogamy was the norm and the ideal, polygyny, having more than one wife, is evident in the Old Testament.[36] Polygyny was not common practice, but it seems to have been accepted for leaders where it was connected with their official responsibilities and polygamy among royalty was allowed since marriage alliances were political arrangements. Notably the concubines of a ruler were passed on to his successors, for example, after driving David out of Jerusalem Absalom publicly had intercourse with his father's concubines.[37] Indeed, polygamy was only critiqued where it involved the marriage of foreign wives in the case of Solomon, or the illegal seizure of property in the case of David.[38] In spite of this apparent acceptance of polygamy, various biblical examples suggest that polygyny always led to disaster and bitter rivalry, for instance between Sarah and Hagar and the exile of Hagar and Ishmael; between Leah and Rachel and their jealousy of Jacob's concubines; the tragedy of Bathsheba's husband and David; and the problem of idolatry and Solomon's wives.

Adultery was seen as a transgression against the husband's right to exclusive access to his wife. The woman was committed to her prospective husband after betrothal and so intercourse with any other man before marriage was also regarded as adultery. According to Deuteronomy 22:23–24, and reflecting ancient near eastern practice, both the man and woman could be put to death if the act took place in the city since the woman could have cried out to be saved; otherwise only the man was put to death. Following Leviticus 19:20 intercourse with a slave 'assigned' to a man was not seen as adultery but the man had to make a sin offering.

Following the general culture of the near east, marriage and so divorce were not merely private affairs. Nevertheless, although divorce was tolerated in the Old Testament as a concession to human weakness,[39] divorce was not approved of nor was it recommended. The prophet Malachi reports that Yahweh 'hates divorce' because divorce breaks faith and breaks a covenant to which Yahweh has been a witness, and it removes the possibility of 'God-given' offspring.[40] In an effort to see where Jesus stood within the tradition the Pharisees asked Jesus for his views on the text of Deuteronomy 24:1–4 that allows divorce. As R. Gane points out, the text is limited to certain cases and it deals with remarriage of the same husband to the same wife after he has divorced her and she has remarried and either divorced again or become a widow.[41] The Deuteronomy text suggests that there was already legislation that permitted the husband to divorce his wife, however, the text does not allow him to take her back after she remarried. The grounds for divorce are that the husband can no longer love his wife because she has committed some 'indecency', *ervat daœbaœr*,[42] or he finds something 'obnoxious' about her. The phrasing 'he finds ... about her' takes the form of a legal charge connected to betrayal of trust. However, the scope of 'obnoxious' is not at all clear and the exact meaning was the subject of much debate,[43] hence the Pharisees question to Jesus. Given that the penalty for adultery was death it would seem that 'indecency' was something other than adultery. On the one hand, unlike divorce in the ancient Near East where it seems the husband could divorce his wife for any reason, in the case of Israelite marriage there must be a significant reason; on the other hand, the husband need not succumb to, for instance family pressure, and he could decide to forgive his wife. Notably, and despite the injunction in Deuteronomy 24:1–4, God calls Israel and Judah who have both gone after false gods and 'committed adultery with stone and with wood', to repent and turn back to him.[44]

Divorce was a public act and the husband presented his wife with a bill of divorce, a document of separation sending her away from his house. This probably took the legal formula 'she is no longer my wife nor am I her husband.'[45] If a wife was divorced she took her dowry with her and she was free remarry without a charge of adultery being brought against her. However, to avoid losing the dowry a husband might claim that his wife was not a virgin at marriage. If this charge were to be proved true, then she would be stoned. But if this charge was false the husband was flogged and had to pay a fine to his wife's father. Moreover, the husband could not divorce her again.[46] Again if a man raped a virgin who was not betrothed, he had to marry her, pay a fine to her father, and he could never initiate divorce proceedings against her.[47]

Following Leviticus 21:7 and Ezekiel 44:22 there was a higher standard for priestly families. Priests could not marry prostitutes or women who had been divorced by their husbands, though they could marry widows.[48] The reason given is that 'the priest is consecrated to his God.' It has been suggested that Jesus had this in mind when he prohibited remarriage after divorce in Luke 16:18, after all Christians, like the priestly families of old, are called to be holy.

In some cases, marriages that were illegal from the beginning could be dissolved. Following Deuteronomy 7:3–4 in order to combat idolatry, Israelites were not to take foreign wives or husbands.[49] Thus, the leaders of the Israelites with the scribe Ezra, who was charged with re-establishing the Mosaic Law on the people returning to Jerusalem after their exile, make a covenant with God to send away all foreign wives and their children.[50] Marriages where the spouses were related to one another within prohibited degrees of kinship were void, considered as incest, and may have been punishable by death.[51] It seems that marriage between a Jew and a *mamzer*, a person born as a result of incest, possibly adultery, or a prohibited union, was also prohibited and so void.[52]

Unlike the ancient near eastern custom, wives were not inherited should their husbands die. However, if the marriage had not produced sons then the widow was still bound to her husband's family as long as there was a surrogate relative who could provide the deceased husband with children. Under the levirate law the brother-in-law had owed a particular duty to the widow, *levir* being the Latin translation of *yabam*, brother-in-law.[53] To be eligible, a brother-in-law had to have the same father as his deceased brother and the requirement did not apply to a brother-in-law born after his brother's death. The widow did not remarry, and her deceased husband was considered to be the father of any children provided biologically by his relative.[54] This procedure of Levirate 'marriage' ensured that the family name did not die out and kept the estate within the family. If however the brother-in-law refused to follow the Levirate duty, the widow had to begin the severance ritual and if he did not relent there was a ceremony of contempt for his failure to keep the memory of the deceased. The widow pulled the sandal off his foot, spat in his face and recited the formula 'thus shall be done to the man who will not build up his brother's house'.[55]

While there are similarities and differences in the marriage processes of the Old Testament and the ancient Near East, the underpinnings of marriage in the Old Testament are significant and give marriage and family a special theological context beyond social or cultural custom.

The Old Testament: blessing and covenant

Throughout the troubled history of Israel as recounted in the Old Testament, marriage and family were central because marriage grew the bonds of community, it kept the community alive, it helped to form the extended family of God's People, the People of Israel: marriage and family were a matter of identity. As Deuteronomy 6:1–9 and 11:18–21 explain, the commandments, laws, customs and traditions of Israel are to be passed down through the generations from parents to children. Significantly God's love for the People of Israel is compared to marital love and family love becomes a paradigm for God's love. God's saving love for his people is described in terms of a wedding: 'as the bridegroom rejoices in his bride, so will your God rejoice in you.'[56] Using the metaphor of a faithful husband and adulterous wife, the prophets Hosea, Jeremiah and Ezekiel as well as the 'messenger', Malachi, speak of the ever-faithful God who loves with a steadfast love his wayward people. As É. Levine notes, the ancient Israelites were particularly tempted by the pagan god Hadad, also known as Baal, meaning both husband and master.[57] The Old Testament prophetic tradition is very dependent on the demands of the Covenant, and marital infidelity is often spoken of in terms of covenant infidelity using symbolic language of the covenantal marriage between Yahweh and his people. The most sustained metaphor can be found in Hosea. In a very practical symbolic action, the prophet Hosea (c.700 BCE) describes how he was told by God to marry a prostitute, Gomer. Hosea loves Gomer, and when Gomer deserts him he takes her back. The image of God as the bridegroom and Israel as the bride, found in the prophets Isaiah, Ezekiel and Hosea[58], develops the idea of covenant: after a time of exile for unfaithfulness[59], God does what husbands are not permitted to do under the Deuteronomic law—he marries his divorced wife again.[60]

While marriage in pagan cultures in the Near East often involved divination and the gods of fortune, marriage in the Old Testament was associated with God's blessing. The Hebrew term *bãrak*[61], to bless, refers also to the verb to kneel, and it is used in Genesis 1:22 when God blesses the first human beings and tells them to be fruitful and multiply. God's blessing here indicates that human beings are dependent on God down the generations. God's blessing continues through the covenants God makes with Noah after the Flood in Genesis 9:1, with Abram in Genesis 12:2–3 and then with the Israelites. Similarly, fathers blessed their own children.[62] Indeed, blessings from fathers were so significant that Jacob obtains Isaac's blessing by pretending to be his brother Esau and this blessing makes Jacob master of his brother.[63] Blessings carry with them a sense of spiritual and actual potential for the future. The Jewish practice of reciting frequent blessings in thanksgiving is a reminder of the connectedness of the Jewish people to God.

When the *Catechism* speaks of marriage as a blessing[64] it reminds us of the importance of a blessing as 'a divine and life-giving action, the source of which is the Father.' Blessings have a two-fold aspect: from one dimension they are gifts given to us from God and from creation through the economy of salvation so that 'the whole of God's work is a blessing.' Notably God blessed 'all living beings, especially man and woman.' From the other dimension and on the part of human beings, blessings bring forth adoration, thanksgiving and also offering blessings back to God.

The notion of marriage as a blessing is also played out in the understanding of marriage as a covenant. The idea of covenant in the Old Testament is complex and it seems to involve a number of elements: the forming of a relationship that is not based on an already existing natural relationship; the creation of obligation; agreement possibly made under oath or given divine sanction.[65] In addition to the contractual element of marriage through arrangements made between the families, the feasting together seems to have cemented the new covenantal relationship.[66] Notably, the giving of a hand in the form of a hand shake or lifting the hand seems to have been a symbolic gesture of covenants in general[67] and may have been a part of the marriage agreement signifying making a common cause with someone.[68] While the contractual elements of exchange of gifts or the paying of a bride price may give the impression that marriage was a matter of purchase, sexual union appears to have been the final ratifying feature making marriage a binding covenant rather than merely a contract between families.[69]

Love in marriage

While marriage was a major concern between families, love also had a significant place even though there could be a marriage without love, as the marriage between Jacob and Leah shows.[70] One of the themes of the Book of Tobit (4th century BC) is the joy of family life. Marriage within the same clan is encouraged. Unlike the previous seven husbands who died on their first evenings with Sarah, Tobias marries for good reasons: not only is Sarah destined for him by God but Tobias also falls deeply in love with her so that 'he could no longer call his heart his own.'[71] He marries out of love and 'singleness of heart', not lust.[72] Tobias and Sarah pray to God for grace and protection, thus placing their marriage in a religious context as the will of God.

Although different words are used to describe different aspects of love, the two words *ahab* and *hesed* are particularly relevant for marriage.[73] To love, in the sense of *ahab*, is the love that a woman has for a man and a man for a woman. Understood within the relationship of marriage, *ahab* expresses love rooted in sexual desire and emotional attachment, the way Isaac loved Rebekah.[74] *Ahab* also refers to family love between parents and children, the love that Abraham had for Isaac.[75]

The book the Song of Songs, thought to be written by the young Solomon,[76] and known as the greatest of all songs, was traditionally part of the Jewish canon even though there is no explicit mention of God. The Song of Songs is a collection of poems about human love probably in the context of wedding celebration, and its inclusion into the canon indicates the significance of love and marriage for ancient Israel. At the same time it reflected the theme of the love of God for Israel and the relationship of husband and wife developed by the prophets from Hosea onwards.[77] This human love, *ahab*, gives the couple their intimate connection and identity, 'set me like a seal on your heart' and their love is 'strong as Death', 'love no flood can quench, no torrents drown.'[78]

In both theology and ethics *hesed* is considered to be an extremely important term.[79] Difficult to translate, *hesed* has the sense of steadfast love and loving kindness.[80] *Hesed* is associated with the idea of covenant, a reciprocal relationship, rather than simply a general loving kindness and it is a frequent attribute of God.[81] God's steadfast love is eternal and his acts of *hesed* will always continue.[82] *Hesed* encompasses mercy, grace, strength, kindness, loyalty, reliability, faithfulness and blessing. Thus, it goes beyond sentimentality, desire, or simply contractual fulfilment of a commitment. Although *hesed* refers to relationship, the relationship may not be equal and there may be a weaker party and a stronger party. *Hesed* then also relates to generosity and the steadfast commitment of the stronger party to implement the promises of their covenant. This aspect of *hesed* is played out in the story of the prophet Hosea whose steadfast love for his unfaithful wife is used by Hosea as an analogy to describe the faithful love of Yahweh for his unfaithful and weak people. And at the end times the coming of the Messiah is like a bridegroom coming to his wedding celebrating with a wedding feast.[83]

The goods of marriage

Although the goods of marriage, children, union of the spouses and fidelity, are usually associated with the later Christian tradition of marriage, these goods are implicit in the major themes in the Wisdom literature of the Old Testament. Children are a sign of God's blessing on the marriage.[84] Both father and mother are their child's first teachers[85] and there are obligations of respect between parents and children. Parents have the significant duty to pass on the traditions of Israel, especially the Shema, the prayer to carry out the requirements of the Torah:[86]

> Listen, Israel: Yahweh our God is the one, the only Yahweh. You must love Yahweh your God with all your heart, with all your soul, with all your strength. Let the words I enjoin on you today stay in your heart. You shall

tell them to your children, and keep telling them, when you are sitting at home, when you are out and about, when you are lying down and when you are standing up.[87]

The relationship between the spouses and the way in which they can live happily with each other is something in which God and all people delight.[88] Certainly there are a number of negative texts about women highlighting the impact that a querulous wife or a wife lacking in virtue can have on the home and husband. However, there are also texts showing that finding and marrying a good and virtuous wife brings joy; she is a pillar of support and provides stability in the home.[89] Infidelity, whether by husband or wife dishonours the marriage.[90] Fidelity is threaded through and central to the Old Testament.

Marriage and friendship

The significance of marriage as an analogy for God's love for his people is rich and has a depth of meaning that cannot be reduced to one interpretation. However, ancient notions of friendship raise interesting perspectives. The Old Testament covenant relationship of God and his people hides within it what will later be revealed in the New Testament: human beings are called to be friends with God, and more than that, adopted children and brothers and sisters of Christ. Key for the moral life is love, friendship with God that is a love between friends. Such a friendship was a cause of scandal to philosophy because in the ancient world friendship could only exist between equals. According to Aristotle perfect friendship is 'the friendship of men who are good and alike in virtue', each receives the same as he gives, and it is rarely found. Moreover, friendship was essentially between two men. Aristotle also identifies friendship for pleasure and friendship for utility that lasts only as long as the pleasure or usefulness lasts. For Aristotle the friendship between husband and wife or parent and child inevitably is one of inequality, and in these relationships Aristotle thinks that the better party, that is the husband or the parent, should be loved more than he loves.[91] It is the role of the superior party to receive love not to give it.

But in the Christian tradition, building on the Old Testament, it is God who loves us first. God communicates this love and God raises human beings into the supernatural order where there can be person to person love. And God is the first to give totally of himself. He sends his Son. Love in marriage is not for pleasure or utility, lasting only as long as those aspects last. Love in marriage is a form of friendship, the love of another 'self', where each person wants the good of the other as if it were their own good. It is a love characterised by total self-gift.

According to St Thomas Aquinas, both the Old Law and the New Law are from the one God of the Old and New Testament. However, the Old Law is more severe than the New Law because the Old Law imposes many external observances and obligations. Christ fulfils the Old Law with the New Law, a law of the heart, of love. Quoting St Augustine, Aquinas points out that laws are not heavy to the person who loves.[92]

So, from the beginning

From the very beginning marriage has been a part of God's plan of salvation. Each human being is at the same time unique and irreplaceable yet also created for communion with God and with other human beings. The union of a woman and a man in marriage as 'one flesh' expresses the intimate communion between two people that is not inward looking but looks outward to a community of persons, the family. This community is not a social grouping like a colony of ants or a hive of bees. Rather the family as the first human community signifies that we each need other people to help us to be fully human and more truly the persons that God wants us to be. Marriage then is a vocation, a calling that enables people to grow together. In the Old Testament marriage goes beyond the contractual obligations of its Near East neighbours because it involves the concepts of covenant, blessing and fruitfulness, steadfast love, and faithfulness. Moreover, as a relationship that everyone can understand even if they come from relationships that are less than perfect, marriage signifies the faithful relationship that God has with his people through a love, *hesed*, that is holy and can never be quenched.

Significantly, the wisdom of the Old Testament is not human wisdom, or something attained simply by the efforts of human beings. God's wisdom discloses itself to the people of Israel. Then, in history, God's wisdom gives himself to the world by breaking open the gates of heaven and making his dwelling place here on earth. God descends not because of any request by human beings but out of pure love and gift. Notably, St Matthew's gospel begins with the 'roll of the genealogy of Jesus Christ, son of David, son of Abraham', and a genealogy also figures in St Luke's gospel.[93] This genealogy shows that Jesus is connected through his Israelite descent to the messianic line and to the royal line of David through the legal paternity of Joseph. Jesus is thus embedded in family history as God's plan of salvation is embedded in human history and played out in marriage and the community of the human family.

Jesus: developments from the Old Testament and later rabbinical debate

When the Pharisees ask Jesus where he stands on the question of divorce and remarriage this is not a simple question. Rather the question is heavily laden and from the response of Jesus the Pharisees would have expected to learn about not only his moral leanings but also his politics. We saw that there was considerable disagreement on how to interpret the text of Deuteronomy 24, noting that the text does not legislate for divorce but only gives guidelines about the remarriage of a divorced wife with her former first husband. The dispute crystalized around the Houses or schools of two first century BCE rabbis, Hillel and Shammai. These two Houses offered contrary interpretations of the rabbinic tradition: the 'softer' tradition of Hillel and the more rigid tradition of Shammai.⁹⁴ Followers of Hillel tended to be more accommodating towards circumstances and times. During the Roman occupation both Houses objected to the imposed tax burdens. However the followers of Shammai found support with the Zealots, the political group who sought to oppose the Romans by any means.⁹⁵

It is difficult to piece together the whole debate between the Hillel and Shammai traditions because these traditions were transmitted orally and so were subject to the principles of rabbinic abbreviation. These principles recommended short phrases that were easy to remember and what was obvious in the debate was often omitted.⁹⁶ In the tradition of Shammai 'a man should not divorce his wife except if he found a matter of indecency in her, since it says: *for he found in her an indecent matter.*' In the tradition of Hillel a man may divorce his wife 'even if she spoiled his dish, since it says: *for he finds in her an indecent matter.*'⁹⁷ In a further explanation, it appears that the Shammai tradition understood 'an indecent matter' whereas the Hillel tradition accepted 'any matter.' The Shammai followers argued that in the Hillel interpretation 'indecency' was superfluous; the Hillel followers responded that 'indecency' was necessary in order to show that remarriage was allowed also for those who were divorced for indecency.⁹⁸ Recalling the discussion in the previous section on marriage in the Old Testament, the notion of 'indecency', *ervat daœbaœr*,⁹⁹ denotes something 'obnoxious' such that the husband can no longer love his wife.¹⁰⁰ For the House of Shammai it seems that 'indecency' or unchastity refers to adultery.¹⁰¹

Jesus does not take the side of one rabbi over the other, nor does he dismiss the Torah. Indeed, he does something entirely different.¹⁰² There are three accounts of the question and the response of Jesus: the account in Luke 16:18 is short and to the point; Mark 10:1–12 is slightly longer; Matthew 5:31–32 and then Matthew 19:3–12 give a fuller account.

Writing perhaps to gentile communities evangelized by St Paul,¹⁰³ the author of Luke's gospel takes a straightforward approach to divorce and remarriage: Jesus taught that 'everyone who divorces his wife and marries another is guilty of adultery, and the man who marries a woman divorced by her husband commits adultery.'[104] In 16:17 Luke reports Jesus as saying 'it is easier for heaven and earth to disappear than for one little stroke to drop out of the Law.' By his absolute prohibition of remarriage after divorce Jesus then did not seek to replace the law, rather he follows God's declaration in Malachi 2:16, 'I hate divorce.' Moreover, and perhaps following Leviticus 21:7 and Ezekiel 44:22 Jesus calls his followers to the high standards expected of priestly families who are called to be holy.[105] With Jesus everything changes. However, we may want to consider that if Jesus comes for every human being and calls every human being to holiness, if he brings the fulfilment of God's plan of salvation, and if he is the incarnation of the Father's *hesed*, then all who are called to the state of marriage are also called to its vocation to holiness.

The author of Mark's gospel, writing possibly to gentiles under Roman rule,[106] sets out the teaching of Jesus on divorce and remarriage in the context of the demands of discipleship. The transfiguration in Ch 9:2–8 reveals the glory of the hidden Messiah, Jesus, who can cast out demons and who says that 'everything is possible for one who has faith.'[107] Jesus foretells his passion[108] and says that the greatest are children[109] but anyone who leads astray 'little ones who have faith, would be better thrown into the sea with a great millstone hung round his neck.'[110] Those who follow Jesus do not look to concessions tolerated by the law, rather they aim to do the will of God. M. Hooker points out that Jesus does not contradict the Torah in his teaching on remarriage after divorce. Rather Jesus indicates the true fulfilment of the law.[111] The Pharisees ask Jesus if it is lawful for a man to divorce his wife and in return Jesus asks his questioners what Moses commanded. The Pharisees reply that Moses allowed a writ of divorce to be drawn up. Jesus does not dispute the validity of this ruling. But he does see it as a concession for their hardness of heart. Jesus then returns to the original principle that 'from the beginning of creation he [God] made them male and female. This is why a man leaves his father and mother, and the two become one flesh.'[112] As A. Thatcher explains, 'leaving and cleaving are the basic activities that help human societies to organize themselves.'[113] The teaching of Jesus returns to God's plan in Genesis so it appears to be *haggadah*, traditional teaching for couples inscribed in the very fabric of humanity. Jesus then adds 'they are no longer two, therefore, but one flesh. So, then, what God has united, human beings must not divide.' The time for the 'new creation' has arrived.[114] This teaching is reinforced for the disciples 'in the house', and as Hooker suggests, for the new Christian community since the ruling applies to both husbands and wives, reflecting Roman law which, as opposed to Jewish law, allowed both parties to divorce.[115] The teaching of Jesus not only goes beyond the legalism of the Mosaic law, it is also counter-cultural. The discussion of divorce and remarriage is followed by the blessing on children and the search of the rich young man for holiness and eternal life.

The author of Matthew's gospel, writing to Jewish Christians and in the light of Jewish rather than Roman law,[116] presents two teachings about divorce and remarriage. The text 5:31–32 follows the teaching of the Sermon on the Mount and the Beatitudes and the context is the fulfilment of the law and the new standard demanded now that Jesus has come. As part of the list of 'it has been said', 'but I say' Jesus explains:

> it has also been said, anyone who divorces his wife must give her a writ of dismissal. But I say this to you, everyone who divorces his wife, except for the case of an illicit marriage, makes her an adulteress; and anyone who marries a divorced woman commits adultery.[117]

The exception of 'illicit marriage' has been interpreted as marriage within the prohibited degree of kinship, therefore making the marriage void.[118] The text 19:3–12 is more detailed. Like Mark's account the Pharisees test Jesus to see where he stands theologically and politically. From the start Jesus returns to God's plan in Genesis, answering the Pharisees:

> have you not read that the Creator from the beginning made them male and female and that he said: this is why a man leaves his father and mother and becomes attached to his wife, and the two become one flesh? They are no longer two, therefore, but one flesh. So, then, what God has united, human beings must not divide.[119]

Notably, Jesus combines Genesis 1:27 and Genesis 2:24. As E. Lövestam points out, this combination was common in rabbinic literature and reflects Genesis 7:9, the animals going two by two, male and female, into the ark, in order to emphasize that monogamy is the principle of creation.[120] The expression 'one flesh' does not simply refer to the sexual relationship of the couple nor to any resulting children. Rather, their entire existence is now one of a unity of complementary difference. The emphasis thus moves away from an account of monogamy to an inseparable unity that is the work of God himself.[121] Divorce then is not compatible with God's will. The Pharisees then raise the issue of the concession given by Moses.[122] Jesus replies that this concession was due to their hard-heartedness, 'but it was not like this from the beginning.' Jesus then follows this with his own teaching, giving it *halakic* legal flavour:[123] 'now I say this to you: anyone who divorces his wife—I am not speaking of an illicit marriage [*porneia*]—and marries another, is guilty of adultery [*moicheia*].'[124] The New Jerusalem Bible translates *porneia*, as 'illicit marriage' rather than unchastity. Porneia certainly bears a range of meanings centring on illicit sexual intercourse[125] and it could refer to a sexual relationship outside marriage such as living together, or a sexual relationship before marriage, or a marriage invalid because it was within prohibited relationship. In these cases, the couple could separate since these are not marriage. Acts 15:20 uses *porneia* to refer to pagan marriages that would be incestuous under Jewish law. *Porneia* could also refer to any sexual infidelity and in particular to adultery. D. Instone-Brewer suggests that *porneia* is simply a synonym of *moicheia*, adultery.[126] J. C. Laney interprets *porneia* as incestuous marriage.[127] It seems that if Matthew meant adultery then he would have used the technical term *moicheia*, a term he uses in 15:19. Moreover, if Jesus was simply repeating the saying of Shammai then it seems unlikely that the disciples would respond with such concern when they say 'if that is how things are between husband and wife, it is advisable not to marry.'[128]

The New Testament scripture scholar B. Viviano offers three possible solutions to Matthew's exception clause:[129] assuming that the exception clause is not an interpolation, the first solution is that *porneia* is a real exception to the absolute prohibition of remarriage after divorce. This seems to be the Greek Orthodox position. However, the text refers to *porneia* not *moicheia*, and moreover is not different from the view of Shammai. The second solution is that the clause does not contain a real exception because it refers to separation from an adulterous wife without remarriage: the husband can only divorce on the grounds of adultery but if he remarries after he has divorced his wife then he commits adultery. In the third solution again the clause does not contain a real exception because *porneia* is understood as marriage within forbidden degrees of kinship, *zenut*, and so the marriage is not a true marriage and it would be subject to a decree of nullity not divorce.[130] However as Lövestam points out, the Greek *porneia* is equivalent to the Hebrew *zenut* and there is no evidence that the terms would have automatically been interpreted as only to do with degrees of kinship as opposed to sexual unfaithfulness.[131] The fourth solution offered by Lövestam is that the exception clause refers to Jewish marriage law that forced a man to divorce an unfaithful wife.[132] If the wife was unfaithful then she was responsible for the divorce and her husband had no say in the matter. Thus, Jesus neither sanctioned divorce nor allowed remarriage but he did absolve men of the responsibility of breaking the unity of married life.

The uncompromising nature of the teaching of Jesus on remarriage seems to be confirmed by the disciples who say in v.10 'if that is how things are between husband and wife, it is advisable not to marry.' However, Jesus explains in v.11 that faithfulness in marriage is a gift from God, and v.12, to others there is the gift of celibacy.[133] This leads on to the teaching of Jesus on celibacy in Matthew 19:10–12.

Celibacy

The claim that 'from the beginning' human beings were created male and female, expected to leave their parents and cleave to another to become one flesh may seem to suggest that marriage is the essential way of life. However, although the significance of some form of marriage exists and has always existed in different cultures,[134] this does not mean that every person should be married. Thatcher views the relationship of the two becoming one flesh as paradigmatic for loving relationships and relationships that reflect both the source of love who is God and the image of God as a Trinity of Persons.[135] In this context celibacy 'for the kingdom' is also a matter of love.

Responding to his disciples, Jesus lists three kinds of eunuchs: those eunuchs from birth, that is those unable to have sexual intercourse; those made eunuchs through the cruelty of men and for the use of harem guards or courtiers;[136] and those who choose not to marry 'for the sake of the kingdom of Heaven.'[137] Jesus accepts that his teaching is difficult though it is unclear whether he is referring to the discussion on remarriage as adultery or the comment of the disciples that it is advisable not to remarry and so Jesus is referring to celibacy. If Jesus is referring to the comment of the disciples then v.12 is his explanation of what it means not to marry.[138] F. Moloney thinks that Jesus refers to his stringent teaching on remarriage and he explains that the followers of Jesus may never remarry because they are now Christians and so have been given the grace to remain faithful. The text about eunuchs as those who choose not to marry refers to the cases of converted gentiles who had married incestuously under Jewish law and so their marriages had to be dissolved.[139] When people in this situation choose not to remarry or when they remain celibate after divorce, they effectively make themselves eunuchs.[140] D. Instone-Brewer understands the text as Jesus giving permission for people not to marry rather than commending the single life.[141] R. J. Van Tine interprets the text as saying that disciples who had divorced illegitimately and then choose to remain without a spouse in order to avoid a charge of adultery have in effect made themselves eunuchs and they make this sacrifice as a witness to the Kingdom.[142] According to Van Tine Ambrose, Ambrosiaster and Jerome removed vv.10–12 from the context of the discussion on remarriage after divorce in order to support a broader notion of celibacy in keeping with the Pauline understanding of celibacy found in, for instance, 1 Corinthians 7.[143] Whatever the outcome, as R. France observes, vv. 10–12 'emphasize that whether one is married or not is not a matter of "better" or "worse", but of God's gift, which is not the same for all disciples.'[144]

Was Jesus married?

Whether or not Matthew 19:10–12 commends celibacy over marriage, it seems that Jesus himself did not marry.[145] Some think that this may be related to the circumstances of his birth. Gossip about the paternity of Jesus circulated early on with Origen reporting the commonly quoted tradition that Mary had an adulterous affair with the father of Jesus, a Roman soldier named Panther.[146] The idea that Jesus was a *mamzer*, a child produced from a sexual relationship that could never be valid under Jewish law, has gained some currency,[147] particularly since *mamzers* were marginalized in society. Although the meaning of *mamzer* is uncertain, it may refer to the hybrid population of Ashdod,[148] a child conceived either as a result of adultery or incest[149] or with a non-Israelite for a father, which is why, it has been argued, Joseph decided to divorce Mary quietly to spare her shame.[150] A child simply born outside wedlock to unmarried parents was not a *mamzer*: choosing not to marry did not have the same stigma as being unable to marry. *Mamzers* were not admitted into the 'congregation of the Lord', the national governing body,[151] and they were not eligible to marry unless with another *mamzer*, and this might explain why Jesus was not married. However, before the late second century CE when the first Mishnah, the oral Torah, was published, it seems that *mamzers* were forbidden to enter Jerusalem or the temple, and they were not allowed either to be taught or to learn the Torah.[152] This does not seem to be the case for Jesus and there is nothing in the gospel narratives to indicate that Jesus was considered to be marginalized or an outcast. Moreover, Joseph marries Mary, adopts Jesus as his son, names him, settles his family in Nazareth where Jesus is known as 'the carpenter's son.'[153]

Certainly, celibacy was unusual in Jewish society at the time of Jesus and it did not have the approval of the rabbis since celibacy seemed to contradict the command in Genesis to go forth and multiply. Indeed, the suggestion that not all men are expected to marry may have shocked first century Jews since it was the duty for every Jewish man to marry and have children.[154] However there were some exceptions as indicated by the celibate lifestyle of some of the prophets and some minority communities such as the Essenes.[155] France argues that the comments by Jesus on voluntary celibacy in Matthew 19:10–12 reflected the actual situation of Jesus and acted as a form of 'apologia.'[156] Jesus is not celibate for the sake of celibacy or even for the ease of his mission. Jesus steps beyond history where people marry and are given in marriage to declare that the Kingdom of God is here.[157]

Significantly, the discussion about marriage and celibacy is immediately followed by a pericope about Jesus welcoming children, Matthew 19:13–15. This raises the question of the teaching of Jesus in general about family life and marriage.

Jesus on family life

Bringing a child to an elder for a blessing was a common event, though it is not clear whether this applied at the time of Jesus or later since the evidence only appears in a Talmudic tract composed after the New Testament.[158] The statement that the disciples objected to people bringing little children to Jesus 'for him to lay his hands on them and pray' may indicate that the disciples did not want Jesus to be regarded in the same way as any other elder. Moreover, the disciples appear to be scolding the children rather than their parents.[159] However, as D. Harrington points out, what was unusual was not that parents brought children to Jesus. Rather Jesus took children 'seriously as persons' and presented them as models for the Kingdom.[160] Indeed, the welcome Jesus gave to these little ones as recounted in all three synoptic gospels,[161] seems to have been unprecedented.[162] Naturally, during the time of Jesus parents loved and cherished their children and children were valued as economically important for the future. Nevertheless, childhood was regarded as a state of immaturity, a state out of which to grow. Children were vulnerable, ignorant and deficient. They could be ill-treated and they had no rights.[163] In contrast to Satlow's negative view of Jesus on marriage and family, Jesus understands that children, who in ancient times did not have power or status, are receptive to God by the very fact of their dependence on others. They know how to receive. They have an ultimate significance for discipleship. As Harrington explains, 'the kingdom must be received as a gift, for no human power or status can create it or force it.'[164] Indeed, God hides the mysteries of the kingdom from 'the learned and the clever' and reveals them to little children.[165] Moreover, in Matthew's gospel it is children, not the disciples, who recognize and proclaim Jesus as they cry 'Hosanna to the son of David' on his entry into Jerusalem.[166]

Jesus appreciates the significance of intergenerational bonds of family life. On the one hand he welcomes children and he sees children as a model of discipleship and trust.[167] He heals children and restores them to their distraught parents.[168] Implicitly Jesus acknowledges the close bond between parents and their children, even when children have grown to adulthood. He feels great compassion for the widow of Nain whose only son has died, perhaps recalling that he himself is an only son. He brings the son back to life, giving him back to his mother.[169] On the other hand, in both Matthew's and Mark's gospels following on from his blessing of the children, Jesus meets the rich young man and he reminds the young man that the commandments forbidding adultery, murder, theft and false witness include the positive commandments to honour father and mother and to love one's neighbour.[170] Jesus criticises the practice whereby some Jews circumvent the commandment and avoid helping their parents by claiming that what they have is *korban*, dedicated to God, and so not available to use for supporting parents.[171]

Jesus also uses parent and child analogies. Despite the severe limitations of analogy, family relationships are some of the best resources we have for describing the depths of love and Jesus builds on the tradition of Proverbs and the Psalms where 'as tenderly as a father treats his children, so Yahweh treats those who fear him.'[172] Jesus knows that parents love their children: no one would hand his son 'a stone when he asked for bread' or 'a snake when he asked for a fish.' However how much more will God the Father give 'good things' to those who ask.[173]

Jesus begins two of his parables with the words 'a man had two sons.'[174] For his hearers this introduction would have instantly raised expectations. After all, in the Jewish tradition the younger son wins over the older son—Ishmael over Isaac, Jacob over Esau, Joseph over his older brothers.[175] It was the offering of Adam's youngest son, Abel that found favour with God causing his older brother, Cain to grow jealous enough to kill him.[176] However Jesus overturns Jewish expectations in story-telling. In one of the two sons stories of Jesus the first son refuses to do what his father asks but thinks better of it later and does what his father wants, the second son says yes to his father but then does not act.[177] Unlike the second son, the first son knew that he had to repent. This story expresses faithfulness to God and challenges Jewish attitudes to Jesus. In probably the most well-known parable, the Prodigal Son,[178] the youngest son in the parable is not successful and loses his dignity as a Jew by being reduced to feeding pigs; the oldest son is invited to the feast. However, at the end of the story the oldest son shows anger and a deep resentment for his father. He sees his relationship with his father as like slave and master and he complains bitterly about the treatment of his profligate brother. The parable focuses on the sorrow and then rejoicing of the father and the lost and found of both sons. Yet in the end, and despite the generosity, forgiveness and faithful love of God, we do not know if the righteous person can bring himself to rejoice with the sinner. Nevertheless, the father's offer remains open.

Jesus 'the bridegroom' and the wedding feasts

In the gospels of Matthew, Mark and Luke, and in the same context, Jesus refers to himself as 'the bridegroom.'[179] In Matthew's account the disciples of John the Baptist and the Pharisees were known to fast beyond what was prescribed by the Law, and some people ask Jesus why it is that his disciples do not follow this practice. Notably, they do not ask Jesus about what he himself does. Jesus states that his companions cannot fast because the bridegroom, Jesus himself, is still with them. He also clearly foretells his impending death 'when the bridegroom is taken away from them, and then they will fast.' In pointing out that no one sews a piece of unshrunken cloth onto an old cloak because the tear would get worse, nor is new wine put into old wineskins because the skins would burst, Jesus is telling the people that he has not come to add or to patch: the old is passing away and with his coming the new messianic age has arrived.[180] It is perhaps significant that just before Matthew relates the context in which Jesus calls himself the bridegroom, Jesus replies to the Pharisees who complain that he is eating with tax collectors and sinners. Jesus quotes Hosea 6:6 on mercy and the prophet Hosea of course speaks of faithful love.

Faithful love returns in the form of the metaphor of a wedding feast representing the kingdom of heaven. The prophets Hosea, Isaiah and Jeremiah saw Israel as the bride of God. In the parable of the wedding feast Jesus points to the marriage of God and his people and the need for people to be properly prepared.[181] Being properly prepared and vigilant is the message of the wise and foolish virgins, the attendants who go out to wait for the bridegroom.[182] Testifying to Jesus as 'the Christ, the Chosen One of God', John the Baptist calls himself 'the bridegroom's friend' who is 'filled with joy at the bridegroom's voice.'[183] Of course analogy and metaphor attempt to compensate for poverty in language and they do not directly parallel what they attempt to express. In the case of the marriage metaphor Jesus is the celibate bridegroom and so both marriage and celibacy are found in creative tension even if this appears to be incongruous. In this metaphor the relationship is not between master and servant or king and subject. Moreover celibacy, which was unusual now belongs to the economy of everyday living and celibate men or virginal women become someone's, Jesus's, spouse.[184]

The ministry of Jesus takes place in everyday life, in walks through towns, visiting people in their houses, going to the temple, meals with friends. In John's gospel, 2:1–12, Jesus is also invited to celebrations, notably the wedding at Cana. The action of Jesus at this wedding is the first 'sign' in John's gospel.[185] For John 'sign' is a highly significant moment. John begins his gospel with relating seven 'signs' whereby Jesus the Word reveals himself to the world and his followers. Jesus, his disciples and his mother Mary are invited to a wedding. The wine is used up and Mary observes to

Jesus 'they have no wine.' The reply of Jesus seems rather brusque, 'Woman, what do you want from me? My hour has not come yet', though in fact the term 'woman' is a very polite form of address. Mary, confident in her trust in Jesus says to the servants 'do whatever he tells you', an instruction directed to all those who follow Jesus. Jesus turns water into wine. There have been many interpretations of this story. Mary's *Magnificat* demonstrates that Mary was well aware of God's faithful love and God's promise to his people.[186] Moreover, for the many years that Jesus spent in Nazareth living under the 'authority' of his parents, Mary had time to reflect on the 'great things' that God has done as she 'stored up all these things in her heart.'[187] Her observation that they have no wine may also indicate that the whole people of Israel lack wine and all Israel is waiting for the Messiah and the great wedding feast. For John, the 'hour' refers to the glorification of Jesus and it is determined by the Father. However now perhaps is the time to begin his mission that will lead eventually to the cross. Significantly, the next time that Jesus calls his mother 'woman' is when she stands at the foot of the cross and Jesus entrusts the beloved disciple to her, 'woman, this is your son.'[188] John's gospel interprets this form of address as a reference to Genesis 3:15, 20: Mary is the new Eve and spiritual mother of all the faithful.[189]

This interpretation that places the relationship of Mary and Jesus beyond the mother son relationship may help when it comes to Jesus's apparent dismissal of mother and family. Matthew tells of the occasion when Jesus was speaking to the crowds and his mother and 'brothers' (*adelphoi* refers to close relations) were standing outside 'anxious to have a word with him.' The account does not say that Jesus did not go to speak with them. But Jesus does reply 'who is my mother? Who are my brothers? Anyone who does the will of my Father in heaven is my brother and sister and mother.'[190] Human ties of relationship are important, but they give way to spiritual relationships with God. Thus, Jesus makes it clear that the demands of discipleship mean that the family is not the ultimate reference point. Indeed, the disciple must 'hate' anything that stands in the way of relationship with Christ and this includes father, mother, wife, children, brothers and sisters,[191] perhaps predicting the coming times of persecution when family members were set against each other.

Finally, Jesus says that marriage does not continue after death and there is no marriage in heaven.[192] This saying, and the saying about hating family members seem to cement Satlow's view that Jesus rejects the value of marriage and family. However, C. S. Lewis provides another answer to this. Lewis explains,

> our present outlook might be like that of a small boy who, on being told that the sexual act was the highest bodily pleasure, should immediately ask if you ate chocolates at the same time. On receiving the answer "No" he might regard absence of chocolates as the chief characteristic of sexuality. In vain would you tell him that the reason why lovers in their carnal raptures don't bother about chocolates is that they have something better to think of. The boy knows chocolate: he does not know the positive thing that excludes it. We are in the same position. We know the sexual life; we do not know, except in glimpses, the other thing which, in Heaven, will leave no room for it.[193]

There is an understandable tendency to idolise the other person in marriage, to think that one person can make us truly and completely happy. This is understandable because of the very nature of human love, a love that reflects God's love. But human love is only a reflection. If we see marriage as a path to holiness, then we do not marry in heaven because we do not need to. Moreover, there are no sacraments in heaven. Sacraments prepare us in this world for heaven; they are signposts. There are no sacraments in heaven because we do not need signposts, we, God willing, are there, at the eternal banquet, in communion with the communion of saints, where every tear will be wiped away.

In Scripture and Ancient Times 55

So, from Jesus

Jesus uses familiar images in his teaching: householders, fathers, and their children. He encounters parents seeking help for their children, and children themselves. He meets people in difficult relationships like the Samaritan woman at the well. Even though Jesus was not married he recognizes the significance of marriage and family relationships. Indeed, he refers to himself as the bridegroom and in doing so taps into the very powerful Old Testament image of God and his faithful love for his people. Many of those who speak about marriage in the Christian tradition were and are not married but lived and live a celibate life. However, this does not rule out what they have to say. Their encounters with Jesus as the Way, Truth and Life gives them real insights into the human condition, the dignity of being human, and marriage and family life as one of the ways to holiness.

To St Paul

On the road to Damascus in about 34AD everything changed for the Roman citizen Saul of Tarsus. From avid persecutor of the early Christians, Saul became a passionate apostle of Christ. As Saul began his mission to the Gentiles he began to use the Roman version of his name, Paul. After his conversion, everything St Paul does and says is 'under Christ's law' and 'for the sake of the gospel.'[194] St Paul's overarching concern is to proclaim the significance of Christ for all human beings: 'if we believe Jesus died and rose so too will God, through Jesus, bring with him those who have fallen asleep.'[195] He teaches the *kerygma*, that Christ who was crucified has been raised from the dead as foretold in the scriptures, and this is the faith held by all the apostles.[196] St Paul's focus is on the one common faith and one common hope for the Christian community that has been enlivened by the Holy Spirit. In what are probably his earliest letters, his two letters to the Thessalonians, St Paul advises watchfulness for the imminent return of Christ, the *Parousia*.[197] Indeed he seems to have expected the *Parousia* to come in his lifetime and only later came to realize that he might die before it. The kingdom, then, is here but not yet. Whatever St Paul has to say on the subject of marriage then is framed in his belief that he has been captured by Christ.[198] This entails a transformation of all relationships of power: the weak and strong, Jews and Greeks, slaves and free, male and female, are 'all one in Christ.'[199]

St Paul's teaching is not simply urging communities to act in a particular way or within a certain ethical framework. His teaching is profoundly theological and focussed on the Christian community as the Body of Christ. However, St Paul did not write theological treatises. His writings have come down to us as letters addressing particular occasions that often presuppose previous oral communications or other responses. It is a one-sided conversation. Moreover, the order of his letters traditionally given in the bible reflects not the order of the letters in time but rather the diminishing length of the letters. Some of the letters may be collated from a number of letters sent to the same community. Importantly it is well-nigh impossible to reconstruct a historical social reality without importing some underlying assumptions and presuppositions. With these provisos, we begin with St Paul and his correspondence to the Corinthians.

St Paul and the Corinthians

In antiquity the port of Corinth was an important city both militarily and commercially.[200] At the time of St Paul Corinth had a thriving Greco-Roman culture and economy and attracted travellers, traders, and tourists. As with many Greek and Roman cities Corinth was marked by religious diversity.[201] Some ancient writers made derogatory remarks about the promiscuity to be found in the city, but it was probably no more or less virtuous than any other ancient cosmopolitan city.[202] The Christian community in Corinth seems to have been made up of Jew and Gentile converts who probably met in private homes.[203]

It seems that St Paul had a lengthy correspondence with the Christians at Corinth and the two letters we have now may well be an amalgamation of five letters. There are also hints of some missing letters.[204] St Paul had written a letter 'in agony of mind' over some issue, possibly a painful confrontation with someone in Corinth, but it is not clear whether this letter was incorporated into 2 Corinthians or was lost.[205] St Paul probably dictated his first letter to the Corinthians before signing it and it was to be read out aloud to the assembly.[206] There seem to be some urgent problems facing the new converts and these included not only questions of morality, marriage and virginity, but also the relationship of the community to the Corinthian pagan society, in particular eating food sacrificed to idols, and divisions among the community itself. There has been much debate on the religious and philosophical cultures that influenced the Corinthians, and a tendency to spiritualism or possibly early Gnosticism or Epicureanism has been identified.[207] This tendency may in part account for some of the views, often presented as opinions or slogans[208] on marriage and virginity with which St Paul deals. Gnostic[209] and spiritualist currents tended to show disdain for people regarded as weak and to disparage matter and human sexuality.[210] In contrast, St Paul takes a realistic attitude to sexuality and urges unity in the community.[211] He uses the language of the family, 'brothers' and 'sisters', *adelphoi,* and household language that shows the importance of the household in early Christianity to emphasize the ties that bind the community together.[212] Not only was the household the basic structure of society, it was also where the church assembly took place and the place of evangelization.[213]

For St Paul the Corinthian Christians had been 'consecrated in Christ Jesus and called to be God's holy people.'[214] Therefore the moral life can be summed up simply as 'you belong to Christ.'[215] The community should be the holy people God has called them to be.[216] As R. Collins explains, St Paul takes as the foundation for his teaching on marriage and sexuality anthropology anchored in the tradition of scripture, the union of the people in Christ, and the *parousia*, the impending end times.[217]

The Corinthian community itself brought St Paul's attention to one major issue, the issue of sexual immorality, and in particular incest or relationships within prohibited degrees.[218] In part the problem may have arisen among those who did not think that the body or morality concerning the body mattered since they were overly concerned with a spiritualised Christianity. Certainly, as St Paul had preached, Christ had freed his followers from the snares of the world. Yet this seems to have led some Christians to believe that they were therefore freed from any prohibitions, hence the case of the Christian man living with his stepmother.[219] As we have seen the age gap between women and men on marriage may have been considerable and on her husband's death the wife may have been closer in age to her husband's son from a previous marriage. Although both Roman law and the Old Testament forbade marriage to a stepmother, this practice, associated with converted gentiles, had been tolerated by some rabbis and the Corinthians were not subject to Roman law.[220] St Paul observes that not even pagans would do such a thing and he notes the troubling reaction of some in the Corinthian community who seem more than happy that social conventions have been flouted.

For St Paul, all behaviour should be patterned on Christ[221] and St Paul recommends that the community expel the offender so that he will eventually realize what he has done and repent.[222] As J. Murphy-O'Connor points out, for St Paul sin in not purely a private affair but has a social dimension.[223] St Paul takes issue with the Corinthian saying that 'for me everything is permissible' and that therefore whether the action involves food or sex, anything goes, after all, the Corinthians argued, God allows the destruction of the body and so the body does not matter. Sin for the Corinthians seems to be a matter of intention not specific action.[224] St Paul's reply, framed as 'do you not know' begins by accepting the freedom of the Christian under Christ but it is a freedom in community, and some actions, notably those that involve sexual immorality especially of prostitution, destroy community. St Paul points out that for Christians the body cannot be irrelevant precisely because God raised Jesus from the dead and he will raise those who are in Christ as well. Moreover, and referring to Genesis 2:24 and the one-flesh aspect of sexual intercourse as intended by the Creator, sexual intercourse with a prostitute deliberately excludes permanence and is a sin against a person's own body because he fails to use the body for the purpose intended by God.[225] In a further challenge to the Corinthian elitist spiritualisation of Christianity St Paul brings them back to the reality that as Christians we are 'members of Christ's body', the body is 'the temple of the Holy Spirit.'[226] As Murphy-O'Connor explains, this way of being in the world was brought about by the physical presence of Christ in history, that historical presence was a part of God's plan, and so the very bodies of Christians have a part to play in the mission of Christ.[227] 'So use your body 'for the glory of God.'[228]

Having established the significance of the body as an aspect of the whole person, St Paul then deals with further questions raised by the Corinthian community, and he does not simply tell them what to do. Notably, St Paul is not presenting a general treatise on marriage, rather he is responding to specific questions.[229] He begins by referring to another Corinthian saying that 'it is a good thing for a man not to touch a woman.'[230] Certainly St Paul finds affinity with an ascetic way of life since he is convinced that this is the way someone like him can be totally devoted to God.[231] However and in contrast to the idealism of some Corinthians, he realistically understands that this way of life is not for everyone and he does not think that there is anything morally wrong with marriage or sexual relations in marriage.[232] Thus celibacy is good but it cannot be imposed, especially on those for whom it would be too difficult. Moreover, both celibacy and marriage are gifts from God and 'everyone has their own gift.'[233] St Paul's injunction for people to 'stay as they are' may have reflected Paul's belief in the imminent *parousia*.[234] Notably, St Paul's conviction that it 'is good' to be unmarried seems to undermine the Genesis view that it is not good for man to be alone. But for St Paul the Christian is never alone since he or she is both united to Christ and to other Christians.[235]

Possibly because of reported cases of sexual immorality St Paul states that each husband should have his own wife and each woman her own husband. However, St Paul seems to be counter-cultural in recognizing the marital rights of both wives and husbands. Moreover, he rules out selfish use of the other person.[236] In confirming a legal obligation to conjugal rights on both parties St Paul may have been thinking of situations where one of the couple had accepted total abstinence and the other had not agreed. St Paul rejects the idea that celibacy can be forced on the other person and any abstinence can only be by mutual agreement for a definite time period and for a particular reason.[237]

Next St Paul responds to what may have been an actual case of divorce for a Christian couple in Corinth. Murphy-O'Connor suggests that the case may have involved an ascetic who decided not only on abstinence but on a complete breakup of the marriage. Presumably the wife did not agree and wanted to accept a writ of divorce which would give her the right to marry again.[238] St Paul draws attention to the ruling which is not his but is 'the Lord's': the wife should not accept a writ of divorce, but if she had to, she should not see herself as free to remarry. Rather the couple should think about a reconciliation.

The second case that St Paul considers is that of a marriage where only one of the parties is a Christian. Murphy-O'Connor speculates that there may have been some in Corinth who insisted that the marriage be broken since the presence of an unbeliever threatened the community of all.[239] Again St Paul takes a practical approach and he distinguishes between a situation where the unbeliever is content to live with the Christian convert and a situation where the unbeliever refuses and leaves the marriage.[240] In the first situation St Paul says that the couple may not divorce because, it seems, the unbelieving spouse has already shown a draw towards the Christian community and there may be conversion and a growth in holiness. In the second situation if the unbeliever has issued a writ of divorce then it stands, and the Christian spouse is no longer tied to the marriage.[241] The initiative for separation is with the non-believer who cannot live at peace with believer.[242]

In contrast to the Corinthians who seem to think that the married would have a better relationship with God if they were celibate, or that those in mixed marriages would be better to separate, essentially what matters for St Paul is belonging to the Lord. This is why he advises each person to live the life that the Lord has assigned to him, to keep the commandments and to avoid pagan vices,[243] and to live out their commitment to the Lord in their spiritual and moral life.

The section of St Paul's letter relating to virginity and marriage, 1 Cor 7:25–40 is difficult to interpret because in this passage the situation at Corinth is not at all clear. Murphy-O'Connor deduces that the question raised by some in the Corinthian community concerns spiritual marriages, that is marriages where the couple had made a vow of celibacy, but now were finding it difficult to adhere to their commitment.[244] St Paul understands the question in terms of the *parousia*, 'the time has become limited' and 'this world as we know it is passing away.'[245] St Paul therefore urges people to stay as they are, though if they do marry it is not a sin. Given that the end is coming St Paul advises people not to become overly attached to or engrossed in things or people.[246] It is in this context that he observes how easy it is for people who are married to become absorbed in each other and perhaps he is reflecting the situation of those in Corinth who think they know what is best for other people rather than concerning themselves with giving 'undivided attention to the Lord.'[247]

St Paul's view of the matter of the equality of women in worship is the cause of some debate and consternation in some quarters.[248] It is clear that in Corinth women had leadership roles and St Paul works with them as he does in other Christian communities, though it may well have been that Corinthian women were promoting a more extreme ascetic viewpoint.[249] Moreover St Paul expects men as well as women to behave appropriately in the liturgical assembly and he seems particularly concerned that the appearance of both men and women should conform to traditional standards.[250] This may be because any sign of novelty or eccentricity might detract from proclaiming the message of Christ, indeed the message may be obscured or even highjacked by faddish behaviour. Therefore, it is better to keep to traditional hierarchies, especially since this world is passing away. Nevertheless, ultimately there is equality because 'in the Lord, though woman is nothing without man, man is nothing without woman; and though woman came from man, so does every man come from a woman, and everything comes from God.'[251]

St Paul, household codes, the Colossians and the Ephesians

The Colossians may have lived in or near the city of Colossae, a city marked by a syncretic culture of Judaism, paganism and philosophical strands of Stoicism and Pythagoreanism, as well as some troubling forms of asceticism.[252] The letter to the Ephesians seems to have been destined to reach a number of Christian communities with a focus on gentile converts.[253] The authorship of both letters is a matter of debate and it may be that even if St Paul did not actually compose the letters himself, they were written with his approval or at least were attempts to summarise his teaching.[254]

By the time the letter to the Colossians is written belief in the imminent *parousia* seems to have faded, though the 'here-but-not-yet' paradox of the kingdom still remains.[255] As with other early Christian communities there were those who rejected anything to do with the world and who saw anything material, especially the body, and anything related to the body such as marriage, as obstacles to be overcome.[256] On the one hand the author of Colossians reinforces the belief that Christians belong to another world, the world of Christ and so the dominance of the world is rejected. On the other hand the author insists that Christians should be integrated into the social order.[257] This perhaps reflects the discourse in John's gospel when Jesus talks about his followers as not belonging to the world but being sent into it:[258] Christians are in but not of the world. Teaching on household codes then is part of this integration.

In Colossians 3:18–21 the author offers what seems to be traditional advice for households of believers reflecting the wider social reality. It seems that the conversion of women, children and slaves may have caused tension in households. Reaffirming traditional household codes may have been a way to refute the pagan complaint that early Christians overturned household ordering, notably by speaking to children and 'some stupid women', and so were a disrupting influence in society.[259] As M. MacDonald explains the household code served as a survival strategy in an environment hostile to Christianity.[260] According to the author of the letter to the Colossians wives are called to subject themselves to their husbands as is common in patriarchal societies. In the culture of the time wives were subordinate but here the author suggests a new way of being since he addresses women as free persons asking them to conform freely to the will of God in relation to their husbands 'as you should in the Lord.' Husbands are urged to love their wives and be kind. Love was not a required ingredient of marriage, but a special bond of love comes with a life in Christ. Children are addressed directly suggesting that they were present at the assembly and they are to obey parents. Fathers had ultimate authority in the culture of the time including over their adult children and they could choose to accept or reject, even kill by exposure female or defective infants. Here fathers are not to provoke or exasperate their children. In following conventional household ordering Christians did not draw attention to themselves and they could live peacefully alongside unbelievers even in the same family. They could still live a distinctive life in Christ in society. Moreover, at a time when the head of the household, the *paterfamilias*, decided the religion of the family, Christian women could have a real influence in evangelization by remaining in the home.[261]

Significantly, and at a time when some forms of asceticism rejected the world out of hand, the notion of the body of Christ is central for Christians who are after all in the world though not of the world. The liturgical hymn inserted into the letter to the Colossians, 1:15–20 proclaims that not only the universe but also the Church is centred on Christ.[262] The overarching context of authority and obedience for the Christian can be found in Colossians 1:18 where ultimate authority is in Christ who is the Head of his Body, the Church, and 'in him all things hold together.' Christians then are 'ambassadors for Christ' and in the new world order God is 'in Christ reconciling the world to himself.'[263]

By the time of the letter to the Ephesians there appears to be more of a separation from non-believers with Christians urged not to go on living 'the empty-headed' life that the gentiles live but to live as 'children of light.'[264] Moreover there is little to suggest that Christians had to defend their beliefs against non-believers and it is more likely that the community was becoming inward looking.[265] Christians generally are asked to be 'subject to one another out of reverence for Christ.'[266] Key to the household code that follows is the analogy of Christ and church, husband and wife, and it has resonance with the steadfast love of God for his people from the writing of the prophet Hosea.[267] Simultaneously Christians are asked to keep to the patriarchal values of the time yet see their relationships as transformed by the new love found in Christ who nourishes and cherishes his people in the same way a loving husband takes care of his wife and family. Instead then of an emphasis on rule and authority, the focus is on love. MacDonald notes that the language of sanctification by Christ of the Church reflects baptismal rites; sanctification in marriage may point to the ritual washing of a Jewish bride before the ceremony and it also seems to refer to the understanding that a husband was the protector of the honour of his wife.[268] Building on the idea that Christ loves and saves his body, the Church, husbands are to 'love their wives as their own bodies',[269] and by speaking of bodies the author may have intended to stem any ascetic tendencies that denigrated the body.[270] The idea that as Christians 'we are members of his Body' explains why Christ loves the Church and underscores the reality of the way in which Christians are nourished by his body. The reference to the husband's own body also anticipates the later quote of the two-in-one-flesh of Genesis 2:24. As well as explaining the origin of the union between husband and wife, the Genesis quote establishes marriage as part of God's plan of salvation. The same seems to be said of the union of Christ and his Church and both are a mystery.

While the obedience of children to their parents was a part of the general social outlook, the author of Ephesians addresses children directly and says they are to be obedient to their parents 'in the Lord.'[271] In quoting the commandment to honour father and mother, it is clear that this instruction is from God. However, the further injunction to fathers not to drive children to resentment illustrates an element of respect for even the weakest of the family.

The tensions of being in the world are perhaps demonstrated in the way that marriage operated both in the theological and secular sphere. Certainly, we have to remember that the ancient world was complex and multicultural and so we can only have a snapshot of the realities of marriage and family life. Nevertheless, in most cultures some form of marriage, as well as procreation and the bringing up of children, have always been regarded as fundamental to the wellbeing of society as a whole.

Marriage in the ancient Greek world

In the ancient Greek world men and women could live together informally but there was no transfer of a dowry and any children were not regarded as citizens, nor did they have any claim on the father.[272] Marriage therefore offered a stable situation for wives and for children. Marriages in the ancient Greek world were arranged between families. Literary sources suggest that the ideal age of the husband to be was about thirty and the bride twelve, so often the husband negotiated the marriage himself.[273] Moreover it appears that only the formal consent of the bridegroom was required. A dowry was decided upon and this would support the wife in the event of divorce or the death of her husband. The betrothal took place before witnesses and, as if to emphasize the youth of the bride and her passing into marriage, her toys were dedicated to the goddess Artemis. Most weddings took place in the winter month of Gamelion, January, and at the full moon. During the ceremony the bride gave a lock of her hair as a sacrifice to the gods of marriage, Zeus and Hera. After a ritual bath, the girl was veiled and was taken by torchlight to where the guests were assembled. After feasting the husband and his supporters accompanied his wife to her husband's home where there were further celebrations before the couple entered the wedding chamber.[274]

Divorce in Athens was a simple procedure and required no formalities.[275] The husband did not even have to give his wife any warning or declare grounds for divorce. However, if his wife had committed adultery he was obliged to divorce her.[276] Unless he claimed some wrongdoing on her part, the husband had to return the dowry and her belongings; the wife went back to her family home. If the wife wished to initiate divorce, she had to approach the courts through her male relatives and provide good reason for her petition. A Greek father had the right to remove his daughter and initiate divorce proceedings for any reason. Notably, if the wife's father had died and the couple did not have any sons to inherit his property, the wife's male relatives could force her to divorce her husband and she had to marry one of her father's relatives in the hope that there would be sons to keep the property in the family.

Marriage in the ancient Roman world

In Latin marriage, *matrimonium,* has reference to *mater,* mother, reflecting the importance of marriage for the production of legitimate children.[277] The ideal age for women at marriage was early to middle teens and for men mid to late twenties.[278] However marriage was more a matter of fact than a matter of law. In the *Twelve Tables,* Rome's first code of law created in about 450 BC marriage was a serious issue because it conveyed power to the head of the family or clan, the *paterfamilias,* who was the oldest male ancestor. Indeed, a person subject to the power of a *paterfamilias* could not marry without his consent.[279] Power over the wife and over the wives of sons was called *manus,* over children (and slaves), *potestas.*[280] *Manus* meant that the woman passed from her father's family to the family of her husband and in practice this was said to occur after the bride was brought to the house of the bridegroom and the union had continued for a year.[281] This transfer of the woman may have been the result of a religious ceremony, *confarreatio,* possibly named after the sacrifice of a spelt, *far,* cake made to Jupiter and accompanied by a formal set of words and the presence of witnesses. *Confarreatio* may have been only open to patricians or socially elite citizens. The secular practice of *coemptio* was open to other citizens, the plebians, and was a formal act transferring ownership. *Usus* came about if the woman remained with the man for a year; to avoid passing into *manus* she had simply to be absent for three nights.[282] The implication here is that there had to be an intention to remain married, it was not merely a matter of living together. However, once it became possible for property to pass to a woman on the death of her paterfamilias, then the three night absence may have been a strategy to keep property in the family of the woman.[283]

Since marriage was a question of fact it could end simply by separation of husband and wife. Since *manus* was a legal transaction it could only be broken by a legal act, and the same applied to the religious act of *confarreatio.* This separation possibly also took the form of a set of words and may have required the husband to call a family council with representatives from his wife's family to show grounds for the husband's action. Probably there was no recourse to divorce by the wife in early law though this may have become a possibility later.[284]

As the law developed to keep pace with the expanding empire, marriage became preceded by a betrothal which took the form of an exchange of promises between the husband to be or his father and the father or guardian of the woman. Initially this agreement was not enforceable though possibly in later rules there could be an action for damages if either party broke off the engagement.[285] After about 31 BC *manus* became the exception and living together became enough to make marriage though the intention to live together was often accompanied by ceremonies of bringing the woman to the husband's house, lifting her over the threshold and giving her gifts of fire and water.[286] The parties had to have *conubium,* the right to contract a fully legal marriage, and at various times marriage between certain people was forbidden, for instance the *Twelve Tables* did not allow marriage between a patrician and a plebeian,[287] though this was later legalised in 445 BC. Only Roman citizens had the right of *conubium*. If either party lacked this right, for instance the two were slaves, the marriage was a *contubernium* co-habitation. Unlike concubinage where legal marriage may have been socially unacceptable, in the case of *contubernium* the couple were not able to marry rather than choosing not to. For *conubium* the couple had to be above the age of puberty, be of sound mind and not related within prohibited degrees, though again these degrees were later relaxed.[288] For divorce to take place there had to be a declared intention to separate and it seems that by the end of the Republic by about 30 BC the divorce rate was high among the Roman elite.[289]

When Augustus took charge of the Roman Empire in 31 BC he made the restoration of Rome to its former glory his aim. This involved addressing moral degeneration and reinvigorating

Roman society.²⁹⁰ To this end Augustus declared marriage to be a civic obligation. He imposed penalties and the loss of inheritance for the unmarried or those who did not remarry after divorce or the death of their spouse and this applied to women between twenty and fifty years of age and men between twenty-five and sixty. In part this obligation was to address the decline in population however fines went into imperial funds.²⁹¹ Augustus also imposed penalties for marital infidelity.²⁹² Notably, adultery was defined as sex between a married woman and a man other than her husband. A citizen could bring a charge of adultery against any married woman, or against a man who committed adultery with a married woman; the man's marital status was legally irrelevant.²⁹³ The laws implemented by the Emperor Augustus penalizing celibacy and promoting the producing of children remained in force through the third century although initially they only applied to Roman citizens.²⁹⁴

By the time of the jurist Gaius who wrote his *Institutes* of Roman law around the time of Hadrian (ruled 117–138 AD), Pius (ruled 138–161 AD) and Marcus Aurelius (161–180 AD), the older Roman law of marriage had given way to the *jus gentium*, the law of all people not just Roman citizens. Now, *consensus facit nuptias*, consent rather than possession of the wife made marriage and husband and wife were regarded more as partners. Consent was not simply consent to sexual relations. Rather consent was also to living a married life, *affectio maritalis*.²⁹⁵ Notably, this *affectio* was a matter of intention and did not imply affection or love.²⁹⁶ If there was no intention to live a married life the relationship was considered to be co-habitation and if the *affectio maritalis* ceased, that is if there was no longer continuous consent, then the couple could divorce.

However, in the provinces of the Empire many people who were often ignorant of Roman law simply followed their own local laws and customs. Moreover, given the many political crises affecting the Empire, for the third century emperors enforcing the law of marriage was not a priority.²⁹⁷

Summary

Jesus knew the scriptures. He knew about the depth of the Father's love for his people. This love was so counter-cultural that instead of God the Almighty staying aloof or waiting for people to come to him, God came to them time and again in his faithful steadfast love. God revealed this love to his people in words they could understand: words of marriage and family life. All of this was to build up to the greatest gift, the gift of God himself in his son Jesus Christ. Christ as bridegroom to the Church his bride, unites himself in a way with all believers who, under the influence of the Holy Spirit can call God *Abba* Father.[298] Marriage and family life are great goods and blessings from God. But they are not the final good. In the historic situation of people they foreshadow something still greater to come: the eternal marriage, the 'marriage of the Lamb.'[299] Marriage and family life then are historic realities, they are 'in the world' but not purely 'of the world'.

The Christian understanding of marriage and family life as presented by the early church fathers inevitably shares the civil context of Greek and Roman life. We shall see that gradually a shift in the understanding of consent began to appear such that *affectio maritalis* moved away from the legal state of mind whereby the couple considered themselves to be living a married life to a matter of the will whereby consent was defined by the will, and then to modern times where marriage is shaped by feeling. However, the civil law of marriage was very much a human law and it stood in distinction to the divine law of marriage. The tension between the demands of human and divine law thread through much of the subsequent teaching on marriage and family life. Indeed, the relationship of Christians and society, the 'in the world but not of it', and the 'here but not now', ripple under the surface of much of the discussion on marriage and family life. Christian marriage is not simply a life-style choice. Marriage, like celibacy, is a gift from God and a part of God's plan.

Nevertheless, the message found in the letter to the Ephesians demonstrates that an unbreakable relationship of love is understandable to all whether or not they are theologically minded, and that such a relationship is foundational also for secular societies.

Notes

[1] M. Satlow, *Jewish Marriage in Antiquity* (Princeton: Princeton University Press, 2001), pp. 24–25; p. 282 footnote 137.

[2] Pope St John Paul II, *Veritatis splendor*, 88.

[3] Mt 19:3; B. Viviano, 'The Gospel According to Matthew' in *The New Jerome Biblical Commentary* (London: Geoffrey Chapman, 2000), pp. 642–643; p. 662.

[4] St Augustine, *Questions on the Heptateuch* Ex, 73; *Catechism of the Catholic Church*, 129.

[5] Mk 10:6.

[6] W. G. Lambert, 'Mesopotamian Creation Stories' in *Imagining Creation* (Leiden: Brill, 2008), pp. 15–60.

[7] *Myths from Mesopotamia: Creation, the Flood, Gilgamesh and Others* (Oxford: Oxford University Press, 2000), p. 15.

[8] W.E. Vine, M. Unger, W. White Jr, *Vine's Complete Expository Dictionary of Old and New Testament Words* (Nashville: Thomas Nelson, 1996), pp. 51–52.

[9] Pope St John Paul II, *The Theology of the Body, Human Love in the Divine Plan* (Boston: Pauline Books, 1997), pp. 246–249.

[10] *The Jewish Study Bible* (Oxford: Oxford University Press, 2004), pp. 3–7.

[11] *Ibid.*, p. 16.

[12] See for instance P. Ricoeur and E. Levinas.

[13] *The Jewish Study Bible*, p. 16.

[14] *Ibid.*, p.17.

[15] M. Stol, *Women in the Ancient Near East* (Berlin: De Gruyter, 2016), pp. 62–65.

[16] *Ibid.*, pp. 66–70.

[17] *Ibid.*, p. 70.

[18] *Ibid.*, p. 86.

[19] *Ibid.*, pp. 93–95.

[20] *Ibid.*, p. 162.

21. *Ibid.*, p. 234.
22. *Ibid.*, p. 236.
23. *Ibid.*, p. 235.
24. *Ibid.*, pp. 209–211.
25. É. Levine, *Marital Relations in Ancient Judaism* (Wiesbaden: Harrassowitz Verlag, 2009), p. 34.
26. *The Jewish Study Bible, p.* 420.
27. Gen 24:22, 53.
28. D. Instone-Brewer, *Divorce and Remarriage in the Bible (*Grand Rapids: Eerdmans, 2002), pp. 5–6.
29. Ex 21:10–11.
30. *Vine's Complete Expository Dictionary*, p. 12.
31. See for instance Ex 21:22 where a fine was to be paid to the husband, 'owner', of a pregnant woman who miscarried after being accidentally hit during an altercation between men.
32. Ho 2:18.
33. Dt 20:7.
34. Aristotle, *Historia Animalium* 3, 2; *De Generatione Animalium* 1. For a comprehensive analysis of the complexity of Aristotle's embryology see S. Connell, *Aristotle on Female Animals* (Cambridge: Cambridge University Press, 2016).
35. Gn 27:29–30.
36. *The Jewish Study Bible, p.* 16. For an account of polygamy and monogamy in the Old Testament see G. Hugenberger, *Marriage as a Covenant: Biblical Law and Ethics as Developed from Malachi* (Eugene, Oregon: Wipf and Stock, 1994), pp. 106–121.
37. 2 S 16:20–22.
38. Levine, *Marital Relations in Ancient Judaism*, p. 30.
39. Dt 24:1–4.
40. Ml 1:10–16.
41. R. Gane, 'Old Testament Principles Relating To Divorce and Remarriage' in *Journal of the Adventist Theological Society* 12/12 Autumn (2001), pp. 35–61.
42. For an analysis of the range of meanings see Gane, 'Old Testament Principles Relating To Divorce and Remarriage' pp. 41–43.
43. *The Jewish Study Bible*, p. 420.
44. Jr 3:8–14.
45. Ho 2:4.
46. Dt 22:13–21.
47. Dt 22:28–29.

[48] In Ezk 44:22 this is restricted to widows of priests.
[49] In ancient Israel marriage with foreigners was not forbidden, Gn 41:45; 48:5.
[50] Ezr 10.
[51] Lv 18:6–17.
[52] *The Jewish Study Bible*, p. 418.
[53] *New Jerusalem Bible p.* 253, footnote 25.a.
[54] Levine, *Marital Relations in Ancient Judaism*, pp. 34–35.
[55] *Ibid.,* p. 35.
[56] Is 62:5.
[57] Levine, *Marital Relations in Ancient Judaism*, p. 16 footnote 16.
[58] Is 54:5; Ho 2:16; Ezk 16:6–14.
[59] Ezk 7:15–34.
[60] Is 54:6–8, 62:4–5; Ho 16:2–20; Ml 2:10, 14.
[61] *Vine's Complete Expository Dictionary*, pp. 18–19.
[62] For instance, Laban, Gn 32:1; Jacob, Gn 49:28.
[63] Gn 27:1–40.
[64] *Catechism of the Catholic Church*, 1077–1083.
[65] See Hugenberger, *Marriage as a Covenant*, especially Introduction, also pp. 171–174.
[66] *Ibid.,* pp. 205–210.
[67] *Ibid.,* pp. 211–212.
[68] For the significance of hand gestures in oath taking see *Vine's Complete Expository Dictionary*, p. 104. In medieval Europe handfasting, a ritual joining of hands, was a sign of commitment during betrothal.
[69] Hugenberger, *Marriage as a Covenant*, pp. 248ff; p. 343.
[70] Gen 29:30.
[71] Tb 6:18.
[72] Tb 8:7.
[73] *Vine's Complete Expository Dictionary*, pp. 141–143.
[74] Gn 24:67.
[75] Gn 22:2.
[76] *The Jewish Study Bible*, p. 1563.
[77] *Ibid., p.* 1565.
[78] Sg 8:6–7.
[79] *Vine's Complete Expository Dictionary*, p. 142.
[80] *The Jewish Study Bible*, p. 149.
[81] *Ibid.,* p. 1288.
[82] Ps 136; *The Jewish Study Bible*, p. 1434.
[83] Is 54:1–8; 61:2–10.

84 Ps 128.
85 Pr 1:8.
86 *The Jewish Study Bible*, p. 380.
87 Dt 6:4–7.
88 Si 25:1.
89 *Ibid.*, 36:25.
90 *Ibid.*, 23:19; 23:22.
91 Aristotle, *Nicomachean Ethics*, VII.
92 Aquinas, *Summa Theologiae*, I, II, 107.
93 Mt 1:1–17; Lk 3:23–38.
94 See Y. Buxbaum, *The Life and Teachings of Hillel* (New York: Rowman and Littlefield, 1994), p. 4.
95 A. Kasher, *Jews, Idumaeans and Ancient Arabs* (Tubingen: J. C. B. Mohr, 1988), p. 63.
96 Instone-Brewer, *Divorce and Remarriage in the Bible*, pp. 162–164. Instone-Brewer seems to move quickly away from a thorough investigation of scripture to a rather more speculative account of rabbinic teaching when he claims that by the first century CE 'the rabbis agreed that the grounds for divorce were childlessness, material neglect, emotional neglect, and unfaithfulness', p. 85.
97 *Ibid.*, p. 162; J. Neusner, *The Rabbinic Traditions About the Pharisees Before 70 Part II: The Houses* (Oregon: Wipf & Stock, 1971), pp. 36–38.
98 Instone-Brewer, *Divorce and Remarriage in the Bible*, p. 164.
99 For an analysis of the range of meanings see Gane, 'Old Testament Principles Relating To Divorce and Remarriage', pp. 41–43.
100 *The Jewish Study Bible*, p. 420.
101 J. Neusner, *The Rabbinic Traditions About the Pharisees Before 70 Part II*, 38; *The Literature of the Sages First Part* (Netherlands: Brill, 1987), p. 170.
102 Though Jesus may be in agreement with the Qumran Essenes, see D. Harrington, *The Gospel of Matthew* (Collegeville Minnesota: Liturgical Press, 1991), p. 275.
103 R. Brown, *An Introduction to the New Testament* (New York: Doubleday, 1997), pp. 269–270.
104 Lk 16:18.
105 *Commentary on the New Testament Use of the Old Testament* G. K. Beale and D. A. Carson (eds.), (Grand Rapids Michigan: Baker Academic, 2007); Lv 21:7; Ezk 44:22.
106 R. Brown, *An Introduction to the New Testament*, pp. 161–163.
107 Mk 9:25.

[108] Mk 9:30–32.
[109] Mk 9:33–37.
[110] Mk 9:42–48.
[111] M. Hooker, *The Gospel According to St Mark* (London: A & C Black, 1991), pp. 234–235.
[112] Mk 10:6–7.
[113] A. Thatcher, *God, Sex and Gender* (Oxford: Wiley-Blackwell, 2011), p. 99.
[114] Hooker, *The Gospel According to St Mark*, p. 236.
[115] *Ibid.*
[116] Brown, *An Introduction to the New Testament*, pp. 212–216; A. Cohen, *Matthew and the Mishnah* (Tubingen: Mohr Siebeck, 2016), p. 35.
[117] Mt 5:31–32.
[118] *The New Jerusalem Bible*, p. 1617 footnote n.
[119] Mt 19:4–6.
[120] E. Lövestam, *'Divorce and Remarriage in the New Testament'* in *The Jewish Law Annual* Volume 4 (Leiden: Brill, 1981), pp. 49–50.
[121] *Ibid.*, p. 51; see also C. Blomberg 'Matthew' in *Commentary on the New Testament Use of the Old Testament* (Grand Rapids Michigan: Baker Academic, 2007), p. 59.
[122] Blomberg points out that the Pharisees may not have presented an accurate interpretation of the Mosaic law, 'Matthew', p. 61.
[123] See Cohen, *Matthew and the Mishnah*, p. 189.
[124] Mt 19:7–9.
[125] Instone-Brewer, *Divorce and Remarriage in the Bible*, pp. 275–278; J. C. Laney, 'No Divorce and No Remarriage' in *Divorce and Remarriage: Four Christian Views* (Illinois: Intervarsity Press, 1990), pp. 33–37.
[126] Instone-Brewer, *Divorce and Remarriage in the Bible*, p. 278.
[127] Laney, 'No Divorce and No Remarriage' pp. 36–37.
[128] Mt 19:10.
[129] Viviano, 'The Gospel According to Matthew' p. 643.
[130] This is the interpretation followed by F. Moloney, *'A Hard Saying' The Gospel and Culture (*Collegeville Minnesota: Liturgical Press, 2001), p. 39.
[131] Lövestam, *'Divorce and Remarriage in the New Testament'*, pp. 55–56.
[132] *Ibid.*, p. 61.
[133] Blomberg, 'Matthew' p. 60.
[134] *Catechism* 1603.
[135] Thatcher, *God, Sex and Gender*, pp. 100–101.
[136] Following Dt 23:1 these men were excluded from the assembly and priesthood, J. Blenkinsopp, 'Deuteronomy' in *The New Jerome Biblical Commentary* (London: Geoffrey Chapman, 1990), pp. 94–109, p. 105.

137 Mt 19:12.
138 Moloney, *'A Hard Saying' The Gospel and Culture*, p. 42.
139 *Ibid.*, pp. 43–44.
140 *Ibid.*, p. 44; see also Q. Quesnell, 'Made Themselves Eunuchs for the Kingdom of Heaven' in *Catholic Biblical Quarterly* 30/3 (1968), pp. 335–338.
141 Instone-Brewer, *Divorce and Remarriage in the Bible*, pp. 169–170.
142 R. J. Van Tine, 'Castration for the Kingdom and Avoiding the αἰτία of Adultery (Matthew 19:10–12)' in *Journal of Biblical Literature* 137/2 (2018), pp. 399–418.
143 *Ibid.*, pp. 417–418.
144 R. T. France, *The Gospel According to Matthew: An Introduction and Commentary* (Grand Rapids Michigan: Eerdmans, 1985), p. 283.
145 G. Holland, 'Celibacy in the Early Christian Church' in *Celibacy and Religious Traditions* (Oxford: Oxford University Press, 2008), p. 66; Harrington, *The Gospel of Matthew*, p. 276.
146 Origen *Against Celsus* 1, 2; B. Chilton, 'Mamzerut and Jesus' in *Jesus From Judaism to Christianity* (New York: T&T Clark, Continuum, 2007), p. 26.
147 Chilton, 'Mamzerut and Jesus' pp. 31–32; for a definition of *mamzer* see R. Eisenberg, *Dictionary of Jewish Terms* (Rockville Maryland: Schreiber, 2008), p. 248.
148 Blenkinsopp, 'Deuteronomy', p. 105.
149 *The Jewish Study Bible*, p. 418.
150 Mt 1:19; Chilton, 'Mamzerut and Jesus' p. 22.
151 *The Jewish Study Bible*, p. 418.
152 S. Fishbane, *Deviancy in Early Rabbinic Literature* (Leiden: Brill, 2007), pp. 5–6.
153 Mt 1:24–25; 2:23; 13:55.
154 Instone-Brewer, *Divorce and Remarriage in the Bible*, pp. 168–169.
155 C. Olson, 'Celibacy and the Human Body: An Introduction' in *Celibacy and Religious Traditions* (Oxford: Oxford University Press, 2008), p. 10.
156 France, *The Gospel According to Matthew*, p. 283.
157 See Mt 12:28.
158 J. M. Gundry-Volf, 'The Least and the Greatest: Children in the New Testament' in *The Child in Christian Thought* (Grand Rapids, Michigan: Eerdmans, 2001), p. 37 footnote 35.
159 France, *The Gospel According to Matthew*, pp. 283–284.
160 Harrington, *The Gospel of Matthew*, p. 276.
161 Mt 19:13–15; Mk 10:13–16; Lk 18:15–17.
162 Viviano, 'The Gospel According to Matthew', p. 662.

163 Gundry-Volf, 'The Least and the Greatest: Children in the New Testament', pp. 31–32.
164 D. Harrington, 'The Gospel According to Mark' in *New Jerome Biblical Commentary* (London: Geoffrey Chapman, 1993), pp. 617–618.
165 Mt 11:25.
166 Mt 21:15.
167 Mt 18:1–5; Mk 9:36–37; Lk 9:48.
168 Mt 9:18–25; Mk 5:22–43; Lk 8:41–56; Mt 15:21–28; Mk 7:24–30; Mt 17:14–18; Mk 9:17–27; Lk 9:38–43; Jn 4:46–52.
169 Lk. 7:11–15.
170 Mt 19:16–19; Lk 18:19–20; Mk 10:17–19.
171 Mk 7:9–13; Mt 15:4–6. J. Fitzmyer, *Essays on the Semitic Background of the New Testament* Vol. 1. (Grand Rapids, Michigan: William Eerdmans, 1997), pp. 93–100.
172 Ps 103:13; Pr 3:12.
173 Mt 7:7–11; Lk 11:9–13.
174 Mt 21:28–32; Lk 15:11–32.
175 Gn 21:8–14; Gn 25:27–34, 27:1–36; Gn 37:1–4.
176 Gn 4:1–16.
177 Mt 21:28–32.
178 Lk 15:11–32.
179 Mk 2:18–22; Mt 9:14–17; Lk 5:33–39.
180 See *New Jerusalem Bible*, p. 1623, footnotes g, h, i and j.
181 Mt 22:1–14.
182 Mt 25:1–13.
183 Jn 1:32–34, 3:29.
184 E. Clark, 'The Celibate Bridegroom and His Virginal Brides: Metaphor and the Marriage of Jesus in Early Christian Ascetic Exegesis' in *Church History* 77 1, (March 2008), pp. 1–5.
185 Jn 2:1–12.
186 Lk 1:46–55.
187 Lk 2:52.
188 Jn 19:26.
189 *New Jerusalem Bible*, p. 1747 footnotes c, d, e; p. 1787 footnote l.
190 Mt 12:46–50.
191 Lk 14:25–27.
192 Mt 22:30; Lk 20:35.
193 C. S. Lewis, *Miracles* (London: Centenary Press, 1947), pp. 190–191.
194 1 Co 9:19–23.
195 1 Th 4:14.

[196] 1Co 2:2; Ga 3:1; Ga 1:6–9.
[197] 1 Th 4–5.
[198] Ph 3:1–13.
[199] Ga 3:28.
[200] D. Horrell and E. Adams, 'The Scholarly Quest for Paul's Church at Corinth: A Critical Survey' in *Christianity at Corinth: The Quest for the Pauline Church* (Louisville: Westminster John Knox Press, 2004), pp. 1–43, p.2.
[201] *Ibid.*, pp. 5–6.
[202] *Ibid.*, pp. 7–8; R. Collins, *First Corinthians* (Collegeville Minnesota: Liturgical Press, 1999), pp. 22–24.
[203] Horrell and Adams, 'The Scholarly Quest for Paul's Church at Corinth', pp. 10–11; J. Murphy-O'Connor, *1 Corinthians* (Dublin: Veritas, 1980), pp. ix-x.
[204] Collins, *First Corinthians*, p. 4.
[205] 2 Co 2:4.
[206] 1 Co 16:21; 1 Co 1:1; see Collins, *First Corinthians*, pp. 2–3.
[207] Horrell and Adams, 'The Scholarly Quest for Paul's Church at Corinth', pp. 17–23; Collins, *First Corinthians*, pp. 16–17.
[208] Collins, *First Corinthians*, p. 5; 1 Co 1:11–13.
[209] Collins notes the 'amorphous' nature of early Gnosticism, *First Corinthians*, p. 97.
[210] Murphy-O'Connor, *1 Corinthians*, p. xiii.
[211] Collins, *First Corinthians*, p. 17.
[212] 1 Co 1:10–11; Collins, *First Corinthians*, pp. 20–21.
[213] Collins, *First Corinthians*, pp. 73–74.
[214] 1 Co 1:2.
[215] *Ibid.*, 3:23.
[216] Collins, *First Corinthians*, p. 25.
[217] *Ibid.*, p. 28; 1 Co 7:29; 7:31.
[218] 1 Co 5:1–13; 6:12–20.
[219] *Ibid.*, 5:1–5.
[220] *New Jerusalem Bible*, p. 1897 footnote 5a.
[221] 1 Co 11:1.
[222] *Ibid.*, 5:4–5; 5:13; Murphy-O'Connor, *1 Corinthians*, pp. 41–42.
[223] Murphy-O'Connor, *1 Corinthians*, p. 43.
[224] 1 Co 6:12–13; Murphy-O'Connor, *1 Corinthians*, pp. 50–54.
[225] 1 Co 6:16–18; Murphy-O'Connor, *1 Corinthians*, p. 53.
[226] 1 Co 6:19–20.
[227] Murphy-O'Connor, *1 Corinthians*, pp. 53–54.

228   1 Co 6:20.
229   *New Jerusalem Bible*, p. 1897 footnote 7a; Murphy-O'Connor, *1 Corinthians*, p. 59.
230   1 Co 7:1.
231   *Ibid.*, 7:32–35; Murphy-O'Connor, *1 Corinthians*, p. 59.
232   Murphy-O'Connor, *1 Corinthians*, p. 59.
233   1 Co 7:7.
234   *Ibid.*, 7:8.
235   Gn 2:18; *New Jerusalem Bible*, p. 1899 footnote h.
236   1 Co 7:3–4.
237   *Ibid.*, 7:5–7; Murphy-O'Connor, *1 Corinthians*, pp. 60–61.
238   Murphy-O'Connor, *1 Corinthians*, p. 63.
239   *Ibid.*, p. 64.
240   1 Co 7:12–13; 7:15–16.
241   *Ibid.*, 7:15.
242   Later we have the Petrine privilege where a non-consummated marriage between baptised and non-baptised parties can be dissolved; the Pauline privilege is where both parties are unbaptised and one wants to marry a baptised person.
243   1 Co 7:17; Murphy-O'Connor, *1 Corinthians*, p. 67.
244   Murphy-O'Connor, *1 Corinthians*, pp. 71–72.
245   1 Co 7:29; 7:31.
246   *Ibid.*, 7:25–31.
247   *Ibid.*, 7:32–35; Murphy-O'Connor, *1 Corinthians*, pp. 74–75.
248   1 Co 11:2–16; Murphy-O'Connor, *1 Corinthians*, pp. 103–109.
249   Horrell and Adams, 'The Scholarly Quest for Paul's Church at Corinth', pp. 34–36.
250   1 Co 11:2–6; W. Orr and J. Walther, *Anchor Bible: 1 Corinthians* (New York: Doubleday, 1976), pp. 262–264.
251   1 Co 11:11–12.
252   M. MacDonald, *Colossians, Ephesians* (Collegeville Minnesota: Liturgical Press, 2000), pp. 9–13.
253   *Ibid.*, pp. 17–21.
254   *Ibid.*, pp. 6–9; pp. 15–17.
255   *Ibid.*, p. 130.
256   *Ibid.*, pp. 121–124.
257   *Ibid.*, p. 124.
258   Jn 17:16–18.
259   MacDonald, *Colossians, Ephesians*, pp. 161–162.
260   *Ibid.*, p. 166.

261 *Ibid.*, p. 168.
262 *Ibid.*, p. 61.
263 2 Co 5:19–20.
264 Ep 4:17, 5:9; MacDonald, *Colossians, Ephesians*, p. 323.
265 MacDonald, *Colossians, Ephesians*, pp. 337–338.
266 Ep 5:21.
267 MacDonald, *Colossians, Ephesians*, pp. 327–341.
268 *Ibid.*, p. 328.
269 Ep 5:28.
270 MacDonald, *Colossians, Ephesians*, p. 330.
271 Ep 6:1; MacDonald, *Colossians, Ephesians*, pp. 332–333.
272 R. Garland, *Daily Life of the Ancient Greeks* (London: Greenwood Press, 2009), pp. 82–83.
273 *Ibid.*, pp. 72–73; M. Lovano, *The World of Ancient Greece Vol.1* (California: Greenwood, 2020), pp. 278–280.
274 Garland, *Daily Life of the Ancient Greeks*, pp. 75–76.
275 *Ibid.*, p. 82.
276 *Ibid.*, p. 172; Lovano, *The World of Ancient Greece*, p. 253.
277 A. Borkowski, *Textbook on Roman Law* (London: Blackstone, 1997), p. 119.
278 B. Frier and T. McGinn, *A Casebook on Roman Family Law* (Oxford: Oxford University Press, 2004), p. 28.
279 H. F. Jolowicz and B. Nicholas, *Historical Introduction to the Study of Roman Law* (Cambridge: Cambridge University Press, 1972), p. 119.
280 *Ibid.*, p. 114.
281 *Ibid.*, pp. 114–115.
282 *Ibid.*, pp. 115–116.
283 *Ibid.*, p. 117.
284 *Ibid.*, pp. 117–118.
285 *Ibid.*, p. 233.
286 *Ibid.*, p. 234.
287 *Ibid.*, p. 11.
288 *Ibid.*, p. 235.
289 *Ibid.*, p. 236.
290 Borkowski, *Textbook on Roman Law*, pp. 14–15.
291 Frier and McGinn, *A Casebook on Roman Family Law*, pp. 34–39.
292 *Ibid.*, p. 103.
293 *Ibid.*, p. 120.
294 J. E. Grubbs, "'Pagan' and 'Christian' Marriage: the State of the Question" in *Journal of Early Christian Studies* 2/4 1994, pp. 361–412, p. 382.

[295] G. Lind, *Common Law Marriage* (Oxford: Oxford University Press, 2008), pp. 53–57.
[296] S. Treggiari, 'Marriage and the Family in Roman Society' in *Marriage and Family in the Biblical World* (Illinois: Intervarsity Press, 2003), pp. 132–182, pp. 154–155.
[297] Grubbs, 'Pagan' and Christian Marriage', pp. 383–384.
[298] *Vine's Complete Expository Dictionary*, p. 1.
[299] Rev 19:7.

3 'IN THE WORLD' WITH THE CHURCH FATHERS

As Christianity began to spread the early church fathers were keen to stress that they proclaimed, taught and handed on the faith in God the Father, Christ his Son, and the Holy Spirit, as 'received from the apostles and disciples',[1] and that the 'one Physician' is the Saviour, Jesus Christ.[2] The early church fathers were as concerned as their predecessors to work out the meaning of having a life in Christ while also being in the world. At first glance it may appear that the early Christian approach to marriage and family is simply responding to the secular culture of the time and strands within that culture, while attempting to forge Christianity's own specific identity apart from Judaism. Certainly, it is true to say that early Christian writers were addressing pastoral concerns. Nevertheless, marriage matters theologically, and challenges to Christian marriage touched upon significant theological questions such as the goodness of the material world, the title of the Virgin Mary Mother of God, biblical interpretation, and especially the path to holiness. Moreover, early Christian theologians also played a part in the unfolding of marriage as part of God's plan of salvation.

In the ancient world pagan religions were polytheistic and pagans could happily add gods to their personal worship without having to relinquish others first. As St Paul found when he visited Athens, the people worshiped a number of gods and seemed to be open to accepting more, even an unknown one.[3] To a certain extent worship corresponded to whatever was the particular activity to hand so there were gods relating to civic life, to the community, and to family life where a family might have their own particular favourites. In the case of family life, people could choose to which gods they wished to appeal, so in pagan eyes a

Christian marriage rite might have been simply a quirk of that household. However, Judaism was different because Jews profess belief in the one God. Christianity was different because Christians believe in the one God in Three Divine Persons: the Father and Jesus his only begotten Son, and the Holy Spirit. As Christianity emerged, at times painfully, out of Judaism, it had been easy to regard it as simply a sect. The Jews saw themselves as the chosen people and so they were not especially concerned with the worship and lives of pagans. Christians saw Christ as fulfilling that promise made to the Jews and this requires proclamation of the good news. Moreover, Christianity asks for conversion and this involves a putting away with the old, and a putting on with the new, putting on Christ. Christ did change everything.

Christians in the world

St Paul's letters and accounts of the missionary activity of the apostles indicate that there were a number of local communities of Christians scattered across the Roman Empire. St Paul's letters also show evidence of a counter-cultural element in Christianity from the beginning. In one of the earliest apologies for Christianity written in about 179AD, the Roman advocate Marcus Minucius Felix sets up a dialogue between his Christian friend Octavius and the pagan Caecilius. Caecilius gives the case against the Christians: not only are Christians gathered from the dregs of society, including illiterate people and gullible women, and indulge in fasts and strange feasts, in particular Christians do not make sacrifice to the gods, indeed they despise the temples and laugh at pagan sacred things.[4] Sacrifice to the gods was seen as necessary to guarantee the peace and prosperity of the Empire.

Although the Emperor Nero (54–68AD) persecuted some Christians in Rome, the first time that persecution took the shape of public policy appears to be during the reign of the Emperor Domitian (83–96AD). In order to build up the treasury Domitian ordered worship at Imperial temples to bring in funds, and since the Jews were regarded as a separate group exempt from the traditional Roman cults, he enforced a Jewish temple tax. However, Christians soon came to the attention of the authorities. Christians worshipped the same God as the Jews but since they were not Jews, they did not pay tax. In addition, the Christian refusal to sacrifice to the gods, who were regarded as the guarantors of peace and prosperity, was seen as a threat to the Empire and Christians were charged with the crime of atheism.[5]

The situation of early Christians being 'in the world but not of the world', and the fact that marriage rested on witnessed consent rather than on a set legalised and obligatory formula gave Christians the scope to develop their own rites without falling foul of civil demands. Marriage could be specifically Christian. Unlike some jurisdictions, there was no ban among Christians on marriages between classes. Moreover, among Christians clearly there was no sacrifice to the gods. It is difficult to ascertain if there was a particular Christian ritual in the first two centuries AD. However, in the letter of St Ignatius of Antioch (d.c.108) to St Polycarp, St Ignatius says that Christians should marry with the permission of the bishop so that they are married 'in the Lord.'[6] Tertullian (c.155–240) also suggests that there was some sort of liturgy with a blessing and permission from the church, possibly also a Mass.[7] By the fourth century there is evidence of a specific rite with a blessing.[8] With perhaps an eye to those who thought that Christianity freed women in particular from any social convention early Christian writers such as St Clement of Rome (d.c.99) praise the hospitality of couples who treat everyone with equal respect and notably wives who love their husbands and manage their households properly.[9] Referring to Ephesians 5, St Ignatius of Antioch urges wives to love the Lord and 'be satisfied with their husbands' and husbands to love their wives as the Lord loves the Church.[10]

Nevertheless, how early Christians viewed marriage was complex. With the deaths of the apostles and of those who had had a direct link with them, the *parousia*, the idea that Christ's return was imminent, began to fade. The world still seemed to be under the sway of sin and death and some Christians began to think more of what it meant to be in the world. For some like St Anthony of Egypt (c251–356) the quest for holiness led to a rejection of marriage and property, and the embracing of an ascetic life in the desert as the first monk. However, some early Christians took the view that only a total renunciation of marriage and sexual intercourse would put an end to this world of sin and thus the new age of the Kingdom would come to be. After all, the world is perpetuated by sex, birth, children, and, for these extreme Christians, of course it was the seductive allure of women that prevented men from being completely free. Certainly, as P. Brown explains, rigorous sexual abstinence, sometimes total renunciation, was a part of the Christian tradition.[11] However an extreme encraticism, a form of radical asceticism, drove a wedge between nature and spirit. Nature and the material world were no longer seen as good, sexuality belonged only to the world of animality and could not even be disciplined, sexuality could not be held in check by society or institutions like marriage.[12]

Tertullian's polemic against Marcion, explains these different strands. Marcion (d.c.154) was from Pontus and the son of a bishop. When in Rome he came under the influence of gnostic thinking and this led him to reject the God of the Old Testament and most of the New Testament apart from the writings of St Paul, who, he believed was the only apostle to understand the message of Jesus. For Marcion it was only by cutting all ties with human society, beginning with the ties of marriage, family, parents and children, that new ties of communion could be forged.[13] Tertullian says that Marcion declares marriage and procreation to be evil[14] and renounces marriage as if it is a bad thing superseded by a good thing. In contrast, Tertullian explains that when some Christian ascetics refrain from marriage it is because they see marriage as a good thing but superseded by something better. Thus, in choosing abstinence Christians do not reject marriage. Tertullian points out that at creation God gave his blessing to marriage though naturally not to the excesses of sexuality such as adultery, covetousness or unchastity. Marriage also offers opportunities for temperance, chastity, continence, and discipline, all the things that help people to grow in holiness.[15] Similarly St Clement of Alexandria (c.150–c.215) calls for chastity in marriage and control rather than unbridled desire in contrast to those who simply hate anything to do with 'the flesh'.[16]

Certainly, marriage and family were placed in a larger framework with, for instance St Perpetua and St Felicity (both d.c.203) choosing martyrdom over motherhood as they each entrust their infant children into the care of others.[17] However as the red martyrdom of persecution lessened and the white martyrdom of the ascetic monastic life gained momentum, it remains important to recognize that neither martyrdom nor monasticism involved hatred of the body. Monasticism acknowledged that restraints have to be placed on the body since the body is ruled by a twisted will. Temperance, balance and chastity are called for to counter greed, the first sin, and uncontrolled desires. Apparently, in a famine-ridden world where people were tempted by avarice and dominance, ravenous greed rather than sex was thought to be the first sin that led Adam and Eve to eat the fruit of the forbidden tree.[18] Moreover the body is also destined for eternal life through the resurrection of the flesh and it is deeply implicated in the transformation of the soul.[19]

Responding to the culture of the time

The early church fathers lived, worked and ministered in a particular culture and context. Their writings are often responses to certain situations or people and are aimed at handing on the good news of Jesus Christ. However, as the dispute between Tertullian and Marcion shows, the early church fathers were not simply responding to challenges from a pagan culture. Certain strands within Christianity itself were also seen as threats. In terms of marriage and family life one real problem came in the form of an extreme encraticism as promoted by Tatian the Syrian (c.120–180) and later by the rise of Manichaeanism.

The encratite movement was associated with an ascetic Syrian theology and St Irenaeus (c.120-c.202) calls Tatian an encratite and follower of Marcion.[20] Tatian was a convert to Christianity and studied for a time in Rome under St Justin Martyr (c.100–165). On his return to the East he founded an encratite sect, the Aquarii, who rejected wine and even substituted water for wine in the Eucharist.[21] Tatian was particularly irritated by what he saw as the immorality of Greek pagans notably expressed in their sculptures. Very little remains of Tatian's writings though a fragment of his *On Perfection According to the Saviour* is preserved by St Clement of Alexandria. According to St Clement Tatian interpreted St Paul's first letter to the Corinthians Chapter 7 strictly: all sexual activity is unbridled, uncontrolled and the work of Satan, and this includes sex within marriage. As far as Tatian is concerned, St Paul only pretended to allow sexual activity in marriage when in fact St Paul regarded it as fornication under a mask of legitimacy. Tatian further believed that Adam and Eve were expelled from paradise because they engaged in sexual intercourse. According to E. Hunt, Tatian did not find marriage a problem, rather it was sexual activity within marriage that was problematic and so Tatian urged that husband and wife live in complete continence as brother and sister.[22] St Irenaeus suggests that the real problem for Tatian was that sex increased the human race.[23] In contrast to theologians like Tertullian and St Irenaeus who see marriage and procreation as part of God's plan for humanity from the beginning,[24] thinkers like Tatian see marriage and procreation as the result of sin and a return to paradise involves rejecting both. For Tatian it seems that marriage means only spiritual union.

Even though Tatian's interpretation went beyond what St Paul actually said, his interpretation demonstrates that St Paul's teaching in 1 Corinthians 7 was hugely influential for early Christians. Certainly, Christian tradition affirms that marriage is a good and a path to holiness. Nevertheless, in the second and third centuries we can chart a growing interest in celibacy and virginity, though this interest can be contrasted with the strict view of Tatian. This interest can be traced in the writings of St Clement of Alexandria, Tertullian, Origen (c.185–253) and Lactantius (c.250–325).

The theology teacher St Clement of Alexandria lived in a rich, leisured and pleasure-seeking society. In his treatise *Who is the rich man that shall be saved?* St Clement advises wealthy people on the demands of following Christ and in his other teachings he points to the counter cultural messages of Christianity. In his practical work *Christ the Instructor or Educator* St Clement writes to Christian men and women alike. He explains that God is the master of both men and women, salvation is for both, and that there is equality in virtue and in marriage since marriage is 'an equal yoke.'[25] Although men and women have an innate equality,[26] and share the same nature, virtue and task of self-control, there are differences between the sexes. Following St Paul's hierarchical ordering the husband is head of the wife and they have different tasks, yet the wife can still engage in philosophy and at times show greater excellence than her husband.[27] In contrast to those who reject marriage out of hand, and to those like the followers of the gnostic Basilides (d.c.140) who appear to claim total moral freedom including freedom to sin since they are already perfect, St Clement says that celibacy is a blessed state gifted by God to some, but marriage is also a state to be admired. However, marriage can be used 'rightly or wrongly':[28] the problem lies in seeing marriage as a licence for unrestrained lust and pleasure unconnected to procreation.[29] Equally celibacy chosen out of hatred for God's good creation is wrongheaded.[30] According to St Clement and following the Genesis command to be fruitful and multiply, the goal of sexual intercourse is procreation and through procreation human beings co-operate with God. Simply seeking pleasure shows a lack of self-control and is an abuse of marriage.[31] St Clement points out that self-control applies not only to sexual desires but to other desires as well.³² Not only the spirit but also behaviour, manner of life and body are subjects for sanctification.³³ Indeed, all work, including the work in the house done by wives, is service not slavery to others.³⁴ St Clement's advice to Alexandrians is to live simply, use what has been given whether it is money, wealth, food, or sex in marriage wisely and properly, and work together since this is God's plan.

Tertullian, an educated convert from Carthage who may have been a lawyer, was himself married to a Christian and, in contrast to St Clement's teachings, Tertullian's writings seem to be more intimate and personal. Indeed, two letters to his wife, Books I and II, and a treatise on marriage are still in existence. In *To His Wife* Tertullian speaks not only to his wife but to other Christian wives and so more broadly about marriage. It seems that in Roman society considerably more aristocratic women than men were becoming Christians and these women had difficulties in finding Christian husbands of the same social standing. If they married beneath their social status, they would lose their noble rank and wealth and, in some cases, might become slaves themselves. The alternatives were to marry a pagan of the same status or to live with a socially inferior Christian without going through a legal Roman marriage.³⁵ Tertullian is especially concerned about the problems that may arise in marriages between a Christian wife and pagan husband, not least that the husband may not allow her to practice her faith. However, Tertullian speaks of his Christian wife as his 'beloved fellow servant in the Lord.'³⁶ While he sees marriage as a 'good thing', 'blessed by God as the seminary of human life' and for 'replenishment of the earth', Tertullian also understands and follows Paul in seeing that celibacy is preferable.³⁷ Moreover Tertullian is full of praise for those widows who do not remarry even though they have the right to do so, but instead 'prefer to be wedded to God', and he recommends this path to his own wife.³⁸ Similarly, when writing to a 'brother' who has been widowed he repeats the same advice.³⁹ Nevertheless, Tertullian also speaks of equality in marriage where both can pray and fast together, visit the sick, give alms and care for the poor: for where the two are there is God.[40] Later on in life Tertullian came under the influence of the Montanists, advocates of the New Prophecy, who taught a strict Christian discipline. By this stage Tertullian had concluded that remarriage after widowhood was absolutely forbidden.[41]

While Tertullian's rigorous outlook increased, Origen began from a strongly ascetical view, indeed he interprets the advice to become eunuchs for the Kingdom literally. Origen sees the one-flesh union of husband and wife in the context of Ephesians 5 and the love Christ has for the Church. In the same way as a husband should not leave his wife, the Church and possibly the believer should not be separated from the Lord.[42] Origen uses the image of the unity of Christ and the Church to comment on the 'divorce of Israel' where 'the mother of the people separated herself from Christ without a bill of divorce.' In effect, he says, the New Covenant with the gentiles is a bill of divorce written out for Israel, and the sign that Israel had received this bill was the destruction of Jerusalem. Moreover, following the law of Moses, Israel committed something 'unseemly' by choosing Barabbas over Jesus and sending Jesus to his death. However, since 'the Son of man is Lord of the Sabbath', unlike the people, the Lord can reform the law.[43]

Origen notes with evident disapproval that, 'contrary to what was written', some 'rulers of the Church' have allowed people to remarry while their first spouse was still alive.[44] Moreover, he seems to despair of the practice of remarriage after widowhood, indeed, sometimes even third and fourth marriages, and he thinks that those in ecclesiastical orders should not be married twice.[45] Nevertheless, Origen thinks that absolute chastity is a gift from God and so cannot be attained by ascetical practice alone.[46] But he also thinks that since in marriage God joins a woman to a man whereby two become one, there is a 'gift', just as there is a gift in celibacy.[47] However Origen does not believe that grace is extended to a pagan spouse. Rather the graces of marriage obtain only where both are Christians. Origen thinks that a Christian spouse can sanctify his or her pagan spouse; but the pagan spouse might also 'corrupt' the believing spouse, and so Origen counsels the believer should consider carefully whether to marry at all.[48] In a reflection perhaps of the difference in age, Origen admits that there is some equality,[49] yet he also sees that the harmony between husband and wife is expressed by the wife's submission to her husband who is her guide.[50] Similarly, while Origen sees harmony and blessing in the union of male and female as expressed in the Genesis command to go forth and multiply, on a more spiritual level of reading, he regards male and female as an illustration of the 'inner man' who has both a spiritual and a more inferior material aspects.[51] Origen's Platonic belief that human beings come into existence through their souls falling into bodies suggests a negative view of sexuality. Sex, after all becomes the means of providing bodies for souls, and Origen also thinks that an addiction to the flesh came into existence as a result of the Fall.[52] However in his analysis of Origen's commentary *On the Song of Songs* J. C. King argues that Origen offers three positive judgments on marriage: that marriage is 'a lawful option' for Christians; that 'God has marked genuinely Christian marriage with a theological character' so that it points as a type to spiritual realities; and that marriage is 'a theological reality in its own right.'[53] Notably, Origen uses marriage imagery to discern his Christology: he compares the unity in Christ with the one-in-flesh of man and wife and concludes that the Word is even more in one flesh with the soul of Christ because it is more becoming for this specific loving soul to be united with God, and this analogy is followed by other theologians.[54]

Emperor Diocletian (c.244-c.316) appointed Lactantius head of rhetoric in Diocletian's chief residence, Nicodemia but Lactantius resigned his post when or just before he became a Christian. Lactantius later became tutor to Crispus, the son of Constantine. The talents of Lactantius lay very much in challenging the errors he saw in pagan philosophy, and in attempting to present Christianity as attractive to pagan thinkers. In order to demonstrate the superiority and moral advantage of Christianity over pagan philosophy Lactantius critiques the pagan understanding of the gods that has them behave like humans, including gods taking goddesses in marriage yet there not being more gods as a result.[55] He takes to task the practice of holding wives in common advocated by Plato. This area of pagan philosophy was an easy target since polygamy was not the usual practice of the time and many of Lactantius's readers, pagan or Christian, would agree with his position. Lactantius praises monogamy as necessary for society, for the proper love of children, and for preserving the love between the couple: 'what husband will love his wife, or wife her husband unless they have always lived as one, unless deliberate devotion and steadfast exchange of loyalty have produced a mutuality of love?'.[56] Moreover, Lactantius charges pagan philosophy for promoting double standards in punishing as adultery a woman's sexual relations outside marriage while allowing men to have as many sexual relationships as they liked as long as these relationships were with slaves, prostitutes or women of low social standing.[57] In his wide ranging discussion that embraces homicide, infanticide, exposure of children, violence and all actions subject to the passions and excesses of the senses, Lactantius says that pagan philosophers mistake virtues for vices. He thinks that if there is a risk that people could not look after children, they would do better not to marry in case they resort to exposure of their children.[58] In terms of emotions, Lactantius claims that people who do not know God are either like the Stoics obliged to 'uproot' affections as if they are diseases or are unable to set limits on their anger, desires and lusts. In contrast, God gives people the gift of virtue so that they can keep desires and pleasures within the prescribed limits.[59] In the context of sexual desire, Lactantius explains that God created the two sexes and the attraction between them is part of his plan as sex is ordained towards procreation. However, he condemns inordinate desire and sex is to be kept strictly within marriage.[60] For Lactantius the gift of celibacy for spiritual reasons is the ideal but is not for everyone.[61]

Notably, and in contrast perhaps to the objection to double standards expressed by Lactantius, the Council of Elvira in Spain between 305 and 314 gave canonical penalties almost exclusively concerning sexual misconduct of women. However, this focus on women may have been because the council was responding specifically to a law passed by Diocletian allowing women to initiate divorce simply by writing a bill of divorce. A woman who had committed an act of adultery had to do penance for five years before she could be readmitted to communion but an adulterous woman who left her husband in order to remarry was excommunicated for life. A woman who left her adulterous husband could not remarry, and if she did remarry, she could not receive communion until her first husband died or she herself was close to death. An unmarried woman who had premarital sex had to abstain from communion for one year because she had 'violated only the marriage rites', assuming of course that she would then marry her lover. Fornication applied to those who had sexual relations with more than one man, and the penalty here was penance and excommunication for five years. A widow who had sexual relations with a man and then married him was excommunicated for five years, but if she married someone else then the penalty was life-long excommunication. Virgins who had dedicated themselves to God but then broke their vows had to do penance and live for the rest of their lives in celibacy or else they risked life-long excommunication. Married bishops, priests and deacons had to refrain from all sexual activity.

The rise of Manichaeism

Rejection of marriage because it resulted in children, yet acceptance of sexual activity outside marriage appears to be a feature of a new movement, the 'Religion of Light', Manichaeism. Although a radical encratite idea had been rejected in mainstream Christianity, in the third century this new religion began to emerge out of a mix of Zoroastrian dualism, Buddhism, Babylonian myth and

Christianity. Named after its founder, Mani (c.216-c.274), Manichaeism spread through the missionary activity of ascetic monks from Persia.[62] According to Mani, the revelations given to Jesus, Buddha and Zoroaster were incomplete and it was he himself who was to bring divine revelation fully into the world.[63]

In his treatise *Contra Faustum* St Augustine (354–430) takes issue with the Manichaean Faustus who had attacked the Old Testament and some New Testament scripture and in particular denied the reality of the Incarnation.[64] St Augustine himself had formerly been attracted to Manichaeism, attending their meetings as a 'hearer' for at least nine years,[65] and his treatise gives a good account of what he regards as the pseudo-Christian Manichaean theories.[66] Manichaeism professed to be a religion of reason. Faustus argues that the Manichaeans believe in one God.[67] However since a good being could not create evil, it was believed that two beings, one of Light, God, and one of Darkness, Hyle or the devil were involved in the beginning of the world. In the battle between the two forces man was defeated by the darkness and lost some of his light and the world now became a mixture of good associated with the spiritual and evil linked to the material. Good and evil were in constant chaos and warfare with the power of the Light residing in the sun and moon.[68]

The devil caused two demons to bring forth Adam and Eve as their offspring with the aim of trapping as much light as possible in the visible world through the generation of children.[69] Since every living being expressed this primordial battle between good and evil, light and dark, human beings consisted of both a good and an evil nature, the body being the 'workmanship' of darkness and a 'prison' for the 'captive deity', the soul.[70] Only God could awaken the chosen ones to the spiritual light within them, and in response these enlightened human beings, the Elect, were to avoid lust and anything associated with the material world, in particular activities connected to the flesh.[71] In contrast to Christians who fast as a matter of discipline, for the Manichaeans eating meat was forbidden for the priestly class since they believed that animals were made by the devil and meat is the result of generation.[72] However some particles of light were trapped in vegetables, especially grains, lentils, beans and yellow fruit like melons,[73] and these were to be eaten since the task of these enlightened human beings was to set free every possible particle of light.

Notably taking up the imagery of Christ the bridegroom and the Church as bride, Faustus claims that the Manichaean religion was the true and chaste bride of Christ.[74] Faustus suggests that Manichaeans did not forbid marriage for those reluctant to embrace virginity, but they did encourage virgins to remain as they were.[75] However, as St Augustine points out, the Manichaeans did not teach that marriage is good and virginity better. Rather, the Manichaeans seem to allow for sexual intercourse for those unable to be continent or for mere pleasure, yet forbid marriage since marriage concerns procreation and in the Manichaean doctrine through birth the soul, 'god' is 'bound' to a body instead of 'released.' This is why the Manichaeans refuse to acknowledge the birth of Christ but do recognize his death which they regard as the release of the soul from the prison of the body.[76] Indeed St Augustine charges the Manichaeans with saying that the procreation of children is a greater sin than cohabitation, and if a 'second grade' follower marries, then he should avoid sexual intercourse at times when his wife may be likely to conceive.[77]

Marriage and celibacy

In contrast to the Manichaeans whose creation story described matter as evil and Adam and Eve as the production of the devil, the early church fathers returned to the scriptures and Genesis. St John Chrysostom (c.344–407) once lived an ascetic life as a monk but due to ill health returned to city life as a priest. Chrysostom criticizes those 'heretics' who say that the present world is evil.[78] Chrysostom explains that the whole of creation is made out of God's 'surpassing love' for humanity. He pointedly tells his congregation 'so, when you hear that "God saw that it was good," presume no longer to contradict Sacred Scripture.'[79]

Chrysostom says he speaks about the honourable state of marriage to counteract those, presumably like the Manichaeans, who despise marriage while allowing licentiousness.[80] Chrysostom presents a view of marriage that includes the significance of properly ordered desire, strength of love, and family harmony that comes about when the family embrace a virtuous and balanced life. Indeed Chrysostom promotes a well-ordered household where all its members including servants are 'intent on the same things' and live in moderation.[81] Much of what Chrysostom has to say on the guidance of wives by their husbands suggests that there could have been a considerable age gap since husbands are called to speak philosophy to her 'receptive' soul, to inculcate a sense of modesty, reserve and detachment from extravagances, and to 'mold her well.'[82] Chrysostom seems to be especially concerned about the corrupting influence of wealth, and so avarice rather than inordinate sexual desires taints marriage.[83] Indeed he urges the men in his congregation not to consider marriage lightly or casually or for financial gain: 'you must consider that marriage is not a commercial venture but a fellowship for life.'[84]

Countering those who claim that procreation is the work of the devil, Chrysostom draws attention to the Genesis text where the command to increase and multiply is 'a blessing' from God.[85] The desire in love is 'deeply implanted in our nature' and 'nothing so welds our lives together as the love of man and woman.'[86] Following Genesis plus the general patristic view that Eve bore the greatest responsibility for tempting Adam, Chrysostom explains that in the beginning Adam and Eve were created equal and were entrusted equally with control of everything. However as a result of succumbing to temptation Eve, and so women, are now subject to their husbands.[87] However while the wife seems to be the loser because she has to submit to her husband, following Ephesians 5 she is the gainer because her husband has to love her, and the 'measure' of this love is Christ's love for the Church.[88] Moreover, husband and wife, as head and body form a close union like Christ and the Church.[89] Again, referring to the heretics, Chrysostom points out that if St Paul condemned marriage then he would not have called Christ a bridegroom and the church a bride.[90]

Presumably a comment on the behaviour of the men in his congregation, Chrysostom notes the damage caused by a husband who uses violence or makes his wife afraid. Indeed he suggests that the permission to separate in Matthew 5 may have been to protect wives from the wrath of their husbands.[91] Instead the husband should 'act like a man who has been entrusted with the care of a sacred image.'[92] He says that even if his wife shows disdain, her husband should sway her not with threats but with the power of his love for her, since she is his 'life's partner' and mother of his children.[93] Unusually, Chrysostom does not condemn second marriages that is another marriage after the death of the first spouse, though he regards this as a concession.[94] Addressing perhaps the excesses of the time and presumably lavish ceremonies, Chrysostom reminds his congregation that marriage is 'not a theatre', it is 'a mystery' and this is shown by the fact that when the couple come together they produce an image of God, a child, 'and the child is a sort of bridge, so that the three become one flesh, the child connecting, on either side, each to other.'[95] Chrysostom reminds husbands and wives to support each other in living good virtuous lives, to pray together, to go to church, and to live with each other in mutual kindness.[96]

By analogy, Chrysostom further associates marriage with entry into the Church through baptism. The conversion in baptism reflects the human reality that a young bride had to completely change her way of life. In his first instruction to those about to be baptised he tells them that the days of their 'spiritual marriage' are close at hand. Referring to the bride of Ephesians 5, in his unfathomable compassion Christ accepts the catechumen in all his sinfulness and hurries to save his soul. On the part of the catechumen the 'dowry contract' in this spiritual marriage is obedience and the agreement made with the Bridegroom; the gift of the

Bridegroom is the magnitude of his love poured out in his sacrifice on the cross.[97] Chrysostom urges the newly baptised to 'keep the marriage robe in its integrity, that with it you may enter forever into this spiritual marriage.' Just as marriage between man and woman are celebrated with feasting for seven days, so too is there feasting for seven days for the newly baptised, setting before them the 'table of mysteries.' And this banquet is prolonged 'through all time', provided they keep their bridal robes 'inviolate and radiant.'[98]

While the Manichaeans allowed sexual intercourse for pleasure but objected to it, and therefore to marriage, when it involved the production of children, the question of abstaining from intercourse also vexed Christians. Interpretations of St Paul's First Letter to the Corinthians 7, and especially 7:5 that married couples should abstain from sexual intercourse for a time to devote themselves to prayer were varied. In the early church clerical celibacy was optional. Gradually married bishops, priests and deacons were expected to refrain from conjugal relations with their wives and this developed into the requirement of perfect and perpetual continence.[99] St Ambrose, bishop of Milan (c.340–397), whose elder sister Marcellina (c.327–398) had taken a vow of consecrated virginity, thinks that more is required of the clergy than of lay people. Following Old Testament ritual purity, St Ambrose therefore expected the clergy to remain pure and so refrain from all conjugal intercourse.[100]

However, what about the case of married lay couples? For biblical theologians like St Jerome (c.347–420) wives have to please their husbands and are concerned with the affairs of the world.[101] In contrast a virgin does not have to please her husband or engage in worldly affairs and so can spend her time with Christ as his bride.[102] Referring to regulations on Jewish ritual purity, St Jerome thinks moreover that the demands of married life mean that lay people cannot pray properly unless they abstain from sexual relations.[103] St Jerome points to St Paul's injunction that we are called to pray always, and from this St Jerome deduces that St Paul's deepest wish is that all Christians should practice permanent sexual continence: either Christians are virgins or they cease to pray in order to be obedient to their marriage vows.[104]

The question of celibacy within marriage also had bearing on another theological issue current at the time: in what way was Mary the mother of Jesus a model for Christians. As D. Hunter explains, some saw Mary as a model for virgins until the birth of Jesus and then as a model for married life since, they claimed, she and Joseph had a normal married relationship. Thus, virginity and marriage were equal in honour. Others saw Mary as ever virgin because her perpetual virginity expressed her total consecration to her son, the Son of God. Thus, virginity was superior to marriage.[105] The concern of those who held that Mary and St Joseph had a normal married relationship was that an emphasis purely on her virginal status would mean that she could not be a model for all Christians.

The question of Mary's virginity came to a head in about 383 when an argument erupted between a monk, Carterius, and a Roman layman, Helvidius who was associated with the Arians. Carterius had written a pamphlet arguing that virginity was superior to marriage. In response Helvidius claimed that Mary did not remain a virgin.[106] Helvidius used scriptural passages about the 'brothers' of Jesus and the statement of Matthew 1:25 that 'Joseph took his wife, but knew her not until she had borne a son; and he called his name Jesus' to support his views. However, Helvidius also explicitly attacked the view that Mary is ever virgin on the grounds that those who held this view also believed that birth was shameful and degrading. As a logical consequence, this meant a denial that God had been born of a virgin's womb. Hunter explains how Helvidius built up his claims to the point of suggesting that ascetics who considered virginity to be superior to marriage in effect had a negative view of sexuality, therefore denied the goodness of creation and so denied the Incarnation, leading to a charge of Docetism. In the early church such charges were particularly sensitive since the discernment that Jesus is truly God and truly man was under threat from those like the Ebionites and

Arians who questioned his full divinity, and those like the Docetics and Apollinarians who questioned his full humanity.

In his tract *Against Helvidius* St Jerome refutes the arguments levelled against the perpetual virginity of Mary. The attribution of Virgin was an early title given to Mary.[107] Since the virginal conception of Jesus[108] affirms his divine sonship, Mary's virginal motherhood is not linked to any mistrust of sexual intercourse. However, some translations of Matthew 1:25 suggest that St Joseph had intercourse with Mary after the birth of Jesus and so Jesus had brothers and sisters. But Matthew's intention was to emphasize that Mary was a virgin when Jesus was born; the 'until' need not suggest virginity only up to his birth. This can be illustrated by other scriptural passages, for instance Psalm 110.1 states, 'Yahweh declared to my Lord, "Take your seat at my right hand, until I have made your enemies your footstool"': it cannot be concluded from this that the Lord will not sit at God's right hand once his enemies have been conquered. Matthew's gospel also speaks about the brothers (*adelphoi*), James, Joseph, Simon and Jude, and sisters of Jesus living in Nazareth.[109] The term *adelphoi* carries the meaning of close relatives. Various scriptural texts speak of 'Mary the mother of James and Joseph' or Joset standing with other 'Marys' and Salome at the foot of the cross,[110] and this Mary was the wife of Clopas who may have been related to Mary the mother of Jesus.[111]

While disputing with Helvidius on Mary's virginity, St Jerome is also keen to point out that in praising virginity he does not intend to disparage marriage,[112] though at times his language does not seem to bear this out. St Jerome argues that a virgin is 'holy in body and in spirit', whereas married women have to please their husbands. Although he accepts that there are some virgins who are not holy because they do not live up to their virginal state, St Jerome also thinks that widows and married women can be holy, but in the case of the married, only if they 'have ceased to be wives' or 'imitate virgin chastity.'[113]

St Jerome's tract silenced Helvidius. However, an even more serious attack on virginity came from another monk who had come to Rome from Milan: Jovinian.

Jovinian and Jerome

Jovinian (c.340s, d.c.398) not only attacked virginity and sexual renunciation but he also criticised asceticism. Moreover, his attacks raised serious questions on the theology of salvation itself. Jovinian's views were condemned in about 390–392 by Pope St Siricius (c.334–399) at a synod in Rome, and this condemnation was confirmed by St Ambrose.[114] Although most of Jovinian's writings are no longer in existence, St Jerome quotes him in his refutation *Against Jovinian*. Notably, St Jerome's refutation was so full of extreme language and bitter invective against Jovinian that St Jerome's friend Pammachius attempted to have the refutation withdrawn from circulation to save St Jerome's reputation.[115]

According to St Jerome, Jovinian made six dubious claims: first that 'virgins, widows and married women, who have been once passed through the laver of Christ, if they are on a par in other respects, are of equal merit'; second, that 'they who with full assurance of faith have been born again in baptism, cannot be overthrown by the devil'; third, that 'there is no difference between abstinence from food and its reception with thanksgiving'; fourth, that 'there is one reward in the kingdom of heaven for all who have kept their baptismal vow'; fifth, that all sins are equal; and six, that Mary did not remain ever virgin.[116] Jovinian's claims then also have a bearing on grace and co-operation with grace and indeed fed into the Pelagian controversy.

St Jerome once again asserts that he does not condemn marriage. St Jerome explains that Christians do not follow Marcion or the Manichaeans who disparage marriage, nor do they follow Tatian and the encratites who think that all intercourse is impure: 'while we honour marriage we prefer virginity.' To support this St Jerome compares virginity to gold and marriage to silver, where obviously gold is to be preferred. Indeed, he says, even philosophers prefer virtue to sensuality.[117] In contrast, St Jerome claims that it is Jovinian who promotes the excellence of marriage in order to disparage virginity.[118] Moreover he argues that Jovinian is a 'common enemy' to virginity and marriage because he thinks that a first marriage is the same as a second or third marriage (marriage taking place after the death of one of the spouses).[119] On the matter of grace, St Jerome says that 'Christ loves virgins more than others, because they willingly give what was not commanded of them. And it indicates greater grace to offer what you are not bound to give, than to render what is exacted of you.'[120]

Apparently one major problem for St Jerome was not a married couple where one becomes a believer. Following St Paul, the believer ought not to separate from the unbeliever. Indeed, St Jerome says that 'a husband may be an adulterer or a sodomite, he may be stained with every crime and may have been left by his wife because of his sins; yet he is still her husband and so long as he lives she may not marry another.'[121] However as far as St Jerome is concerned, when Christian women marry pagan husbands in effect they 'prostitute the temples of Christ to idols.' After all, Christians are part of the Body of Christ, and their bodies are temples of the Holy Spirit.[122] For St Jerome this was a very current problem since in the fourth century there still seems to have been opposition to Christianity in aristocratic circles. Frequently the women of the family were Christians whereas the men and sons remained pagan.[123]

Despite comparing marriage to silver, St Jerome's view of marriage appears harsh. In answer to his contemporaries who suggested that he condemned marriage, St Jerome replies that it is one thing not to condemn and another to commend, and he thinks that he has dealt 'more gently' with marriage than 'most' Latin and Greek writers.[124] Nevertheless St Jerome firmly believes that the joys of marriage are only transient, that marriage brings with it cares and tribulations.[125] He claims that in paradise Adam and Eve were virgins[126] and the command to increase and multiply was to be fulfilled after the Fall. Marriage accompanies the punishment of sweat, toil and the land choked with thorns. In short, virginity is natural and so is superior to marriage since it was the pre-lapsarian state: marriage follows guilt.[127] St Jerome's only real praise for marriage comes because it gives virgins.[128] His clinching argument against marriage is framed in terms of true discipleship: 'no soldier goes with a wife to battle.'[129]

Responding to Jerome

St Jerome's harsh view of marriage is perhaps influenced by his undoubted caustic attitude towards women. This in turn appears to be influenced by the prevailing pagan culture that saw women as generally weak, unreliable and changeable.[130] However St Jerome also follows scripture in thinking that men and women are both called to salvation.[131] Criticized by his contemporaries for surrounding himself with aristocratic wealthy women, St Jerome replies that they, unlike many men, are at least interested in the scriptures.[132] Moreover he says that he judges people's virtue not by their sex but by their minds.[133] According to V. Novembri, for St Jerome the traditional acceptance that women were weaker than men meant that in order to attain holiness they had to strive even more to overcome their natural tendencies towards frivolities, luxuries, and bodily adornments. Indeed, devotion to meditation, scripture and an ascetical life was the only sure way forward. In St Jerome's eyes his cruel mockery of the vanity of women served to draw a sharp contrast between worldly women and the virtuous Christian woman.[134]

Certainly, the institutional structures of Greek and Roman societies gave women and men an unequal status. The age difference at marriage also contributed to this as the older man was seen as responsible for the guidance and education of his much younger wife. Moreover, some scriptural texts cause problems, so for instance in Genesis 2:22 Eve was created from Adam's rib and Genesis 3:16 says that Eve was justly given the punishment of submission. Perhaps most difficult is the complicated text from St Paul's 1 Corinthians 11:7–10 where St Paul says that man is 'the image of God' and 'woman is the reflection of man's glory.' The Pastoral Epistles to Timothy and to Titus seem to have taken the accepted view that women are to be respected and are equal in honour, yet for practical purposes, that is, for peace in the household, the man is held to be superior. Remembering that for St Paul now that faith has come 'all are one in Christ Jesus,' and all, slaves and free, male and female, are Christs,[135] the church fathers also had the difficulty of reconciling texts.

The theologian, philosopher and archbishop St Gregory of Nazianzus (c.330–389) is particularly concerned about laws that entrench inequality between men and women. He refuses to accept legislation that 'restrained' women but 'indulged' men and that severely punished wives for adultery but ignores the infidelities of husbands.[136] According to Gregory the serpent deceived both Adam and Eve, and Christ saves both men and women. As they become one flesh in marriage so then 'let the one flesh have equal honour.'[137] Gregory affirms that marriage is a legitimate and honourable condition, but, he adds, it is not 'more lofty' than virginity. After all, a virgin is 'altogether Christ's.' Virginity is a greater good, but it can only be a greater good because marriage is a good.[138] Although Gregory thinks that marriage and the desire for children are good, he also thinks that it is not good if more than 'due honour' is given to the 'flesh': marriage should be pure and free of lust.[139] Similarly, virginity is not good if it engages in 'spiritual adultery' through sins such as pride or impiety.[140] However, his injunction to both virgins and wives is the same: be 'one in the Lord.'[141]

St Basil of Caesarea (c.329-c.379), theologian, bishop and friend of St Gregory, seems to have dealt with a number of pastoral situations around marriage.[142] To begin with he recognizes that there is a real problem when families put forward young girls to be professed as virgins and the girls themselves have 'no inner impulse' for a celibate life. He suggests that careful discernment should be made to ensure such professions are genuine and he extends this also to men who wish to live a celibate life but not as monks. Husbands who are unfaithful, men who seduce or carry off women are to be suitably punished. St Basil reluctantly accepts the custom that if a husband returns to his wife, she must accept him but if she is the adulteress then she is to be expelled from the home. St Basil accepts the possibility of second or even third marriages, but it appears this only refers to situations for widowers and widows, where the first spouse has died.[143] Only widows who remain unmarried are given support (presumably material or financial) from the community. For a husband who has left his wife and formed a new union, St Basil says he lies under the charge of adultery and so is subject to a lengthy process of penance after which he can be considered worthy of Holy Communion. Notably, St Basil does not say whether the husband had to separate from the second or third union, but since St Basil calls the second union adultery presumably this is the case.[144] St Basil acknowledges the reality of unmarried couples living together but this too is subject to canonical penalties.[145]

While the fathers accept the good of marriage, as a whole they do not recommend second or third marriages. These are marriages after the death of one of the spouses. Given that the age difference between husband and wife could be considerable, presumably there were a number of young widows. However, as St Gregory explains, and relying on the belief that marriage bears a resemblance to the union of Christ and the Church, 'if there were two Christs, there may be two husbands or wives', but there is only one Christ. Although a first marriage is legal, a second is accepted only as an 'indulgence.' [146]

To a certain extent, responses to St Jerome were also related to disputes about methods of biblical translation. St Jerome's method was 'to give sense for sense and not word for word.'[147] St Jerome's method allowed him to argue that St Paul's rebuke of St Peter in Galatians 2:11–14 was only a pretence.[148] For St Augustine this interpretation had serious repercussions: if St Paul was not speaking the truth then how could any of the scriptures be trusted? Moreover, this interpretation plays into the hands of the Manichaeans who also argue that some scripture is false. As St Augustine points out, what then is the Christian answer to those who forbid marriage? As a result, St Augustine is very concerned to maintain the truthfulness of St Paul's teaching on marriage and to correct false understandings.

St Augustine: On the Excellence of Marriage and On Holy Virginity

St Augustine was well aware of the 'heresy' of Jovinian who called Catholics Manichaeans for preferring holy virginity to marriage. Moreover, the Pelagians also called Catholics Manichaeans because Catholics hold that original sin was introduced by the first married couple, Adam and Eve. In contrast to the Pelagians 'who believe that infants stand in no need of Christ as their Physician,'[149] and referring to St Paul's letters to the Romans and Colossians to support his position,[150] St Augustine championed baptism for infants. St Augustine then was charged with condemning marriage and procreation because of his preference for virginity and his assertion that infants inherit original sin.[151]

St Augustine was not the first theologian to acknowledge the existence of original sin. However, without a proper context St Augustine's view, and thus also his approach to marriage, appears pessimistic. And the proper context is the context of grace. Reflecting on Romans 7 and the pervasiveness of sin St Augustine concludes that all people are prone to the same thing: 'what I do I do not want to do.' St Augustine observes that the parts of the human body that have been created expressly for the procreation of children (and here he means the male sex organ) are a good example of this: they do not seem to obey the will, and indeed even act against the will and respond to lust.[152] His observation of the powerlessness of the will and lack of self-control when it comes to sexual desire is the reason why St Augustine says that there is always an element of dominion or lust, and therefore sin, in the sexual act. However, within marriage this is the very least of sins and one that can be forgiven in the same way as we pray the Our Father and ask God to forgive our daily debts.[153]

Nevertheless, St Augustine does not end there. He offers not only a doctrine of sin but also grace: 'who will rescue me?' This is realism rather than pessimism. Original sin is a division within the self, causing a battle and a conflict of desires where the will is torn apart.[154] The effect of original sin and this weakening of the will are found in the tendency of the person to incline towards sin, concupiscence. Sin is choosing a lower good over a higher good.[155] Of course things in the world are attractive because God has made all things beautiful. Friendship, 'a nest a love and gentleness because of the unity it brings' is one great good. However, an 'immoderate urge' towards lower things such as sensual pleasure is a temptation to make a lower choice over the higher choice of a spiritual good.[156] Moreover, St Augustine is well aware that a distorted will leads to distorted passion and passion forms habit, creating a 'chain' that holds the person a prisoner. Notably for St Augustine this was not only a 'chain of sexual desire' but also of ambition and pride. Lust is not simply found in fornication. It is present in all inordinate desires of the body such as drunkenness and gluttony, and these desires are overcome by continence which heals these evils by goods. In the case of marriage, moderation and limiting the lust of the flesh out of permission for the other spouse or for children, are God's way of using evil lust for good. St Augustine asserts that lust after the flesh is lesser a lust than lust against the spirit because the first lust is at least after what is good of flesh.[157] And in the last analysis only God, he says, can heal this wounded will.[158]

To avoid complaints St Augustine wrote two treatises, first one on marriage followed by one on virginity. To leave his readers in no doubt, St Augustine calls his first treatise *On the Excellence of Marriage*. St Augustine begins by observing that human nature is social, friendship is a great and natural good and the first natural union of human society is husband and wife. The naturalness of this union is a great good that goes back to Genesis and it is shown in the way husband and wife walk together, looking in the same direction.[159] Although St Augustine does not expand on this, the idea of husband and wife not simply looking at each other but going forward together looking in the same direction is a beautiful expression of married life.

St Augustine identifies three goods of marriage: children, the fidelity of the couple, and indissolubility or *sacramentum*, the sacramental bond that is the sign of marriage.[160] These three goods are all animated by conjugal love which is the bond of marriage and this bond remains in infirmity and old age, whether or not there is the ability to produce children.[161] Notably, St Augustine thinks that marriage is for the procreation of children, but he seems here to link this not so much to the production of the next generation as to children 'spiritually regenerated', having children who are 'born again in Christ.'[162] However St Augustine also points out that it is not permissible to divorce a wife who is infertile in order to marry another who may produce children: this is adultery.[163] Given that for St Augustine concupiscence taints everything that humans do, marriage includes the genuine good of being a remedy for concupiscence because it channels sexual desire towards the good of children. Fidelity does not simply mean no adultery. Fidelity is a good distinct from the good of children and, as the positive duty of one spouse to meet the needs of the other fidelity gives stability to sexual desire. Fidelity is a social bond and it is a good even if the relationship comes about through a desire for pleasure rather than children. For St Augustine *sacramentum* does not mean the sacraments as we now have them. Rather *sacramentum* is related to the divine, a visible sign of something invisible.[164] Referring to St Paul's letter to the Ephesians the sacrament is a sign of the unity of all who belong to the one City of God and like the case of Christ and the Church marriage is therefore indissoluble.[165] However St Augustine understands Matthew 5:32 to permit separation on the grounds of fornication and he suggests that idolatry is an instance of fornication. It is one thing to separate on the grounds of religious infidelity or pagan idolatry, nevertheless St Augustine thinks that remarriage of either husband or wife still amounts to adultery and so is not permitted.[166] St Augustine thinks that if either the possibility of children or fidelity is excluded then the relationship is not marriage.[167] However, he also thinks that the marriage between Mary and St Joseph was a true marriage even though Mary remained ever virgin, since in their case there was never meant to be 'any carnal connection' and as a result of his conjugal fidelity St Joseph and Mary were both parents of Jesus.[168]

In response to the Pelagian charge that Catholics show a distrust of the material in their affirmation of original sin, St Augustine begins his defence of the faith by explaining that sin is the work of the devil, however human beings are always the 'work of God.' Indeed marriage and procreation would have existed even if there had not been the first sin, after all children are brought about through sexual intercourse.[169] Chastity in the married state, meaning the appropriate use of sexual desire, is one of God's gifts, and the union of the couple to produce children is 'the natural good of marriage.'[170] Inordinate desire, lust, is not a good use of marriage.[171] The shame felt by Adam and Eve indicates the evil of lust, no longer having reasoned control, and lust is the result of the first sin of Adam.[172] As St Augustine notes, a man's body reacts to lust and is not always controlled by his will.[173] However St Augustine does not think that in censuring lust he condemns marriage. Rather he thinks that as a result of the first sin concupiscence is always present in human actions: the taint of original sin follows humanity but it is not from the goodness of marriage.[174] While for St Augustine the procreation of children is the 'proper end' of marriage and so is not sin, 'the nuptial embrace' for the sake of the couple's desires is permissible and pardonable as long as the possibility of children is not impeded.[175] Indeed St Augustine recognizes the fears and sorrows of childlessness within marriage.[176] According to St

Augustine the root of sin is weakness of the soul not the body. This means that St Augustine looks first to other sins than the sensual ones, for example pride, 'the wish to be feared or loved by people for no other reason than the joy derived from such power', idle curiosity or lust.[177]

To balance his treatise on the good of marriage and address concerns in society about people who deliberately remained unmarried St Augustine writes *On Holy Virginity*. While acknowledging that married people have more earthly cares, St Augustine reiterates that it is not a sin to be married.[178] Addressing perhaps unmarried people who personally feel superior St Augustine tells them that they should not judge marriage as an evil and they should not avoid marriage as if it is a 'pitfall of sin.' Rather, if it is gifted to them, they should take the 'greater good' of continence.[179] St Augustine points to the errors of thinking either that marriage is to be condemned or that marriage is equal to virginity.[180] Possibly responding to St Jerome, St Augustine affirms that virginity is a greater good because Holy Scripture and St Paul cannot lie, but it is greater because the great good of marriage is surmounted.[181] However, and returning to his concerns about more spiritual sins, St Augustine says that Christians chiefly war against pride. Virgins are tempted to pride and to thinking that their virtue is due to themselves when in fact it is only achieved with grace. In order to avoid pride no Christian virgin should consider herself superior to any married person. In fact, we can ask who more easily follows the Lamb: humble married people or proud virgins.[182] Whether married or virgin, no one should boast but all should pray 'forgive us our debts.'[183]

St Augustine faced specific pastoral challenges and one such challenge that had significant bearing on his writings on marriage was the pastoral problem of one spouse who decided to renounce sexual relations in marriage especially without the consent of the other. It seems that this applied particularly to married Christian converts.[184] St Augustine therefore stresses the importance of marital fidelity and the reciprocity of conjugal rights. Couched in the terms of paying the marital debt to the other, St Augustine asks for fidelity and sees this payment as an act of charity and mercy that is in itself virtuous and merits sanctification.[185]

Commenting on holiness, St Augustine thinks that human nature is good but wounded and in need of healing and that both continence and chastity in virginity and marriage are gifts from God.[186] St Augustine points out that marriage is not a hindrance to eternal life and that married people also follow Christ's path even if not in exactly his same footsteps.[187] Moreover, and following St Paul, husbands are to love their wives as Christ loves the Church.[188] With a sense of realism St Augustine says that hypocrites are found in every section of Christian life: there are sinners also in monasteries. To illustrate this, he conflates the saying of Jesus about two people in the field or grinding meal or in bed where only one is taken in Matthew 24:40–41 and Luke 17:34–35 to demonstrate that married people have a valid claim to salvation and celibates should not be so convinced. Those working in the field are the good and bad clergy, grinding meal are good and bad lay people who are bound to temporal things, those in bed are the good and bad monks resting in the quiet monastery. The lay person who is saved is:

> someone who is exercised in good works, attentive to the needs of God's servants of God, and of the poor, steadfast in the confession of the faith, unswervingly joyful in hope, and mindful of God, one who calls down curses on nobody and as far as possible loves not only friends but enemies as well. This kind of person has sexual relations with no woman except his wife, or with no man except her husband. He or she will be taken from the mill, but one whose life is not like this will be left there.[189]

In commenting on the differing vocations that all the faithful have, St Augustine says that 'the garden of the Lord...includes not only the roses of martyrs but also the lilies of virgins, and the ivy of married people, and the violets of widows.'[190]

As St Augustine points out, 'no life is free' from passing and trivial sins, and everyday prayer makes satisfaction. Reciting the Our Father in particular blots out these daily, everyday sins.[191] For St Augustine everything comes back to love. The standard of love is that of proper love of God and neighbour under the grace of the Spirit and ultimately loves increases when there is no trace of cupidity.[192]

In spite of the complexities of sexual desire and married love, for St Augustine the union of husband and wife in marriage is a key for grasping other truths. In one of his Christmas sermons St Augustine says that Christ comes as a bridegroom; and the womb of the Virgin Mary is like a 'bride chamber…where the Word of God was united to human creation by a marriage which it is impossible to define.'[193] In his attempts to discern the Trinity, St Augustine says that love is the key because when a person loves they love God who is Love: you see the Trinity if you see love. He says that although the Trinity remains a mystery, there is a trace of the Trinity in the one that loves, the beloved and love. The Holy Spirit is 'gift' of both the Father and the Son and signifies the unity of love between them. He adds that this analogy is imperfect because husband and wife are one-flesh but two separate people.[194] St Augustine also applies the marriage analogy to the truth of Christ, his Church and the faithful. Just as God put Adam into a deep sleep in order to fashion Eve from his side, so 'in Christ's case, a bride was made for him as he slept on the cross, and made from his side. With a lance his side was struck as he hung there, and out flowed the sacraments of the Church.'[195] Just as married Christians are incorporated into each other becoming one flesh, through baptism believers are incorporated into the Church as Body of Christ.[196]

Roman Law to the Theodosian Code

It is difficult to piece together a full picture of the law of marriage because little remains of texts, apart from the *Institutes of Gaius* and some fragments from classical jurists. Moreover, it is unlikely that the Roman law of marriage was observed, known or indeed enforced throughout the whole of the Roman Empire. However, legislation from the emperors became important sources of law.[197] Various attempts were made to collate general laws into collections such as the Theodosian Code containing laws dating from 306–437 and, notably the Justinian Code (c.528).[198] The Theodosian Code collected the laws of the emperors from Constantine I to Theodosius II (ruled 408–450) and new laws were added until the end of the fifth century.[199]

Although the laws implemented by the Emperor Augustus remained in force through the third century there was a noted shift in marriage laws away from the Augustan view of marriage as a civic duty towards marriage as a personal choice.[200] Moreover, by the fourth and fifth centuries consent to marriage by the woman takes on more prominence.[201] Some of the Augustan laws were finally abrogated by the Emperor Constantine I (ruled 306–337) in about 320, however the ban on interclass unions remained.[202] Constantine removed some of the penalties possibly because of the number of Christians who were choosing not to marry. For practical reasons there was not the need to raise taxes through marriage penalties because there were new inheritance restrictions on heretics that compensated for the loss of revenue and people were able to leave their property to non-relatives including the church. Co-habitation was not prohibited but, reflecting the emphasis on consent, the practices of coercion of women into marriage, abduction of women for marriage, or consecrating a woman to lifelong virginity without her consent were condemned.

In the early Empire marriage began by and depended on *affectio maritalis* and so it could be ended once that affection or ongoing consent ceased. However, the liberal divorce laws of early Roman law gave way to a greater emphasis on indissolubility of marriage except for serious breaches.[203] Under Constantine a person who sought a divorce for trivial reasons would be subject to a criminal charge. A woman could only divorce her husband if he was a murderer, sorcerer, or tomb robber but not if he was a gambler, drunkard or frequenter of prostitutes; a man could divorce his wife if she was an adulteress, sorceress or procurer of prostitutes.[204] Some thirty years later the Emperor Julian allowed divorce by mutual consent but the stricter law on divorce was reinstated, abrogated briefly once more in the mid-fifth century under Theodosius II, then again reinstated.[205] However generally divorce seems to have been rare outside the aristocracy and most Greeks and Romans did not approve of it.[206] In the fourth and fifth centuries adultery was treated seriously and was prosecuted as a criminal offence.[207] Apart from Augustan laws to encourage remarriage, remarriage had generally been discouraged in antiquity not least because of the complications of inheritance and marriage payments. Fourth and fifth century legislation returned to the older view.[208]

From the fourth century it was expected that priests should not marry. However, women whose husbands became priests after marriage were not to be deserted. Increasingly in the West husbands who became priests were expected to live celibate lives with their wives. There were very few cases of attempts at same-sex "marriage" and under a law enacted in 342 any man entering such a union would be subject to the death penalty.[209] It is unclear to what extent Christianity influenced Roman legislation on marriage and divorce or indeed the legislation influenced Christianity. However, undoubtedly Roman law and its development greatly influenced society and understandings of marriage through the Middle Ages.[210]

The domestic church

Throughout the Old Testament marriage carries the covenant. The covenant is expressed in the Jewish *shema*, from Deuteronomy 6:5–9, and it is passed down through the family, to children and the children's children. This domestic link is not lost in the new covenant. In early Christianity the idea of domestic church has two interlocking strands: one strand is linked to comparisons of Church to the home, particularly in organisation; the other strand sees the home as carrying on activities in the church notably in educating members of the family so that they grow in holiness.[211]

Through baptism Christians become sons and daughters of God and brothers and sisters in Christ and the early liturgical assemblies seem to have taken place in people's houses. St Paul send his greetings to Priscilla, Aquilla and the church at their house, presumably a reference to one such assembly.[212] In describing the qualities of a good bishop St John Chrysostom explains that like families, churches consist of men, women and children. The Church is 'a small household' and a good bishop shares the same qualities as a good father.[213] Similarly St Augustine says that fathers have a role like bishops to care for the spiritual welfare of their families.[214] Again, St John Chrysostom calls for harmony in households where its members can grow in holiness: a house is, he says, 'a little Church', and those who 'seek first the kingdom', and can regulate their own household affairs are also fit for the management of the Church.[215]

St Augustine bridges the distance between church and home when he asks to be included in the prayers of Juliana 'with all your household Church', referring not to the church that happens to meet in the home but to a home church.[216] Moreover he thinks that Juliana's adherence to Catholicism makes her household 'no insignificant Church of Christ.'[217] In the home setting the early church fathers recognized the significance of parents in transmitting the faith. Fathers are to educate their children 'in the Lord' and teach them the scriptures.[218] St John Chrysostom urges families to read the scriptures, wives to learn, children and servants to listen, and thus to 'make your home a church to put the devil to flight.'[219]

Summary

When marriage was the expected way of life it did not have to be commended. However, the emergence of celibacy as a higher way of living out the Christian life and the challenges brought by the likes of Helvidius and Jovinian meant that theologians had to think more deeply about marriage. It is clear that in a culture where marriage was seen as little more than another legal contract, for the early fathers this was not so. In defending marriage as a covenant, the fathers took a counter-cultural approach preaching against divorce and even sometimes against second marriages after widowhood. Marriage and family life were significant not only for individuals and for society as a whole, but also for describing important theological truths and for living out a life in Christ. Marriage with its characteristics of faithfulness, unity and fruitfulness was a way in which each spouse could lead the other in love to holiness. Moreover, promotion of sexual relationships without maintaining an intrinsic link to procreation hinted at a Manichaean hatred of the material world or a failure to see fruitfulness as co-operation with God. As with other areas of life, marriage was to be lived under virtuous self-control, though as St Augustine pointed out it is naïve to think that sexual desire is uncomplicated. Sexual pleasure all too easily falls into power, domination, self-absorption, and pride instead of truly seeking the good of the other. While the church fathers did discuss the relative merits of virginity and marriage much of their discussion also centred on the nature of conversion, repentance, Christian perfection and on growing in holiness. With the coming of Jesus everything changes and for the faithful earthly realities are transformed. Moreover, taking the idea of the image of God seriously, the early fathers thought that the marriage relationship could say something about God's love, not only in terms of steadfast faithfulness, *hesed*, but also in terms of the gift of his coming as man, and his founding of the Church as his Body.

Notes

1. St Irenaeus, *Against Heresies*, I, 10.
2. St Ignatius of Antioch, *Epistle to the Ephesians*, 7.
3. Ac 17:16–34
4. Marcus Minucius Felix, *Octavius*.
5. Justin Martyr, *First Apology*, 5.
6. St Ignatius of Antioch, *To Polycarp*, 5.
7. Tertullian, *To His Wife*, 2, 9.
8. See D. Hunter, *Marriage and Sexuality in Early Christianity* (Minneapolis: Fortress Press, 2018): Ambrosiaster, *In Ep ad Cor primam* 7, 40; St Ambrose, *Epistle* 62, 7; *Letter of Pope Siricius to Bishop Himerius*, Paulinus of Nola.
9. St Clement of Rome, *Letter to the Corinthians*, 1.
10. Ignatius of Antioch, *Letter to Polycarp*, 5.
11. P. Brown, *The Body and Society* (New York: Columbia University Press, 2008), pp. 83–86.
12. *Ibid.*, pp. 92–95.
13. *Ibid.*, p. 89.
14. See also St Clement of Alexandria, *Stromata*, III, iii.
15. Tertullian, *Against Marcion*, I, 29.
16. St Clement of Alexandria, *Stromata*, III, vii.
17. *The Passion of the Holy Martyrs Perpetua and Felicity*.
18. Brown, *The Body and Society*, p. 220.
19. *Ibid.*, pp. 213–240.
20. St Irenaeus, *Against Heresies*, I, 28.
21. W. Jurgens, *The Faith of the Early Fathers Vol.1* (Collegeville, Minnesota: Liturgical Press, 1970), p. 65. For a discussion of the extent of Tatian's involvement with Syrian encratism see E. Hunt, *Christianity in the Second Century: the Case of Tatian* (New York: Routledge, 2003), pp. 145–150. Hunt thinks that extreme asceticism rather than encratism characterized Syrian Christianity, pp. 154–155.
22. Hunt, *Christianity in the Second Century, p.* 154.
23. St Irenaeus, *Against Heresies*, I, 28.
24. Tertullian, *Against Marcion*, 1, 29; St Irenaeus, *Against Heresies*, I, 28.
25. St Clement of Alexandria, *Christ the Educator*, I, 4.
26. St Clement of Alexandria, *Stromata*, III, ii.
27. *Ibid.*, IV, viii.
28. *Ibid.*, III, xvii.

29 *Ibid.*, III, xv.
30 *Ibid.*, III, xviii.
31 St Clement of Alexandria, *Christ the Educator*, II, 10.
32 St Clement of Alexandria, *Stromata*, III, i.
33 *Ibid.*, III, vi.
34 St Clement of Alexandria, *Christ the Educator*, III, 10.
35 P. Lampe, *Christians at Rome in the First Two Centuries: From Paul to Valentinus* (Minneapolis: Fortress Press, 2003), pp. 119–121.
36 Tertullian, *To His Wife*, I, 1.
37 *Ibid.*, I, 3.
38 *Ibid.*, I, 4.
39 Tertullian, *Exhortation to Chastity*.
40 Tertullian, *To His Wife*, I, 8.
41 Tertullian, *On Monogamy*, 1.
42 Origen, *Commentary on Matthew*, 14, Ch.16.
43 *Ibid.*, 14, Ch.19–20.
44 *Ibid.*, 14, Ch.23.
45 Origen, *Homily 17*; *Commentary on Matthew*, 14, Ch.22.
46 Origen, *Commentary on Matthew*, 14, Ch.25.
47 *Ibid.*, 14, Ch.16.
48 Origen, *Commentary on 1 Corinthians*, 60–62.
49 *Ibid.*, 59.
50 Origen, *Commentary on Matthew*, 14, Ch. 16.
51 Origen, *On Genesis*, Homily 1, 14, 15.
52 J. C. King, *Origen on the Song of Songs as the Spirit of Scripture* (Oxford: Oxford University Press, 2005), p. 181.
53 *Ibid.*, p. 93.
54 Origen, *De Principiis*, II, 6.3; St Ambrose, *Exposition on the Christian Faith*.
55 Lactantius, *Divine Institutes*, 1, 16–17.
56 *Ibid.*, 3, 21.
57 *Ibid.*, 6, 21.
58 *Ibid.*, 6, 20.
59 *Ibid.*, 6, 17, 19–20.
60 *Ibid.*, 6, 23.
61 *Ibid.*, 6, 23.
62 P. Brown, *The Rise of Western Christendom Triumph and Diversity, AD 200–1000* (Oxford: Wiley-Blackwell, 2013), pp. 81–82.
63 J. K. Coyle, *Manichaeism and Its Legacy* (Leiden: Brill, 2009), p. xiii.
64 St Augustine, *Contra Faustum*, III, 1.

65 St Augustine, *On the Morals of the Manichaeans*, 19, 68.
66 St Augustine, *Contra Faustum*, I, 3.
67 *Ibid.*, XXI, 1.
68 *Ibid.*, XX, 2.
69 Coyle, *Manichaeism and Its Legacy*, pp. xiv-xv.
70 St Augustine, *Contra Faustum*, XX, 22, 15.
71 S. Schafer, *Marriage, Sex and Procreation: Contemporary Revisions to Augustine's Theology of Marriage* (Eugene, Oregon: Pickwick, 2019), *p.* 27.
72 St Augustine, *Contra Faustum*, XXX, 1, 5.
73 St Augustine, *On the Morals of the Manichaeans*, 16, 39; 18, 66.
74 St Augustine, *Contra Faustum*, XV, 1.
75 *Ibid.*, XXX, 4.
76 *Ibid.*, XXX, 6.
77 St Augustine, *On the Morals of the Manichaeans*, 18, 65.
78 St John Chrysostom, *Homily 1 On Galatians*, 4.
79 St John Chrysostom, *Homily on Genesis*, 7, 16.
80 St John Chrysostom, *Homily 12 On Colossians*.
81 St John Chrysostom, *Homily 20 On Ephesians*, 6, 7.
82 *Ibid.*, 7, 8, 9.
83 *Ibid.*, 3.
84 St John Chrysostom, *How to choose a wife*, 96.
85 St John Chrysostom, *Homily on Genesis*, 7, 12.
86 St John Chrysostom, *Homily 20 On Ephesians*, 1.
87 St John Chrysostom, *Homily on Genesis*, 17, 36.
88 St John Chrysostom, *Homily 20 On Ephesians*, 5, 2.
89 *Ibid.*, 4.
90 *Ibid.*, 5.
91 St John Chrysostom, *Homily XVII Gospel of Matthew*.
92 St John Chrysostom, *Homily 20 On Ephesians*, 7.
93 *Ibid.*, 2.
94 *Ibid.*, 5.
95 St John Chrysostom, *Homily 12 On Colossians*.
96 St John Chrysostom, *Homily on Genesis*, 17, 38; *Homily 20 On Ephesians* 9.
97 St John Chrysostom, *Baptismal Instructions*, First Instruction, 23–30.
98 *Ibid.*, Sixth Instruction, 102–103.
99 G. Selin, *Priestly Celibacy: Theological Foundations* (Washington: Catholic University of America Press, 2016), pp. 18–24.
100 St Ambrose, *On the Duties of the Clergy*, I, 258–259.

[101] St Jerome, *Against Jovinian*, I, 13.
[102] St Jerome, *Letter* 22, 21.
[103] St Jerome, *Against Jovinian*, 1, 34.
[104] *Ibid.*, I. 7; Jerome, *Letter* 22, 22.
[105] D. Hunter, 'Helvidius, Jovinian, and the Virginity of Mary in Late Fourth Century Rome' in *Journal of Early Christian Studies* 1/1 (1993), pp. 47–71.
[106] *Ibid.*, 48–49.
[107] For instance, St Ignatius of Antioch, *To the Smyrnaeans*, I, 1; *To the Trallians*, IX, 1; *To the Ephesians*, XIX, 1; St Justin, *Dialogue with Trypho*, 43, 66–68 and *Apology* 1, 33; St Irenaeus, *Against Heresies*, III, 21; Origen, *Against Celsus*, 1, 34.
[108] Lk 1:34–36; Mt 1:18–25.
[109] Mt 13:55; Mk 6:3.
[110] Mt 27:56; Mk 15:40.
[111] Jn 19:25. The text speaks of Jesus's mother, and his mother's sister, Mary the wife of Clopas, and Mary of Magdala. However, it is unclear whether sister refers to Salome, also present in the other gospel accounts, or to Mary the wife of Clopas.
[112] St Jerome, *The Perpetual Virginity of Blessed Mary, Against Helvidius*, 22.
[113] *Ibid.*, 23.
[114] Pope Siricius, *Epistola* 7; St Ambrose *Epistolae* 41 and 42.
[115] *St Jerome, Letter* 49, 2.
[116] St Jerome, *Against Jovinian*, I, 3.
[117] *Ibid.*, I, 3, 4.
[118] *Ibid.*, I, 3.
[119] *Ibid.*, I, 4.
[120] *Ibid.*, I, 12.
[121] St Jerome, *Letter* 55, 3.
[122] St Jerome, *Against Jovinian*, I, 10.
[123] Lampe, *Christians at Rome in the First Two Centuries*, pp. 149–150.
[124] St Jerome, *Letter* 48, 3.
[125] St Jerome, *Against Jovinian*, I, 13.
[126] *Ibid.*, I, 4.
[127] St Jerome, *Letter* 22, 19.
[128] St Jerome, *Letter* 22, 20; *Against Jovinian*, I, 12.
[129] St Jerome, *Letter* 22, 21.
[130] For St Jerome's attitude to women see V. Novembri, 'Philosophia and Christian Culture: An Antidote for Female Weakness in Jerome's Letters' in *Papers Presented at the Fifteenth International Conference on Patristic Studies, 2007 Studia Patristica XLIV* (Leuven: Peeters, 2010), p. 475.

131 St Jerome, *Commentary on Isaiah*, XV, 56.3.
132 St Jerome, *Letter* 65, 1.
133 St Jerome, *Letter* 127, 5.
134 Novembri, Philosophia and Christian Culture, pp. 479–480.
135 Ga 3:26–28
136 St Gregory of Nazianzus, *Oration 37*, vi.
137 *Ibid.*, vii.
138 *Ibid.*, x.
139 *Ibid.*, ix; *Oration 40*, xviii.
140 St Gregory of Nazianzus, *Oration 37*, xix.
141 *Ibid.*, x.
142 St Basil, *Letter* 199.
143 St Basil, *Letter* 160.
144 St Basil, *Letter* 217; *Letter* 188, iv.
145 St Basil, *Letter* 217.
146 St Gregory of Nazianzus, *Oration 37*, viii.
147 St Jerome, *Letter* 57, 5.
148 St Augustine, *Letter 28 To Jerome*, 3.4.
149 St Augustine, *On Marriage and Concupiscence*, II, xxiii.
150 *Ibid.*, I, i.
151 *Ibid.*, I, i.
152 *Ibid.*, I, vi.
153 *Ibid., I, xxiv*; St Augustine, *Sermon 9, 18*; St Augustine, *Sermon* 354A.
154 St Augustine, *Confessions*, VIII, 10.
155 *Ibid.*, II, 10.
156 *Ibid.*, II, 10.
157 St Augustine, *On Continence*, 28, 27, 23.
158 St Augustine, *Confessions*, VIII, 10, 13.
159 St Augustine, *The Excellence of Marriage*, 1.
160 *Ibid., 32*; St Augustine, *On Marriage and Concupiscence*, I, x, xvii.
161 St Augustine, *Contra Faustum*, 23, 8.
162 St Augustine, *On Marriage and Concupiscence*, I, viii.
163 *Ibid.*, I, x.
164 St Augustine, *Letter 138, 1*; St Augustine, *On the Catechising of the Uninstructed*, 26, 50.
165 St Augustine, *The Excellence of Marriage*, 21; St Augustine, *On Marriage and Concupiscence*, I, x.
166 St Augustine, *The Excellence of Marriage*, 21; St Augustine, *On Marriage and Concupiscence*, I, x; St Augustine, *On the Sermon on the Mount*, I, 45–48; St Augustine, *On Holy Virginity*, 15.

167 St Augustine, *The Excellence of Marriage*, 5.
168 St Augustine, *On Marriage and Concupiscence*, I, xi.
169 *Ibid.*, I, i.
170 *Ibid.*, I, iv.
171 *Ibid.*, I, iii, v.
172 *Ibid.*, I, vii, viii; II, v.
173 *Ibid.*, I, vi.
174 *Ibid.*, I, v, xvii.
175 *Ibid.*, I, xiv, xv.
176 St Augustine, *On Holy Virginity*, 16.
177 St Augustine, *Confessions* X, 36.59.
178 St Augustine, *On Holy Virginity*, 14.
179 *Ibid.*, 18.
180 *Ibid.*, 19.
181 *Ibid.*, 20–21.
182 *Ibid.*, 52.
183 *Ibid.*, 48.
184 St Augustine, *Psalm 149*.
185 St Augustine, *Sermon 354A*; St Augustine, *Psalm 149*.
186 St Augustine, *On Continence*, 18, 1.
187 St Augustine, *On Holy Virginity*, 21, 28.
188 St Augustine, *On Continence*, 22.
189 St Augustine, *Psalm 99*, 25.
190 St Augustine, *Sermon 304 on the Feast Day of St Lawrence*.
191 St Augustine, *The Enchiridion on Faith, Hope, and Charity*, 71.
192 *Ibid.*, 121.
193 St Augustine, *Christmas Sermon 10* and *Sermon 13*, 115–116; 127–128.
194 St Augustine, *The Trinity*. VIII, 12–14; V, 12; VI, 7; IX, 6.
195 St Augustine, *Psalm 56*.
196 St Augustine, *On the Good of Widowhood*, 13.
197 W. Kaiser, 'Justinian and the Corpus Iuris Civilis' in *The Cambridge Companion to Roman Law* (Cambridge: Cambridge University Press, 2015), p. 120.
198 *Ibid.*, pp. 121–123.
199 M. Kuefler, 'The Marriage Revolution in Late Antiquity: The Theodosian Code and Later Roman Marriage Law' in *Journal of Family History* 32/4 (2007) pp. 343–370, p.344.
200 *Ibid.*, pp. 345–347.
201 *Ibid.*, p. 350.
202 J. E. Grubbs, 'Pagan and Christian Marriage: the State of the Question' in

Journal of Early Christian Studies 2/4 (1994) pp. 361–412, pp.386–387.

[203] Kuefler, 'The Marriage Revolution in Late Antiquity', p. 355.
[204] *Ibid.*; J. E. Grubbs, 'Emperor Constantine' in *Christianity and Family Law: An Introduction* (Cambridge: Cambridge University Press, 2017), pp. 52–68, p. 58.
[205] Kuefler, 'The Marriage Revolution in Late Antiquity', 356.
[206] Grubbs, 'Emperor Constantine', p. 60.
[207] Kuefler, 'The Marriage Revolution in Late Antiquity', pp. 356–357.
[208] *Ibid.*, pp. 357–358.
[209] *Ibid.*, p. 362.
[210] For a discussion of these influences see Kuefler, 'The Marriage Revolution in Late Antiquity', pp. 362–364.
[211] See J. Atkinson, *Biblical and Theological Foundations of the Family Domestic Church* (Washington DC: Catholic University of America Press, 2014), Ch. 9.
[212] Rm 16:5; 1 Co 16:19; Col 4:15; N. Widok, 'Christian Family as Domestic Church in the Writings of St John Chrysostom' in *Studia Ceranea* 3 (2013), pp. 167–175, p. 167.
[213] St John Chrysostom, *Homily 10 On First Timothy*.
[214] St Augustine, *On John's Gospel*, 51, 13.
[215] St John Chrysostom, *Homily 20 On Ephesians*.
[216] St Augustine, *On the Good of Widowhood*, 29.
[217] St Augustine, *Letter 188*, 3.
[218] *Apostolic Constitutions*, IV, 2, xi.
[219] St John Chrysostom, *Homily On Genesis*, 2, 4.

4 MARRIAGE RULES: AFTER THE EARLY CHURCH FATHERS TO THE COUNCIL OF TRENT

ST PAUL REMINDS the community in Rome that Christians follow not a law but a person: Jesus Christ.[1] Certainly, the early church fathers saw marriage as a part of living out faith in Christ. However, there is a significant strand of thinking claiming that 'before the twelfth century, the church had little to do with marriage,'[2] at least in terms of ritual, or that sees early Christian understandings of marriage as essentially concerned with a contractual and secular approach to the detriment of a more interpersonal and theological approach. In part this thinking rests on the fact that marriage was not explicitly defined as a sacrament prior to the twelfth century. However, as W. Kasper points out, this fact does not mean that marriage was seen 'simply as a secular reality and only later sacralized.'[3]

Since marriage takes place "in the world" it does have the characteristics of worldly affairs. Nevertheless, as Catholic social teaching reminds us, the 'importance and centrality of the family with regard to the person and society is repeatedly underlined by Sacred Scripture' and, 'enlightened by the radiance of the biblical message, the Church considers the family as the first and natural society.'[4] Christians are "in" the world even if not "of" the world. This chapter begins by tracing the development of church rules concerning marriage up to the emergence of canon law in the twelfth century and some marriage practices that fed into these rules. However, a focus on the contractual or legal elements of marriage in one era of history should not lead to the assumption that marriage was seen primarily or indeed only as a matter of contract. True, the period after the church fathers and into the medieval and reformation era saw the emergence of a body of canons and ultimately the growth in canon law, hence perhaps a view of marriage that focuses on the legal. Nevertheless, marriage is not only informed by rules and regulations. The chapter therefore considers the clear pastoral concern of medieval popes and theologians for the everyday life of lay Christians, and this includes their life following Christ as married people on a path to holiness. The chapter goes on to explore the path to recognizing marriage as a sacrament where grace is a central concern. Marriage and married love are then situated in the integrated vision of St Thomas Aquinas and his understanding of the human person. However, developments in the method of moral theology after St Thomas tended towards a more legalistic approach to marriage. Finally, the chapter moves from Martin Luther and the attitude of the reformers to marriage, and the Catholic reforms of the Council of Trent. This chapter demonstrates that not only legislation and practices but also the spiritual and pastoral formation of Christians has shaped marriage.

Marriage and a rule book?

In his book *The First Thousand Years: A Global History of Christianity* R. L. Wilken observes that Christianity has always been a 'rule-making community.'[5] Of course this does not mean that the rules were the most significant aspect of Christianity. Nevertheless, the writings of St Paul and the pastoral epistles illustrate how important order was for the emerging Christian Church. Some communities had used scripture to draw up handbooks to deal with questions of liturgical practice, morality, leadership, and standards. Some early examples of these handbooks are the *Didache*, probably written in Greek for a Syrian community and claiming to express the teaching of the Twelve

Apostles; the *Traditio Apostolica* (c.218), written in Greek possibly by Hippolytus (c.170-c.235) giving an account of practices in the Roman Christian community; and the *Didascalia Apostolorum* (c.230) written in Syriac for Syrian communities. Said to be the work of the Apostles, the *Apostolic Constitutions* was a fourth century collection of guidance for clergy and it included some of the earlier handbooks. The very early handbooks cannot really be described as evidence of laws as such since the institutional structure to encourage and support law had not yet fully emerged.

By the early third century councils were being held to decide important questions. As Tertullian states, it was 'customary practice' for bishops to issue mandates, and local councils were gathered 'out of the universal churches' where 'the actual representation of the whole Christian name is celebrated.'[6] There was thus an underlying presumption that all local churches belonged to a spiritual community and each was in harmony with what was believed, confessed and practiced in all the others.[7] However in practice this harmony was not always in evidence as shown by the dispute between Bishop St Cyprian (d.258) and Pope Stephen (d.257) on the question of the baptism of heretics and the seventh council of Carthage in 256.[8]

Bishops also began to draw upon the writings of leading theologians, bishops, and popes to build up a body of authoritative sources and these included canons from councils. From the third century written verbatim records were made at synods and councils in the form of *dixit-placet*, statements of consensus expressing the solidarity in agreement of the bishops present, and *placuit*, 'it pleased us.'[9] The Greek *kanon* originally meant a rod used as a measuring standard and came to refer to summaries of orthodox Christian teaching. It seems that the early councils used canon in the sense of ecclesiastical standards that were more weighty than simple custom.[10] Moreover, there was the sense that God was actively present at these councils[11] thus strengthening the sense of a growing body of authoritative tradition.

In the West the fifth century monk from Rome, Dionysius Exiguus, (the Little or Humble, c.470–544) collected canons from the East and West councils to ensure they were accessible for Latin speakers, and he included papal decretal letters, that is, letters that responded to specific questions.[12] In the East the lawyer and priest from Antioch, John Scholasticus (c.503–577) created a further collection of canons from general councils, local synods, and encyclical letters from Eastern bishops, and he included elements of Roman civil law relevant to church institutions. The collection by Scholasticus later became the basis for canon law in Christian Slavic countries.[13] The collection by Dionysius was widely distributed and canons were regrouped into themes. Additionally, specific questions on cultural practice or individual problems were sent to the popes for guidance.

In the late fifth and sixth centuries Irish monks began to offer the possibility of penance for ordinary lay people along the lines of their own monastic practice. The penitential books grew out of this practice and took the form of a series of lists of sins and their remedies, often in the form of vices and their remedies, the virtues. While the object was to create an easy to use resource enabling priests to offer guidance in the confessional, the idea that sins and their remedies had to be specified comes from medical analogy: a doctor cannot give a healing remedy unless he knows the illness; so too for a doctor of the soul. There is evidence in some penitentials that the marriage ceremony should be followed by a period of prayer, fasting and almsgiving. It is not clear whether this reflected a form of purification or the model of Tobias and his wife who were advised by the Angel Raphael to follow their wedding with a time of prayer to ensure healthy children. Couples were also expected to refrain from sexual intercourse on certain fast and feast days.[14] In 668 St Theodore of Canterbury (c.602–690) included in his penitential the view from St Basil that a wife could not separate from her husband even if he has been unfaithful. St Theodore adds his own opinion, which he says is not canonical, that by mutual agreement a spouse could give permission for their partner to join a monastery.[15] Notably, there was rewriting of some penitentials to reflect Church concern that marriage had to have the free consent of bride and groom.[16]

While the canonical collections had flourished, Roman law was not so well known. As part of the growth in education and universities Gratian (d.c.1159), who may have been a monk and later a bishop, began to teach canon law and Roman law in Bologna in the early twelfth century. Although there had been further compilations of the canons, Gratian was the first to produce a textbook, the *Concordia discordantium canonum* or *Decretum* in c.1130.[17] However the first official papal compilation of church law only appears in the early thirteenth century under the pontificate of Innocent III (1198–1216).

Although there were Christians in England before the mission of St Augustine of Canterbury (d.c.605) in 597, the missionaries brought with them Roman law and in time this law significantly influenced the emerging English law. The contact with Roman Christendom encouraged the Anglo-Saxons to align their practices more with Rome and the Western Church. Certainly, from the seventh century in Anglo-Saxon England the leaders of the English church regarded laws as an essential part of Christian life. However, as R. H. Helmholz points out, it is one thing to acknowledge the existence of laws, and another to demonstrate government of the church by law, especially since there were no groups of professional ecclesiastical lawyers and no legal education available. Instead, the church relied more on sacramental and theological norms.[18] Nevertheless, when it came to conforming to Church regulations, Helmholz identifies four points of principle on marriage that the Church held to almost from its inception. These principles were not found in the pre-missionary territories of the Germanic or Anglo-Saxon people and differed from the 'essentially private nature' of Roman marriage. First, marriage was indissoluble; second, some form of clerical regulation was desirable; third, men and women should be able to have freedom in entering marriage; fourth, there were prohibitions of marriages between men and women who were related within certain degrees of blood or marriage.[19]

Cultural practices

The reach of the Roman Empire may have been great, but to the north were settled tribes of barbarians. These tribes had different customs and practices now in part lost to history. There is some literary evidence from Ireland through poetry, sagas, and the lives of the saints. The Irish saints themselves travelled throughout northern Europe in attempts to convert the pagans. Irish society consisted of tribes further divided into kindred groups called *septs*, and these groups consisted of individual households led by a chief that might have numbered between one hundred and twenty to two hundred and fifty people and so included servants, slaves and men at arms.[20] Marriage was usually monogamous but that did not preclude other sexual relationships and both parties could divorce. Indeed, some of the Irish saints were born illegitimate.[21] In the Germanic lands the equivalent of the *sept* was the *sippe*, again a kin group led by a chief who controlled a particular territory and probably consisting of about fifty families.[22] In both the *sept* and the *sippe* there was frequently a high concentration of women in the noble households to the deprivation of other family groups. Again, although monogamy was the usual practice there is evidence of polygamy and husbands could divorce their wives but not wives their husbands.[23] It seems that Roman law may have influenced some Germanic practice since there were two forms of marriage, *in manu* transferring authority over the wife to the husband, and *sine manu* without such a transference. Moreover, the marriage custom followed the same pattern of betrothal, payment of dowry and handing over of the bride to the groom.[24] The dowry was paid by the groom to the bride's family along with other gifts and further gifts were given to the wife after consummation of the marriage.[25] Marriage *sine manu* did not involve a dowry and seems to have been similar to a form of abduction though with the consent of the woman. Although this form of marriage was publicly recognized, by the early sixth century these marriages were discouraged. The problem was that they were often clandestine and so difficult to prove or enforce. Despite a decree at the Council of Arles in 524 forbidding marriage without a dowry or without a public wedding, clandestine marriages remained common.[26] Since marriages were frequently contracted to protect property or keep property within the clan, marriages between close relatives were common, hence questions on consanguinity or affinity, including issues of the spiritual relationship of godparents became important and often conflicted with practice.

By the time of the late Roman Empire the ages for marriage had changed somewhat with the age of husbands falling and women delaying marriage. This seems to match the Germanic age of marriage.[27] There is more written evidence after about 750 mostly in the form of administrative documents. Many families lived on family farms as serfs paying rents to their lords.[28] As Christianity spread to these more settled areas the rules on marriage also began to take hold. In particular, rules on monogamy and prohibited degrees of kindred in marriage had significant impact in cultures where noble households had a disproportionate number of women compared to lower class households.[29]

It is unclear how marriage practices in medieval Western Christendom crystallised into monogamous and indissoluble marriage where questions were referred to ecclesiastical courts. Indeed, Helmholz suggests that there was some compromise with cultural practices in Anglo-Saxon England and the general acceptance of church competence in marriage and divorce law emerged only gradually.[30] There has been lively discussion on the relationship of secular and ecclesiastical law regarding marriage and it is probably useful to see this relationship in terms of co-existence.[31] S. McDougall[32] outlines three possible theories: first, that clergy imposed their view of marriage onto a reluctant laity; second, the laity accepted this imposition since it matched their own interests; third, the change was a compromise between laity and clergy. However, as McDougall points out these theories mistakenly assume that there was a clear division between clergy and laity in terms of consciousness and ideology or indeed that there was a power struggle between clergy and noble lay people. She argues that the shift involved a number of complex elements. Moreover, there is a question of actual evidence, and it is not helpful simply to consider unusual marriage practices such as the apparent marriage of the five to seven year old Prince Henry of England to his distant cousin the two or three year old Princess Margaret of France, or scandalous marriages of abbesses or bishops from noble families called back to the secular world in order to take over family estates and provide an heir. Undoubtedly, marriage laws were flexible, open to finding annulments, and noble marriages at least were strategic business, including marriages that might be regarded as within prohibited degrees, as in the case of the young Prince Henry and Princess Margaret. Nevertheless, there are some comments that can be made more generally on marriage and there were some obvious concerns that provided impetus for greater regulation of marriage, notably clandestine marriages.

Questions to the popes

At a time when acceptance of the regulations around marriage were still fluid, questions concerning local customs provide an invaluable window into marriage practices and problems, and the assimilation of Christianity into different countries and cultures. As an example, St Augustine of Canterbury raised a number of questions with Pope St Gregory I (c.540–604) concerning church law and Anglo-Saxon practice, mainly to do with prohibited degrees of relationship, and Pope St Gregory I replied in what is now known as the *Libellus responsionum*. As Helmholz explains in the Middle Ages there was no one body of church law governing marriage and the church generally followed existing local customs. Marriage disputes were probably settled informally, possibly with the involvement of the local priest or bishop if necessary.[33] Nevertheless, questions were sent to some church authorities, notably on the issue of indissolubility.

The number of questions concerning divorce and remarriage suggests that these may have been common practices, but, as A. Bevilacqua's painstaking research shows, the replies of the popes over the centuries remain constant. Himerius (fl.380), Bishop of Tarragona, sent a question to Pope St Siricius (c.334–399) and in his response the pope said that it is forbidden for a husband to marry the wife of another not least because the original blessing given to the bride by the priest would be violated.[34] In his reply to Victricius Bishop of Rouen (c.330-c.407) Pope Innocent I (d.417) explained that a second marriage while the first spouse was still alive was adultery, and that marriage for a wife was dissolved only on the death of her husband.[35] In another letter this time to Exsuperius the Bishop of Toulouse (d.410) Pope Innocent stated that the Church condemns adultery in equal measure for husbands and wives though he admitted that it was more difficult for wives to prove this. Those who have divorced and remarried were to be denied communion.[36] In another case a wife was captured by the Goths and during her captivity her husband contracted another marriage. On her return to Rome she went to Probus, a civil official who sought the help of Pope Innocent. The pope ruled that the husband's second marriage was unlawful since his first wife was still alive and noted that the husband had not obtained a divorce, so presumably the second marriage was also unlawful under civil law.[37] The pope's decision seems to show that both church and civil law agree in this case. Similar problems this time of husbands taken captive and then returning, arose under the reign of Pope St Leo I (d.461). Pope St Leo agreed that the second marriages of their wives had to be terminated but the wives would not be punished by excommunication as long as they returned to their first husbands.[38] St Bede (673–735) accepted that a wife could be dismissed for unfaithfulness or for a religious reason, however her husband could not marry another while she was still alive.[39] St Boniface (c.672–754) sent a question to Pope St Gregory II (d.731) regarding a wife whose illness meant that she could not have sexual intercourse. It is not clear from the text, but it may have been that no consummation of the marriage was possible and on this ground Pope Gregory allowed the husband to marry another, but the husband had to continue to support her.[40] Pope St Zacharias (d.752) wrote to Pepin (714–768), the leader of the Franks, to explain church teaching on divorce and remarriage. Quoting canon 8 of the Council of Carthage XI in 419, Pope Zacharias re-emphasized that although separation was possible, remarriage entailed excommunication and penance.[41] It is unclear whether the second marriage was terminated. Pope John VIII (d.882) responded to Ethelred, Archbishop of Canterbury (d.888) on the practice of divorce in England. It seems that the only reason for separation was unfaithfulness but in that case the parties should either remain single or be reconciled. Remarriage to another was forbidden.[42]

Written in 866, the *Letter of Nicholas I to the Bulgars* (*Letter 99*) offers further insight into marriage practices. The Bulgars occupied lands in the areas of Bulgaria, and south of the Danube. Their situation seems to have been typical of the time. From the sixth century the Bulgars had had some contact with Christianity through normal trade and diplomatic relations with other countries including Byzantium. The Christian population increased and at times was persecuted. The Bulgar Khan, Khan Boris who reigned from 852–889, converted to Christianity taking the baptismal name Michael and the title Prince. However, and possibly not wishing to be subject to the emperor in Byzantium, Prince Michael wrote to Pope St Nicholas I (820–867) in order to reconcile Bulgar and Christian practice and clarify certain matters of faith. In his response to Prince Michael, Pope St Nicholas I lists essential elements of marriage that reflect very much the traditional legal formalities of Roman law. The betrothal required the consent of both parties freely given as well as the consent of their parents. There was a dowry agreement that was witnessed by the guests. A religious rite followed later in church with a Eucharistic liturgy and nuptial blessing as long as this was the couple's first marriage, presumably meaning the previous marriage had been ended by the death of the first spouse. Notably Pope St Nicholas says that according to Roman law consent is the essential element, other elements, including the religious ceremony, are optional extras.[43] Whether the marriage ceremony took place in a domestic setting or in a church, consent made marriage. However, in the East the Byzantine Emperor Leo VI (866–912) ruled that a nuptial liturgy was necessary for validity.[44]

Papal responses to local questions suggest a growing recognition of the need to unify liturgy and practice. Still, the popes and pastors showed that pastoral care, encouragement on the path to holiness, and concern for the daily lives of people remained clear priorities.

Grace and the path to holiness

St Paul's letters and the pastoral epistles demonstrate the importance of order in the Church and lay people are a part of that order. Additionally, the pastoral epistles and the early church fathers show a keen interest in the pastoral care of their flocks and many of the early writings are framed in this care for the realities of people's lives. Following this path, in about 590 shortly after he became pope, St Gregory I (c.540–604) wrote a pastoral treatise, *Regula Pastoralis, Pastoral Rule Book* outlining guidance to clergy, primarily bishops, as 'physicians to the sick.'[45] Good pastors should teach according to the needs of their flocks and Pope St Gregory I gives comprehensive advice covering different groups of people. He arranges this advice in opposing pairs to underline the need to give appropriate rather than blanket care and the groups range from men and women, the impudent and bashful, the humble and haughty, to the gluttonous and abstinent.

In his advice on the care of married and single people Pope St Gregory I notes that while married people 'take thought for each other's good' they should not neglect the 'things of God.' Earthly love is, he says, after all fleeting and they should live in hope of eternal life. Husband and wife should bear with each other's foibles with 'mutual patience' and 'mutual exhortations.' He adds, 'they are also to be admonished to give heed, each of them, not so much to what they have to bear from the other as to what the other has to bear from them.' Following in the footsteps of the early church fathers, Pope St Gregory I reminds married people that marriage is for children and that although pleasure is allowed there are dangers in immoderate sexual intercourse that goes beyond what is due in marriage because such use of marriage betrays an uncontrolled element that is not befitting.[46] Pope St Gregory I sent a copy of his *Pastoral Rule Book* to his old friend, Leander, bishop of Seville, brother of St Isidore.[47]

Alongside Pope St Gregory I, St Isidore of Seville (c.560–636) was also influential throughout Christian Europe and St Isidore was especially interested in order in the church.[48] St Isidore wrote *De ecclesiasticis officiis, On the Origins of Offices* as part of the enterprise to forge a Christian kingdom in Spain by unifying liturgical practices including the marriage liturgy[49] and the practice of anointing of kings. This last practice gave the Church authority over civil leaders and a focus on liturgical practice was a method of educating clergy and so re-establishing church order.[50] *De ecclesiasticis officiis* was written for bishops and clergy and considered to be official teaching rather than simple guidance for the pastoral care of the faithful. St Isidore relied in particular on the writings of St Augustine.[51] Following St Augustine, St Isidore states that marriage was a part of God's plan from the beginning, and he agrees with St Paul that marriage brings with it cares of the world, nevertheless, following Hebrews 13.4, 'the beds of the married are not dishonourable.'[52] According to St Isidore, marriage came about by mutual consent and[53] he lists three reasons for marriage, roughly corresponding to three goods:

children, the good of mutual help, and to enable self-restraint.[54] Significantly St Isidore classes married people among the 'orders' of the Church[55] giving them a special place in the life of the Church alongside monks, penitents, virgins and widows. As P. Reynolds observes, 'thus Isidore thought marriage to be a religious vocation,' and Reynolds relates this back to St Augustine's three classes of Christians.[56]

Reynolds notes that this inclusion of married people into the life of the Church was not unusual. He cites the view of St Bede who described the hierarchical ordering of the Church by allegory with the Temple of Solomon. The three floors of the temple are arranged upwards from broad to narrow. The top narrow floor corresponds to the narrow life of consecrated virgins and religious who have renounced marriage and the world to embrace a life dedicated to prayer; the second floor are the ascetics, *continentes*; the broad ground floor are married people. St Bede explains that less is expected of married people because they live in the world, they are not asked to sell their possessions, but they are asked to keep the commandments. Yet this floor is integral to the whole building.[57]

Noting that lay people were the only order in society that did not have instructions or guidance, Jonas, Bishop of Orleans (d.c.841/2) wrote *De institutione laicali* a treatise on secular morality modelled on those written for monks, possibly expecting his treatise to have a legislative effect.[58] Jonas wrote in a common literary style, the *speculum* or mirror style which aimed to show, to quote St Paul 'through a glass, darkly,' both what the situation actually was and what it should be.[59] As part of the project to advance a cohesive view of society the *speculum* took the form of instructions for a model way of life where everyone had a part to play. Although ostensibly written at the request of Count Matfrid of Orleans who had asked for guidance on how to live a Christian upright married life, Jonas used some of his earlier material and set about writing on the whole of lay morality from the entrance of the person into Christian life in baptism through to the sacraments. In the section on marriage Jonas addresses men but sees marriage as a partnership where parents look after their whole household, their little flock, as bishops have care of their people. Married people then are also involved in bringing people to salvation.[60] Relying on St Augustine, Jonas repeats that marriage is one of the goods of creation but, he adds, human beings tend to abuse goods. According to Jonas marriage is for upbringing of children even though men tend to use it for lustful reasons. Nevertheless, Jonas thinks that married life as well as celibacy has a place in the body of Christ; they share one virtue, chastity, and this differs not in kind but in degree. In a similar vein, Alcuin (735–804) the abbot of St Martin of Tours wrote his moral treatise *De virtutibus et vitiis, On Virtues and Vices* at the request of an influential count and military man, Guy Wido. Alcuin reassures Guy that the life of a lay person is a truly Christian way of life and a way of holiness.

From the time of Charlemagne (d.814) there was a concerted effort to reform the life of people, lay and religious alike and moral texts and instructions were written specifically addressed to lay people in general.[61] Practical pastoral manuals to help the priest with *cura animarum,* care of the soul, began to appear by the end of the twelfth century, perhaps inspired by the reforms of the Fourth Lateran Council 1215. Confession by lay people to a priest had been encouraged through the penitentials. But Canon 21 of the Fourth Lateran Council mandated confession at least once a year for all the faithful of either sex once they had reached the age of discretion. Priests were urged to impress on their flock the importance of confession for their salvation.[62] The pastoral manuals not only informed priests and confessors. They also served to teach the laity through the priest's advice on daily living. Certainly, by their very nature the manuals specified particular sexual sins, sometimes in detail. However, the manuals also tempered theory with experience and practice. For instance, pastoral concern for married women in the confessional and notably privacy and confidentiality were particularly delicate since wives were under the authority of their husbands and confidential meetings with the priest or certain penances might raise the suspicions of the husband. Penances were therefore often tailored to the person's situation.[63]

Moreover, and in contrast to some harsher views of women as irrational and leading men into sin, some of the manuals speak about the complementarity of husband and wife, the importance of the dignity of women and love and respect owed to them. Reflecting the Pauline idea that wives contribute to the holiness of their husbands, wives were encouraged to 'soften' the hearts of their husbands and persuade them to both merciful and more upright behaviour. Husbands and wives were assured of the moral rightness of fulfilling the marital obligations to each other, with an added emphasis on mutual support and partnership.[64]

St Aelred: marriage as spiritual friendship

In what has been called a uniquely 'personalist understanding' of marriage,[65] St Aelred Abbot of Rievaulx (c.1110–1167) sets marriage more broadly into spiritual friendship, though as we have seen, spiritual friendship has already been, at least implicitly, an important aspect of marriage. From the age of about fourteen and before entering Rievaulx as a monk in 1134, St Aelred had been at the court of King David I of Scotland eventually becoming the king's steward. As abbot St Aelred had to put to use the diplomatic skills he had learnt at court in both the secular and ecclesiastical spheres and he was a well-known public figure. Not long after becoming abbot, St Aelred wrote a treatise on *Spiritual Friendship* in the form of a dialogue with Ivo, a young monk.[66] Spiritual friendship is obviously a central concern in monastic life. However, St Aelred explains that nature itself gives the human soul a desire for friendship, experience increases that desire, and the law confirms it.[67] St Aelred returns to the creation of Adam and Eve in Genesis. He affirms that it was not 'good' that man should be alone. The creation of woman from man was an equality, demonstrated by a desire for friendship, and charity in the human heart that is the characteristic of true friendship. However, as a result of the Fall charity grew 'lukewarm' and cupidity 'crept in and let private gain supplant the common good.' Cupidity 'corrupted the splendour of friendship and charity' through avarice, envy and a host of other sinful attitudes.[68] Nevertheless, St Aelred sees that marriage is for the good of society and the common good, and the creation of woman made this possible.[69] St Aelred further stresses that the friendship between the spouses, a friendship characterized by charity, is a sharing in the divine life of God. St Aelred is concerned when marriage becomes a purely private matter where individual satisfaction takes over from the common good. In a further explanation of this communitarian nature of love St Aelred says:

> Almighty God can immediately bring to perfection anyone he pleases and bestow all the virtues on any one person. But in his caring way of dealing with us he causes each person to need the other and to have in the other what one does not possess in oneself. Thus, humility is preserved, charity increased, and unity recognized. Therefore, each belongs to all and all belong to each.[70]

According to St Aelred in true friendship 'a friend loves always' despite all difficulties.[71] True friendship is spiritual and 'is desired not with an eye to any worldly profit or for any extraneous reason, but for its own natural worth and for the emotion of the human heart, so that its fruit and reward is nothing but itself.'[72] St Aelred agrees that the virtue of virginity, surpasses the virtue of widowhood and widowhood surpasses conjugal chastity. However, he affirms that conjugal chastity remains a virtue.[73] In his earlier treatise *The Mirror of Charity* St Aelred explains that the experience of love consists of three elements: first, attraction, the spontaneous desirable effect that the other has on a person and this can be spiritual, rational or irrational; second, intention, as the person makes a specific decision to pursue the other; third, fruition, which involves the joy of attaining one's goal. In a world without sin these elements would always tend towards the good. However, in the world corrupted by sin the powers of the soul are weakened and any one of these elements may tend towards evil. Only Christ's grace can heal the weakened soul.[74] As a pastor as well as an abbot St Aelred is well-aware of the difficulties besetting marriage. He explains, 'like a boat is marriage contracted in faith in Jesus Christ. But this boat is flimsy and rickety and ships great quantities of water in its hold; and unless it is bailed out all the time it quickly sinks.'[75] Almsgiving, works of mercy and faith in the Cross of Christ are the things that bail out marriage from the worldly preoccupations and sins that threaten marriage.

What makes marriage?

That consent made marriage and couples were thus free to marry, subject to certain forbidden degrees of kinship, can be found in Anglo-Saxon legislation: regulations in 1008 allowed a widow to do what she willed, and woman could not be forced to marry someone she disliked.[76] To ensure public acknowledgment of marriage a council at Winchester in 1076 ruled that the blessing of the priest was a requirement for legitimacy. A council in London in 1102 presided over by St Anselm Archbishop of Canterbury (1034–1109) decreed that a disputed clandestine marriage was void.[77] Rites of marriage were beginning to emerge in the eleventh century in lands influenced by the Carolingian liturgical books and the *Decretum* of Gratian.[78] In northern France and Anglo-Saxon England the traditional betrothal formality was celebrated at the door of the church before the nuptial liturgy. The priest specifically inquired into the consent of both parties.[79] Significantly this form of marriage before the Church was both physically in front of the church and a public celebration before the Christian community. Moreover, in 1200 a council of Westminster decreed that no marriage could be contracted without the publication of banns on three occasions. This served not only to prevent clandestine marriages but also to discover whether there were any impediments to the marriage.[80]

The twelfth century saw not only economic and population growth but also urbanisation, and a flourishing of learning in cathedral schools.[81] This interest in learning led to further discussion on marriage and marriage was a particularly interesting case because it fitted into both the secular and sacramental order. One major question focused on what made marriage: was it consent or consummation.[82] Roman law favoured consent while the Germanic and tribal cultural traditions looked to consummation.[83] Gratian distinguished between consent that initiated marriage and consummation that ratified it. According to Gratian a legitimate marriage was celebrated according to the local law or custom, with public rites and the transfer of a dowry. Although Gratian thought that a clandestine marriage was therefore illegitimate since it was celebrated secretly, given the pronouncement from Pope St Nicholas that consent made marriage, Gratian agreed that a clandestine marriage was nevertheless valid.[84]

Peter Lombard, (c.1100-c.1164) was a former student at Bologna and knew the works of Gratian. Lombard became famous for his theological work the *Book of Sentences,* a series of questions that systemized the whole of Christian teaching. Over the centuries, collections of sayings and sentences from the church fathers had been handed down but considerable confusion was created where these authorities did not agree, and questions of interpretation naturally arose. Books of sentences were produced to give reasoned argument for agreement or disagreement over the various authorities.[85] Lombard's *Sentences* became the textbook for universities in Europe until the sixteenth century.[86] Written in about 1150, the *Sentences* quote Gratian and diverge from some of Gratian's opinions. On the matter of marriage Lombard argued that spoken consent was all that was required. As in the patristic era, there was a real concern about how to include the case of Mary and St Joseph into an understanding of marriage. Indeed, the marriage of Mary and St Joseph was invoked by both Gratian and Lombard, and according to both approaches, by consent Mary and St Joseph had a true marriage. On the question of consent, Lombard decided that the consent of their lord was required for the marriage of serfs.[87] However, a lord could not impose marriage or the monastic life on his serfs. Lombard's view on marriage became the standard and eventually feudal lords and parents lost control over who could marry whom. The couple were still expected to seek blessing from the church and the Fourth Lateran Council 1215 insisted on the publication of banns of marriage. However, failure to approach the church meant that the marriage was illicit but not invalid, so the marriage stood, and the couple were liable to penance.

The different approaches presented by Gratian and Lombard were eventually brought together by Pope Alexander III (d.1181). Pope Alexander had studied under Gratian, but he favoured the consent approach. Pope Alexander decreed that marriage comes about through the free and mutual exchange of consent to be husband and wife. Lack of free consent from both parties is a barrier to a valid union. This mutual consent creates a binding relationship and as such is indissoluble in principle, though this does not mean absolute indissolubility. Consent is ratified by sexual intercourse so that a consummated valid marriage is indissoluble in fact. Consummation completes the process of forming an absolutely indissoluble union.[88]

However, interest in marriage was not only in the essentials that made marriage. St Augustine's view of marriage had taken central place in collections from the fathers because he had written extensively on marriage.[89] According to T. Finn, St Augustine's ambivalent attitude to marriage was conveyed in many commentaries on his work although inevitably these commentaries did not convey the nuances of his thought. In addition to the questions around consent and consummation, Finn lists other central questions such as, what were the benefits of, and offences against marriage; who were legally qualified to marry; marital rights; marriage in relation to orders and holy vows; disparity of cult; and degrees of kinship both physical and spiritual.[90] Nevertheless, how marriage was a sacrament was one of the most pressing questions. Thus, when thinking about marriage two strands emerge: first is the more juridical based strand that focuses on questions to do with what makes marriage and how marriage is a sacrament; second is the strand that considers marriage in a pastoral and personal context. An approach that sees the first strand as central or indeed the only strand in the development of Western thinking on marriage will inevitably suggest that church thinking is essentially contractual and juridical.

Marriage: a sacrament

E. Schillebeeckx points out that marriage was regarded as a sacrament not because of the liturgy that surrounded it but by the very nature of marriage itself.[91] St Augustine had called marriage a *sacramentum* and this term had a double meaning.[92] *Sacramentum* pointed to the indissoluble sacred obligations that the spouses had taken upon themselves, reflecting the oath of loyalty made by a Roman soldier and his physical branding as an outward sign of this pledge, or money placed by litigants in a sacred space.[93] *Sacramentum* was also a sacred sacramental sign referring to the mystery of the unity of Christ and his church. For the early church fathers, since *sacramentum* involved permanent obligations not to destroy the sacramental sign of marriage or the unity of the spouses, dissolution of the marriage was not permitted. As sacramental theology developed *sacramentum* began to be seen as an effective sacramental sign that brought something about. In the case of marriage, it brought about an objective bond that could not be broken, so dissolution of marriage was not possible.[94] This is not to say that for the early fathers *sacramentum* was merely metaphorical. As J. Martos explains, the fathers used the language and concepts of their time in order to put into words the non-verbal experience of the sacred as opened up by the sacraments.[95] Martos notes that as the

Church emerged from the chaos of the collapse of the Roman Empire, invasion by Germanic tribes, and the subsequent mission to Christianize Europe, liturgical practices centring on seven major rituals became simplified. By the twelfth century sacramental practices and rites concerning the seven sacraments, baptism, confirmation, eucharist, penance, holy orders, anointing of the dying, and also marriage, began to have a more stable form and the seven were also being recognized as the principal sacraments.

In his *Sacraments of the Christian Faith* Hugh of St Victor (d.c.1141) gives an overview of the Christian faith and he observes that the 'first guilt of man was pride.' This was followed by the three punishments of mortality, concupiscence and ignorance. Human beings need to be freed through grace and the remedy consists of three things: faith, sacraments and good works.[96] Hugh explains that not every sign of a sacred thing is a sacrament. Hugh identified four essentials for a sacrament: first there had to be a material element; second there had to be some real resemblance to that which the sacrament signified; third a sacrament had to be instituted by Christ; fourth, a sacrament conferred grace. Hugh states that marriage is a sacrament but unusual among the sacraments because unlike the other sacraments marriage was established before sin.[97] Marriage is good because the author of marriage is God, moreover, marriage was 'consecrated' and so instituted by Christ through the miracle at Cana.[98] Hugh thinks that marriage was instituted as a 'compact of love' for the union of souls, much like the union of a soul with God, so that it helps the couple to love God; for the bringing forth of children; and as a remedy against concupiscence.[99] Marriage brings with it three blessings: faith, hope of children, and sacrament.[100] Using the example of Mary and St Joseph, Hugh says that marriage is made by consent. He then notes the double consent in marriage to live a communal life in mutual love and consent to the sexual act.[101] In 1136 Peter Lombard had studied with Hugh at the Abbey of St Victor in Paris and was undoubtedly influenced by Hugh's thinking on the sacraments.[102] The popularity of Lombard's sentences led theologians to focus their discussions on Lombard's definition: 'something is properly called a sacrament because it is a sign of God's grace, and is such an image of invisible grace that it bears its likeness and exists as its cause.'[103]

However, Lombard thought that marriage was not like the other sacraments. He accepted that marriage was a sign of the sacred, but he did not think it caused grace. Martos identifies three reasons in particular for this difficulty: since financial arrangements were inextricably tied into marriage it might seem that grace was the subject of a financial transaction; unlike the other sacraments, marriage existed before the coming of Christ so it could not easily be said to have been instituted by Christ; more significantly marriage involved sexual intercourse so while marriage was good, it was also tainted and seen as a remedy for concupiscence rather than a path to holiness. However, Martos explains that three factors led theologians to re-examine these views: the rise of the Albigensians and Cathars; the development of a Christian wedding ritual and blessings that seem to sanction sexual relations in marriage; the rediscovery of St Augustine's writings on marriage as a sacramentum.[104]

The Albigensians and Cathars both shared similar beliefs with the Bogomils, though in varying degrees of severity.[105] Bogomil was a priest who lived during the reign of the Bulgarian Tsar Peter (927–969). Like the Manichaes and dualists of previous centuries, the Bogomils believed that the material world was the creation of an evil deity and they rejected the Old Testament. They refused the sacraments and veneration of the Cross as symbols of material things. They avoided wine, sexual intercourse, and also meat, possibly because they believed in transmigration of souls into animals.[106] The Cathars were led by perfects, people considered to be holy, who embraced simple lives of poverty, abstained from sexual relations, and followed a rigorous diet. They believed that the body was 'a cruel prison' and sexual difference was imposed by an alien power. Marriage and the procreation of children were part of a diabolical plot to perpetuate physical life and trap the spirit.[107]

Some of the more severe Cathars believed that children perpetuated humanity and by renouncing sexual intercourse they looked forward to the extinction of the human race. Whether or not Manichaenism was the root of Albigensian and Cathar beliefs, these beliefs raised the same kind of challenges, notably to the goodness of creation and of children. As a result, theologians proposed even more strongly that intercourse for children was a good.[108]

Once it was established that mutual free consent was the *sacramentum* in marriage then medieval theologians could relate marriage to the threefold distinctions they had developed in sacramental theology. The *sacramentum tantum*, sacramental sign, represented by the symbolic words, gestures and objects in the rite was the element that was 'only a sign'; the *sacramentum et res*, sacramental reality, was the element that was 'both sign and reality' and represented the change in the subject of the person, received by participation in the rite; the *res tantum*, sacred reality, was the element that was 'only a reality' representing God's freely bestowed grace. The bond of marriage produced by the rite is the sacramental reality, creating a real change in the man and woman as they become husband and wife. The bond is also a sign of the love Christ has for the Church and the grace the couple need to fulfil their obligations to each other.[109]

The first enumeration of the seven sacraments including marriage was formally made in *The Profession of Faith of Michael Palaeologus* from the Second Council of Lyons in 1274.[110] Nevertheless, there were still questions about the grace conferred by the sacrament. Some theologians continued to follow Lombard who had thought that marriage did not confer grace and it was only remedial. Moreover, Lombard said that Christ did not institute marriage though he did approve of it.[111] Others thought that it was simply the grace to avoid sin. However, the view that since marriage was a sacrament and all the sacraments bestowed grace therefore marriage did as well, ultimately prevailed. At the Council of Florence in 1439 Pope Eugenius IV (1383–1447) issued the *Bull of Union with the Armenians* and this comprised a summary of the doctrine of sacraments in general, including marriage as one of the seven, based on a treatise from St Thomas Aquinas (1225–1274). The summary referred to Ephesians 5 and affirmed that mutual consent is the efficient cause of marriage. Following St Augustine, the three goods of marriage are children and their education, faithfulness and indissolubility. Separation in cases of adultery was allowed, but not remarriage. Implicit is that grace is given.[112]

St Thomas Aquinas is perhaps best known for his *Summa Theologiae*, a lengthy summary of Christian theology and philosophy written for his students, and his *Summa contra Gentiles*, an apology on the truth of the Catholic faith. St Thomas also wrote a series of scriptural commentaries and *opuscula* or little treatises that served as explanations of the faith. The *Catechetical Instructions* are a later collection made up of St Thomas's catechesis and *opuscula*. It includes the *Explanation of the Seven Sacraments* which was part of the treatise *De fidei articulis et septem sacramentis* that St Thomas had written at the request of the Archbishop of Palermo and this was quoted in the *Bull of Union with the Armenians*. St Thomas's various catechetical instructions were used as textbooks for priests and teachers.

St Thomas's comments on the sacraments appear under the heading *The Tenth Article: the Communion of Saints, the Forgiveness of Sins*. St Thomas sets a review of sacraments here because Christ's communication of grace takes place through the sacraments and this unites all Christians in the communion of saints. Marriage is listed as the seventh sacrament and as a sacrament it brings salvation. Certainly, St Thomas sees the sacraments as medicinal, but he does not think that marriage is merely a remedy against concupiscence. According to St Thomas marriage is also a basic human good because of the natural desire for children, their education and upbringing, and for human companionship.[113] Marriage also gives the couple grace to live their married life.[114] Referring to St Paul, marriage is not only an honourable state of life, it is also 'meritorious for eternal life' for those in a state of grace.

St Thomas Aquinas: happiness, virtues and the passions

St Thomas thinks that marital intercourse for children is an act of virtue, intercourse for the intention of 'rendering mutual comfort' is an act of justice. However, if intercourse excites lust within the limits of marriage it is a venial sin. But if lust goes beyond these limits 'so as to intend intercourse with another if possible' it becomes a serious sin.[115] Perhaps in more personalistic terms, this intending intercourse with another reflects the objectifying of the other spouse to the extent of no longer seeing the person. St Thomas adds that according to St Gregory 'sins of the flesh are more shameful and less blameful than those of the spirit.'[116] Abuse is of course a particular evil in itself. According to Pope St Gregory I, two sins hold 'cruel sway' over the human race: pride, the sin of the spirit, and lust, the sin of the flesh. St Gregory observes that the sin of pride is more insidious because people think of pride as less disgraceful than lust and so they do not regard it as serious and therefore they do not even attempt to avoid it.[117] St Thomas notes that through baptism Christians belong to the body of Christ and so therefore, in agreement with Pope St Gregory, any misuse of the body is a sin. Following Matthew 22:30, plus the belief that in the resurrection bodies will be raised in a 'different quality,' St Thomas further observes that there will be no need for marriage in heaven.[118]

St Thomas calls the unity in marriage the 'greatest friendship.' According to St Thomas there are four characteristics of friendship: it is based on benevolence, it involves communication, it is mutual, and it is a form of charity.[119] Marriage in particular also involves equality and regard for the other.[120] He thinks that polygamy cannot convey this friendship, arguing that marriage was 'at no time a perfect state' until the coming of Christ because Jewish men could have many wives, but women could not have several husbands, and therefore there was no equality or proper friendship.[121] St Thomas further explains that marriage is indissoluble: the couple become one in marriage, parents are one in producing children and in caring for them and divorce is contrary to justice due to the children and to the spouses.[122] He points out that adultery is forbidden to both husband and wife because they are 'one body,' and that the sin of adultery is equally serious for both. Adultery shows both a lack of faith to God's law of 'one body' union of the spouses, and the sacrament 'because marriage is contracted before the eyes of the Church, and [adultery is] a betrayal of faith to the other partner.' However, he also notes that adultery by the wife steals children from her husband.[123] St Thomas makes it clear that the great and deep friendship of marriage is more than the conjugal acts between the spouses and has a spiritual element. It also includes the distinctively human acts of sharing a life together and sharing in the entirety of domestic activities.[124]

St Thomas did not live to complete his *Summa Theologiae* and a supplement was compiled probably by his friend Fra Rainaldo da Piperno from St Thomas's commentaries on the Sentences of Peter Lombard. Marriage is affirmed as a sacrament, and the form of the sacrament is the mutual consent of the couple rather than the blessing of the priest. Moreover, marriage reflects the Paschal Mystery in terms of charity, since Christ suffered for the Church, his spouse.[125] The supplement refers to marriage as a *coniunctio*, a joining together directed to the procreation and upbringing of children and to one family life. Thus, this joining together of bodies and souls is a joining together of complementary persons that makes them one, and so marriage is indissoluble.[126]

For St Thomas an understanding of human beings and human interaction is incomplete without considering happiness, virtues, and the passions. St Thomas says that human happiness is two-fold: one happiness is related to human nature and can be gained in this life. A person can obtain this by natural means and there are natural principles, the virtues, that enable the person to act well in pursuit of this happiness. However, this happiness is imperfect. Although St Thomas does not discuss marriage in relation to earthly happiness, he does say that in this life evil can never be totally excluded. Indeed, we cannot have true happiness in this life because 'the goods of the present life pass away; since life itself passes away.'[127] Anyone who has been bereaved perhaps would recognize this. The other happiness surpasses human nature. A person can obtain this only by the power of God, by a 'kind of participation of the God-head.' The natural principles are not sufficient to direct a person towards this other happiness, so the person needs additional principles provided by God. These additional principles are the theological virtues of faith, hope and charity, *caritas*: they direct us to God, they are infused in us by God alone, and we know them by divine revelation.[128]

In addition to the theological virtues, there are four cardinal virtues, prudence or practical wisdom, justice, temperance, and fortitude. Prudence and justice are concerned with the very act of reason; temperance and fortitude put the order of reason into the passions because at times the passions act against reason. Thus, when the passions incite the person beyond reason and so need to be curbed, the virtue of temperance steps in; when the passions urge the person to withdraw from reason either through fear of danger or extra effort, the virtue of fortitude steps in.[129] The cardinal virtues are the hinges, *cardo* meaning hinge, on which all the other virtues turn. The intellectual virtues perfect reason; the moral virtues perfect our 'appetites,' inclinations, in obedience to reason.[130] For a human being to be properly integrated the person needs both reason and inclinations to be well disposed and so the person needs both intellectual and moral virtues. Thinking in terms of marriage and relationships, a fully mature person has affective and intellectual maturity and can integrate his or her weaknesses and strength: the person has self-control and is fully in possession of themselves.

Significantly, for St Thomas the passions have an important and positive role in human psychology.[131] Passions are not obstacles to be overcome or suppressed. Rather they are a God-given aspect of being human and are naturally related to reason.[132] Passions are involved in human action and are the subject of the virtues, so they contribute to human flourishing.

Passions, or as St Thomas calls the subject of passions, sensitive appetites or inclinations, are morally neutral as they move through a person in response to the objects that are experienced. This movement is not simply something that happens without any direction. Instead, it is a movement towards or away from something perceived with the senses as good or evil. St Thomas also thinks that passions belong to both the body and the soul because affective experiences result in emotions and feelings and are accompanied by bodily changes, after all, the emotive experience of shame coincides with the body going red. St Thomas identifies two sorts of passions that are complementary: concupiscible and irascible. Concupiscible passions are simply inclinations towards something desired or away from something hurtful. There are six such passions: love and hatred, desire and aversion, pleasure and pain. It is important to note that concupiscence refers to a yearning for something good and so concupiscence is not in itself sinful. However, since this yearning desire could be inordinate or directed at a lower good instead of a higher good, it could, and often does struggle against reason, and acts as a 'tinder for sin'[133]: as St Paul says lamenting this inward 'battle,' 'the good thing I want to do, I never do; the evil thing which I do not want, that is what I do.'[134] Irascible passions are directed towards the good that is difficult or arduous because these passions have to overcome obstacles. Irascible passions counteract the tendency of concupiscible passions to turn away from their fulfilment because of obstacles. There are five such passions: anger, hope and despair, courage and fear. When passions are under the control of reason they can contribute powerfully to help the intellect and will because they intensify the inclination towards the good. But we need a balance of both: simply focusing on concupiscible passions leads to egoism and emptiness as the person seeks transient or immediate pleasures; simply focusing on irascible passions leads to fear and anxiety. However, because passions are susceptible to being disordered, we need virtues, settled dispositions, to direct the passions to the appropriate objects. As Aristotle explains, virtue is having emotions at the right time, with reference to the right objects, towards the right people, with the right motive, and in the right way.[135]

Connected to the virtues St Thomas sees the specific gifts of the Holy Spirit as additional graces that help the person to be amenable to the promptings of God.[136] Four of the seven gifts belong to reason and three to appetite, inclination. So, to grasp the truth speculative reason is perfected by understanding and practical reason by counsel; to judge rightly speculative reason is perfected by wisdom and practical reason by knowledge; the appetitive power regarding a person's relations with another is perfected by piety, to relate to other people as children of the same Father; and regarding the self, perfected by fortitude against fear of dangers, and against inordinate lust for pleasures by fear, to avoid sin.

In the integrated approach of St Thomas human beings and their action involves the whole person, physical, intellectual, emotional, social, moral and spiritual. However as moral theology developed in its method, later commentators on St Thomas separated out some of these aspects, neglecting others. Moreover, according to the reformers, concupiscence is always sinful because it is part of the sinful corruption of human nature. The integrated approach surfaces again, but not until the twentieth century.

Theological method: changes and challenges

Trends in theological method are also significant in the development of the understanding of marriage, not least because marriage is a part of moral living. In the history of moral theology there is a clear movement from a morality based on happiness and human flourishing, the kind seen in the system of St Thomas, towards a morality based on obligation. Furthermore, new ways of presenting theological ideas meant that the writings of theologians like St Aelred could appeal more to a lay audience.

The way of organising theology from at least the ninth century, though possibly as far back as Boethius (477–524),[137] is known as scholasticism. Scholasticism was informed by a balance of reason and appeal to the authority of Aristotle, other classical authors, the early Church fathers through quotation, and biblical commentaries.[138] Twelfth century theology continued the scholastic approach, and this followed the kind of methodology advised by Peter Abelard (d.1142) in the preface to his book *Sic et non*. Abelard's book is a selection of authoritative texts, mostly from the Church fathers, and he arranged the quotations so that they gave, *sic et non*, a 'yes and no' approach with a view to reconciling or distinguishing the different authorities.[139] Although the methods of dialogue and disputation were already current,[140] Abelard is recognized as applying a strict logic, dialectic, to the process.[141] In this process a text was selected, ensuring that it was not corrupted through errors of copying; a check was made that it was the latest thinking of the author on the subject at issue and not another source he had cited; the context and circumstances of the text were considered; and then the text was discussed with reference to issues of the day.[142]

Although the scholastic method remained dominant into the seventeenth century, it had come under some pressure from a different methodology, humanism, in the sixteenth century. In contemporary understanding, humanism is considered a secular or at least non-religious worldview, where God is at best irrelevant.[143] Unlike modern secular humanism, early humanism was not non-religious nor was it in opposition to Christianity. Rather, humanism and Christianity were seen as complementary[144] and any humanistic social criticisms were regarded as judgments on cultural values of the time rather than on Christianity itself.[145] However, there were undoubted tensions between humanism and scholasticism.

Humanism and the *studia humanitatis* was primarily a literary and cultural programme,[146] characterized by the call for a return to original texts rather than commentaries on them.[147] Humanist methods were disseminated principally through the new technology of the printing press and through personal letters.[148] The kind of skills found in these texts, skills of rhetoric and persuasion, skills needed for a ruling elite, as well as the social values expressed in these texts, held great appeal. In contrast to the speculation and abstract logic of the traditional form of learning, humanistic studies had practical application. The *studia humanitatis* fostered the skills of politics and moral decision-making required for judges, lawyers and lay people interested in governance.[149] This perhaps in part explains why treatises directed specifically to lay people, such as treatises on marriage, became so important. Gradually the intellectual approach to learning changed. Throughout late antiquity and the Middle Ages, classical texts were regarded as authorities, as factual statements.[150] In their attention to grammatical analysis of religious texts, the humanist scholars rejected what the scholastics considered to be the authoritative value of the tradition as expressed by the fathers.

In addition to challenges to textual authority, the traditional scholastic approach was challenged by nominalism,[151] considered to be the *via moderna*, the new way forward. From the early church fathers through to St Thomas Aquinas character, virtues and human flourishing as a fulfilment of being human, had been central to moral thinking. Certainly, law and grace were significant, but these were treated alongside the understanding that human beings are drawn towards the good, and human beings act for a particular end. In this attraction to the good passions and desires hold a significant place, even if at times they lead us to mistake a lower good for a higher one. Nominalism developed from the thinking of William of Ockham (c.1285). According to Ockham any notion of the nature of things or of final ends was an unnecessary multiplication of ideas. Instead, Ockham insisted that there were no natures, just names we give to things. God was said to create out of his sovereign will.[152] From this, Ockham developed a theory of human freedom that focused entirely on the exercise of choice,[153] and such a move contributes to a notion of the person as purely a subject of desires and wants. Earlier thinking was concerned with ways of leading to true happiness, friendship with God, where obligation had an instructive role in the initial stages of moral progress; the greatest role was given to the exercise of virtues.[154] Rather than being guided by practical wisdom shaped by the pursuit of virtues, according to nominalism human beings are simply free to decide one way or another, a freedom of indifference. Acts are moral when they conform to God's law and this means acting morally became an act of the will rather than a matter of wisdom. The passions were regarded with deep suspicion since they could sway the will

Nominalism adopted a covenantal idea of agreement imposed by God between God and believers whereby God accepts individuals if they have first fulfilled his demands[155] thus the understanding of obligation becomes the essence of morality.[156]

Martin Luther and the Council of Trent

Certainly, marriage was always regarded as important for social order and this view did not change during the religious turbulence of the sixteenth century.[157] However, ecclesiastical jurisdiction over marriage, the rule of celibacy for the clergy, and especially the Catholic definition of marriage as a sacrament became the sources of much contention. For many marriage in the sixteenth century had become a corrupt and immoral practice with many young people forced into celibacy as priests or nuns by their parents on the grounds that marriage brought with it too many worldly trials and celibacy was a higher vocation.[158] The Catholic Church recognized the need for reforms. However, the Protestant reformers located the decay in canon law and in Catholic theology of marriage.[159]

Although Martin Luther (1483–1546) saw his own marriage with a former nun as 'defiance of the Devil,'[160] as far as Luther was concerned marriage was a 'divinely noble business,' fit for everyone, and celibacy was not of a higher order. Indeed, marriage was a higher vocation than celibacy.[161] Luther's elevation of marriage to the truly religious order above celibacy seems to be a part of his argument for the priesthood of all believers.[162] Eventually Luther rejected the sacramental character of marriage and its scriptural provenance.[163] In particular Luther objected to the plethora of church regulations concerning prohibited degrees of relationship.[164] As Luther explains 'whoever is ashamed of marriage is also ashamed of being human.' Moreover, he saw that God's power was already present in the sexual instinct and marriage was a way of living out faith in God.[165] Nevertheless, Luther also thought that the state of human beings was so corrupt that sexual intercourse was never without sin.[166] Marriage then was a remedy for disordinate sexual desires and should be declined only by those rare people who could embrace complete continence.[167] Since marriage was mandated by creation it belonged to everyone, not just Christians, and as such should be maintained by the state rather than the church. Divorce could therefore be allowed albeit on limited grounds. For Catholics divorce meant separation of the couple 'from bed and board,' the sacramental bond of marriage remained and neither spouse was free to remarry. For the reformers divorce meant dissolution of the marriage and there was no scriptural basis to prohibit remarriage.[168] The reformers referred to the early church practice of civil marriage in order to refuse the sacramental nature of marriage and the church's jurisdiction.[169] Additionally, the reformers argued that since people lived in the sinful earthly kingdom civil authorities should both promote marriage and allow for divorce and remarriage.[170]

The Council of Trent was convoked in 1545 and after a series of interruptions due to political unrest it was concluded in 1563. Since the Council was called some twenty-five years after the start of the Protestant reformation, it is unlikely that its aim was to prevent or even possibly heal the split in Western Christendom. Instead, it may be more fruitful to see Trent as a reform council.[171] The Council set about a practical reform of the Catholic Church and among its many decrees it dealt with the sacraments, looking at marriage in more detail in its last session in 1563. The Council reaffirmed that marriage was one of the seven sacraments and that sacraments convey grace. Marriage, then, is a source of grace and holiness. Referring specifically to scripture, the fathers at Trent affirmed that the indissoluble and monogamous bond of marriage was established by God in the 'one flesh' of Genesis. This natural bond of love was confirmed by Christ in Matthew 19:6 and Mark 10:9, instituted by Christ and sanctified in Ephesians 5:25, and brought to perfection through his passion. Thus, marriage is a sacrament of the 'new law.'[172] Although separation from bed and board might be possible a valid marriage remained indissoluble and issues concerning marriage remained under church jurisdiction. Moreover, the married state did not surpass virginity or celibacy.[173] In order to deal with clandestine marriages the fathers at Trent reformed the marriage ceremony in its *Tametsi* ('although') decree, declaring null a marriage that took place without the presence of a priest or his representatives and two witnesses,[174] except in places where the Council decrees had not been promulgated or where priests were not available. Banns were to be read three times and the marriage registered.[175] In answer to claims by the reformers that marriage lawsuits are exclusively the concern of secular courts, Trent set the ecclesiastical legal form of marriage but did not deny civil competence, and notably 'praiseworthy customs or ceremonies' could be retained.[176] There was thus a distinction, even if not a separation, between the marriage contract and the sacrament of marriage. According to W. Roberts, the fathers at the Council of Trent did not intend to develop further a theology of marriage. Instead, they sought to correct misconceptions, errors and abuses, and so the Council 'assumed the theological understanding of the meaning of marriage that had been handed down for a number of centuries.'[177]

One of the claims condemned at Trent was the proposition that 'the commandments of God are impossible of observance by the one who is justified.' Instead, the fathers at Trent explained that 'God does not command the impossible, but in commanding he admonishes you to do what you can and to pray for what you cannot, and he gives his aid to enable you.'[178] Although the fathers at Trent had Calvin in their sights, they refer here to St Augustine's treatise *On Nature and Grace*[179] written in response to Pelagius. According to St Augustine, Pelagius taught that 'a person can be without sin and easily keep the commandments of God if he wishes.'[180] In perhaps an early form of nominalism, Pelagius says human beings have intelligence and free will and can choose between alternatives.[181] Since they have been given the moral law, they should follow it.[182] Indeed, Pelagius argues that human beings can be without sin if they want and they can keep the commandments if they so choose.[183] The claim that human beings tend naturally towards sin is, according to Pelagius, an excuse made by those who do not want to face the moral struggle and the only reason why we find it difficult to follow the law is because of our bad habits.[184] In response St Augustine explains that some aids are indispensable: just as 'no one sails without a ship,' human beings need grace to live rightly.[185] Unlike Pelagius who sets grace in opposition to human nature, St Augustine sees grace as liberating and building on nature. According to St Augustine freedom with a good will is a 'great good' but the will cannot be upright unless it has been freed by God's grace.[186] St Augustine distinguishes between two sorts of freedom: *liberum arbitrium captivatum* is free will influenced by the tendency to sin; *liberum arbitrium liberatum* is graced free will, the freedom to make the right choice.[187]

Clearly this discussion about the impossibility of the commandments is significant when it comes to marriage, especially when people talk in a polarized way about either simply following church teaching on marriage without acknowledging struggle, difficulties and the need for grace or thinking that the teaching asks the impossible that no one can fulfil so therefore teaching can only be aspirational. This issue surfaces throughout the discussion on marriage.

Summary

It is all too easy to dismiss the medieval era as a time of upheaval, religious dissent, theological hair-splitting, and a hardening of Catholic Church legislation as a response to the Protestant reformers. However, in the tradition, as outlined by St Thomas Aquinas, moral theology looks at the person as a whole: in his or her physical, intellectual, emotional, social, moral and spiritual dimensions. In terms of marriage, church law indicates the significance of marriage for society as a whole, the importance of equality between men and women, and free consent for the dignity of the human person. The church's pastoral concern for the care of souls seen also in treatises written for married people, demonstrates that marriage and family life is indeed a path to holiness. Moreover, marriage has a spiritual quality. Nevertheless, the idea that marriage is more about contract than covenant or a vocation to holiness began to emerge and this way of thinking had its roots in a major shift in theological thinking—nominalism. This contractual and covenantal appreciation of marriage perhaps reflects the reality that marriage is both a matter of state and religion. Married people are in the world even if as Christians in their married vocation they are not of the world. However, this is not a question simply of authority or a turf war over who should control marriage—church or state. Rather it reflects the way of being a Christian in the world, and pastoral concern for a person's growth as a Christian, especially a married Christian, and how to be leaven in the world.

Happiness may be sought for in relationships and in marriage, the fulfilment of our created nature. And different people have different ideas of happiness. However, our created nature has been raised by grace, as has marriage been raised to the dignity of a sacrament. This means that through grace human beings can attain their final end, not just happiness, but the good itself that must be loved above all things, including the love of self. This good is not only related to the good as right in the moral order or an ideal of the good. The final end for human beings is beatitude, friendship with God, who is Good. We are asked to love the Good more than happiness. Yet, this end is where our ultimate happiness lies. Moreover, holiness in marriage, and in the Christian life, is not attained by a kind of moral athleticism of the practice of ascetics or virtues. Rather holiness is a gift of God's love and grace.

Notes

[1] Rm 7; 10:1–11.
[2] G. Duby, 'The Knight, the Lady and the Priest: the Making of Modern Marriage in Medieval France' in *Contesting Christendom: Readings in Medieval Religion and Culture* (New York: Rowman & Littlefield, 2008), p. 91.
[3] W. Kasper, *Theology of Christian Marriage* (New York: Seabury Press, 1980), p. 32.
[4] Pontifical Council for Justice and Peace, *Compendium of the Social Doctrine of the Church* (Washington DC: Libreria Editrice Vaticana, 2004), 209, 211.
[5] R. L. Wilken, *The First Thousand Years: A Global History of Christianity* (New Haven: Yale University Press, 2012), Ch. 18, p. 174.
[6] Tertullian, *On Fasting*, 13.
[7] Wilken, *The First Thousand Years* p. 176.
[8] Seventh Council of Carthage.
[9] H. Hess, *The Early Development of Canon Law and the Council of Serdica* (Oxford: Oxford University Press, 2002), pp. 60–73.
[10] *Ibid.*, 77; Wilken defines 'canon' as a rule or law, *The First Thousand Years*, pp. 179–180.
[11] Hess, *The Early Development of Canon Law*, p. 76.
[12] Wilken, *The First Thousand Years*, p. 180.
[13] *Ibid.*, p. 181.
[14] S. Jurasinski, *The Old English Penitentials and Anglo-Saxon Law* (Cambridge: Cambridge University Press, 2015), pp. 127–136.
[15] M. Alamichel, *Widows in Anglo-Saxon and Medieval Britain* (Oxford: Peter Lang, 2008), p. 32.
[16] Jurasinski, *The Old English Penitentials and Anglo-Saxon Law*, p. 122.
[17] M. Hoeflich and J. Grabher, 'Normative Legal Texts' in *The History of*

Medieval Canon Law in the Classical Period (Washington: Catholic University of America Press 2008), p. 7.
18 R. H. Helmholz, *The Oxford History of the Laws of England Vol.1 The Canon Law and Ecclesiastical Jurisdiction from 597 to the 1640s* (Oxford: Oxford University Press, 2004), pp. 1–3.
19 *Ibid.*, p. 44.
20 D. Herlihy, *Medieval Households* (Cambridge Massachusetts: Harvard University Press, 1985), pp. 32–34.
21 *Ibid.*, pp. 37.
22 *Ibid.*, pp. 44–48.
23 *Ibid.*, pp. 49.
24 *Ibid.*, pp. 49.
25 *Ibid.*, pp. 49–50.
26 *Ibid.*, pp. 50–51.
27 *Ibid.*, pp. 72–73.
28 *Ibid.*, pp. 60.
29 *Ibid.*, pp. 61–62.
30 Helmholz, *The Oxford History of the Laws of England*, pp. 44–45.
31 C. McCarthy, *Marriage in Medieval England: Law, Literature and Practice* (Woodbridge: Boydell, 2004), pp. 5–6.
32 S. McDougall, 'The Making of Marriage in Medieval France' in *Journal of Family History* 38/2 (2013), pp. 103–121.
33 Helmholz, *The Oxford History of the Laws of England*, pp. 16–17.
34 See A. Bevilacqua, 'The History of the Indissolubility of Marriage' in *Proceedings of the Catholic Theological Society of America* 22 (2012), pp. 253–308, p. 280; Pope St Siricius, *Letter to Bishop Himerius of Tarragona*.
35 See Bevilacqua, 'The History of the Indissolubility of Marriage', p. 280; Pope Innocent I, *Letter to Victricius*.
36 See Bevilacqua, 'The History of the Indissolubility of Marriage', p. 280; Pope Innocent I, *Letter to Exsuperius*.
37 See Bevilacqua, 'The History of the Indissolubility of Marriage', p. 281; Pope Innocent I, *Letter to a Certain Probus*.
38 See Bevilacqua, 'The History of the Indissolubility of Marriage', pp. 282–283; Pope St Leo I, *Letter to Nicetas of Aquileia*.
39 See Bevilacqua, 'The History of the Indissolubility of Marriage', p. 268; St Bede, *On St Mark* 10.
40 See Bevilacqua, 'The History of the Indissolubility of Marriage' p. 285; Pope St Gregory II *Replies to Questions Put By Boniface* (22 November, 726). See also W. Kelly, *Pope Gregory II On Divorce and Remarriage* (Rome: Universita Gregoriana Editrice, 1976).

41 See Pope St Zacharias, *Epistola VII ad Pipinum Majorem Domus itemque ad episcopos, abates et proceres Francorum* in Bevilacqua, 'The History of the Indissolubility of Marriage', p. 286. See also Codex Canonum Ecclesiae Africanae, canon 102.
42 See Bevilacqua, 'The History of the Indissolubility of Marriage'.
43 Pope St Nicholas I *Letter to Answer the Bulgarians' Questions* (866).
44 T. Finn, 'Sex and Marriage in the Sentences of Peter Lombard' in *Theological Studies* 72 (2011), p. 46.
45 Pope St Gregory I, *Pastoral Rule*, I, 9.
46 *Ibid.*, III, 27, admonition 28.
47 P. U. Rabaneda, 'Leander of Seville and His Influence on Isidore of Seville' in *A Companion to Isidore of Seville* (Leiden: Brill 2020), pp. 101–132, p. 118.
48 T. Knoebel, 'Introduction, Isidore of Seville' in *De ecclesiasticis officiis* (New York: Newman Press, 2008), p. 11.
49 E. Schillebeeckx, *Marriage: Human Reality and Saving Mystery* (London: Sheed and Ward, 1965), p. 265.
50 Knoebel, 'Introduction, Isidore of Seville', pp. 8–12.
51 *Ibid.*, p. 13.
52 St Isidore of Seville, *De ecclesiasticis officiis*, 93, 98.
53 Schillebeeckx, *Marriage*, p. 289.
54 St Isidore of Seville, *The Etymologies*, IX, vii, 27; 211–212.
55 Knoebel, 'Introduction, Isidore of Seville', p. 14.
56 Reynolds, *Marriage in the Western Church*, pp. xvi-xvii, 14.
57 *Ibid.*, pp. 14–15.
58 F. Veronese, 'Jonas of Orleans' in *Great Christian Jurists and Legal Collections in the First Millenium* (Cambridge: Cambridge University Press, 2019), pp. 413–428.
59 1 Co 13:12; M. Franklin-Brown, *Reading the World: Encyclopedic Writing in the Scholastic Age* (Chicago: University of Chicago Press, 2012), p. 272.
60 Veronese, 'Jonas of Orleans', p. 420.
61 R. Stone, *Morality and Masculinity in the Carolingian Empire* (Cambridge: Cambridge University Press, 2012), p. 3.
62 B. A. Barr, 'Three's A Crowd: Wives, Husbands, and Priests in the Late Medieval Confessional' in *A Companion to Pastoral Care in the Late Middle Ages (1200–1500)* (Leiden: Brill, 2010), pp. 214–215.
63 *Ibid.*, pp. 213–234; J. Murray, 'Thinking About Gender: The Diversity of Medieval Perspectives' in *Power of the Weak: Studies on Medieval Women* (Chicago: University of Illinois Press, 1995), pp. 7–8.
64 Murray, Thinking About Gender, pp. 10–14.

65. A. M. Mayeski, 'Like a boat is marriage: Aelred on marriage as a Christian way of life' in *Theological Studies* 70 (2009) 92–108; according to Mayeski, St Aelred offers a 'personalist understanding of marriage, significantly different from the thought of other theologians, both prior to and contemporaneous with Aelred, who begin with contract and law.' Mayeski also thinks that St Augustine has in mind marriage as essentially a contractual bond, pp. 99, 96.
66. St Aelred, *Spiritual Friendship* (Collegeville, Minnesota: Liturgical Press, 2010).
67. *Ibid.*, I, 51.
68. *Ibid.*, I, 57–58; see Mayeski, Like a boat is marriage: Aelred on marriage as a Christian way of life, pp. 98–99.
69. St Aelred, *Spiritual Friendship*, I, 57.
70. St Aelred, *Sermon VIII*, 10.
71. St Aelred, *Spiritual Friendship* I, 23, 24.
72. *Ibid.*, I, 45.
73. *Ibid.*, I, 66.
74. St Aelred, *The Mirror of Charity*, III, 11–29.
75. St Aelred, *Sermon XXII For the Nativity of Mary*, 4.
76. M. Sheehan, *Marriage, Family and Law in Medieval Europe* (Toronto: University of Toronto Press, 1996), p. 84.
77. Alamichel, *Widows in Anglo-Saxon and Medieval Britain*, p. 54.
78. E. Hall, *The Arnolfini Betrothal: Medieval Marriage and the Enigma of Van Eyck's Double Portrait* (Berkeley: University of California Press, 1994), pp. 22–24.
79. Sheehan, *Marriage, Family and Law in Medieval Europe*, pp. 113–114; Alamichel, *Widows in Anglo-Saxon and Medieval Britain*, p. 154.
80. Alamichel, *Widows in Anglo-Saxon and Medieval Britain*, p. 155.
81. Finn, Sex and Marriage in the Sentences of Peter Lombard, p. 41.
82. Herlihy, *Medieval Households*, pp. 80–82.
83. Hall, *The Arnolfini Betrothal*, p. 25.
84. *Ibid.*
85. Finn, Sex and Marriage in the Sentences of Peter Lombard, p. 43.
86. *Ibid.*
87. Sheehan, *Marriage, Family and Law in Medieval Europe*, p. 233.
88. J. Kamas, *The Separation of the Spouses with the Bond Remaining: Historical and Canonical Study with Pastoral Implications* (Rome: Editrice Pontificia Universita Gregoriana, 1997), pp. 100–102.
89. Finn, Sex and Marriage in the Sentences of Peter Lombard, p. 50.
90. *Ibid.*

91 Schillebeeckx, *Marriage*, p. 280.
92 *Ibid.*, pp. 281–286.
93 See J. Martos, *Doors to the Sacred: A Historical Introduction to Sacraments in the Catholic Church* (Missouri: Liguori, 2001), pp. 3–4.
94 Schillebeeckx, *Marriage*, p. 284.
95 Martos, *Doors to the Sacred*, p. 44.
96 Hugh of St Victor, *Sacraments of the Christian Faith* (USA: Insight, 2015), Part 8, 1, 193.
97 *Ibid.*, Part 11, 398–449, 1.
98 *Ibid.*, Part 11, 2.
99 *Ibid.*, Part 11, 3.
100 *Ibid.*, Part 11, 7.
101 *Ibid.*, Part 11, 5–7.
102 Finn, Sex and Marriage in the Sentences of Peter Lombard, p. 42.
103 Martos, *Doors to the Sacred*, pp. 48–51.
104 *Ibid.*, pp. 374–375.
105 for an account of these beliefs see M. Costen, *The Cathars and the Albigensian Crusade* (Manchester: Manchester University Press, 1997), pp. 58–76.
106 J. Sumption, *The Albigensian Crusade* (London: Faber, 1978), p. 30.
107 C. Lansing, *Power and Purity: Cathar Heresy in Medieval History* (Oxford: Oxford University Press, 1998), pp. 4–5, 12.
108 Martos, *Doors to the Sacred*, p. 375.
109 *Ibid.*, pp. 54–55.
110 P. Reynolds, *Marriage in the Western Church: The Christianization of Marriage During the Patristic and Early Medieval Periods* (Leiden: Brill 2007), p. 10.
111 P. Lombard, *The Sentences*, 2, 1, 1.
112 Reynolds, *Marriage in the Western Church*, pp. 728–729.
113 St Thomas Aquinas, *Summa Theologiae* I-II q.94, a. 2c.
114 *Ibid.*, III q.62, a.1, q.65, a.1; Supplement 42, a. 3.
115 St Thomas Aquinas, *Explanation of the Ten Commandments: the Sixth Commandment; The Tenth Article: the Communion of Saints, the Forgiveness of Sins: The Seven Sacraments, a Review.*
116 *Ibid., Explanation of the Ten Commandments: the Sixth Commandment.*
117 Pope St Gregory I, *The Books of the Morals, An Exposition on the Book of Job* III, XXXIII, ii, 9; xii, 25.
118 St Thomas Aquinas, *Benefits of the Resurrection: Qualities of the Risen Bodies.*
119 St Thomas Aquinas, *Summa Theologiae* II.II, 23.

[120] St Thomas Aquinas, *Summa contra Gentiles*, III, 123.
[121] St Thomas Aquinas, *Explanation of the Ten Commandments: the Sixth Commandment*.
[122] St Thomas Aquinas, *Summa contra Gentiles* III, 123.
[123] St Thomas Aquinas, *Explanation of the Ten Commandments: the Sixth Commandment*.
[124] See C. Haar, 'Tomás Sánchez and Late Scholastic Thought on Marriage and Political Virtue' in *The Concept of Law (Lex) in the Moral and Political Thought of the 'School of Salamanca'*, (Leiden: Brill, 2016), pp. 81–105, p.91.
[125] St Thomas Aquinas, *Summa Theologiae* Supplement 42, a. 1.
[126] *Ibid.*, 44.a.1; 44.a.3; E. C. Brugger, *The Indissolubility of Marriage and the Council of Trent* (Washington DC: Catholic University of America Press, 2017), p. ix.
[127] St Thomas Aquinas, *Summa Theologiae* I.II, 5, 3.
[128] *Ibid.*, on happiness, I.II, 5, 5; on the theological virtues, I.II, 62, 1.
[129] *Ibid.*, I.II, 61, 2.
[130] *Ibid.*, II.II, 1–170.
[131] *Ibid.*, I.II, 22–48.
[132] *Ibid.*, I.II, 56, 4.
[133] *Catechism of the Catholic Church*, 1264.
[134] Rm 7:1.9.
[135] Aristotle, *Nicomachean Ethics*, 2, 6.
[136] St Thomas Aquinas, *Summa Theologiae* I.II, 68, 4.
[137] See S. Nash-Marshall, 'Boethius' Influence on Theology and Metaphysics to c.1500' in *A Companion to Boethius in the Middle Ages* (Leiden: Brill, 2012), pp. 170, 173 and 175.
[138] C. Nauert, *Humanism and the Culture of Renaissance Europe* (Cambridge: Cambridge University Press, 2006), p. 9. For examples of some of the authorities for early scholastics, see M. Colish, *Studies in Scholasticism* (Aldershot: Ashgate, 2006), p. 4.
[139] See J. Marenbon, *The Philosophy of Peter Abelard* (Cambridge: Cambridge University Press, 1997), pp. 61–62.
[140] For a discussion of the different forms of scholastic disputation from the eleventh century See A. Novikoff, 'Towards a Cultural History of Scholastic Disputation' in *The American Historical Review* 117/2 (2012), pp. 331–364.
[141] Marenbon sees this rigor of logic as something that characterised Abelard's approach. However, he also notes that Abelard can be credited with attempting to build a whole and coherent ethical system, *The Philosophy*

of Peter Abelard, p. 338.
[142] See Colish, *Studies in Scholasticism*, p. 3.
[143] Humanism has been called secular in that it is a philosophy that is non-religious, see C. Lamont, *The Philosophy of Humanism* (New York: Humanist Press, 1997), or religious in that it identifies 'god' with mankind, see T. Molnar, *Theists and Atheists: a typology of non-belief* (Hague: Monton Publishers, 1980), p. 62.
[144] W. Ruegg, 'Epilogue: The Rise of Humanism' in *A History of the University in Europe. Vol. 1 Universities in the Middle Ages* (Cambridge: Cambridge University Press, 2003), p. 449; A. McGrath, *Historical Theology* (Chichester: Wiley-Blackwell, 2013), p. 86; Nauert, *Humanism and the Culture of Renaissance Europe*, p. 64.
[145] See J. Hankins, 'Humanism and modern political thought' in *The Cambridge Companion to Renaissance Humanism* (Cambridge: Cambridge University Press, 2003), p. 125.
[146] For a discussion on the different interpretations of *studia humanitatis* see R. Black, 'Humanism' in *Renaissance Thought: A Reader* (London: Routledge, 2001), pp. 68–94, especially p. 72.
[147] Nauert, *Humanism and the Culture of Renaissance Europe*, pp. 17–19.
[148] See E. Rummel, 'Introduction: Scholasticism and Biblical Humanism in Early Modern Europe' in *Biblical Humanism and Scholasticism in the Age of Erasmus* (Leiden Netherlands: Brill, 2008), p. 1.
[149] See Nauert, *Humanism and the Culture of Renaissance Europe*, pp. 10–16.
[150] *Ibid.*, pp. 17–18.
[151] R. Pasnau discusses the appellations of *via antiqua* and *via moderna* in his book, *Metaphysical Themes, 1274–1671* (Oxford: Oxford University Press, 2011), pp. 84–85. He also points out that today nominalism is usually associated with the problem of universals. However, he adds that although there is a 'family resemblance', the thinking of those labelled nominalists, is diverse, pp. 85–86. According to McGrath, the *via moderna* is 'now becoming generally accepted as the best way of referring to the movement once known as 'nominalism'", *Historical Theology*, pp. 118.
[152] See L. Chapp, *The God of Covenant and Creation: Scientific Naturalism and its Challenge to the Christian Faith* (London: T&T Clark, 2011) pp. 89–90.
[153] In terms of moral theories, and the rise of freedom that looks merely to choice, the theologian Servais Pinckaers locates the roots of the decisive break between patristic, early scholastic thinking, and later thinking, in Ockham's notions of freedom and morality, *The Sources of Christian Ethics* (Edinburgh: T&T Clark, 2001), p. 329.
[154] Pinckaers, *The Sources of Christian Ethics*, pp. 251, 334.

[155] McGrath, *Historical Theology*, pp. 118–119, where the covenantal notion in nominalism is also linked to Pelagianism.
[156] Pinckaers, *The Sources of Christian Ethics*, p. 251.
[157] J. Harrington, *Reordering Marriage and Society in Reformation Germany* (Cambridge: Cambridge University Press 1995), pp. 26–27.
[158] J. Witte, 'The Reformation of Marriage Law in Luther's Germany: Its Significance Then and Now' in *Journal of Law and Religion* 4/2 (1986), pp. 293–294.
[159] *Ibid.*, p. 294.
[160] H. A. Oberman, *Luther: Man Between God and the Devil* (New Haven: Yale University Press, 1989), p. 280.
[161] S. Hendrix, 'Luther on Marriage' in *Lutheran Quarterly XIV* (2000), pp. 337–338.
[162] *Ibid.*, p. 338.
[163] *Ibid.*, p. 337; Witte, The Reformation of Marriage Law in Luther's Germany, p. 312.
[164] Martin Luther, *The Estate of Marriage* Part 1.
[165] Oberman, *Luther: Man Between God and the Devil*, pp. 272–275.
[166] Martin Luther, *The Estate of Marriage* Part 3; Hendrix, Luther on Marriage, p. 342.
[167] Witte, The Reformation of Marriage Law in Luther's Germany, p. 309.
[168] *Ibid.*, pp. 336–337.
[169] Schillebeeckx, *Marriage*, p. 361.
[170] Witte, The Reformation of Marriage Law in Luther's Germany, p. 339.
[171] R. Bulman, 'Introduction: The Historical Context' in *From Trent to Vatican II: Historical and Theological Investigations* (Oxford: Oxford University Press, 2006), pp. 3–4.
[172] Council of Trent 1563, Session XXIV; W. Roberts, 'Christian Marriage' in *From Trent to Vatican II: Historical and Theological Investigations* (Oxford: Oxford University Press 2006), pp. 209–210.
[173] Council of Trent 1563, Session XXIV.
[174] H. Vorgimler, *Sacramental Theology* (Collegeville Minnesota: Liturgical Press, 1992) pp. 297–300.
[175] Schillebeeckx, *Marriage*, pp. 365–367.
[176] Council of Trent 1563, Session XXIV.1.
[177] Roberts, *Christian Marriage*, pp. 210–211.
[178] Council of Trent 1547, Session VI.XI *Decree on Justification*; St Augustine, *On Nature and Grace*, 44.
[179] St Augustine, *Retractions*, II, 42; *On Nature and Grace*, 50.
[180] As reported by St Augustine in *The Deeds of Pelagius*, 30, 54.

[181] Pelagius, 'Letter to Demetrias' in B. R. Rees, *Pelagius: Life and Letters*, Vol. II, *The Letters of Pelagius and his Followers* (Woodbridge: Boydell, 1998), 2, 2–3, 2.
[182] *Ibid.*, 3, 2.
[183] St Augustine, *The Deeds of Pelagius*, 16.
[184] Pelagius, *Letter to Demetrias*, 8, 3.
[185] St Augustine, *The Deeds of Pelagius*, 3.
[186] St Augustine, *Retractions*, I, 9, 3; I, 9, 4.
[187] St Augustine, *Retractions*, I, 9, 6.

5 POST TRENT TO THE 1917 CODE OF CANON LAW

CHRIST BROUGHT SOMETHING new and indeed scandalous to the ancient world: the real possibility of friendship with God, a friendship in the strongest sense of love between friends. This is one reason why married love, the strongest of human loves, is used as an analogy, albeit limited, for God's love. The whole of the moral life depends on love, love of God and love of neighbour, loving as Jesus loves. As St John of the Cross says, referring to our judgement before God, 'when evening comes you will be examined in love.'[1]

However, it is an all too human tendency to believe that the moral life depends solely on human will where salvation is gained purely by obedience to the law, and to dwell not on love but on the joys of reward and the pains of punishment. This tendency to rely on the will feeds into the question of whether God commands the impossible, a question that resurfaces often in the teaching on marriage. This chapter explores marriage as it unfolds in moral theology up to the promulgation of the 1917 Code of Canon Law. After the Council of Trent there were significant developments in moral theology and in interpretations of the natural law. In terms of marriage, these developments have perhaps led to an overly legalistic presentation that focused on obedience and licit or illicit acts to the detriment of understanding marriage as a Christian vocation. However, it is important to recognize that these developments affected every area of the moral life, not just marriage. Moreover, the question of the impossibility or possibility of following God's law, the kind of questioning involved today when considering marriage as indissoluble, became especially prominent as the theology of grace was tested and deepened.

Early Christian thinking has always considered marriage to be under its remit because marriage is a sacrament and a Christian state of life. Since marriage is concerned with how we live life, the virtues, what is good, what values are important, what should and should not be done, marriage also comes under the umbrella of moral theology. Moral theology applies theology to action. This means that it does not simply provide lists of dos and don'ts. However, since moral theology is concerned with right and wrong then it also involves law even if it cannot be reduced to law. The problem comes when thinking that obedience and law represent the whole of moral theology or if the moral order is separated from the theological order. Moral obligation and the law are always present but the law is not a yoke or a burden.

Inevitably, developments in moral theology have influenced approaches to marriage. Especially significant developments have been the emergence of nominalism and its focus on obligation, law and obedience; changes in interpretations of natural law; and a reduction of moral theology to dictates of the law. These developments have also influenced catechesis and practical teaching. On the one hand marriage has been treated in terms of law and obedience to rules, and on the other hand in terms of a state in life which involves certain specific goods and acts that are ultimately directed to our final end, happiness with God. The former need not demand a life in Christ; the latter does not refuse a place for the law.

The perception that after the Council of Trent marriage was understood in a legalistic and contractual way requires further thought as does the belief that the Church's reforms were essentially only a response to the criticism of the Protestant reformers. While the Protestant reformers believed that Christian decay was due to deficient doctrine, Catholic reformers also recognized deficient practice and attributed this not to doctrine but to ignorance and misunderstanding of doctrine. Before the Council of Trent there were moves to restore and renew the

Catholic Church notably through better education of the clergy, a deepening understanding of the theology of the sacraments, and a recurrent concern for pastoral care of lay people. During the Protestant reformation Catholic theologians saw that instruction for lay people was vital to counteract the confusion created by new protestant theologies and to address ignorance of church teaching. Catechisms taking the form of question and answer became a particularly successful method of teaching. For the fathers at the Council of Trent catechesis was a priority. However, in addition to catechetical teaching there was a turn towards developing lay spirituality and developing the holiness of life in whatever state the person was in, married or celibate, in the world or in religious life. After all, marriage and the virtues inherent in the marriage relationship and in family life formed the basis for the political community.

Catechism and practical spirituality

The combination of catechetical and practical teaching after the Council of Trent demonstrate that marriage was considered a significant state of life and a real part of Christian living. The pastoral concern showed in practical teaching varies since it reflects the pastor's response to challenges facing his own flock. But this teaching does not question the belief that marriage is a vocation to holiness.

Concerned with correcting misconceptions, errors, and abuses through education, the fathers at the Council of Trent had taken the traditional understanding of the meaning of marriage that had been handed down to them over the centuries as a given.[2] Treatment of marriage in Catholic catechisms then followed this traditional understanding, and as is the nature of catechisms, this treatment is concise and to the point. The *Catechism of the Council of Trent*, the *Roman Catechism* was a manual for clergy and versions were soon produced for the people as well. The *Roman Catechism* notes that marriage is 'gifted with great and divine blessings' and so is truly and properly a sacrament.³ Although called a 'contract' since marriage concerns consent, the *Roman Catechism* recognizes that other contracts differ 'essentially' from marriage. Marriage is not invented by human beings but is instituted by God as a natural indissoluble contract and raised to perfection as a sacrament. The 'ends' of marriage include companionship and mutual assistance, children and family, and a remedy for lust.

In addition to catechetical teaching, leading figures like St Ignatius of Loyola (1491–1556) developed practical ways in which to deepen the spiritual life of Christians. St Ignatius notes that to think, judge and feel as the Church does means, among other things, that 'we should strongly praise religious institutes, virginity and continence, and marriage too, but not as highly as any of the former.'⁴ Moreover, St Ignatius points out that marriage, like other states of life, is a matter of proper spiritual discernment founded on how best to serve God.⁵ This emphasis on the significance of marriage as a way of holiness was further brought out by St Charles Borromeo (1538–1584) who took seriously interior personal conversion to Christ and the Church: reform beginning with 'me' would then ripple out to reform in other areas of life, family life, society and church. Seeking to live a life of holiness is possible in every state of life, and in marriage it is by living out marriage vows faithfully, and by living a life in Christ in the home and at work, not only in church.⁶

Not only did St Robert Bellarmine (1542–1621) write two catechisms on *Christian Doctrine* specifically for teaching lay people,⁷ he also gave practical spiritual advice. In his *Art of Dying Well* St Robert speaks of the sacrament of marriage alongside the other sacraments because the sacraments enable people 'both to live well and to die well.'⁸ St Robert acknowledges that marriage has a 'twofold institution: one as a civil contract by the natural law, and the other as a sacrament by the law of the Gospel.' In keeping with tradition St Robert begins from Genesis, affirming that God is the author of marriage, that the two become one flesh, and, referring to Matthew's gospel, that the bond is indissoluble.

A further reason for indissolubility is that the sacrament signifies the union of Christ with his Church. St Robert then talks about the exaltation of marriage 'to the dignity of a sacrament' found in Ephesians 5 and adds St Augustine on the significance of marriage as 'the sanctity of the sacrament.' He gives the traditional three blessings of marriage as 'children, fidelity and the grace of the sacrament.' Merely seeking 'carnal pleasure' is not a good use of marriage and is a sin. Although children are a good of marriage, St Robert is concerned for families who are too poor to support their children. Moreover, since having children includes their proper upbringing St Robert upbraids those who neglect their family. He allows for a couple to separate 'from the marriage-bed' by mutual consent, and 'spend their days in prayer and fasting.' St Robert is clear that the grace of the sacrament and 'the other blessings it brings with it', 'helps in a wonderful manner to produce love and peace between married people.' Returning to Ephesians 5, St Robert enjoins husbands to love their wives, 'not with a love of concupiscence' but in imitation of Christ, seeking not 'utility or pleasure' but the good of the spouse. St Robert urges wives to love their husbands with reverence and not as tyrants, presumably reflecting his pastoral experience.

St Francis de Sales (1567–1622) provides perhaps one of the most directly personal and extended teaching on marriage. St Francis, Bishop of Geneva in exile in Annecy was keen to put the principles of the Council of Trent into action in his diocese and 'regain' Geneva for the Church by the force of charity.[9] He was especially interested in the clear mandate from Trent for the catechetical instruction of the faithful and this seems to have fuelled his writings to and for people 'in the world.' Like many of his contemporaries he used the real and indissoluble union of husband and wife in marriage to illustrate other religious truths. He took marriage to describe the relationship of love and the will,[10] the soul's relationship to God the faithful spouse who will never abandon us, the promises given to Christians on earth of the divine marriage to come, and the indissoluble union of the soul with God in heaven.[11] As he explained, 'try as hard as you like, but in the end only the language of the heart can ever reach another heart.'[12] However, as a pastor and spiritual director St Francis also wrote specifically on marriage and, as his letter to a wife who thinks marriage hinders holiness shows, his argument was simple: 'let us be what we are, and let us be it well, to do honour to the Master whose work we are.'[13]

In addition to letters to a number of people 'in the world', St Francis wrote *Introduction à la Vie Dévote* or *Philothea* ostensibly to a noble lady, but he includes advice to people in different classes and states of life. He explains that all Christians, the 'living plants' of God's Church, are called to 'bring forth the fruits of devotion, each according to his calling and vocation.' All are called to holiness. Yet the practice of devotion must be adapted to the capabilities, engagements, and duties of each person, and what is fitting for one person will be different for another. St Francis adds that it is 'not merely an error but a heresy' to suppose that holiness and a life of devotion is incompatible with any state of life, and that includes life at 'the domestic hearth.'[14] Nevertheless, although he thinks that 'God's will is found in marriage and in virginity', he is clear that marriage is not above virginity and celibacy.[15] The task for all is to be in the world and yet serve and love God.

The spiritual life requires patience, courage, and struggle against sin. Nevertheless, this is not a lonely struggle: living a life of devotion implies love of God and divine love, grace, enlightens the person enabling them to do good and to love more.[16] According to St Francis a life of devotion is incorrectly characterized as something gloomy or unsociable when in fact it is 'a lovely, a pleasant, and a happy life.' Indeed, he calls true devotion 'spiritual sugar' that sweetens difficulties in life.[17]

In his advice to married people,[18] St Francis closely follows and quotes Ephesians 5. St Francis explains that marriage is a great sacrament, 'honourable to all, in all, and in everything'. Marriage is holy, 'the orchard of Christianity' because it produces children, and it is necessary for the good of society. Therefore, it is to be 'preserved inviolate.' However, and perhaps reflecting a more worldly approach to the ceremony, St Francis wishes that Christ 'were always invited to all marriages' as to Cana so that 'the wine of consolation and benediction would never be lacking.' Again, referring closely to the love Christ has for the Church, St Francis urges married people to cultivate more than 'natural' or 'mere human love.' Rather they should 'cherish a love which is holy, sacred, and divine'. The first result of this love is an 'indissoluble union of your hearts'; the second 'inviolable fidelity'; the third the birth and upbringing of children as souls for God. St Francis speaks of the need for husbands to 'preserve a tender, constant, and heartfelt love' for their wives, though he also presumes the ordering where the wife is her husband's 'companion,' yet he remains 'her superior.' Wives are urged to love 'tenderly, heartily, but with a respectful love and full of reverence', stressing their dependence on their husbands. Children are to be dedicated to God and trained in virtue so that parents build up a 'good house.' St Francis realizes that wives are in charge of households and he recognizes the importance of their devotion for the whole family, as 'more effectual' than their husbands.

Notably, St Francis encourages 'mutual caresses—caresses truly loving but chaste, tender and sincere'. Although through holy devotion husband and wife 'mutually lead and sustain each other', St Francis thinks that it is the wife who softens her husband with 'the sugar of devotion.' The 'union' of marriage guides each to virtue and 'the faithful husband and wife sanctify one another in the sincere fear of the Lord.' St Francis suggests that wedding anniversaries be marked with confession, communion, and prayer, 'commending their married life to God, and renewing their resolutions of sanctifying it by mutual faithfulness and love, thus, through Christ, taking breath, as it were, in the midst of the cares attending their vocation.' It is worth noting that the emphasis that St Francis de Sales places on the practicalities of married life and tenderness in marriage has clear resonance with the approach of Pope Francis in *Amoris Laetitia*.

In discussing the 'undefiled' marriage bed, St Francis uses the analogy of eating. Eating to preserve life is similar to sexual intercourse to produce children. St Francis acknowledges that what is 'requisite in marriage' for bringing children into the world is 'a good thing, and very holy' since the 'principal end' of marriage is children. Like eating for social reasons is legitimate, the mutual 'debt' owed by the spouses is 'both lawful and just' and not to be withdrawn without consent, not even for 'exercises of devotion', still less for a pretence of virtue or anger. This debt should be rendered cheerfully, faithfully, and freely even if there is no expectation that children will result. St Francis thinks that eating to 'content the appetite' is tolerated, as is to content 'the pleasure of the sensual appetite.' However, just as eating to excess or indeed eating not enough, or at the wrong time is dangerous for health, so too is the immoderate sexual appetite dangerous for the health of the soul. Moreover, anything that is done to prevent bringing children into the world is a sin, but the sexual act remains 'just and lawful' even when that end cannot come about. Just as people always thinking about food makes 'a god of their belly', so too is constantly dwelling on 'corporal pleasures' to the detriment of serving God. In essence, St Francis urges 'let that, then, which is holy be done holily.'

The real pastoral concern shown by some of the significant figures in the tradition demonstrates a clear commitment to seeing marriage as a path to holiness. Similarly, in the story of marriage, the idea of moral theology as leading people towards God is a constant thread even if it is sometimes obscured by a focus on obligations and rules. However, developments in the natural law tradition where notions of the good and human flourishing through the virtues gives way to notions of the right as defined by law, plus developments in moral thinking towards the dominance of sheer obedience, explain how marriage took on a more legalistic framework in the Catholic tradition.

Developments in the Natural Law tradition

Founded in the classical philosophical view that there is an ordering in the universe,[19] that everything has its place, theologians like St Augustine developed the idea that things in the world, be they 'stones, waves, wind or flame', show a desire for their own place and order: heavy things like bricks tend downwards not so much because of gravity but because of their nature as heavy. The adjective 'good' makes sense in the context of what a thing is, in reference to what is it for: a brick is a good brick when it fulfils its function as a brick; a brick that is so light that it floats around would not be a good brick. This ordering in the world allows us to reason about what we should and should not do, since human beings also are a part of the world order. However, the full truth about human beings, as expressed in the understanding that humans are made in the image of God, means that human beings are not simply one element among many in the world: human beings are 'called to communion with the living God, the person transcends the whole cosmos while integrating himself in it.'[20] Human beings are in the world but not of it. There is also an ordering brought about by the two great commandments to love God and love neighbour. These two commandments as expressed in the Ten Commandments encompass deeds towards God and neighbour, words concerning God and neighbour, and the heart's response to God and neighbour.[21] The four virtues of prudence that informs good reasoning, justice that ensures what is due is rendered appropriately, temperance that there is a proper balance, and fortitude that gives the strength required, aid the internal order of a person to fulfil this order of love. For the church fathers, natural law is further understood in the framework of the history of salvation and so the natural law is realized in different ways given the different states of nature: original nature, fallen nature, and restored nature.[22] As we have already seen, the church fathers consider marriage and the procreation of children in all these varying different 'natures' as well as seeing marriage and procreation as part of the God ordained order, subject to the commandments of love and practice of virtue.

For St Thomas Aquinas knowing and accepting that we are created by God and destined for friendship with God is to observe the law of our nature, natural law. St Thomas explains that there are four laws[23]: the law of nature, the law of concupiscence, the law of scripture, and the law of charity and grace 'which is the law of Christ.' Since knowledge of the law requires much effort, St Thomas adds that 'Christ gave an abridged law which all can know, and no one can be excused from observing it because of ignorance. And that is the law of divine love.' For St Thomas, the inclination for procreation and for mutual love belong to the law of nature; the sacrament belongs to the divine law of Christ. Indissolubility is thus grounded in both natural law and divine law.[24]

St Thomas describes the law of nature as 'nothing other than the light of the intellect implanted in us by God, by which we know what should be done and what should be avoided.' This law is implanted by God at creation. However, St Thomas points out that the devil has 'sown in man' another law on top of the law of nature, and that is the law of concupiscence. The law of concupiscence frequently corrupts the law of nature and the order of reason: in St Paul's words:

> in my inmost self I dearly love God's law, but I see that acting on my body there is a different law which battles against the law in my mind. So I am brought to be a prisoner of that law of sin which lives inside my body.[25]

The law of scripture then is needed to bring people back to a life of virtue and away from a life of vice. But the law of Moses that leads to the good and away from evil does so through fear of final judgment. Therefore, in addition, the law of Christ which is a law of love enables people to act with freedom not fear, the freedom of children who desire to do the good. Significantly, these different laws operate in all areas of life, not just the area of marriage, and this includes the law of concupiscence.

Indeed, for St Thomas human love between two people helps us to understand divine love. St Thomas lists a number of benefits when human acts match up to the standard of divine love, using by analogy human love: the person grows spiritually; is prompt to obey in a similar way in which 'we see lovers doing great and difficult things for the sake of their beloved'; finds strength in adversity; finds happiness; is ready to forgive 'for it is clear that the more we love someone, the more we are sorry if we offend him'; hearts are enlightened; there is joy and peace; and dignity is enhanced by becoming friends. Of course, for St Thomas charity is a gift from God because we love because God loved us first.

Natural law, then, is the knowledge of what should be done and what should be avoided, and it is accessible by human reason: as St Paul says even the gentiles, who do not have the Law of Moses, have a law 'engraved on their hearts to which their own conscience bear witness.'[26] Natural law is natural because it accords with our nature: people are naturally capable of knowing the natural law. But Revelation through scripture and Church tradition help in the sense that without Revelation some truths would be known only by a few, after a long time and at the risk of making errors on the way.[27] Natural law involves practical reason because it concerns action, and it is not an imposition on us because it is to do with what we need to do to flourish as the kind of beings we are. Thus, we can work out that some things, for instance murder, can never lead to our flourishing as human beings. Not only can we work out what is good for us, we can also work out how to achieve that good. St Thomas also says that the natural law is our participation in the Eternal Law of God.[28] Reason does not create its own truth or invent truth. Rather reason discovers truths. While natural law is concerned with both the order in the world and with the moral order governing human action, notably, something is not part of natural law simply because it is observable in the animal world. Nor is the natural law a "gut feeling". The natural law refers to essential inclinations in us and the human capacity to discern principles in the order of nature. Natural law is a law of reason, and this discernment enables us to flourish as beings of a particular kind. However, reason does not create its own laws and so natural law is not a rationalist law in the sense of reason being absolutely autonomous. The natural law is proper to the human race as a *ius*, a principle of law, rather than as a specific regulation, a *lex*. And an aspect of this being of a particular kind is the human tendency to seek out and form friendship which is part of the very definition of human life.

As we saw in the previous chapter, the emergence of nominalism as the *via moderna* marked the philosophical divide between the *via antiqua* and a new way of thinking about the concept of being. The *via antiqua* accepted universals based on the proposal that there was something in common between one kind of things, say human beings, that distinguished them from other kinds of things. The *via antiqua* understood notions like "beings of a particular kind" and "nature" as describing true realities. The new way of thinking regarded universals as irrelevant and accepted only particulars: individual human beings, and for the purposes of moral theology, unconnected individual acts. As M. A. Gillespie observes, the term 'modern' means to be new, 'a novel way of being in the world', where one's being is defined in terms of time, rather than in relation to a land, people, place or religious tradition. He argues that 'modern' has 'something Promethean' about it, a self-liberating understanding of the self.[29] This Promethean modern understanding further became disassociation from God.

This 'more vivid sense of moral subjectivity' grew within a complex cultural context. With the growth of universities and theoretical disputation, doubt, conscience and opinion became prominent concepts. In particular, the discovery of new lands and peoples brought to the fore questions of what it is to be human and what it is to have a human nature. Conquest and colonialism challenged understandings of the natural law as common to all human beings. The status of indigenous peoples in the New World was also questioned and in response the influential Spanish theologians of the sixteenth century concluded that human rights are inherent in human nature and do not depend on the person's situation regarding the Christian faith.[30] Pope Paul III finally declared that 'Indians are truly men'[31] against those who regarded them as brute animals destined to be slaves. But this also led to an interpretation of natural law as 'founded solely on the light of reason common to all people.'[32] It is easy to see how God can drop out of the picture of moral theology.

The focus on the 'naturalness' of natural law, the issue of human rights in the context of specific cultural questions concerning the New World and current affairs underlie the public lecture, *relectio*, of Francisco de Vitoria (c.1486–1546) on marriage. De Vitoria's lecture was written up from the notes of one of his students and published after de Vitoria's death. In his *relectio De Matrimonio* de Vitoria takes it as given that natural law is what is reasonable and commonly accepted.[33] Moreover, he observes that the practice among the heathen people of the New World bears this out, and he includes parenting in this observation.[34] Although de Vitoria was expressing the universality of the natural law through the fundamental inclinations of all human beings, there is a danger that natural law comes to be seen as merely what is natural in the world. However, de Vitoria's appreciation of human partnership avoids this danger. De Vitoria took the view that the primary end of marriage was procreation of children and educating them in virtue. The spousal relationship was secondary to this, though as a result of fallen human nature, the couple had mutual need of each other to fulfil their duties to each other and to their children. The question of polygamy arose not only out of the problem of New World tribal practices and European clandestine marriages but also from some of the more public cases of the time, for instance the situation of England's King Henry VIII. Polygamy was seen to be incompatible with the ends of marriage. In particular, attention was drawn to the equality between spouses and their reciprocal obligations, as well as the importance of the role of the wife in the harmonious organisation of the home. This fundamental equality and the understanding of the wife as a full partner in the relationship and not a servant could only be realized in a monogamous relationship.[35] The contractual dimension of marriage comes out of the reality that marriage creates obligations. As theologians like Francisco Vitoria recognize,[36] where an obligation is created there has to be consent, therefore consent is a necessary part of marriage.

However, marriage and family life were not seen as purely private matters. Rather marriage and the proper upbringing of children were regarded as foundational for good citizenship. As C. Haar points out the spousal relationship was one of 'virtuous friendship' and not a statement of gender roles resting on male superiority: 'friendship in the political sense of virtue was forged in the marriage relationship.'[37] The virtues, friendship, parental responsibilities, and notably virtues relating to the conjugal relationship were indispensable elements for the political community.[38]

Alongside the nascent idea of human rights lay a strong current of voluntarism. Voluntarism emphasizes the absolute freedom of God and consequently that Promethean free self which seeks to be freed from all constraints or conditioning or subjection to the order of the world. This freedom became a freedom of indifference, 'a pure capacity to choose contraries' and disconnected from inclinations or the objective good. Consequently 'nature ceases to be a criterion for knowing the wise will of God' and the law is found in the will of the lawmaker.[39] In conjunction with nominalism's influence on obligations, moral theology took on a legalistic outlook where happiness, growth in holiness, and our ultimate destiny was obscured by obedience to the law. Natural law became separated from faith and more like a series of regulations where an act was designated licit or illicit.

Modernity is also tied into the notion of progress in terms of superiority to what has gone before[40] and modernity is often related to the shift from theology in relationship to philosophy to a rupture between theology and philosophy. Of course, in contrast to the claims of modernity, progress does not necessarily result in something superior. The early church fathers engaged critically with philosophy and welcomed philosophy that was in tune with Christian faith. As Pope St John Paul II observes, the fathers 'were not naïve thinkers.' They did not simply transpose truths of faith into philosophical categories. Moreover, they used 'philosophically trained reason' to find meaning and to discover explanations so that they could come to a better understanding of faith.[41] However, this harmony between faith on the one hand and reason and philosophy on the other was disrupted by an exaggerated rationalism that put all religious truth outside the realm of reason and knowledge. Like Paley's watch, in the rationalist system, the world may have been designed and set in motion by God, but it had its own order and coherence and as a result reference to God became optional. In this way of thinking natural law is binding even if there is no God. The 'concrete situation of human persons in the history of salvation, marked by sin and grace' has been bracketed out[42] and natural law became a law of nature understood in purely empirical and observable terms. Instead, then of procreation being the co-operation of parents in the wise plan of God for the flourishing of the family, procreation risks becoming simply a matter of the functioning of the human body.

The interpretation of natural law as a law of nature is found especially in the work of the protestant jurist Hugo Grotius (1583–1645). Greatly influenced by Vitoria, Grotius was interested in finding common ground between different Christian denominations. For Grotius a common legal understanding of marriage based on natural law was an important part of this project.[43] Protestant political leaders had already moved the jurisdiction over marriage from the Church to the state but there were tensions with this in practice among Lutherans, Anglicans and Calvinists.[44] Therefore finding a common legal understanding of marriage could contribute to unity. Moreover, Grotius recognized what has always been held, that marriage is the first natural society where good citizens are formed.[45] Although Grotius had respect for scripture and theological reasoning, he decided to base his work on the law of nature and he separated out those features of traditional Christian marriage that were necessary to the law of nature and those that required a scriptural foundation.[46] His confidence was such that he believed that natural law would exist even if God did not.[47] To begin with, Grotius observes that certain Christian practices are shared by non-Christians, and he includes monogamy and the prohibition against adultery. He also notes animal practices to inform what is natural. According to Grotius, incest is not common among 'brute' animals and so therefore is unnatural.[48] However he observes that animals naturally pair up to look after their young, and he argues that what is natural in the 'brute' animal world is reasonable but better practised in the human world.[49] Following St Thomas, Grotius adds that monogamy is reasonable and natural because it provides for the sexual needs of the couple, it ensures that parents know their children and children know who are their parents, and it enables the proper upbringing and education of children through the efforts of both parents. Moreover, activities such as adultery or extra-marital sexual behaviour, prostitution or unilateral divorce are unreasonable because they are destructive of the good inherent in monogamy.[50] However, on the grounds that in the animal world polygamy existed successfully, and some of the Old Testament patriarchs had polygamous relationships, Grotius feels that polygamy in the human world cannot be condemned without recourse to the law of Christ. Grotius nevertheless thinks on purely conventional theological grounds that polyandry (one woman with multiple husbands) to be unnatural because husbands have dominion over their wives.[51]

Setting aside the problems of simple observation of nature, the ingredients of rationalism, individualism and nominalism come together in the seventeenth century conception of the law of nature. The law of nature depended on a concept of the state of nature, an imaginary concept describing how human beings lived before communities and social customs. For instance, for J. Locke (1632–1704) the idea of 'man' is an individual who is 'absolute lord of his own person and possessions, equal to the greatest and subject to nobody' and the law of nature here is the right of self-preservation of life, liberty, and property. The only limitation to this right is the equal rights of others.[52] Unlike the nascent rights of Vitoria that are grounded in the moral order derived from the essence of human nature, Locke's right is a symbol of self-interest. For T. Hobbes (1588–1679) the law of nature is understood in purely empirical terms as a primitive state of fact. Human beings are like individual atoms and the state of nature is 'war.' To get out of this state of war Hobbes advocates the social contract, mutual agreement to enter into community relationships and to be governed by consent. In contrast to the natural law contention that the community and the individual flourish together and are not in competition, the common good of Locke and Hobbes is simply the security of self-preservation and possession of property. Government becomes a power that checks individual power and consequently the concept of the juridical omnipotence of the state, including over marriage legislation, takes shape. The Church becomes one more element in this power struggle among many. In its denial of a natural inclination towards social life beginning with the family, and its presentation of the human being as a solitary atom that seeks society purely as a means to protect himself from others, this development of the law of nature totally neglects the natural law.

The moral law then is no longer founded on the good or on being and human flourishing. Instead, various competing theories arise with utilitarianism weighing up and designating what is perceived to be the good according to the utility of pleasure or happiness; with a morality where action is based solely on feeling; and reacting to this, with Kantian ethics relying on sovereign reason and duty to inform right action. The eighteenth-century age of reason, the Enlightenment, that nurtured Kantian ethics set reason as the source of all knowledge. Reason is absolutely autonomous and cannot be subject to any other law, and that includes any notion of a final end. Passions and emotions have to be excluded because they are subjective, arbitrary and cloud reason. Reason seeks rules and principles that can be consistently universalized, and if rules apply to everyone then it is not a matter of whether a person can or cannot obey them: morality becomes a matter of the will—you will to obey them. What matters for the moral life is a good will. The now autonomous and self-sufficient person presents to God all his acts of good intention and purity for the final reckoning. Rather than the search for the good, morality becomes concerned about the data of conscience, reward, and punishment. The law of freedom where duty is to be done for duty's sake, is set against the law of nature and the desire for happiness. Grace seems to disappear. In traditional moral theology a good person does what is good, or in keeping with the law of reason, for love of the final good. In the emerging moral philosophy, the final good disappears and the person follows the law for the law's own sake. Moreover, in the rationalist system to love God or to love another cannot be a matter of disinterested duty because it is still to act out of self-interest. Thus, morality is no longer a morality of love.

Alongside the shift away from natural law as a law of reason that is a participation in God's eternal plan, towards natural law as a law of nature there were further developments in moral theology that led to a more legalistic view of marriage.

Developments in moral theology

From the sixteenth and seventeenth centuries manuals of theology were drawn up as part of the task to educate the clergy, a task identified as vital at the Council of Trent. It is crucial to realize, as T. Slater explains, that the manuals are 'technical works' to help priests and confessors in their duties. Manuals are 'not intended for edification, nor do they hold up a high ideal of Christian perfection for the imitation of the faithful. They deal with what is obligation under pain of sin; they are books of moral pathology.'[53] The manuals covered human acts in general, conscience, law, sin, virtues and vices, the precepts of the Decalogue, contracts and commandments of the Church. Sins in marriage are dealt with under the vice of lust, sins of thought, sins of impurity and failures of obligation of children and parents under the fourth commandment. Since the object is to help priests in the confessional, the focus is on specifying sins and consequently sex is seen in negative terms where even licit sexual intercourse is framed in terms of the obligation to fulfil the marriage debt. On the positive side, the manuals did serve to help establish culpability, and invincible, vincible or innocent ignorance, as well as formal and material cooperation and coercion in order better to form consciences. Significantly, if Church teaching on marriage is seen only through the prism of the manuals then this would be a distortion.

However, the legacy of the manuals indicates the direction of moral theology towards legalism and what is licit and illicit. The writers of the manuals were influenced by nominalism and its focus on law and obligations and ultimately conscience. Instead of the law being a guide, through nominalism the law had become opposed to freedom and one of the roles of conscience was to mediate between law and freedom. Moral theology became essentially concerned with interpreting the law. Nominalism provided the roots for casuistry, an approach to moral theology that had already begun prior to the Council of Trent but proved very influential for the fathers at Trent. Casuistry, as its name suggests, makes the case by taking a problem, finding analogies, examining the circumstances, resolving doubt and giving a solution.[54] Moral theology involved arguing on cases of conscience and eventually came to depend on summaries of cases focusing on intention and the sinfulness of actions.[55] In doubtful cases where there was no clear law, where there were no obvious solutions and where there was a range of opinions, it seemed appropriate to follow the solution offered by the greatest number of theologians. Known as probabilism, a doubtful law cannot impose a certain obligation, but a person could follow the better grounded or more probable opinion.

Faced with many difficult questions coming from the New World concerning marriage between pagans where one becomes a Christian, and the increasing number of decrees and rules, the Jesuit Tomás Sánchez (1550–1610) found probabilism particularly congenial to moral theology. Sánchez wrote *Disputationes de matrimonio,* a ten-volume treatise on marriage and his systematic treatment became influential for later teaching and for canon law.[56]

Notably Sánchez dealt with questions of dispensations, impediments to marriage, the significance of consent including the problem of coerced or insufficient consent, and reasons for separation. In order to identify principles and clarify situations, Sánchez included thorough and detailed accounts of all aspects of sexual acts, to the horror of those who saw this display of intimate knowledge as incompatible with his vocation as a Jesuit. Although Sánchez says that procreation and education of children is the intrinsic and primary end of marriage, he acknowledges that pleasure is a legitimate aspect of sexual intercourse, though pleasure alone cannot be an end in itself.[57] Sánchez became known for his liberal interpretation of the principle that otherwise mortal sexual sin could become venial depending on the intention and circumstances. His precise depiction of licit and illicit marital acts became a model for the manuals to enable confessors to identify what was and was not a sin, mortal or venial.

The particularly liberal approach of Sánchez was taken further, and by the end of the sixteenth century probabilism had slipped into laxity whereby any opinion could be followed regardless of its grounding or indeed whether or not the law was doubtful. Partly in response to laxism, seventeenth century Jansenism took a rigorist view claiming that only direct and clear moral certainty against a law allowed its non-observance. The Jansenists claimed they were disciples of St Augustine and followed the traditional teaching of the Church. Questions of obedience to the law and questions about grace supplying what is needed for people to act rightly became particularly pressing. In his controversy with St Augustine, Pelagius had simply set aside any notion of grace: Christians had no excuse not to follow God's commandments and everything could be accomplished by free will. The fathers at the Council of Trent followed St Augustine and explained that God does not command the impossible, but God asks us to do what we can and to pray for grace to enable us to do what we think we cannot do. However, in the seventeenth century a dispute about grace and free will erupted through the followers of Jansenism. In its extreme form, Jansenism holds that as a result of the Fall human nature is corrupt and depraved. Therefore, human beings are utterly incapable and even the just are unable to obey God's commands by their own efforts. Moreover, many people are tempted beyond their strength. The will is faced with the delights of heaven provided by sufficient grace, and the delights of the world, each vying for control over the passive will. If, through efficacious grace, the heavenly delights are stronger then the will has an irresistible impulse to the good. If the delights of the world are stronger, the will becomes unable to resist concupiscence and falls into sin.[58] Unlike St Augustine who sees grace as building on nature and regards free will as good and graced free will better, in the Jansenist system free will becomes at best passive, at most irrelevant.

The moral theologian St Alphonsus de Liguori set out a detailed response to the many arguments on the possibility or impossibility of obeying God's commandments. He takes great pains to distinguish the teaching of St Augustine from the claims of the Jansenists and to root his responses to Jansenism in St Thomas Aquinas and the decrees made at Trent. Beginning with pelagianism, St Alphonsus identified the Jansenist issue: either the commandments are possible, and we observe them by the strength of our free will alone, or they are impossible, and no one is bound to observe them since no one is obliged to do impossibilities. In the view of St Alphonsus, 'all these precepts are impossible to us without Grace, but are quite possible with the assistance of Grace.' St Alphonsus next considers the semi-pelagians who hold that human strength of will has been weakened by original sin and so grace is needed to do what is right, nevertheless they deny grace is necessary for the beginning of faith or the desire for salvation. In response St Alphonsus believes, 'with the Catholic Church', that every beginning of faith and good desire is the working of grace in us.[59] Quoting St Augustine, St Alphonsus explains that God gives everyone the grace to pray, and through prayer the means of obtaining grace to fulfil the commandments.[60] Turning to Luther, Calvin and the Jansenists, St Alphonsus identifies that their main contention is that free will has been totally extinguished by sin. Therefore, human co-operation is not required, and faith alone in the merits of Christ alone brings salvation. This fallen will means that it is impossible for human beings to obey the commandments. Moreover, 'movements of concupiscence' are themselves sins so everything preceding consent or reason is also sinful. In response, St Alphonsus says that 'movements of concupiscence' are 'natural defects proceeding from our corrupt nature, and for which God will not blame us.' Though, he adds, we should make positive resistance to 'movements of carnal delectation' because 'there is great danger of consenting to them.'[61] In contrast to the Jansenists, St Alphonsus, quoting St Paul, says that God does not suffer people to be tempted beyond what they are able and this applies to all people, not simply to those few predestined for salvation as claimed by the Jansenists.[62] Notably, and perhaps in keeping with the rationalistic tone of the time, St Alphonsus is suspicious of the passions rather than seeing them, as St Thomas does, as a positive and God-given aspect of human beings. Moreover, it is the will rather than the exercise of the virtues that controls passions.

Although Jansenism was condemned by Pope Alexander VIII (1610–1691) in 1690 the different moral systems of probabilism represented by the liberal followers of Sánchez, and rigorism that grew out of Jansenism, jostled alongside probabiliorism. As a less lax form of probabilism, probabiliorism holds that the stricter opinion of a range of opinions should be followed. However, probabiliorism was not adequate and to resolve the problem of the direction of moral theology St Alphonsus supported equiprobabilism. Following equiprobabilism, in cases where the law was doubtful, an opinion in favour of liberty had to be equally probable with an opinion in favour of the law before it could be followed. Given the plethora of laws, decrees and responses that might overwhelm the 'ordinary priest', St Alphonsus wrote his *Moral Theology* as a resource for confessors, detailing which principles should be used in solving many different cases.⁶³ Although in *Moral Theology* St Alphonsus had followed in the tradition of the manualists and had himself presented a detailed account of licit and illicit marital acts, St Alphonsus was drawn to equiprobabilism not so much through legalism as through his experience in the confessional.

For St Alphonsus the salvation of souls depends to a great extent on the guidance given to people in confession. St Alphonsus was opposed to both rigorism and laxism, urging confessors to be 'neither too indulgent nor too severe'.⁶⁴ Priests are to be kind fathers, doctors who can diagnose sickness and prescribe the right medicine, careful teachers, and judges who help penitents examine their conscience and who provide absolution and penance. Confessors are not to inquire too deeply into whether or not a married couple render 'the marriage debt' to each other, and as to 'other things' concerning married life, he should not say anything unless he is asked.⁶⁵ In contrast to the extreme rigorists who would often deny absolution, St Alphonsus starts from the position of kindness, telling penitents that 'God's mercy is bigger than your sins', after all, people are saved by love.⁶⁶

State and Church tensions

From ancient times we have seen that marriage is a public matter. State regulation of marriage indicates that marriage is important for society. Marriage and family are the first building blocks of society and the place where new citizens are formed. On a purely worldly level, regulation protects children and spouses, it provides a framework for the distribution of property, and it ensures that people do not evade their obligations. As different states began to exert their own authority over the institution of marriage the contractual aspect of marriage was further emphasized.

In sixteenth century protestant countries such as England the marriage ceremony had to take place according to the rites of the Church of England. Catholic marriages were not recognized because they followed a religious practice not accepted by the state. Previously, clandestine marriages were marriages contracted in secrecy. In England, clandestine marriages became marriages that did not comply strictly with Anglican canon law.[67] Moreover, marriages contracted by informal arrangement were common especially among poorer people who wished to avoid the costs of the calling of banns, the marriage certificate, and a large celebration. These informal arrangements took the form of an exchange of vows *per verba de praesenti* 'in words of the present tense' that created a binding contract.[68] In England the Marriages Act 1753 sought to regulate marriage by ensuring public registration and by insisting that marriage took place in an Anglican church after banns had been called or a license purchased. Notably these stipulations did not apply to Quakers or Jews, however Catholics were not exempt. By the nineteenth century English law accepted that even in religious traditions where marriage was regarded as a sacrament, the religious ceremony only arose out of the civil contract. Therefore, the validity of marriage could be established by purely civil contract. The increasing emphasis on registration for a valid marriage contract created the problem of recognizing a Protestant marriage in a Catholic state or Catholic marriage in a Protestant state. However, the question of marriage between Catholics and non-Catholics was also pressing for the Church. In his 1748 encyclical addressed to the bishops of Poland, *Magnae nobis*[69] Pope Benedict XIV (1675–1758) notes general disapproval of mixed marriages because they put strain on the Catholic spouse when it comes to adherence to the faith. But he reiterates that the bond of marriage is permanent, that the Catholic spouse should not be 'perverted' by the non-Catholic spouse, and that all the children, male and female, should be brought up as Catholics. In addition, state requirements for registering marriages as contracts also raised the possibility of the state dissolving such contracts. As Pope Pius IX (1792–1878) notes in his allocution *Acerbissimum vobiscum* delivered in a secret consistory on 27 September 1852,[70] moves to consider marriage as a civil contract only and to allow divorce in certain cases ignores the mystery, dignity and sanctity of the sacrament of marriage. Marriage between the faithful is always a sacrament.

Modernity and Pope Leo XIII

By the time of Pope Leo XIII (1810–1903) growing secularism had given way to a more outright derision of the sacred and an active promotion of agnosticism. The problem of the provision of adequate education for clergy still remained. There was significant concern that couples had lost the sense of marriage as a sacrament and the possibility of divorce became more acute where there seemed to be simply a civil contract. In Italy and France there were bills in place for civil marriage and divorce[71] and the idea that marriage involved both the goodness of creation and the action of grace lost its centrality as the power of the state and state legislation grew.

In response to this growing agnosticism, Pope Leo XIII promoted the restoration of Christian philosophy emphasizing its intellectual respectability and he sought to enhance Catholic engagement with the world through a return to the patristics and the thinking of St Thomas Aquinas. Pope Leo XIII believed that this method would enable dialogue with modern science, philosophy, and theology.[72] In this restoration project Pope Leo XIII acknowledges that it is Jesus Christ who divinely renews the world, and Jesus who has entrusted his work to the Church.[73] For Pope Leo XIII marriage is an essential aspect of this project since marriage is foundational to the Christian order and to the flourishing of society. Moreover, God intends the divine institution of marriage to be 'a most fruitful source of individual benefit and of public welfare.'[74] As Pope Leo XIII points out 'the family and society at large spring from marriage.' However, Pope Leo XIII is especially concerned that 'the most excellent ideal of marriage' which is found in both nature and in the sacrament, is becoming gradually extinct by civil authorities who have used this link of marriage to society to make marriage purely a civil contract under civil jurisdiction.[75] Moreover, there is the perception that Church power over marriage is not God-given but rather 'by favour of the civil authority or to its injury.'[76] Pope Leo XIII identifies the main characteristic of civil jurisdiction over marriage as the ease with which divorce can be obtained. According to Pope Leo XIII, an understanding of marriage as simply human law without the support of the Church means that spouses all too easily find the demands of marriage unbearable and they see freedom in being loosed of the ties of the marriage bond. Divorce, says Pope Leo XIII, brings with it a lessening of kindness, family break-up, harm to children, and an erosion of the dignity of women especially where women run the risk of being deserted.[77] Responding to the way in which attitudes to marriage risked being reduced to the merely secular or pragmatic, Pope Leo XIII decided to write his 1880 encyclical *Arcanum Divinae*. Central to the Pope's encyclical is that marriage and family life have not only a vital role in society, but they are also true paths to holiness, and that marriage is divinely instituted and not merely a human construct.

Reiterating the teaching of the Council of Trent, Pope Leo XIII states that God is the 'author' of marriage and, from the very beginning in its very nature marriage is 'a kind of foreshadowing of the Incarnation of His Son; and therefore there abides in it something holy and religious.'[78] By emphasizing the sacred nature of marriage from the first human communities Pope Leo XIII asserts the jurisdiction of the Church, and he categorically states that 'marriage is holy by its own power, in its own nature, and of itself' and so is not subject to the will of civil rulers.[79] Moreover, marriage has been raised to the dignity of a sacrament by Christ[80] and on this basis the Church has full competence over its regulation. Due to this inseparable link between the nature of marriage as both contract and sacrament Pope Leo XIII brooks no distinction or severance of contract and sacrament and therefore refuses to accept the suggestion that the state regulates the contract and leaves questions of the sacrament to the Church:

'the contract cannot be true and legitimate without being a sacrament as well.'[81] Thus, among Christians 'every true marriage is of itself, and by itself, a sacrament.'[82]

For Pope Leo XIII the divine institution and therefore holiness of marriage is indisputable: marriage is a 'great sacrament', 'honourable in all.'[83] Again stressing the aspect of marriage for 'the public welfare', Pope Leo XIII points out that marriage is for children, and also that 'the lives of husbands and wives might be better and happier.' He suggests that this happiness is brought about 'by their lightening each other's burdens through mutual help; by constant and faithful love; by having all their possessions in common; and by the heavenly grace which flows from the sacrament.' He adds the importance of proper and virtuous upbringing of children as good citizens for the benefit of society.[84] Pope Leo XIII establishes that the noble purpose of marriage is to bring forth 'children for the Church' not in the sense of increasing numbers in the pews but rather as 'fellow citizens with the saints' for the worship of God.[85] Secondly, the duties of husband and wife are 'to have such feelings for one another as to cherish always very great mutual love, to be ever faithful to their marriage vow, and to give to one another an unfailing and unselfish help.' Simultaneously Pope Leo XIII repeats the traditional hierarchy of husband and wife.[86] Moreover, God gives couples 'power to attain holiness in the married state', and by making marriage 'an example of the mystical union between himself and his Church' God perfects natural love. Thus, the bond of divine love strengthens human love, and the union of two in one is holy and indissoluble.[87]

Canon Law

The 1917 Pio-Benedictine Code of Canon Law was the result of an ambitious project to gather into one all the sacred canons of ecclesiastical law. Huge and unwieldy collections of the 'old law', ancient law promulgated before the time of Gratian, the 'new law' from Gratian to the Council of Trent, and the 'newest law' that came out of the Tridentine Synod were already in existence, leading many fathers at the First Vatican Council in 1869 to protest 'we are weighed down by law', and to call for a reform.[88] The process of reform was begun in 1904 under the pontificate of Pope St Pius X and completed in 1917 under the pontificate of Pope Benedict XV.

Marriage is covered in Book 3 Title VII of the 1917 Code[89] and the Code begins by stating that Christ raised the contract of marriage between baptized persons to the dignity of a sacrament. Therefore, it is impossible for a valid contract of marriage between baptized persons to exist without it being a sacrament: if both parties are baptized and it is a valid marriage contract then it is a sacramental marriage.[90] The 1917 Code is clear that marriage of baptized persons 'is ruled not only by divine law but also by canon [law], with due regard for the competence of civil power concerning the merely civil effects of said marriage.'[91]

Implicit in the 1917 Code is the traditional canonical distinction between *matrimonium in fieri*, 'marriage in the act of being constituted', and *matrimonium in facto esse*, 'marriage in the act of being lived out.' *Matrimonium in fieri* is the act of consent and the contract that gives rise to the *matrimonium in facto esse*, the marriage bond. If there is a fundamental flaw in the *matrimonium in fieri* then no *matrimonium in facto esse* results. However once the *matrimonium in facto esse* has been constituted by the legitimate consent of the parties then the bond of marriage continues 'even if seas of troubles cause the shipwreck of the existential relationship of the spouses.'[92] Indeed, marriage 'enjoys the favour of the law' so if there is any doubt the validity of the marriage is to be upheld until the contrary is proven.[93] Marriage comes into effect by the consent of the couple as long as it is 'lawfully expressed' by the two who have legal capacity to consent.[94] The Code defines matrimonial consent as 'an act of the will by which each party gives and accepts a perpetual and exclusive right to the body for acts which are of themselves suitable for the generation of offspring.'[95]

The 1917 Code seems to be the first official document to set out the ends of marriage in terms of primary and secondary ends:[96] procreation and education of children is the primary end, mutual help and 'the allaying of concupiscence' are secondary ends.[97] By delineating the ends of marriage as primary and secondary, it would appear that the secondary end of marriage, mutual help or love, could be excluded from the consent to marry without invalidating marriage because the secondary end is not absolutely necessary for the primary end. Having identified the ends of marriage the Code outlines its 'essential properties': unity and indissolubility. The sacramental character of marriage gives these essential properties 'a special firmness.'[98]

Canon law cannot be seen merely as a set of rules and regulations. The codification of canon law serves the mission of the Church and aids in the renewal of Christian life. In *Arduum sane munus*, Pope St Pius X's *motu proprio* that set up the project to codify the law, Pope St Pius X explains that this tremendous task of governing the Church is for the good of souls and to restore all things in Christ.[99] In *Providentissima Mater Ecclesia*, the Bull to promulgate the new code, Pope Benedict XV regards Church laws as guidance and direction for clergy and the faithful, as well as a source of wisdom for the world.[100] Nevertheless, canon law is not the only word on the Christian life. In the tradition canon law is complemented and deepened by pastoral and theological reflections on marriage and family life.

Summary

Understandings of Christian marriage as it has developed through the centuries has very many different interwoven threads. There are the strands of the civil and secular, the Christian and Church, as well as historical contexts and evolving traditions. A cursory look at post Trent teaching on marriage may suggest that this teaching tended to be left to moral theologians who dealt with the morality of physical sexuality, and to canon lawyers who dealt principally with the validity of consent. The emphasis from this teaching seems to fall on procreation as the primary end of marriage with unity of the spouses and indissolubility treated in relation to this end. In this period the very pastoral and practical teaching on marriage and family life are often neglected because of the emphasis on the law. Nevertheless, the pastoral approach is still present not least because teaching and law have always had the care of people at their heart. Moreover, teaching has always presented marriage as sacred and as belonging to the mystery of Christ and his Church.

Significantly, understandings of marriage are influenced by developments in moral theology and philosophy as well as dominant trends in thinking. However, the many secular challenges to the Church's jurisdiction and in particular the secular claim that marriage as a contract gives the state jurisdiction in the same way as it has control over other contracts, has led the Church to affirm the inseparable identity of the marriage contract and the marital sacrament for the baptized. Sacrament belongs to the very essence of marriage.[101] Nevertheless, it seems that the way in which the 1917 Code of Canon Law set out a hierarchical ordering of the ends of marriage reflects the tendency towards legalism in moral theology itself. This in turn led some theologians to call for a more personal understanding of the theology of marriage, and later a revisiting of natural law and a return to the virtues. However, in yet another strand to the story of marriage, marriage and the family have been subject to more pressures and promises in the brave new world of twentieth century science and technology.

Notes

1. St John of the Cross, 'The Sayings of Light and Love' in *The Collected Works of St John of the Cross* (Washington: Institute of Carmelite Studies, 2017), 60, p. 90.
2. W. Roberts, 'Christian Marriage' in *From Trent to Vatican II: Historical and Theological Investigations*, (Oxford: Oxford University Press, 2006), pp. 210–211.
3. *The Catechism of the Council of Trent, The Roman Catechism.*
4. St Ignatius of Loyola, 'The Spiritual Exercises' in *The Spiritual Exercises and Selected Works* (New York: Paulist Press, 1991), 356, p. 211.
5. *Ibid.*, 169, p. 161.
6. St Charles Borromeo, *Charles Borromeo, Selected Orations, Homilies and Writings* (Oxford: Bloomsbury 2017), 17.
7. St Robert Bellarmine, *Doctrina Christiana* [1597] (Prague: Mediatrix Press, 2016), p. xii.
8. St Robert Bellarmine, *The Art of Dying Well.* [1620] (Manchester New Hampshire: Sophia Institute Press, 1998), Ch 1, 3; Ch 15, pp. 113–120.
9. A. Ravier, *Francis de Sales: Sage and Saint* (New York: DeSales Resource Centre, 2007), pp. 57–58.
10. St Francis de Sales, *Treatise on the Love of God.* [1616] (Rockford Illinois: Tan, 1997) Book I, Ch IV, 67.
11. *Ibid.*, Book III, Ch V, 137–139.
12. St Francis de Sales, *St Francis de Sales: Selected Letters* (New York: DeSales Resource Centre, 2011), p. 22.
13. St Francis de Sales, 'Letter: To a wife who thinks that marriage hinders holiness' in *Thy Will Be Done: Letters of St Francis de Sales* (Manchester New Hampshire: Sophia Institute Press 1995), pp. 21–22.
14. St Francis de Sales, *Philothea or an Introduction to the Devout Life.* [1608] (North Carolina: Tan, 2010), Ch 3 9–10; St Francis de Sales, *Treatise on the Love of God* Book VIII, Ch VI, 258.
15. St Francis de Sales, *Treatise on the Love of God* Book IX, Ch V, 280; Book VIII, Ch IX, 262.
16. St Francis de Sales, *Philothea* Ch 1, 4.
17. *Ibid.*, Ch 2 6–7.
18. *Ibid.*, Chs 38, 39, 231–239.
19. See J. Mahoney, *The Making of Moral Theology* (Oxford: Clarendon Press, 1987), pp. 72–77.
20. International Theological Commission, *In Search of a Universal Ethics: A New Look at the Natural Law* (London: Catholic Truth Society, 2009), 26.

21 St Thomas Aquinas, *Summa Theologiae* IaIIa, q.100,a.5.
22 International Theological Commission, *In Search of a Universal Ethics*, 26.
23 St Thomas Aquinas, 'On the Ten Commandments' in *The Catechetical Instructions* Prologue, 1.
24 C. Haar, 'Tomás Sánchez and Late Scholastic Thought on Marriage and Political Virtue' in *The Concept of Law (Lex) in the Moral and Political Thought of the 'School of Salamanca'* (Leiden, the Netherlands: Brill, 2016), pp. 89–90.
25 Rm 7:23.
26 Rm 2:14–15.
27 St Thomas Aquinas, *Summa Theologiae* I.q1.a.1c.
28 *Ibid.*, IaIIae. q.91.2.
29 M. A. Gillespie, *The Theological Origins of Modernity* (Chicago: University of Chicago Press, 2008), p. 2.
30 International Theological Commission, *In Search of a Universal Ethics* 28–30.
31 Pope Paul III, *Sublimus Dei* (1537).
32 International Theological Commission, *In Search of a Universal Ethics* 31.
33 See J. Witte, *Church, State and Family: Reconciling Traditional Teachings and Modern Liberties* (Cambridge: Cambridge University Press, 2019), pp. 65–69.
34 Francisco de Vitoria, 'On the American Indians (De Indis)' in *Vitoria Political Writings* (Cambridge: Cambridge University Press, 1991), pp. 231–292.
35 S. Salvi, 'Towards a New Era of Modernity? Late Scholastic Speculation on Bigamy and Polygamy' in *Family Law and Society in Europe from the Middle Ages to the Contemporary Era* (Switzerland: Springer 2016), pp. 169–172; Haar, 'Tomás Sánchez and Late Scholastic Thought on Marriage and Political Virtue', pp. 94–95.
36 See S. Pinon, *The Ivory Tower and the Sword: Francisco Vitoria Confronts the Emperor* (Eugene Oregon: Pickwick, 2016), pp. 112–114.
37 Haar, 'Tomás Sánchez and Late Scholastic Thought on Marriage and Political Virtue', p. 94.
38 *Ibid.*, 82.
39 International Theological Commission, *In Search of a Universal Ethics*, 29.
40 Gillespie, *The Theological Origins of Modernity* p. 6.
41 Pope St John Paul II, *Fides et Ratio*, 41–42.
42 International Theological Commission, *In Search of a Universal Ethics* 33.

43 J. Witte, 'Grotius and the Natural Law of Marriage' in *Studies in Canon Law and Common Law in Honor of R.H. Helmholz* (Berkeley: The Robbins Collection 2015), pp. 239–240.
44 *Ibid.*, pp. 237–238.
45 *Ibid.*, p. 240.
46 *Ibid.*, p. 242.
47 *Ibid.*, p. 241.
48 *Ibid.*, pp. 247–248.
49 *Ibid.*, pp. 242–243.
50 *Ibid.*, pp. 244–245.
51 *Ibid.*, pp. 245–246.
52 J. Locke, *Two Treatises of Government.* [1689] (London: Routledge 1987), Second Treatise Ch 2,6.
53 T. Slater, *A Manual of Moral Theology: Vol.1.* (St Pius X Press, 2012), Preface to the First Edition.
54 J. Keenan, 'Moral Theology' in *From Trent to Vatican II: Historical and Theological Investigations* (Oxford: Oxford University Press 2006), pp. 163–164.
55 *Ibid.*, 168.
56 S. Tutino, *Uncertainty in Post-Reformation Catholicism: A History of Probabilism* (Oxford: Oxford University Press, 2018), pp. 91–92.
57 See Haar, 'Tomás Sánchez and Late Scholastic Thought on Marriage and Political Virtue', Sánchez Disputations On Marriage 9.11.
58 See St Alphonsus Liguori, *The History of Heresies, and Their Refutation: or the Triumph of the Cross* (Dublin: James Duffy 1847), Ch XIII Refutation XIII, pp. 320–321.
59 *Ibid.*, Ch XIII Refutation V, IV; Refutation VI pp. 248–249.
60 *Ibid.*, Ch XIII, VI p. 251.
61 *Ibid.*, Ch XIII Refutation XI, I, II p. 286.
62 *Ibid.*, Ch XIII Refutation XIII pp. 321–322.
63 St Alphonsus Liguori, *Guide for Confessors* (Lulu.com 2018), p. 23.
64 *Ibid.*, p. 8.
65 *Ibid.*, p. 41.
66 *Ibid.*, p. 11.
67 R. Probert, *Marriage Law and Practice in the Long Eighteenth Century: A Reassessment* (Cambridge: Cambridge University Press, 2009), p. 8.
68 *Ibid.*
69 Pope Benedict XIV, *Magnae nobis.*
70 Pope Pius IX, *Acerbissimum vobiscum.*
71 R. Hittinger, 'Popes Leo XIII and Pius XI' in *Christianity and Family Law:*

72.   Pope Leo XIII, *Aeterni Patris*.
73.   Pope Leo XIII, *Arcanum Divinae*.
74.   *Ibid.*, 26.
75.   *Ibid.*, 27.
76.   *Ibid.*, 17.
77.   *Ibid.*, 27–29.
78.   *Ibid.*, 19.
79.   *Ibid.*, 19.
80.   *Ibid.*, 20.
81.   *Ibid.*, 23.
82.   *Ibid.*, 24.
83.   *Ibid.*, 14, 15, 25, 26.
84.   *Ibid.*, 26.
85.   *Ibid.*, 10.
86.   *Ibid.*, 11.
87.   *Ibid.*, 9.
88.   P. Gasparri, 'Preface to the 1917 Code' in *The 1917 or Pio-Benedictine Code of Canon Law* (Edward Peters San Francisco: Ignatius Press, 2001), pp. 1–19.

An Introduction (Cambridge: Cambridge University Press, 2017), pp. 328–329.

89.   E. Peters, *The 1917 or Pio-Benedictine Code of Canon Law*.
90.   *Ibid.*, Canon 1012; Roberts, 'Christian Marriage', p. 211.
91.   *Code of Canon Law 1917*, Canon 1016.
92.   'Title VII Marriage' in *New Commentary on the Code of Canon Law* (New York: Paulist Press, 2000), p. 1240.
93.   *Code of Canon Law 1917*, Canon 1014.
94.   *Ibid.*, Canon 1081, 1.
95.   *Ibid.*, Canon 1081, 2.
96.   M. Lawler, *Marriage and Sacrament: A Theology of Christian Marriage* (Collegeville Minnesota: Liturgical Press, 1993), p. 66.
97.   *Code of Canon Law 1917*, Canon 1013, 1.
98.   *Ibid.*, Canon 1013, 2.
99.   Pope Pius X, *Arduum sane munus*.
100.   Pope Benedict XV, *Providentissima Mater Ecclesia*.
101.   'Title VII Marriage' in *New Commentary on the Code of Canon Law*, p. 1238.

6 GETTING PERSONAL IN THE TWENTIETH CENTURY

WHAT WOULD JESUS do? In 1896 Rev. C. M. Sheldon wrote a novel, *In His Steps: What Would Jesus Do?* Sheldon delivered his story weekly, a chapter at a time, to a packed congregation. In each story the main character is challenged not to do anything without first asking what Jesus would do. The question 'what would Jesus do?' opens up new avenues into a more personal ethic and into social ethics in a brave new world characterized by the promises of scientific and technological progress where often what can be done becomes what should be done. Marriage and family life could not but be impacted by these developments.

Sheldon's question 'what would Jesus do?' also reflected a new turn in biblical criticism and interpretation: the project to find the 'historical Jesus'. Nineteenth century 'biographies' pursuing the quest for the historical Jesus sought to discover what the 'real Jesus' was like. Beginning from the individual and from personal experience are also features of existentialism, and a focus on the person characterizes personalism.

What would Jesus do? Perhaps more than any other century, the twentieth century is marked by the turn to two compelling concepts associated with existentialism: autonomy and authenticity. Autonomy demands that every person must decide how to act based on their own rational deliberation. Authenticity allows that our deepest feelings and desires may trump our rational deliberation and our willingness to follow social norms. In his novel Sheldon has his characters ask about the 'source of knowledge' concerning what Jesus would do, especially since they are living in the twentieth century and there are many perplexing questions not mentioned by Jesus. Sheldon's main character, the Reverend Henry Maxwell replies that the 'test' is to ask the Holy Spirit for guidance and to be 'absolutely honest with ourselves.'[1] Sheldon's individualized ethic has some similarity with situation ethics. In contrast to traditional Christian ethics that has principles and rules, including absolutes such as not deliberately and directly killing the innocent, situation ethics 'keeps principles sternly in their place, in the role of advisors without veto power ... for the situationist there are no rules—none at all.' For the 'pragmatic-empirical temper of situation ethics' there is only the 'rule of love.'[2]

Church thinking on marriage has always been influenced by philosophy or trends in the world. However, this need not be a negative influence. Philosophical ethics that promote personal responsibility and personal response as well as engagement with social justice are good examples of positive developments. As Pope St John Paul II says about philosophy in general, 'faith and reason are like two wings on which the human spirit rises to the contemplation of truth.'[3] However, Church teaching has always recognized the dangers in Pelagian tendencies of thinking that human efforts are all that are needed, that social justice can be reduced to social work, that human beings can simply rely on their own devices. Although the Church sees in philosophy 'the way to come to know fundamental truths about human life',[4] the Church has other resources with which to measure philosophy, resources such as Revelation, tradition, reason and experience. The Church also recognizes the importance of developing an informed conscience, and the significance of the virtues in living out the Christian life. At times Church teaching has taken a critical stand against some philosophical trends and so has responded to counter worrying tendencies such as the Manichaean distrust of the body, extreme asceticism that disparaged sex and marriage, or scepticism about the goodness of creation and the inexhaustible depth of grace. Church teaching also serves philosophy by reminding people of the dangers of reductionism and of philosophy's tendency towards pride, to think that it can fully grasp all of reality from its own imperfect and limited view. Notably, Church teaching reminds us of the wonder that is in the world, and of the mystery that is the human person in relationship with other human persons.[5]

While the 1917 Code of Canon Law could go some way in presenting the essence of Church teaching on marriage and family, new scientific and technological developments brought significant new challenges and pressures. The context for one of the early encyclicals on marriage, Pope Pius XI's *Casti connubii*, written to encourage couples and offer a renewed vision of marriage, had its own specific challenges: eugenics, the apparent burden of children, and the rising divorce rate.

The eugenic context

The response to 'what would Jesus do?' demanded social action and Sheldon's book helped to popularize the Protestant Social Gospel Movement in North America.[6] The Social Gospel Movement developed alongside social reform movements aimed at purifying society of moral degeneracy. For some of these social reformers the object of Christianity became 'a perfect man in a perfect society.'[7] At the dawn of the twentieth century new discoveries in science and technology encouraged the view that with the human creative spirit everything was possible. Sheldon himself was enthusiastic about science and the application of evolutionary theory to social reform.[8] Science and technology were given prominence in every aspect of human life, including marriage and procreation. There was a pronounced optimism that scourges in society from crime, to alcoholism, poverty and disease could be solved by science. T. Malthus (1766–1834) had argued that population growth would always outstrip food supplies, that poverty and famine was the result of overpopulation and the irresponsibility of the lower classes. Pessimism could be overcome by optimism in science, notably by population control.

The idea of eugenics, that humanity could be improved by encouraging the fittest members of society to have more children, or the right to be well-born, had already been proposed by F. Galton (1822–1911), the cousin of C. Darwin, in 1869. By the 1900s early geneticists were thinking of applying techniques used in animal breeding to select desirable human characteristics and to eradicate intellectual and physical disabilities and psychiatric conditions. Science and technology could be used in human reproduction to improve the human population. Reproduction, the production of another individual has replaced procreation, the creation of another through a relationship between parents, and parents and God.

Most of the early eugenic movements aimed to affect reproductive practices often by proposals to prevent life through interventions such as sterilization, contraception, segregation and abortion. Some movements also promoted measures to end life.[9] For thinkers like Galton eugenics was seen as preferable to natural selection. Individuals should manage their own reproduction, and the state could intervene to ensure the best stock.[10] The first International Eugenics Congress took place in 1912 in London. Organised by the Eugenics Education Society which was itself founded in Britain in 1907, the Congress was dedicated to Galton who had died the previous year.[11] The first paper of the conference was from Galton who had argued that the laws of heredity apply equally to human beings as to plants and 'lower animals.' The problem outlined by Galton was that the 'degenerate', that is to say the 'insane', 'imbeciles', habitual criminals, and people with serious diseases seem to be more fertile than 'normal' people and they frequently marry, producing more degenerate children. One of the 'first efforts in practical Eugenics' is 'to restrict the propagation of children by the notoriously Unfit' and promote the propagation of the 'Fit.' In a report published in the *British Medical Journal*[12] it was said that the main task of the Congress was to educate the public on the importance of the new eugenic science. The paramount concern was to establish a 'moral code' to ensure the 'welfare of the unborn' in connection with questions about marriage and the state. The participants presented the 'hope that the twentieth century would be known in future as the century when the eugenic ideal was accepted as part of the creed of civilization.' In terms of marriage, one paper suggested that 'the law should take lessons from biology' based on animal breeding, to avert the 'disaster' of the reproduction of the feeble-minded, alcoholics, and people with other 'tainted conditions' that were closely allied with epilepsy. Sterilization programmes in the United States for 'defectives and degenerates', many of which were compulsory or did not require consent, were put forward as appropriate practical measures. The economic, social and moral 'burdens' of children were seen as not only bound up with 'individual conditions of existence' but also with progress and the transformation of society. The concluding word was given to Major L. Darwin, son of C. Darwin: 'the elimination of the feeble-minded was a policy that they felt should be kept in the forefront of their programme.' With the language of 'unfit' and 'fit', eugenics was 'centrally an evaluative project for the classification of humans.'[13]

Eugenics and the regulation of reproduction and marriage was a part of the new international world. However, the eugenic movement was not without its critics. Some scientists and geneticists objected on scientific grounds, others objected to state interference. Notably, there was significant opposition from Catholics although this opposition to eugenics has often been characterized as opposition to the specific practices of sterilization and contraception since these practices render sex non-reproductive.[14] However, reactions to Pope Pius XI's 1930 encyclical on marriage, *Casti connubii*, suggest that Church opposition went beyond the separation of procreation from the sexual act. For some who promoted birth control like M. Sanger, the opposition of Pope Pius XI was down to a fear of progress.[15] Sanger notes with approval the 'conversion to scientific control' of some religious groups, notably the Church of England, which at their 1930 Lambeth Conference accepted contraception,[16] though she does not refer to the restrictive nature of this Anglican conversion where contraception had only been suggested in specific limited cases. Significantly, until the 1930s most Christian denominations had opposed contraception and the Church of England decision came as a bolt from the blue. According to Sanger, in contrast to the more progressive religious denominations, Pope Pius XI's adherence to Christian tradition was back-ward looking, anti-scientific and controlling. Sanger argued that everyone had the 'right to be well-born', and quoting President Hoover, 'the complete birthright of a sound mind in a sound body.' To achieve this:

> America cannot limit her scientific birth control to the diseased, mentally defective, and poverty-stricken families. Even parents with sound bodies and minds, with education and means and comfortable homes, find that nature must not be allowed to follow her own blind way in breeding.

For Sanger, advances in science 'all tend to emphasize the immediate necessity for human control over the great forces of nature.' Birth control was primarily 'the instrument of liberation and of human development.'[17]

Casti connubii

Pope Pius XI begins his encyclical by situating marriage firmly in both the worldly, sacramental, and religious spheres. He affirms that marriage has a particular dignity as the 'principle and foundation of domestic society', that Jesus raised it to a sacrament restoring it 'to the original purity of its divine institution', and Jesus entrusted marriage to the care of the Church.[18] In no uncertain terms Pope Pius XI declares the divine institution of marriage and states that the divine laws of marriage, its sacramental dignity and perpetual stability, 'cannot be subject to any human decrees or to any contrary pact even of the spouses themselves.' Following scripture, the 'constant tradition' of the

Universal Church, and the Council of Trent, 'God is the Author of the perpetual stability of the marriage bond, its unity and its firmness.'[19] Pope Pius XI recognizes the human element in marriage when he talks about consent, 'the free act of the will', that constitutes 'true marriage', from which 'a conjugal union of a particular man and woman' arises. Nevertheless, he points out that freedom and consent concern the wishes of the 'contracting parties'; the nature of marriage remains subject to divine laws. Quoting St Thomas Aquinas, it is not a true marriage if something contrary to the laws of marriage is expressed in the consent.[20] Pope Pius XI explains that the 'sacred and inviolable bond of marriage arises from the profound joining of the souls and bodies of the "contracting parties", and God's decree.' Notably, and in contrast to some eugenic thinking, the nature of this union and consent which is made 'not by any passing affection of sense of spirit, but by a deliberate and firm act of the will' sets marriage apart not only from non-human animal pairings but also from other human unions.[21] Pope Pius XI accepts that marriage should be regulated by 'legitimately constituted authority.' However, he emphasizes that since the choice to marry 'flows from human nature itself', people should be able to choose their state of life, whether marriage or virginity. Quoting Pope Leo XIII, human law does not have the power to take away the 'natural and primeval right of marriage' or 'circumscribe in any way the principal ends of marriage', notably procreation.[22] It seems that Pope Pius XI had in his sights here those eugenic mandates prohibiting some people from marrying as well as measures to prevent reproduction.

In laying out the 'blessings' that belong to the 'blessing' of true marriage Pope Pius XI refers to St Augustine. These blessings are offspring, conjugal faith or faithfulness, and sacrament or indissolubility. In his high regard for the duty of parenthood, Pope Pius XI thinks that 'children should be begotten of love, tenderly cared for and educated in a religious atmosphere.' Yet he adds that in the event of separation, one of the parties 'should not be joined to another even for the sake of offspring.' Pope Pius XI takes the Code of Canon Law that sees the primary end of marriage to be the procreation and education of children as obvious.[23] Among the blessings, the 'child holds the first place' because through procreation human beings have the privilege of being God's 'helpers in the propagation of life.'[24] In transmitting life parents are 'ministers as it were of the Divine Omnipotence.'[25] To help to bring into life, educate and have baptized human beings who will one day enjoy life forever with God is 'a great gift of divine goodness.' Pope Pius XI considers that parents receive their children 'with joy and gratitude' but also as gifts, 'a talent committed to their charge by God' for not only the benefit of the family and society but also ultimately to be restored to God. The privilege of procreation also includes the right to educate, especially in the faith, aided by the indissolubility of the bond that ensures the mutual help of the parents. The marvellous dignity of co-operating with God and the important duty of procreation and education of children is such that it belongs only in marriage.[26] For Pope Pius XI sin against offspring in the form of contraception or abortion is also sin against conjugal faith since both blessings are 'essentially connected.' Any threats to monogamous marriage destroy mutual fidelity.[27]

The second blessing of marriage is 'conjugal honour' consisting in 'mutual fidelity of the spouses in fulfilling the marriage contract', notably in its 'one flesh' aspect. Conjugal honour not only rules out polygamy but also any infidelity including 'adultery in the heart.' Mutual fidelity in marriage is characterized by the virtue of chastity rooted in a pure love, analogous to Christ's love for the Church.[28] Pope Pius XI spends considerable time on the love between the couple, giving this love what could be termed a personal touch. Pope Pius XI critiques the way in which a notion of love as 'sympathy' or 'a certain vague compatibility of temperament' has been substituted for the 'true and solid love' of marriage. Building marriage on this 'sympathy' is like building a house on sand, and it enables people to argue that once the feeling ceases the marriage is dissolved. Instead, marital love, built on 'mutual conjugal chastity and strengthened by a deliberate and constant union of spirit' can, like the house built on rock, withstand adversity.[29] According to Pope Pius XI this love is a 'deep attachment of the heart which is expressed in action.' In keeping with the traditional formulation of the rights and duties of marriage and the marriage debt, Pope Pius XI calls this a law not only of justice but also charity. However, he says that the 'outward expression of love' manifested in deeds goes further than 'mutual help.' Following the tradition of marriage as a path to holiness, Pope Pius XI explains that the 'primary purpose' of marital love is that the man and woman 'help each other day by day in forming and perfecting themselves in the interior life', growing in love towards God and neighbour. For Pope Pius XI it is this 'partnership in life,' and imitation of Christ, with God's grace that enables the growth in virtue and holiness. Notably, Pope Pius XI explains that this 'mutual moulding of husband and wife, this determined effort to perfect each other, can in a very real sense, as the Roman Catechism teaches, be said to be the chief purpose of marriage', when looking at marriage not in 'the restricted sense' of being instituted for the procreation and education of children, but 'more widely as the blending of life as a whole.'[30] Indeed, 'conjugal faith has always been counted amongst the most priceless and special blessings of matrimony.'[31]

In terms of the family as 'domestic society', Pope Pius XI takes up the traditional hierarchical ordering within the family that placed the husband as the head of the household.[32] In language that today seems to speak of a patriarchal world order, Pope Pius XI goes to great lengths to censure female emancipation. However, he seems to have in his sights the view of emancipation that pits the family against the fulfilment of women as if true freedom for women is freedom from the burdens of home and children; a view that thinks care of the family can only be slavery. He warns that this emancipation debases motherhood and may simply result in a new slavery. In an interesting excursion into human rights, Pope

Pius XI does talk about 'equality of rights' and the need to recognize rights that belong to human dignity and to marriage where 'both parties enjoy the same rights and are bound by the same obligations', though for family ordering there is some inequality and 'due accommodation.'[33] Nevertheless, Pope Pius XI emphasizes that although the wife gives 'ready subjection' and 'willing obedience', she has full human dignity as an adult person including the power to exercise proper and personal judgement. She is a 'companion' not a servant. Pope Pius XI here wishes to avoid an 'exaggerated liberty which cares not for the good of the family' where 'the heart is separated from the head to the detriment of the whole body.' Indeed, Pope Pius XI says that 'if the husband is the head, the woman is the heart, and as he occupies the chief place in ruling, so she may and ought to claim for herself the chief place in love.' In terms of a more personalistic thinking on marriage, this emphasis on the significance of love perhaps goes beyond mere mitigation of a traditional hierarchical ordering. 'Divine charity' should be the guide in all their relations.[34]

Christian marriage is 'crowned' by the 'blessing' of the sacrament, denoting both indissolubility and 'the raising and hallowing of the contract' by Christ who made it an efficacious sign of grace. Since indissolubility was spoken of in the beginning, in Genesis, indissolubility belongs to every true marriage even when the sacramental element is absent. In addition to establishing that a valid marriage is indissoluble, Pope Pius XI lists the benefits of indissolubility. For the couple the 'generous yielding of their persons and the intimate fellowship of their hearts' require the guarantee provided by indissolubility and indissolubility assures security and personal dignity; indissolubility benefits the education and upbringing of children and is a public good for society as a whole.[35] Most important, the sacrament 'perfects natural love' and is a sign and source of grace that sanctifies husband and wife. As a sign of grace constituted by Christ, there is no true marriage between baptized persons that is not therefore a sacrament. Grace assists the couple in understanding, adhering to and putting into practice what belongs to the married state. Since grace requires co-operation, the 'seeds' of grace may remain latent until the couple cultivate them.[36]

Pope Pius XI thinks that of all the blessings of marriage the sacramental aspect of marriage is 'most sharply' attacked. Undoubtedly for Pope Pius XI the rise in secular divorce laws and civil regulation of marriage is but one instance of the way in which the state is encroaching onto the religious territory. The attempt to secularize the institution of marriage is to rob it of its holiness and its dignity. Pope Pius XI thinks that it is 'sufficiently obvious' that all marriages, sacramental and natural, have 'a certain sacredness and religious character' as a result of the very 'nature of things.' The permanent bond for love, mutual support and for children, express this nature and so cannot be dispensed with by any law.[37] Pope Pius XI outlines the dangers in divorce legislation especially when it designates marriage as 'hard and unpleasant' by its rationale that divorce is good for spouses, children and society.[38]

Given that marriage and family life are deeply connected to society, Pope Pius XI expresses deep concern about publications, films and media that present a false picture of marriage either by disparaging it or by romanticizing and trivializing it. Pope Pius XI sees this degradation of marriage as part of a general attack on divine and natural law by those seeking to sow 'cockle amongst the wheat.'[39] He details what he regards are some fundamental fallacies when it comes to marriage. To begin with, there is the pernicious view that marriage is simply invented by humans and the reductive view that marriage is seen 'merely as the means of producing life and of gratifying in one way or another a vehement impulse.'[40] Notably, Pope Pius XI links this reductive view to the secular approach and in condemning it demonstrates that it has never been a part of Church teaching. Pope Pius XI also points to the inconsistency of claiming that the 'seeds' of true marriage such as the permanent bond and the natural end of procreation are inscribed in human nature, yet also claiming that marriage is a human invention. Belief that marriage is the product of human invention and so subject to 'human caprice' allows that other 'temporary', 'experimental' or 'companionate' unions can be designated marriage even though they explicitly deny the indissoluble bond or the procreation of children.[41]

One particular evil identified by Pope Pius XI is the evil of seeing children as 'the disagreeable burden of matrimony', a burden that can be avoided not by 'virtuous continence' which is permitted and still sees children as gifts, but by 'frustrating the marriage act.' Since the conjugal act is by nature destined primarily for the begetting of children, to frustrate the act is to 'sin against nature', and 'no reason, however grave', can alter this. Presumably referring to the 1930 decision at the Lambeth Conference, Pope Pius XI strongly chides those who have departed from 'the uninterrupted Christian tradition' leaving only the Catholic Church to stand firm amid the 'moral ruin.'[42]

Pope Pius XI does consider the case where the mother's life or health would be in danger, but this seems to be in the context of mothers who risk their lives 'with heroic fortitude' to preserve the life of their already conceived unborn child, and so presumably he is referring to abortion. Pope Pius XI notes that the 'great crime' of abortion has been justified both on the mere choice of either parent or on eugenic grounds and that there are calls for its decriminalization. However, abortion is always 'murder of the innocent' and the unborn child cannot be considered an 'unjust aggressor' even when the life of the mother is at risk. Instead, Pope Pius XI urges doctors to guard and preserve the lives of both mother and child.[43]

Referring specifically to eugenics, Pope Pius XI decries attempts to prohibit certain people from marrying, and especially laws for forced sterilization, as examples of the state taking power which it does not legitimately possess. These actions and sanctions unjustly brand certain people as criminals. The family, says Pope Pius XI, is 'more sacred' than the state, and people are destined for eternity not just earthly life. Moreover, sterilization is mutilation of a healthy function and this is not permitted unless it is for the sake of the integrity of the whole body.[44]

Pope Pius XI repeats traditional teaching that there is no sin for spouses who find themselves in situations where they are 'sinned against rather than sinning', but nevertheless they should try to dissuade their partners. Presumably, this refers to marital acts against the conscience of one of the spouses. Indeed, Pope Pius XI recognizes that there are 'secondary ends such as mutual aid, the cultivating of mutual love, and the quieting of concupiscence' which are to be considered in assessing moral action, so long as 'they are subordinated to the primary end and so long as the intrinsic nature of the act is preserved.'[45] However, he observes that the law forbidding intrinsically evil acts cannot be set aside on the grounds of difficulty. Quoting Trent and with reference to the Jansenist 'heresy':

> there is no possible circumstance in which husband and wife cannot, strengthened by the grace of God, fulfil faithfully their duties and preserve in wedlock their chastity unspotted… 'God does not ask the impossible, but by His commands, instructs you to do what you are able, to pray for what you are not able that He may help you'.[46]

Pope Pius XI recognizes that any discussion on marriage requires a firm foundation not only in theology but also in practice and so he presents a forward-looking approach to marriage preparation that would find a place in twenty-first century thinking. For Pope Pius XI, science can be helpful, but a more holistic approach is needed. In particular, dependence on God's grace, participation in the sacraments and the exercise of the virtues are more effective than relying simply on science in living out the marital commitment.[47] Moreover, Pope Pius XI advocates 'wholesome instruction and religious training' to counter the 'exaggerated physiological education' that ignores virtuous living.[48] He recognizes that if children have a poor family experience this is likely to be replicated in their own relationships and he recommends remote and proximate preparation so that couples are well-prepared and children properly educated. Above all Pope Pius XI urges people to pray about their choices, including choice of partner, so that they discern what God wills for them.[49] Finally, 'if ever they should feel themselves to be overburdened by the hardships of their condition of life, let them not lose courage.'[50]

Contract to personalism?

The Church's moral teaching on marriage has often been characterized as 'cold legalism' and an arbitrary list of what not to do, rescued only in the twentieth century by a more personalistic understanding.[51] Partly, this is due to the language of contract and the apparent focus on procreation as the primary end of marriage. Marriage is spoken of in terms of contract primarily because marriage entails consent between the parties, and consent is a characteristic of contractual arrangements. As the sacred discipline dealing with ecclesiastical law, Canon Law does refer to marriage as a contract and consent as its essential aspect. However, since contracts are regulated by state legislation it seems unlikely that contract is the major focus for Church teaching, especially given the constant refrain that marriage belongs within the sphere of Church and not simply secular jurisdiction. Moreover, Popes Benedict XIV, Pius IX, Leo XIII and Pius XI recognize the danger in thinking of marriage in terms of contract only: not only does this imply that the bond could be broken by the contracting parties, it also loses sight of the sacrament and mystery that is inherent in marriage. In addition to language of contract and consent, Pope Pius XI develops a deeper consideration of married love, perhaps as a response to more materialistic, reductive and functional approaches to the human person. The journey of the story of marriage and family shows time and again that the Church responds to the real concerns of married people, that the vocation to holiness is threaded throughout, that spirituality, love, and friendship figure in theology. Marriage is not just about rights, duties, and the procreation of children. Marriage concerns a relationship not simply between bodies but between persons. Pope Pius XI seems to anticipate the move towards personalism in philosophy.

One significant strand of modern philosophical thinking is the twentieth century turn to the person and the other. In what is regarded as an authoritative analysis of modern philosophy, the French philosopher E. Mounier (1905–1950) pointed out that classical philosophy used to leave 'other-person-ness' 'strangely alone.' Philosophy was interested in putting the person in the centre with its focus on subjectivity, and the individual as the 'thinking thing' from the French philosopher Descartes. Other questions also related to the person in terms of what separated the self from things. With existentialism, philosophy began to grapple with the nature of human existence framed around the experience of the human subject as not just a thinking thing, but a feeling, acting, living being. This led to reflection on intersubjectivity, the separation of the self from the other, and then to 'other-person-ness'. As Mounier commented in relation to existentialism, 'we always picture another-person as *someone I can see*. Now, he is also someone *who can see me*.'[52] Persons are not like other things in the world like stones or trees or even other animals.

Since persons are not like things it may seem that persons are completely beyond our comprehension. But that is not the case. Persons may not be the subject of ready definitions and no one can fully grasp the whole reality of another, however much they love that person. Nevertheless, persons do express something of themselves by the way they are and act in the world.

Personalism is considered to be a philosophy and not simply an attitude towards the other because it involves certain positions. However, since there are different approaches to personalism it is better to think of this philosophy as personalisms.[53] After much deliberation the philosopher Boethius (475-c.525) gives a tentative definition of person as 'the individual substance of a rational nature.'[54] This definition has become classic. However, it is often overlooked that Boethius was speaking in the context of the Trinity, hence 'individual' does not refer to a number, otherwise he would be saying that God is not one but three. Instead 'individual' relates to what is unique in the One God, that is, the Three Divine Persons. Additionally, Boethius wrote at a time when the understanding of universals was the norm, hence his idea of 'rational nature' applies to every human being no matter how small and whatever their capacities: if an entity is a human being, it has a rational nature even if it cannot express rationality.[55] Nevertheless, the philosophy of personalism resists defining the concept of person because that would be a reductive approach and Boethius himself says that the concept of the person is 'a matter of great perplexity.'[56]

Personalism gives priority to the human subject. Coupled with the philosophy of phenomenology that lets the phenomena, the thing, speak for itself rather than putting forward theories, personalism places the person and personal experience centre stage. However, as K. Wojtyła, later Pope St John Paul II, discovered in his research into phenomenology, there are real difficulties with some personalisms. Personalisms associated with some phenomenological thinking consider the person as primarily the thinking thing or self-consciousness. Reality is reduced to subjective understanding and interpretation to the point where there is no objective reality. The mind becomes the measure of reality and there is no truth. There are personalisms that make the thinking aspect of the person centre of everything including truth; personalisms that keep body and soul and mind together; personalisms that focus on rights and human dignity; personalisms where the person is in relationship with others. And there are personalisms that recognize the human person in all that person's aspects but also in relationship with others and especially with God. God is the centre of all things and human persons find their selves through the gift of self in imitation of God's gift of his Son.

The contributions of Dietrich von Hildebrand and Herbert Doms

In 1929, a year before Pope Pius XI promulgated *Casti connubii,* D. Von Hildebrand (1889–1977) published his book *Die Ehe,* translated into English from the German as *Marriage: The Mystery of Faithful Love.* Hildebrand's book was based on a lecture on marriage that he gave to the Catholic Academic Association in Germany in 1923. In his lecture Hildebrand made an explicit distinction between the purpose and the meaning of marriage. As Hildebrand's wife later explained, Hildebrand realized that he was 'breaking new ground' and so he sent his lecture first to the papal nuncio in Munich, Cardinal Pacelli, who became secretary to Pope Pius XI. On the death of Pope Pius XI Pacelli was elected pope taking the name Pius XII. Pacelli endorsed Hildebrand's views and Hildebrand published his book.[57] In the later English translation Hildebrand noted that in *Cast connubii* Pope Pius XI 'refers to a passage of the Roman Catechism in which conjugal love is considered as the ultimate meaning of marriage', and Hildebrand suggests that his book may have had some influence on 'bringing about an increased stress on the role of love in Christian marriage.'[58]

Hildebrand studied phenomenology under E. Husserl and M. Scheler, and he converted to Catholicism in 1914. Hildebrand was especially concerned with what he termed a 'terrible anti-personalism, a progressive blindness toward the nature and dignity of the spiritual person.' This anti-personalism was expressed in the reduction of the human person through biological materialism. To counteract this biologism Hildebrand drew attention to the importance of stressing 'the spiritual significance of marriage—and to explain not only its primary end (procreation), but also its primary meaning as the intimate union of two persons in mutual love.'[59] Notably, Hildebrand thought that the role of love in marriage had been underestimated by some theologians, especially given the focus on procreation. Moreover, he thought that the expression 'marriage-contract' was 'not a happy choice of words since marriage differs essentially from any other real contract',[60] and he took *Casti connubii* to endorse conjugal love as the ultimate meaning of marriage.[61]

According to Hildebrand we can understand the nature of love without reference to sex because, after all, the source of love is Divine Love.[62] Nevertheless, conjugal love is 'a completely new kind of love' to, say, love between friends or for children because 'it involves a mutual giving of one's self' in a complete and exclusive manner where they belong to each other, 'not only the heart but the entire personality.' Marital love is not simply a 'return of affection' but a love that 'tends to a unique union', a 'community' of two persons. Using philosophical language originating from M. Buber, Hildebrand distinguishes married love from a 'we relationship' where people walk side by side, instead designating this 'face to face' love as 'the most profound I-Thou relationship': they are united in 'a mysterious fusion of their souls.'[63]

Hildebrand further distinguishes the conjugal relationship from other relationships of love by its 'specific characteristic' of the giving of the self that involves a 'definite decision.' By saying 'I love you' 'we decisively choose a person.' The question of whether a person loves in this sense can be answered quite definitely with yes or no.[64] For Hildebrand love is not 'blind', rather it gives sight because in conjugal love the 'real individuality of the partner is revealed' and the person comes to understand 'the divine plan underlying the creation of this particular individuality.'[65] Conjugal love is not infatuation, an illusion or sensual desire but instead implies an 'intention of duration and strict exclusiveness.' And this 'being in love must be reactualized at specific moments.'[66] The union of two in one flesh is 'a complete spiritual-sensual union.'[67]

According to Hildebrand conjugal love can only come into being between a man and a woman. For Hildebrand complementarity is key and this cannot be reduced to mere sexual biological difference. Hildebrand accepts that every human being is called to 'glorify God by their sanctity.' Nevertheless, 'man and woman represent two different types of mankind, both having their respective significance according to the divine plan and their special value quite apart from their procreative function.' The difference between man and woman is a metaphysical one and is 'two types' of spiritual persons.[68] Man and woman complement each other and 'their meaning for one another is something quite unique. They are made for each other in a special way' spiritually and bodily.[69]

Although Hildebrand details the significance of conjugal love, he does not think that conjugal love is marriage, although it contains 'an anticipation' of the meaning of marriage. Implicitly following the tradition of what makes marriage, Hildebrand explains that marriage is a 'reality in the objective order', constituted by a 'solemn act', presupposing 'a formal act of the will', that is 'fully actualized' in consummation. It is a 'communion of objective validity' that creates duties and persists 'regardless of the sentiments or attitudes of the partners.' Significantly, according to Hildebrand 'the existence of conjugal love between the partners makes marriage desirable and gives it meaning, but does not in itself establish this objective bond.'[70]

Since for Hildebrand marriage is 'in its nature, principally a communion of love', 'the meaning of physical consummation is not restricted to its function as a means of procreation.'[71] Hildebrand draws a distinction between meaning and ends: he says that 'love is the primary meaning of marriage just as the birth of a new human being is its primary end.'[72] He thinks that 'this primary end is not the only meaning of the physical act.' Instead, he locates the meaning of the physical act primarily in 'the realization of the sublime communion of love in which, according to the words of our Savior, "they shall be two in one flesh".' From creation, marriage is 'the mystery of love.' That a new human being comes from this union is part of is 'solemn grandeur': procreation and the communion of love can never be deliberately separated.[73] Hildebrand adds that 'every marriage is fruitful' even when there are no children because 'true love possesses an intrinsic spiritual fruitfulness.'[74] However, the 'justification' of the physical union does not lie in conjugal love. Rather it lies in 'the solemn act of the conclusion of marriage' whereby the person gives themselves 'freely and irrevocably to the beloved for the entire lifetime.'[75] For Hildebrand 'the sexual union is thus the organic expression of wedded love, which intends precisely this mutual gift of self.' Hildebrand thinks that 'modern theories' that exaggerate sex while missing its deeper significance completely fail to understand the 'spiritual structure of personality' and the nature of love. Equally false is the view that physical sex is 'purely an external addition' to married love. There subsists a 'pre-established harmony' between physical sex and married love.[76]

Hildebrand is realistic enough to realize that love in marriage needs to be properly nourished, protected and cherished. This 'task' differs according to whether the marriage is best, imperfect or even troubled. Regardless of the state of the marriage, Hildebrand believes that God gives the required grace.[77]

K. Schemenauer points out that since Hildebrand does not clearly explain what he means when he says that conjugal love is the 'primary meaning' of marriage Hildebrand opens himself up to misunderstandings. According to Schemenauer, the English translation of Hildebrand's lecture *Die Ehe* that became his book *Marriage* dropped a crucial word: Hildebrand's proposal in *Die Ehe* reads that love is 'the primary created meaning of marriage'; 'created' is missing in the English translation. The point here is that the meaning of marriage is not subjective but rather it is rooted in God's intention for marriage. However, it is not clear from Hildebrand's own writing whether he thinks that conjugal love is required for marriage to exist or whether he thinks spouses should foster conjugal love since conjugal love is part of the definition of marriage.[78] Nevertheless, it is important to realize that Hildebrand identifies love not as an end of marriage but as its motivation. Presumably, Hildebrand was aware of the problems concerning the language of primary ends and Schemenauer notes that Hildebrand does not use the phrase 'primary meaning' in his later works. As Schemenauer observes, Hildebrand's focus was 'to show that conjugal love should not be reduced to procreation and to describe the role of conjugal love in marriage.'[79]

H. Doms (1890–1977), a Benedictine priest and admirer of Scheler, read Hildebrand's work but did not think Hildebrand had gone far enough.[80] In his book *The Meaning and End of Marriage* first published in German in 1935, Doms recommends giving up the language of primary and secondary in speaking of the purposes of marriage. According to Doms, 'the constitution of marriage, the union of two persons, does not consist in their subservience to a purpose outside themselves for which they marry. It consists in the constant vital ordination of husband and wife to each other until they become one.'[81] Conjugal love has primacy because children are the fruit of the union and, anyway, not every act of intercourse results in offspring.[82] For Doms the final biological purpose of marriage is procreation, but 'the highest and most important purpose of marriage is undivided community of life for man and woman.'[83] Doms explains that in the conjugal act the 'ontological unity of the spouses is realized by the fact that each one is immediately and totally fulfilled by the *actus secundus* of the other.'[84] In contrast to the I-Thou union presented by Hildebrand, Doms implies that marriage completes and fulfils the other person. This is problematic for an understanding of celibacy since it may imply that the celibate person is somehow incomplete. The thinking of Doms was taken a step further by the Swiss Passionist B. Krempel who advocated one essential end of marriage: the perpetual union of the lives of the two spouses, thus removing procreation from the ends of marriage.[85]

Holy Office statement of 1944

This confusion over the ends of marriage demanded both a clarification and a response. On 1 April 1944 the Supreme Sacred Congregation of the Holy Office decreed on the *dubium*:

can the opinion of certain writers be admitted who either deny that the primary end of marriage is the procreation and rearing of offspring, or teach that the secondary ends are not essentially subordinate to the primary end, but are equally principal and independent?[86]

Dubia ask for a 'yes' or 'no' answer. The answer from the Congregation was in the negative and Pope Pius XII approved the decision. The Congregation confirmed that there is an objective end and a subjective end to marriage. Defining the 'end', the Congregation explained that the *finis* is a good obtained through any action and it is related to both the nature of the act itself and the intention of the agents. An example of this would be a good meal that gives nutrition by its very nature of being food, but also serves human interaction: there are two ends in the same act. The Congregation next drew a distinction between the *finis operis* and the *finis operantis* in marriage.

The *finis operis* of marriage is the good that obtains objectively by its very nature. This good is given by God's design and it is intrinsic to marriage itself. The *finis operis* of marriage is procreation and education of children and it is not in human power to frustrate this good. Procreation and education of children is then the primary end of marriage. However, procreation cannot be seen as something merely biological. Rather procreation is co-operating with God.

The *finis operantis* is related to the intention of the spouses when they enter marriage. Certainly, there can be different reasons for entering into a marriage and usually the reasons agree with the objective end of marriage, to found a family. However, if a couple intentionally enter marriage willing against the objective end of marriage, for instance if they decide not to have children, then no marriage takes place because there is a defect in their consent. Thus, the *finis operantis* is subordinate to the *finis operis*, the objective end. In addition to procreation as the primary end of marriage, there are two secondary ends: the good of the spouses in the form of a common life, and the remedy for concupiscence.

The question of the place of love in marriage resurfaces in later debates. However, it may be useful to point out the universality of Church teaching. If primacy is given to conjugal love, then this seems to threaten the nature of marriage. After all, there can be a valid marriage without conjugal love. On the one hand, in cultures other than that of the West where perhaps great store is placed on love, especially romantic love, love may not be the main ingredient as in the case of consent to an arranged marriage. This does not mean that love is entirely absent or indeed that love does not grow. On the other hand, giving primacy to love and separating out procreation seems to challenge sexual morality, allowing for couples to live together or for same sex unions. And if, as Doms asserts, human beings are incomplete beings without the other, then that challenges the charism of celibacy.

Marriage and scientific progress

As papal nuncio, the future Pope Pius XII may have endorsed Hildebrand's approach to marriage, after all, Hildebrand did see procreation as its primary end. Speaking to the Court of the Sacred Roman Rota in 1941 and so prior to its 1944 statement, Pope Pius XII notes the importance of recognizing both the primary end of marriage and the secondary end that is subordinated to the primary end.[87] Pope Pius XII faced the usual tension between state and Church and keeping to tradition he affirms that marriages, even between the unbaptized are 'in the natural order a sacred thing' so civil courts have no power to dissolve them.[88] However, Pope Pius XII faced other challenges to marriage especially from emerging new technologies coupled with new moral approaches.

For Pope Pius XII scientific technical progress is 'the gift of God' and part of the new world order that requires the collaboration of Christianity to ensure the common good.[89] Moreover,

Pope Pius XII reminds scientists, especially atomic scientists, of the 'wonderful structure of natural laws', that the 'universal law says order in big things as in small ones.' With proper humility 'the people and the scientist' still 'stop in amazement' at the wonder of God's world.[90] Nevertheless, Pope Pius XII observes that the 'technical spirit' has been transformed into 'a serious spiritual danger' by a sense of self-sufficiency that makes a goal out of what is technically possible. The 'technical spirit' leads to a denial of supernatural goods and religious values, and a superficiality in relationships.[91]

Pope Pius XII declared that he was profoundly affected by evidence given at the trials of Nazi doctors who had sacrificed individuals for 'the medical interests of the community' and by reports of the atrocities in the name of medical research done to people in concentration camps. Undoubtedly, the ghost of eugenics was also present. For Pope Pius XII this evidence inevitably led him to ask, and not for the first time, about the 'moral limits' on the nature and extent of what may be done in medicine. Pope Pius XII recognizes that human beings have 'the capacity' to free themselves from their own creation. However, instead of reliance solely on pure freedom Pope Pius XII offers three 'basic ideas' for medical ethics: that it should 'conform to the essence of human nature'; it should 'conform to reason and finality', and be based upon 'positive values'; it should be 'rooted in the transcendental.'[92]

Anticipating the shift in medical ethics to seeing the patient not as a body to be worked upon but as a person, Pope Pius XII reminds doctors that the patient is 'not an isolated creature' but is a person with a life and family. However, Pope Pius XII also points out that there is a prescribed order: 'man is not the owner, the absolute lord of his body.'[93] In terms of marriage and new technologies, Pope Pius XII is especially concerned about artificial fertilization both outside and in marriage. Pope Pius XII places the new technology in the tradition that 'only the spouses have a reciprocal right over their body to generate a new life' and this cannot be transferred to the intervention of another party.[94] Pope Pius XII reminds obstetricians of the right to life and he points out the evil of abortion for reasons including eugenics and the apparent burden of lives designated as worthless. He adds that husband and wife should be supported in their role as parents. Referring to *Casti connubii,* Pope Pius XII says that contraception and direct sterilization are illicit. However, for 'serious reasons' observance of infertile times may be licit. Abstinence is, he says, not impossible though it may seem heroic.[95] The question of eugenics was still current, and Pope Pius XII calls sterilization or the prohibition of marriage for biological, genetic, or eugenic reasons an injustice, though he does accept that advice can be given to people who carry 'a very heavy inheritance.'[96]

Pope Pius XII sees the family as the 'cradle' not only for birth but also for the development, education, and formation of children, especially in the area of the formation of conscience. He critiques the 'new morality' that ignores the natural law and Church teaching in favour of the individual's own determination. While pointing to the importance of the law, he also critiques morality that characterises Church teaching simply in terms of the intransigence of obligation and law to neglect of the 'dynamic of the moral life.'[97] Pope Pius XII may have had in mind the 'new morality' of thinkers like J. Fletcher (1905–1991) who championed the use of technology unfettered by the limits of traditional morality. Inspired by pragmatism Fletcher thinks that the good, like the true, is 'whatever works.'[98] For Fletcher, 'the heart of the matter is control' and the 'key' to control is 'initiative.' We have, he says, the technology to 'change man himself.' Indeed, he adds 'if we refuse to do what we can when we can, on the ground that we may not or ought not to take the initiative, this is ... 'subhuman', because truly human acts are moral, that is free and responsible.'[99] Fletcher may ask 'are we too Promethean, stealing the fire?' and he may warn against being 'trapped by a Promethean intoxication.' Nevertheless, as far as Fletcher is concerned, 'the decision lies with us.'[100] Transcending 'natural restrictions' by technology and choice, especially in the area of artificial reproduction, 'is a human and spiritual victory.'[101]

In addition to his concerns about the moral rather than simply technical aspects of medicine and technology, Pope Pius XII notes the influence of personalism specifically in relation to marriage. He recognizes that a deeper sense of conjugal love sees the conjugal act as a personal act and expression of personal and emotional union. Nevertheless, he is concerned that the emphasis on love and 'techniques of love' found in many publications and marriage guides are being made the centre of marital relations and children are placed either outside or on the periphery of 'the values of the person.' He thinks that this inverts the proper order in marriage. According to Pope Pius XII, 'the truth is that marriage, as a natural institution, by virtue of the will of the Creator does not have as a primary and intimate aim the personal perfection of the spouses, but the procreation and education of new life. The other ends, although they are also understood by nature, are not in the same degree as the first, and even less are superior to them, but are essentially subordinate to it.' Pope Pius XII applies this also to marriage where there are no children. Certainly, Pope Pius XII does not seek to deny or diminish the significance of personal values in marriage. But he nevertheless seeks to ensure that the personal element is not separated from the primary end of marriage, procreation, and indeed takes a proper place in the 'service of new life.'[102] In the light of technologies to address the problem of infertility Pope Pius XII reiterates that 'the constant teaching of the Church' holds that 'the particular ends of the spouses, their common life, their personal perfection' are subordinate to the primary end of fatherhood and motherhood. Yet he also states that Church teaching rules out 'the opposite attitude' which claims to separate 'biological activity from the personal relationship of the spouses in the generation.' Human fertility has 'essential moral aspects.' Notably, Pope Pius XII says that the marriage contract with procreation as its primary end does not give the right to offspring, but to the 'natural acts' capable of generating new life.[103]

The Second Vatican Council

For Pope St John XXIII the singular problem facing the Church's teaching on marriage was the lack of adequate catechesis and proper preparation for people entering marriage. As he explains, the Church 'does not defend interests of outdated castes or customs', rather the Church proposes and defends 'the will of God'. He concludes that therefore it is necessary that 'the Church's doctrine on marriage be better known and spread in all its forms.'[104] Pope St John XXIII's call for a Second Vatican Council can be seen generally in terms of presenting church teaching in a clearer light. As Pope St John XXIII says, 'the Council intends to build a new structure on the foundations laid in the course of history, with the divine and human means that the Church has at her disposal. It is quite obvious that it is not a question of new doctrine, of sensational formulas.'[105] Pope St John XXIII did not live to see the completion of the Council but Church teaching on marriage and the family benefitted from the Council's clearer light. Moreover, the Council fathers situated married couples and families more explicitly into the apostolic activity of the people of God.

In the Council's dogmatic constitution on the Church, *Lumen Gentium*, the church fathers detail the way in which the sacraments bring into operation the 'common priesthood' of the faithful. Referencing Ephesians 5, in the sacrament of matrimony Christian spouses 'signify and partake of the mystery of that unity and fruitful love which exists between Christ and his Church.' By virtue of this sacrament, they 'help each other to attain to holiness in their married life and in the rearing and education of their children.' Their children are 'new citizens of human society' and by baptism, children of God, and so 'the family is, so to speak, the domestic church.' In whatever state of life they find themselves, the faithful are called 'each in his own way' to holiness.[106] The whole of the lives of the lay faithful, including family life, and even in the 'hardships' of life, can be consecrated to God as spiritual sacrifices.[107] Married life has a particular importance in forming the family into 'an excellent school of the lay apostolate' and the spouses have their own 'proper vocation in being witnesses of the faith and love of Christ to one another and to their children.'[108] Moreover, as the 'primary and principal educators' of their children, parents must create 'a family atmosphere animated by love and respect for God and man' so that a well-rounded education is fostered. The family is the first school in human virtue.[109]

The centrality of marriage and family life for the Church and society is brought out in the *Decree on the Apostolate of the Laity, Apostolicam Actuositatem.* In the Church's service to humanity and the building up of the Kingdom, marriage and family life are 'of unique importance' precisely because God has established them as the 'beginning and basis of human society'. Christian husbands and wives are 'co-operators in grace and witnesses of faith for each other, their children and all others in the household' and they form their children in terms of education and vocation. According to the church fathers, 'the greatest part of their apostolate' is to show in their own lives the 'indissolubility and sacredness' of the marriage bond, to affirm their right to educate their children in a Christian manner, and to defend 'the dignity and lawful autonomy of the family.' As the 'domestic sanctuary of the Church', the family is the place from where service to others and justice flow.'[110]

Most of the teaching on marriage and family is found in the Pastoral Constitution *Gaudium et spes,* on the Church in the Modern World. Notably the church fathers speak of the Church *in* the world and not simply *and* or alongside the world. The Church offers a 'service' to the 'human family', to all humankind. And the fathers say it is the human being who is 'the key to this discussion': the person 'whole and entire', body, soul, heart, conscience, mind, will, and not just the spiritual or physical aspects of human beings.[111] One of the 'problems of special urgency' is marriage and the family, and the fathers consider these 'in the light of the Gospel and of human experience.'[112]

Situating marriage and family squarely in the world, the fathers observe that the well-being of the individual, of human and of Christian society is 'intimately linked' to the healthy condition of the community produced by marriage and the family. However, various pressures from polygamy to divorce and excessive self-love have obscured the excellence of marriage.[113] To give clarity to church teaching and to support those who try to preserve the holiness and dignity of marriage, *Gaudium et spes* begins from first principles, though with a twentieth century flavour.

The fathers first affirm that 'the intimate partnership of married life and love has been established by the Creator and qualified by his laws, and is rooted in the conjugal covenant of irrevocable personal consent.' When validly constituted, the 'sacred bond' from this act of mutual self-gift is 'lasting' and no longer depends on human decisions. 'God himself is the author of matrimony' and the benefits and purposes of marriage have bearing on the individual, the family and on society. Having established the covenantal nature of the marriage partnership the fathers next introduce the ends of marriage: 'by their very nature, the institution of matrimony itself and conjugal love are ordained for the procreation and education of children, and find in them their ultimate crown.' The goods or blessings of marriage are presented as an integral whole:

> thus a man and a woman, who by their compact of conjugal love 'are no longer two, but one flesh' (Mt 19:ff), render mutual help and service to each other through an intimate union of their persons and of their actions. Through this union they experience the meaning of their oneness and attain to it with growing perfection day by day. As a mutual gift of two persons, this intimate union and the good of the children impose total fidelity on the

spouses and argue for an unbreakable oneness between them.[114]

Through the sacrament Christ comes into the lives of married Christians, and 'authentic married love is caught up into divine love.' Notably the fathers stress the power of the sacrament that aids the couple in the office of being father and mother, that 'suffuses their whole lives with faith, hope and charity', that advances their sanctification, all of which contributes to the glory of God. Significantly, children also contribute to making their parents holy.[115] The following four paragraphs of *Gaudium et spes* develop the themes set out in the initial presentation of the first principles.

Perhaps in keeping with the turn to experience the fathers begin by discussing the nature of love. True love between husband and wife is an 'eminently human one', and person to person. Notably the fathers describe it as directed 'through an affection of the will.' Linking this love to a 'friendship distinctive of marriage', love involves the good of the whole person and so the expressions of love have a 'unique dignity.' When the love of the spouses is merged with the divine gifts of healing, perfecting, grace and charity, the spouses are led to give a 'free and mutual gift of themselves' throughout their whole lives. In place of the notion of duty, the fathers speak of the conjugal act as 'noble and worthy', and when 'expressed in a matter which is truly human', and with 'a joyful and ready will', these acts promote the mutual self-giving by which they enrich each other.[116] Significantly, Pope St Paul VI and then Pope St John Paul II later go on to interpret what is meant by 'truly human.'

While mutual faithfulness and the sacrament of matrimony keep love 'steadfastly true in body and in mind', certainly, the fathers are aware that in married life the days ahead may be 'bright' or 'dark.' Explicitly calling marriage, a 'Christian vocation', the fathers point out that fulfilling the duties of this vocation demands 'notable virtue', prayer, 'large heartedness' and 'the spirit of sacrifice.' Giving witness to faithfulness and harmony in their love, to their concern for their children, and the proper preparation of young people for the future, will bring about the needed 'cultural, psychological and social renewal' of marriage and the family.[117]

Having explored love and faithfulness, the fathers return to scripture categorically to repeat that 'marriage and conjugal love are by their nature ordained toward the begetting and educating of children.' Perhaps as an antidote to those who see children as burdens or simply ancillary to marriage, the fathers again observe that 'children are really the supreme gift of marriage and contribute very substantially to the welfare of their parents.' Moreover, the fathers explain the theological purpose of marriage: 'while not making the other purposes of matrimony of less account', the 'aim' or end of married love and 'the whole meaning' of family life, is co-operation with God who through the spouses enlarges and enriches God's own family.[118] This theological explanation can be found throughout the tradition but it is often buried in a rather biological account of marriage or exploded into a mistaken critique that Church teaching simply wants more Catholics in the pews.

As co-operators with God and 'in the sight of God', parents make the judgement about the size of their family, taking account of their own welfare, existing and future children, 'the material and the spiritual conditions of the times as well as of their state in life', but in consultation with others including the Church. They cannot proceed 'arbitrarily' but must be governed by 'a conscience dutifully conformed to the divine law itself', and 'submissive toward the Church's teaching office.' Where the marriage does not produce children, despite the desire of the couple, the marriage still maintains its 'value and indissolubility' because marriage 'is not instituted solely for procreation': its very nature is 'as an unbreakable compact between persons, and the welfare of the children', both of which require a growing mutual love.[119]

Again, looking to 'modern conditions' and experience, the fathers recognize that some couples may not feel in a position to increase the size of their families. The fathers acknowledge that a lack of intimacy may put pressure on relationships and there is the problem of recourse to 'dishonourable solutions.' However, the fathers are clear that there is no contradiction between divine laws regarding the transmission of life and those regarding authentic conjugal love. Among these 'dishonourable solutions' the fathers list abortion and infanticide as 'unspeakable crimes.' Moreover, since sex, conjugal love and procreation are not simply biological acts but are truly human acts, exercised 'in accord with genuine human dignity' they must be 'honoured with great reverence.' The moral aspects then of any procedure 'does not depend solely on sincere intentions or on an evaluation of motives, but must be determined by objective standards.' Keeping together the truly human act, mutual self-giving, human procreation 'in the context of true love', and the practice of the virtue of conjugal chastity, as well as the eternal destiny of every person, means that the faithful 'may not undertake methods of birth control which are found blameworthy by the teaching authority of the Church in its unfolding of the divine law.'[120]

Finally, the fathers point to the importance of the proper education of children. This goes beyond intellectual or emotional upbringing since the fathers recognize that 'the family is a kind of school of deeper humanity.' Responsibility belongs jointly to fathers and mothers and education includes inculcating in children an understanding of vocation and choice of state of life. The fathers envisage various generations to be involved in this task. Given the importance of the family for society, everyone notably public authorities, scientists and family associations and organizations, and priests are also encouraged to work for the welfare of the family.[121]

In this rich description of married life the fathers use the language of covenant and present a personal and relational account of marriage that is vocational and grounded in the call to holiness, a call that is a central feature of the Council as a whole. There is no explicit hierarchy of the ends of marriage, though by its very nature marriage is ordained for the procreation and education of children, and no indication of the subordination of the wife and children to the husband in the ordering of the household. Instead, the fathers stress the 'equal personal dignity of wife and husband, a dignity acknowledged by mutual and total love.'[122] The question of artificial birth control is touched upon, but Pope St John XXIII had reserved this to a special commission. Notably, the procreation of children is placed in the theological sphere as co-operation with God for the increase of God's kingdom.

It is interesting to observe that the fathers explicitly state that the Christian family has a particular role in the world, a point that becomes significant for Pope St John Paul II and for Pope Francis. Since the Christian family springs from 'marriage as a reflection of the loving covenant uniting Christ with the Church' the family can 'manifest to all men Christ's living presence in the world, and the genuine nature of the Church.' The three blessings of marriage, 'mutual love of the spouses', 'generous fruitfulness', and their 'solidarity and faithfulness', and in addition 'the loving way in which all members of the family assist one another' tell the world something about Christ and the Church.[123] Moreover, marriage is placed squarely in the Paschal Mystery: 'following Christ who is the principle of life, by the sacrifices and joys of their vocation and through their faithful love, married people can become witnesses of the mystery of love which the Lord revealed to the world by His dying and His rising up to life again.'[124]

Pope St Paul VI: marriage and reserved business

In 1963 Pope St John XXIII created a Pontifical Commission on Population, Family and Birth-rate to prepare for a conference sponsored by the United Nations and the World Health Organisation related to questions of population growth and control.[125] At the same time some Dutch bishops had claimed that 'birth regulation' was purely a matter for the conscience of the couple, and Schillebeeckx had argued that contraception was a 'moral obligation.'[126] In 1964 Pope St Paul VI asked for a confidential inquiry to be circulated among the world's bishops on what was becoming a challenging topic. According to G. Grisez, Pope St Paul VI and the bishops supported the teaching of *Casti Connubii.* However, one question up for debate was whether the birth control pill was a contraception, after all, according to some scientists the pills 'inhibit ovulation, are not sterilizing agents, and they respect the integrity of the marriage act.'[127] Notably the scientific evidence presented to the commission stated that there was no agreement on the way in which the pill was thought to work.[128] If the pill operated by inhibiting the fertilised egg from implanting then it would be an abortifacient. Another area of concern was the way in which the Church should approach governments and the UN on the issue of population growth and control.[129] Pope St Paul VI expanded the commission in 1964 and it included lay people and married couples. The issue for discussion was not the teaching of Pope Pius XI (that contraception is always gravely wrong), but rather the teaching of Pope Pius XII (who had rejected an earlier version of the pill).

The commission recognized that there was some urgency in responding to the question since there was 'a state of confusion' among pastors and the faithful.[130] Moreover, the commission accepted that among theologians the difference of opinion went beyond consideration of conjugal problems.[131] The question also touched upon the nature and methodology of moral theology, conscience, and tradition. However, the commission agreed that an initial document should address four main points so that the questions of 'methods' could be seen in a 'new light.' First, 'the idea of responsibility', especially of husband and wife, in the matter of procreation: 'responsibility' was taken to mean maturity, and any text on responsibility would be 'shielded from any suspicion that it was in favour of the limitation of births.' Moreover, the commission thought that 'the sense of responsibility' took on its 'fullest meaning in education concerning the primary end of marriage.'[132] Second, the place and importance of love in marriage: the commission recognized that love was a recent element, and more prevalent in Western cultures, and that the concept of love had various meanings. The commission further observed that the hierarchy of ends had been formulated for a specific purpose and was 'inadequate' for current thinking.[133] Third, the positive meaning of sexuality: notably, it was important to stress its 'human' character.[134] Fourth, the importance of education and proper preparation for a mature approach to marriage. The commission also acknowledged that the speed with which science was developing meant that a pronouncement on a particular 'method' may soon be outdated.[135] There was discussion and evidence presented on the rise in population rates as well governmental strategies to limit population, and it was noted that there was a general disinterest from developed countries in helping developing countries economically.[136] Going beyond the expected discussion, the question whether the pronouncements of Pope Pius XI and Pope Pius XII were irreformable was raised, and it was admitted that the question was 'far from clear.'[137] It seems that there was considerable debate on whether every contraceptive intervention was intrinsically evil, and this debate demonstrated a significant difference in approaches to moral theology. In effect, the commission was producing 'new thinking' that touched on nature, the principle of continuity on moral matters, interpretation of tradition and morality, and the role of the Magisterium in relation to conscience.[138]

The commission eventually produced a final report outlining all its discussions and including summaries of the views of groups of theologians who thought change was possible and those who opposed change. Part of the final report was leaked under the name of the 'Majority Report'; the theological summary opposing change was not a counterpart to the Majority Report, but was a summary of different views, nevertheless it was referred to as the 'Minority Report'.[139] Following *Gaudium et spes* the Majority Report states that 'marriage and conjugal love are by their nature ordained towards the begetting and education of children.' In contrast to a 'contraceptive mentality' that is egotistically opposed to fruitfulness and therefore to be condemned, responsible parenthood is practised over the course of a 'fruitful married life'; morality does not depend on the individual sexual acts of the couple.[140] In this method of moral thinking, overall intention rather than acts matter. According to one member of the commission, the Jesuit Father J. Ford who was not party to the Majority Report, the only point of agreement in the Majority Report was that contraception should be approved, and the Report gave a variety of conflicting theological and ethical opinions to support this.[141] Ford believed that the 'new morality...in which only love is recognized as an absolute requirement' was 'a key factor.' This new morality allows love to displace nature, does not regard grace as always efficacious, and emphasizes purely individual conscience.[142] From the point of view of J. Fuchs, party to the Majority Report and an advocate for proportionalism, given that all methods of contraception contain some evil, evil can be permitted for some proportionate good.[143] Far more than a question of contraception or even marriage, arguably the commission had exceeded its remit, and was really concerned with fundamental questions of ecclesiology and moral theology.

From Pope St Paul VI's viewpoint, the commission had raised far more problems than it solved, he recognized there was no agreement, and some approaches were at variance with the traditional moral doctrine on marriage.[144] Pope St Paul VI began his long awaited encyclical *Humanae vitae* with an outline of married love. The characteristic features of married love are that is 'fully human' and not merely a question of natural instinct or emotional drive; it is 'total' and a 'special form of personal friendship'; it is faithful and exclusive; and it goes beyond the love of the couple to bring about new life.[145] Responsible parenthood concerns the 'objective moral order which was established by God, and of which a right conscience is the true interpreter'; it does not depend solely on the choices of the couple.[146] Pope St Paul VI explains that the natural law, interpreted by 'constant doctrine' 'teaches that each and every marital act must of necessity retain its intrinsic relationship to the procreation of human life.' The 'inseparable connection' established by God between the unitive significance and procreative significance of the marriage act, both of which are inherent in the act, cannot be broken.[147] To emphasize this connection Pope St Paul VI says that just as imposing the sexual act on a person is 'no true act of love' and a moral offence, so too is impairing the capacity to transmit life. Spouses cannot deprive their acts of marital love which is a 'divine gift' of its meaning and purpose. Human beings do not have 'unlimited dominion' over their bodies but are 'ministers' of God's design.[148] Taking advantage of natural times of infertility in a woman's cycle to control birth as long as children are not totally excluded from the marriage is different to acts of direct contraception since the first respects the natural order of creation whereas the second deliberately frustrates the natural order.[149] Pope St Paul VI explicitly rejects the argument from 'totality' that the Majority Report had favoured, that individual acts do not have relevance but merge into the moral goodness of past and future acts. He then distinguishes the idea of tolerating the lesser evil from the principle that 'it is never lawful, even for the gravest reasons, to do evil that good may come of it.'[150] The Majority Report accepted that contraception was evil yet had allowed that evil could be done for a greater good. While the Majority Report appealed to the Second Vatican Council's spirit of dialogue and to the complexity of modern life to call for change, Pope St Paul VI acknowledges that the Church is destined to be 'a sign of contradiction', and 'cannot declare lawful what is in fact unlawful.'[151]

Covenant to the Code of Canon Law 1983

As Pope St John Paul II explained on the promulgation of the 1983 Code of Canon Law, Pope St John XXIII first proposed the reform and renewal of the 1917 Code of Canon Law and his decision was supported by the fathers at the Second Vatican Council. Pope St John XXIII's decision came out of his awareness of the 'signs of the times' both in terms of the sweeping changes and shifts in the world that had impact externally on the Church, which is also in the world, and other unnamed 'progressive internal factors.' Since the revised Code built upon the previous work of the Council, the revision began after the Council had closed. The process was lengthy not least because it was carried out in the 'collegial spirit' advocated by the Council.

According to Pope St John Paul II, the purpose of the Code is to create order in individual and social life, and in the activity of the Church so that faith, grace, and charisms, which are primary to the law, can develop more easily. As a fruit of the work of the Council, the 'novelty' of the Council is replicated in the 'novelty' of the Code, and the norms were reformed to accommodate 'a new mentality and new needs.' Notable elements are the presentation of the Church as the People of God; authority as 'service'; the Church as a 'communion'; the threefold office of the People of God as priest, prophet and king; commitment to ecumenism; and the duties and rights of the faithful, especially the laity. To foster 'the pastoral care of souls as much as possible', 'charity, temperance, humaneness and moderation' are pre-eminent. Some 'unduly rigid norms' were replaced with exhortation; subsidiarity, human rights and dignity also figure.[152]

The 1917 Code of Canon Law did not offer a definition of marriage. However, it did state the sacramental nature of the marriage contract. In contrast, the 1983 Code very much followed *Gaudium et spes* in presenting the nature of marriage as:

> the matrimonial covenant, by which a man and a woman establish between themselves a partnership of the whole of life and which is ordered by its nature to the good of the spouses and the procreation and education of offspring, has been raised by Christ the Lord to the dignity of a sacrament between the baptized.[153]

Notably there is no hierarchical ordering of the ends of marriage. Rather, like the presentation in *Gaudium et spes* the ends are 'embedded' in the nature of marriage and are objective in the sense that they do not depend on the intention of the spouses.[154] The

Code continues, 'for this reason, a valid matrimonial contract cannot exist between the baptized without it being by that fact a sacrament.'[155] As the canonist J. Beal notes, this causes problems for people who have been called 'baptized non-believers': since they do not have faith, they cannot enter a sacramental marriage; but since they are baptized their marriage, if valid, is a sacrament.[156]

The 1983 Code describes the 'essential properties' of marriage as 'unity and indissolubility, which in Christian marriage obtain special firmness by reason of the sacrament.'[157] As with the ends of marriage, these essential properties are independent of the intention of the spouses. Beal explains that these properties are 'not goals external to marriage but qualities inherent in the institution of marriage itself.' Unity refers to the exclusive relationship between husband and wife and as Beal points out, post-conciliar reflection has allowed for the possibility that unity is violated by, for instance, an unhealthily close emotional relationship of one of the spouses on his or her parent. Indissolubility refers to the perpetual nature of the marriage relationship that not only should not be terminated but cannot be terminated. A valid marriage, whether or not the parties are baptized, is intrinsically indissoluble even if the parties subsequently withdraw their consent.[158]

Following the tradition, 'the consent of the parties, legitimately manifested between persons qualified by law, makes marriage: no human power is able to supply this consent.'[159] Beal notes that the indispensable nature of consent as the moment when marriage is constituted poses problems in cultures where marriage comes about through progressive stages.[160] Like the 1917 Code, in the revised Code matrimonial consent is 'an act of the will.' Whereas the 1917 Code spoke about the will of 'each party', the 1983 Code takes a more personal approach by referring to consent as an act of the will exchanged between 'a man and a woman.' Beal argues that this change was not intended to respond to same sex unions and he adds that nevertheless 'the new wording does suggest that an exchange of consent between persons of the same sex is not truly "marital", and does not, therefore, give rise even to the semblance of marriage.'[161] If consent establishes marriage, for Beal, given the emphasis in *Gaudium et spes* on conjugal love, one question remains: 'whether love is an essential dimension of matrimonial consent.'[162]

Summary

The language of contract has featured in the story of marriage from its beginnings in ancient custom and law as an obvious extension of the requirement of consent and mutual agreement between two people or, looking into the past, two families. However, the scriptural foundations of marriage as God's gift to humanity remind us that marriage is more deeply a covenant between two people, and a covenant between the couple and Christ, and between the couple and the Church, where the couple form a personal community. This personal community is ordained towards a community of persons: children. Embedded in the nature of marriage are certain ends and characteristics. Since these belong to the very fabric of marriage, they are independent of the intention of the spouses. Marriage has a public character and in Christian terms it is a way of living out Christian life in the world. As such couples have a vocation not only within marriage but also for the world: 'the family constitutes, much more than a mere juridical, social and economic unit, a community of love and solidarity, which is uniquely suited to teach and transmit cultural, ethical, social, spiritual and religious values, essential for the development and well-being of its own members and of society.'[163]

According to Pope St John Paul II 'the family is the first and most important' way of the Church.[164] Moreover, he says:

> the history of mankind, the history of salvation, passes by way of the family…the family is placed at the centre of the great struggle between good and evil, between life and death, between love and all that is opposed to love. To the family is entrusted the task of striving, first and

foremost, *to unleash the forces of good,* the source of which is found in Christ the Redeemer of man.[165]

He urges, 'family, become what you are.'[166] Given that through the debates over contraception, the family and marriage became the focus of the struggle for the future of the church in terms of ecclesiology and moral theology, the family may indeed be the way of the Church in more ways than one. It also touches on the *sensus fidei* and the sense God's faithful people have for the truths of the Gospel. This struggle has continued to be played out in the Apostolic Exhortations of both Pope St John Paul II and Pope Francis that responded to the deliberations of synods of bishops on the family.

Notes

[1] C. Sheldon, *In His Steps. What Would Jesus Do?* (Grand Rapids: Revell 1984), Ch 2, pp. 26–27.
[2] J. Fletcher, *Situation Ethics: The New Morality* (Louisville: Westminster John Knox Press, 1966), p. 55.
[3] Pope St John Paul II, *Fides et Ratio*.
[4] *Ibid.*, 5.
[5] *Ibid.*, 4.
[6] C. Rosen, *Preaching Eugenics: Religious Leaders and the American Eugenics Movement* (Oxford: Oxford University Press, 2004), p. 25.
[7] C. Evans, *The Social Gospel in American Religion: A History* (New York: New York University, Press 2017), p. 22.
[8] Rosen, *Preaching Eugenics*, p. 26.
[9] P. Levine, A. Bashford, 'Introduction: Eugenics and the Modern World', in *The Oxford Handbook of the History of Eugenics* (Oxford: Oxford University Press, 2010), p. 3.
[10] *Ibid.*, p. 5.
[11] See *Report of Proceedings of the First International Eugenics Congress London 24th July to 30th July 1912*, vols. 1 & 2 (The Eugenics Education Society: London 1912–1913).
[12] *Ibid.*
[13] Levine and Bashford, 'Introduction: Eugenics and the Modern World', p. 9.
[14] *Ibid.*, pp. 17–18.
[15] M. Sanger, *Birth Control Advances: A Reply to the Pope* 1931.

16. *The Lambeth Conference Resolutions Archive From 1930* Resolution 15.
17. M. Sanger, *The Pivot of Civilisation In Historical Perspective* (Seattle: Inkling Books 2001), pp. 388; 394.
18. Pope Pius XI, *Casti connubii*, 1.
19. *Ibid.*, 5.
20. *Ibid.*, 6.
21. *Ibid.*, 7.
22. *Ibid.*, 8.
23. *Ibid.*, 17.
24. *Ibid.*, 10–11.
25. *Ibid.*, 80.
26. *Ibid.*, 12–18.
27. *Ibid.*, 72.
28. *Ibid.*, 19–22.
29. *Ibid.*, 78.
30. *Ibid.*, 19–25.
31. *Ibid.*, 30.
32. *Ibid.*, 26.
33. *Ibid.*, 74–77.
34. *Ibid.*, 26–29.
35. *Ibid.*, 31–37.
36. *Ibid.*, 39–41.
37. *Ibid.*, 80.
38. *Ibid.*, 85–86.
39. *Ibid.*, 45–47.
40. *Ibid.*, 49.
41. *Ibid.*, 50–51.
42. *Ibid.*, 53–56.
43. *Ibid.*, 58; 64–67.
44. *Ibid.*, 68–71.
45. *Ibid.*, 59–62.
46. *Ibid.*, 61–62.
47. *Ibid.*, 100–101.
48. *Ibid.*, 108.
49. *Ibid.*, 112–115.
50. *Ibid.*, 111.
51. See for instance K. Schemenauer, *Conjugal Love and Procreation: Dietrich von Hildebrand's Superabundant Integration* (Maryland: Lexington, 2011), p. xii.

52. E. Mounier, *Existentialist Philosophies, An Introduction* (London: Rockliff 1948), pp. 72–75.
53. E. Mounier, *Personalism* [1949] (Notre Dame: Notre Dame University Press, 1970), Informal Introduction to the Personal Universe.
54. *Ibid.*, IV.
55. P. Matthews, *Discerning Persons: Profound Disability, the Early Church Fathers and the Concept of the Person in Bioethics* (Steubenville OH: Franciscan Press, 2020), pp. 251–256.
56. Boethius, 'Against Eutyches and Nestorius' in *A Treatise Against Eutyches and Nestorius. Tractes, The Consolation of Philosophy* (Cambridge Massachusetts: Harvard University Press, 1997), II.
57. D. von Hildebrand, *Marriage: The Mystery of Faithful Love* [1929] (Manchester New Hampshire: Sophia Institute, 1984), p. xv.
58. *Ibid.*, pp. xxvi-xxvii.
59. *Ibid.*, p. xxv.
60. *Ibid.*, p. 23.
61. *Ibid.*, p. xxvi.
62. D. von Hildebrand, *In Defense of Purity: An Analysis of the Catholic Ideals of Purity and Virginity* (Eugene Oregon: Wipf and Stock, 1962), p. 8.
63. Hildebrand, *Marriage*, pp. 7–9.
64. *Ibid.*, pp. 10–11.
65. *Ibid.*, p. 12.
66. *Ibid.*, pp. 17–18.
67. *Ibid.*, p. 19.
68. *Ibid.*, pp. 13–15.
69. *Ibid.*, p. 15.
70. *Ibid.*, pp. 21–22.
71. *Ibid.*, p. 25.
72. *Ibid.*, p. 7.
73. *Ibid.*, pp. 26–27.
74. *Ibid.*, pp. 29–30.
75. *Ibid.*, pp. 32, 22.
76. Hildebrand, *In Defense of Purity*, pp. 7–10.
77. Hildebrand, *Marriage*, pp. 32–37.
78. Schemenauer, *Conjugal Love and Procreation*, pp. 1–42.
79. *Ibid.*, p. 46.
80. *Ibid.*, p. xiii.
81. H. Doms, *The Meaning of Marriage* (New York: Sheed and Ward, 1939), pp. 87–88. It seems that the English translator omitted one chapter of Doms' original German text and reduced the title.

82   *Ibid.*, pp. 77–78.
83   *Ibid.*, pp. 85, 95.
84   *Ibid.*, pp. 76–78.
85   J. Noonan, *Contraception: A History of its Treatment by the Catholic Theologians and Canonists* (Cambridge Massachusetts: Harvard University Press, 1986), p. 498.
86   Holy Office, Decree, 1 April 1944.
87   Pope Pius XII, *To the Court of the Sacred Roman Rota* (3 October 1941); Pope Pius XII, *To the Medical-Biological Union San Luca* (12 November 1944).
88   Pope Pius XII, *At the Court of the Holy Roman Rota* (6 October 1946).
89   Pope Pius XII, *Christmas Radio Message* (24 December 1941).
90   Pope Pius XII, *To the Members of the Pontifical Academy of Science* (8 February 1948).
91   Pope Pius XII, *Christmas Radio Message* (24 December 1953).
92   Pope Pius XII, *To Participants in the VIII Congress of the World Medical Association* (30 September 1954) note 3.
93   Pope Pius XII, *To the Medical-Biological Union San Luca*.
94   Pope Pius XII, *To the Catholic Doctors Convened in Rome for their Fourth International Congress* (29 September 1949).
95   Pope Pius XII, *To the Participants in the Congress of the Italian Catholic Union of Obstetrics* (29 October 1951).
96   Pope Pius XII, *To Participants in the First International Symposium on Genetic Medicine* (7 September 1953).
97   Pope Pius XII, *Radio Message on the Occasion of the Family Day* (23 March 1952).
98   Fletcher, *Situation Ethics*, p. 42.
99   J. Fletcher, 'Technical Devices in Medical Care' in *On Moral Medicine: Theological Perspectives in Medical Ethics* [1970] (Grand Rapids: Eerdmans, 1998), p. 279.
100 *Ibid.*, pp. 281–282.
101 J. Fletcher, *Morals and Medicine* (Princeton: Princeton University Press 1954), p. 117.
102 Pope Pius XII, *To the Participants in the Congress of the Italian Catholic Union of Obstetrics*.
103 Pope Pius XII, *To the Participants in the Second World Congress on Fertility and Sterility* (19 May 1956).
104 Pope St John XXIII, *To the Members of the Court of the Sacred Roman Rota* (13 December 1961).
105 Pope St John XXIII, *To Participants in the First European Meeting of Youth*

(2 September 1962).
[106] Second Vatican Council, *Lumen Gentium*, 11.
[107] *Ibid.*, 34.
[108] *Ibid.*, 35.
[109] Second Vatican Council, *Gravissimum Educationis*, 3.
[110] Second Vatican Council, *Apostolicam Actuositatem*, 11.
[111] Second Vatican Council, *Gaudium et spes*, 3.
[112] *Ibid.*, 46.
[113] *Ibid.*, 47.
[114] *Ibid.*, 48.
[115] *Ibid.*, 48.
[116] *Ibid.*, 49.
[117] *Ibid.*, 49.
[118] *Ibid.*, 50.
[119] *Ibid.*, 50.
[120] *Ibid.*, 51.
[121] *Ibid.*, 51.
[122] *Ibid.*, 49.
[123] *Ibid.*, 48.
[124] *Ibid.*, 51.
[125] The background to the setting up of the Commission is from a short biography of Father J. Ford, written by G. Grisez. Father Ford had helped with the consultation of US bishops and was appointed to the commission.
[126] R. B. Kaiser, *The Encyclical That Never Was, The Story of the Pontifical Commission on Population, Family and Birth, 1964–1966* (London: Sheed and Ward 1985), pp. 41, 55.
[127] *Report on the fourth session of the Commission to study the problems of population, family and birth-rate* 25–28 March 1965, p. 13. This has been published by Grisez with an explanation of its source.
[128] *Report on the fourth session of the Commission*, p. 28; Kaiser, *The Encyclical That Never Was*, p. 68.
[129] Kaiser, *The Encyclical That Never Was*, p. 73.
[130] *Report on the fourth session of the Commission*, p. 6.
[131] *Ibid.*, p. 45.
[132] *Ibid.*, pp. 7–8.
[133] *Ibid.*, p. 9.
[134] *Ibid.*, p. 10.
[135] *Ibid.*, p. 14.
[136] *Ibid.*, pp. 17–23.
[137] *Ibid.*, pp. 14–16.

[138] Kaiser, *The Encyclical That Never Was*, pp. 136–137.
[139] http://www.twotlj.org/BCCommission.html.
[140] Final Report of the Pontifical Commission on Population, Kaiser, *The Encyclical That Never Was*, p. 9.
[141] J. Ford, *Memorandum* 4 July 1966.
[142] *Ibid.*, pp. 17–18.
[143] B. Hoose, *Proportionalism* (Georgetown: Georgetown University Press, 1987), pp. 35, 39 footnote 45.
[144] Pope St Paul VI, *Humanae Vitae*, 6.
[145] *Ibid.*, 9.
[146] *Ibid.*, 10.
[147] *Ibid.*, 11–12.
[148] *Ibid.*, 13.
[149] *Ibid.*, 16.
[150] *Ibid.*, 14.
[151] Final Report of the Pontifical Commission on Population, Kaiser, *The Encyclical That Never Was*, p. 4; Pope St Paul VI, *Humanae vitae*, 18.
[152] Pope St John Paul II, Apostolic Constitution *Sacrae Disciplinae Leges*.
[153] Code of Canon Law 1983 Canon 1055, 1.
[154] J. Beal, 'Title VII Marriage', in *New Commentary on the Code of Canon Law* (New York: Paulist Press 2000), pp. 1243.
[155] Canon 1055, 2.
[156] Beal, *New Commentary on the Code of Canon Law*, 1248–1249.
[157] Canon 1056.
[158] Beal, *New Commentary on the Code of Canon Law*, 1249.
[159] Canon 1057, 1.
[160] Beal, *New Commentary on the Code of Canon Law*, 1251.
[161] *Ibid.*
[162] For Beal's discussion on this question see *New Commentary on the Code of Canon Law*, 1252–1253.
[163] *Charter of the Rights of the Family*, 1983, Preamble.
[164] Pope St John Paul II, *Gratissimam Sane Letter to Families*, 2.
[165] *Ibid.*, 23.
[166] Pope St John Paul II, *Familiaris Consortio*, 17.

7 GETTING TOGETHER: THE 1980 SYNOD AND FAMILIARIS CONSORTIO

THE DISCIPLES OF Jesus were known as the men and women who belonged 'to the way':[1] Jesus being the Way, the Truth and the Life.[2] Perhaps a good image here is of the two disciples who meet Jesus on the way to Emmaus.[3] Jesus walks by their side, he listens to them, and then explains everything. The image of the road to Emmaus is useful for the synod process, after all synod comes from the Greek *syn hodos* referring to together and road, on the path together. The Emmaus image is also important for a process that has become essential for the Church: the process of accompaniment. If the disciples had walked in front of Jesus or behind him, they would not have heard what he had to say. Accompanying someone is walking alongside them. St John Chrysostom sees Church as a 'name standing for walking together.'[4] Synodality is a way of being Church. The 1980 Fifth General Synod of Bishops on *The Role of the Christian Family in Today's World* and the resulting exhortation of Pope St John Paul II, *Familiaris Consortio,* are significant milestones in the teaching of the Church on marriage and the family.

Synods and synodality

During the Second Vatican Council it was clear that the involvement of the bishops, meeting and 'walking' together, was invaluable and Pope St Paul VI decided to continue this formally. As the Council ended, he instituted the Synod of bishops a 'permanent Council of Bishops for the universal Church', directly and immediately subject to the power of the pope, with the remit of 'providing information and offering advice.' The synod also has the power to make decisions subject to ratification by the pope.[5] The synod then is a means of promoting close relations between the pope and the bishops, and between the bishops themselves. However, whether the synod is an advisory body that assists the pope in his ministry or something more remains ambiguous.[6] Synodality is still in the process of being worked out. Of course, there is already confusion with *syn hodos* as this may refer to a meeting point on the path or a continuing journey. Nevertheless, as the idea of synodality matured from the heart of the Second Vatican Council, it has come to be associated with the involvement and participation of the bishops gathered in unity *cum Petro et sub Petro*, with Peter and under Peter,[7] and of 'the whole People of God in the life and mission of the Church' and is based on the *sensus fidei fidelium*, the sense of the faith of the faithful.[8]

Indeed, consulting the faithful is not new.[9] A helpful way of looking at the sense of the faith of the faithful in the ministry of the Church can be found in the work of the nineteenth century theologian St John Henry Newman (1801–1890). Newman explained that Christianity exercises three indivisible functions, prophet, priest and king. He also identified the three elements of the pastor and flock in worship; theology and schools of learning; the governing of pope and curia. He adds, 'in man as he is, reasoning tends to rationalism; devotion to superstition and enthusiasm; and power to ambition and tyranny.'[10] Theologians can become too rigid and intellectual in their own beliefs, the hierarchy too concerned with power and control, the laity too prone to follow uninformed opinion. When the prophetic, priestly, and kingly functions are indivisible, there may not be total agreement, but there will be a fruitful dynamic.[11] Newman is often cited for his celebrated toast 'to Conscience first, and to the Pope afterwards.' Certainly, Newman had 'an exalted view' of conscience. Nevertheless, he also recognized that our sense of right and wrong is easily obscured by pride, passion, and level of education: conscience is at once 'the highest of all teachers, yet the least luminous.'[12]

Keeping together the concepts of priest, prophet and king, the International Theological Commission describes the principle of synodality as 'the action of the Spirit in the communion of the Body of Christ and in the missionary journey of the People of God.'[13] On this journey Christians are 'pilgrims and strangers in the world, honoured with the gift and responsibility of proclaiming to all the Gospel of the Kingdom'[14]: the Church is in the world but not of it, and at times will be a 'sign of contradiction'. There remains much still to be done to develop the understanding of synodality,[15] but the process has begun, notably with the synods on the family called by Pope St John Paul II in 1980 and by Pope Francis in 2014 and 2015.

The synod process begins with the choice of the topic from a number of suggestions made by the bishops from the previous synod. A preparatory document, a *lineamenta* is drawn up and circulated worldwide to bishops's conferences inviting comment and recommendations. In preparation for more recent synods questionnaires have been organised for the laity. A working document, *instrumentum laboris* is then produced and sent out to the participants to form the basis for the debates. This working document is precisely a working document and issues can be raised and added, changed or excluded as the synod progresses. The actual synods are closed to the press to ensure that there can be a frank and challenging discussion though the press receive summaries and inevitably sensationalism, hype and speculation happen outside the synod. At the synod each bishop has the opportunity to make an intervention, a short address to the other participants, in the synod hall. The participants also meet in small groups, *circuli minores*, organised according to language, so that they can listen, discuss, and make additional proposals or amendments. The proposals are then sent to a drafting commission who formulate a draft report. This report is presented to the synod as a whole and bishops are able to make further interventions or proposals and the draft is revised where necessary. The final report is read out and the bishops vote on each of the paragraphs. A clear majority is required for a paragraph to stand. The final report or set of propositions is offered to the pope as the workings of the participants. Certainly, the process has not been without its critics. Commenting on the workings of the 1980 Fifth General Synod on the Role of the Christian Family in Today's World, J. Grootaers and J. Selling complained that the procedure to formulate the propositions presented to Pope St John Paul II lacked transparency, did not fully reflect the suggestions of the bishops, and the final text may have been manipulated by those in charge of the synod.[16] Exactly the same charge was brought by different people in relation to the final report presented to Pope Francis at the conclusion of the 2015 synod on the family.[17]

From the outset it is important to remember that the synodal process is not conciliarism, a movement holding that supreme authority lay with an ecumenical council apart from and even against the pope. Nor is it a form of parliamentarianism.[18] Instead, the people who take part are called; they are:

> responding to the summons of the Lord, listening as a community to what the Spirit is saying to the Church through the Word of God which resonates in their situation, and interpreting the signs of the times with the eyes of faith.[19]

The synod process gives bishops the opportunity to learn from each other, to discover what lies beyond their own cultures, to gain a different perspective on questions, to come together as a universal church of many yet one.

1980 Fifth General Synod of Bishops: the role of the Christian family in today's world

Over two hundred bishops from over ninety countries participated in the Fifth General Synod; there were some forty-three lay auditors including doctors and married couples, and members of religious orders, including Mother Teresa. The interventions from the bishops reflected their particular concerns with some from the developed world raising the issue of contraception and citing statistics on the number of Catholics using contraceptives, some from the developing world concerned about government strategies to impose limits on family size and to make birth control a requisite for foreign aid, some noting the prevalence of polygamy in their countries, mixed marriages, and the cultural practice where marriage happens in stages, and some observing that poverty is the root cause of problems in families.[20] The prominent issues were separation, divorce and remarriage as well as pastoral inadequacies in dealing with difficult questions. The English Archbishop B. Hume raised the point that married people were the best theological source or *fons theologica*, 'first, because they are the ministers of the sacrament of matrimony and, second, because they alone have experienced the effects of this sacrament', and he observed that good conscientious people felt unable to accept 'that the use of artificial means of contraception in some circumstances is *intrinsice inhonestum*, as this latter has generally been understood.'[21] Inevitably, perhaps, Pope St Paul VI's encyclical *Humanae Vitae* was raised at almost every press conference,[22] and there was dissatisfaction from some interest groups that questions to do with homosexuality and the demographic question were ignored.

At the end of the synod the bishops presented Pope St John Paul II, who had been present throughout, with a list of agreed propositions that summed up their deliberations and that could be further developed.[23] The forty-three propositions included a theological and anthropological foundation for the sacrament of marriage, and the expected topics of indissolubility and divorce, women and the family, mixed marriages, the role of the family in transmitting and safeguarding human life, marriage in special circumstances, extra-marital relations, marriage preparation and spirituality. Notably, the bishops thought that the need to develop a positive theology of human sexuality was a pressing concern.

Moreover, they recognized the need for compassion and a healing mission where marriages had failed.

Significantly, the bishops began by presenting a proposition on the *sensus fidei*. By a large majority the bishops affirmed the prophetic nature of the witness of the *sensus fidei* which is, they said, the 'fruit of a living faith.' The bishops accepted the importance of opinion polls and statistics to help in the investigation of the truth, even if the *sensus fidei* is not the result of these statistics. However, they also agreed that 'this "supernatural appreciation of the faith" *sensus fidei* is not just a consensus of all Christians. The Church is not subject to majority rule. Christ's disciples seek truth not number.'[24]

Before the final vote and presentation to Pope St John Paul II, proposition 24 was revised. According to the initial proposition:

> the Synod of Bishops cannot ignore the difficult and painful situation of many Christian couples who, despite their sincere goodwill and because of their weakness or objective difficulty, are (*sunt*) unable to fulfil the moral norms of the church. In the pastoral treatment of the married, pastors should hold fast to the law of gradualness.

The verb *sunt* was changed to *sentient*, so that the proposition read 'feel (*sentiunt*) unable to obey the moral norms of the church.' The General Rapporteur, Cardinal J. Ratzinger, who prepared the amendments and final document, explained that this change was in response to the Latin language group who were concerned about overtones of Jansenism, that some of God's commandments are impossible for the just person to fulfil. It was left to Pope St John Paul II to clarify that the 'law of gradualness', that pastors start with people where they actually are, does not mean there are gradations in the law.

Following the usual progression of the synodal process, the bishops invited the Pope to write an exhortation on the role of the Christian family and to develop a bill of rights of the family to be presented to the United Nations.

Familiaris Consortio: On the role of the Christian family in the modern world.

The first words of Pope St John Paul II's exhortation, *Familiaris Consortio*, the fellowship of the family reflects perhaps the Pope's perennial concern with solidarity and a sense of what he terms 'brotherhood', the common supportive relationship people have with each other. As Pope St John Paul II was later to say to young people, 'the world you are inheriting is a world which desperately needs a new sense of brotherhood and human solidarity. It is a world which needs to be touched and healed by the beauty and richness of God's love.'[25] For Pope St John Paul II the family is the place where we first encounter this brotherhood. During the synod Ratzinger had commented on two contrasting approaches, an inductive method based on the experience of married people, and a deductive method based on theoretical principles. Certainly, there are elements of both methods to varying degrees in *Familiaris Consortio.* Nevertheless, as Pope St John Paul II pointed out, when as Father Karol Wojtyła he taught at Lublin University, the theology of the family 'must be pastoral throughout because revelation as the source of theology and of the magisterium of the Church ... is pastoral throughout.' He added that although theological theory, 'vision', of the family is pastoral in one way theological practice in another way, practice has its 'grounds and roots' in the vision.[26]

Pope St John Paul II begins his exhortation with a reminder of the 'precious value' of marriage and the family, and that the Church is 'at the service' of the family.[27] Starting from the real experience of married life in Part One of his exhortation Pope St John Paul II looks at the 'bright spots and shadows for the family today' in order to understand the situation, though Pope St John Paul II also notes that apparently appealing solutions 'obscure in varying degrees the truth and dignity of the human person.'[28] Following the synod,[29] he considers the 'situation' in terms of discernment and the *sensus fidei*, noting that this is not simply a matter of statistics or a consensus of the faithful. However, in perhaps a nod to Archbishop Hume, Pope St John Paul II observes that Christian spouses and parents 'can and should offer their unique and irreplaceable contribution' to this discernment: 'they are qualified for this role by their charism or specific gift, the gift of the sacrament of matrimony.'[30] The bright positive aspects of marriage include personal freedom and the quality of interpersonal relationships. But there is also a host of shadows, negative aspects from divorces, civil unions, abortions, sterilizations and a contraceptive mentality to the view of freedom as the autonomous power of self-affirmation, consumerism and a general sense of uncertainty of the future.[31] Pope St John Paul II thinks that it is vital to form a 'new culture' and a 'new humanism' that takes account of experience and also science and technology. In forming this culture there is a need to recover an awareness of 'primary moral values' which are 'values of the person.'[32] Pope St John Paul II calls for a 'continuous, permanent conversion' and an 'educational growth process' to bring people back to a richer understanding of the mystery of marriage and family life.[33]

Pope St John Paul II recognizes the part played by insights from the Christian tradition in informing this new culture, and in Part Two of the exhortation he explores the plan of God for marriage and the family. Following the request from the synod he outlines the anthropological and theological foundations of marriage.[34] Pope St John Paul II begins by picking up the scriptural themes linking marriage to salvation history: the image of God who is love, the covenant between God and His people, and Jesus the bridegroom. Returning to the beginning and human beings made in the image and likeness of God, Pope St John Paul II says that, as love, God in himself 'lives in the mystery of a personal loving communion.' Made in God's image, love and communion are the human being's fundamental vocation, inscribed in our humanity, and 'love includes the human body.'[35] Appealing to revelation, Pope St John Paul II understands that there are two specific ways of realizing the vocation of the human person to love: the vocation to marriage and virginity or celibacy.

While Pope St John Paul II is principally concerned with marriage and family, celibacy was also raised at the synod.[36] Pope St John Paul II thinks that celibacy or virginity 'for the sake of the kingdom' presuppose and confirm the dignity of marriage. As he explains, 'marriage and celibacy are two ways of expressing the living mystery of the covenant of God with his people.' In stressing the complementarity though not equality of marriage and celibacy, Pope St John Paul II addresses the traditional problem of those who esteem celibacy to the point of negating marriage. Pope St John Paul II observes that when marriage is denigrated or sexuality not valued then celibacy, as the renunciation of these goods, also loses its meaning. Celibacy is in the tradition superior to marriage because the person who is celibate for the sake of the kingdom points the way to the kingdom as 'the only definitive value' and anticipates in his or her flesh the 'new world of the future resurrection.' Pope St John Paul II notes that celibacy too requires the commitment to fidelity, and he sees that celibacy liberates the heart 'in a unique way' both for a deep love of God and spiritual fruitfulness as the spiritual father or mother of many.[37]

According to Pope St John Paul II sexuality is 'not just biological but concerns the innermost being of the person', and therefore relevant to both the married and celibate. Human beings are sexual beings. In marriage sexuality is realized in a 'truly human way' by 'total personal self-giving', which in the marriage relationship involves the commitment to fidelity and 'responsible fertility.'[38] Fidelity is further reflected in the way in which the bond of love in marriage becomes the 'image and symbol' of God's covenant with his people.[39]

Moving to an exploration of marriage as a sacrament, in an echo of the Second Vatican Council's call to root all the sacraments in the Paschal Mystery and to show more clearly the grace of the sacrament,[40] Pope St John Paul II explains that 'like each of the seven sacraments, so also is marriage a real symbol of the event of salvation, but in its own way.' Since the 'definitive fullness' of the gift of love is found in Jesus and in his sacrifice on the Cross, marriage between baptized persons becomes 'a real symbol of that new and eternal covenant sanctioned in the blood of Christ.' The 'intimate community of conjugal life and love', and the 'profoundly indissoluble manner' in which the spouses belong to each other is the 'real representation, by means of the sacramental sign, of the very relationship of Christ with the Church.' Grace helps them put the demands of love into action. Notably, in terms of what is possible, according to Pope St John Paul II 'the Spirit....renders man and woman capable of loving one another as Christ has loved us.' Moreover, the indissoluble marriage relationship is prophetic as it bears witness to the hope of the future encounter with Christ.[41]

Invoking traditional sacramental theology, Pope St John Paul II notes that the *res et sacramentum*, the sacramental reality, and first immediate effect of marriage is the Christian conjugal bond. This 'communion of two persons' 'represents the mystery of Christ's incarnation and the mystery of His covenant.' Thus, the 'normal' characteristics of marriage of total love, and deep personal unity of one flesh, heart and soul, that demand indissolubility, faithfulness, mutual giving and openness to fertility, are endowed with a 'new significance.'[42]

For Pope St John Paul II the bond of love between the spouses is a gift that does not end with the couple. Repeating *Gaudium et spes*, according to God's plan marriage is ordained to procreation and the education of children. Love makes the couple capable of the 'greatest possible gift', becoming co-operators with God in giving life to a 'new person.' Pope St John Paul II sees parental love as a matter of evangelization and a real witness to God's love. He explains that 'parental love is called to become for the children the visible sign of the very love of God', noting that conjugal love does not lose its value even when children are not possible for the couple.[43]

The family as 'a communion of persons' is an important concept for Pope St John Paul II. The family not only introduces each new person into interpersonal relationships and into solidarity and brotherhood, it also brings the new person to another family, 'the great family of the Church'. Certainly, 'Christian marriage and the Christian family build up the Church.' But the relationship of the Christian family and Church is mutual, for as the family is the 'cradle' and 'setting' for each new person, the family is also redeemed in the Church.[44]

Having set out the theological character of marriage in Part Three Pope St John Paul II turns to the role of the Christian family as he urges families to 'become what you are.' To know its mission, Christians need to know what marriage is and to rediscover the truth about the nature of the family, Pope St John Paul II returns to God's plan. As an 'intimate community of life and love' the role of the family is to 'become more and more what it is', to ever deepen that community, 'to guard, reveal and communicate love.' Significantly, 'this is a living reflection of and a real sharing in God's love for humanity and the love of Christ the Lord for the Church His bride.' Following the synod,[45] Pope St John Paul II identifies four tasks for the family: forming a community of persons; serving life; participating in the development of society; and sharing in the life and mission of Church.[46] Love, fidelity and self-gift ground the community of persons. Pope St John Paul II does not forget the bodily aspect of marriage, stating that the conjugal communion, 'the sign of a profoundly human need', 'sinks its roots in the natural complementarity' of man and woman. The nurturing of this communion is, moreover, a life-long project, made perfect in the sacrament of marriage. However, this project is not simply the work of the spouses. The continual deepening of the unity of husband and wife in all aspects of life, reveals to the Church and the world the Spirit's gift of a 'new communion of love.'

Pope St John Paul II points out that polygamy is a contradiction to the unity and total fidelity of husband and wife, and indissolubility is a sign of this communion. Strongly reaffirming the indissoluble nature of marriage that is rooted in 'the total self-giving of the couple' and that is required by the good of children, Pope St John Paul II further locates indissolubility in the love God has for human beings, and the love Jesus has for the Church. In the sacrament a 'new heart' is given so that the couple can share in these loves of God and Christ. Commenting on this task, Pope St John Paul II adds, 'to bear witness to the inestimable value of the indissolubility and fidelity of marriage is one of the most precious and most urgent tasks of Christian couples in our time.' Pope St John Paul II recognizes that at times this witness requires courage, especially when a spouse has been abandoned.[47]

The constant link that Pope St John Paul II makes between marriage and the love Jesus has for the Church as expressed in Ephesians 5 allows him to reflect on the idea of marriage as 'domestic church', an idea amplified in the Second Vatican documents *Lumen Gentium* 11 and *Apostolicam Actuositatem* 11. As a 'natural and human communion' the family itself broadens out to the wider community of other relatives.[48] This 'natural family attitude' begins what Pope St John Paul II later calls 'solidarity between the generations.'[49] Perfected by grace the Christian family is 'a specific revelation and realization of ecclesial communion', a 'domestic church', where every member has a part to play in building up the communion of persons. Pope St John Paul II has a high regard for the transmission of culture, especially culture infused with Christian virtues, values, and belief commitments. He believes that culture is transmitted especially in the family and so he repeats the point from *Gaudium et spes* that the family is a 'school of deeper humanity.' Notably part of this deepening in humanity is the healing experience of forgiveness.[50] In this school of solidarity Pope St John Paul II considers the specific roles of the members of the family. Starting with women Pope St John Paul II speaks of their equal dignity with men, their significant place in society and in the family, and the discrimination they often face. He talks of the important role of men as husbands and fathers. He gives special attention to the rights of children and their personal dignity from the very beginning of their lives noting how they too contribute to building up the family and the holiness of its members. He observes how elderly people have a significant role, especially in bridging the generation gap before it is made.[51]

Pope St John Paul II is well known for championing of life, notably through his 1995 encyclical *Evangelium Vitae*. He also deals with issues of life in *Familiaris Consortio* precisely because for Pope St John Paul II the family is the 'sanctuary of life.'[52] Recalling the injunction in Genesis to be fruitful and multiply, and situating this in the privilege of co-operating with the love of God, Pope St John Paul II says that 'the fundamental task of the family is to serve life.' He explains that procreation is 'the fruit and sign' of conjugal love, yet significantly he adds that the fruitfulness of conjugal love is 'enlarged and enriched by all those fruits of moral, spiritual and supernatural life' that parents hand on to their children, and through children to the Church and the world.[53] Since the love of husband and wife is a unique participation in God's love, Pope St John Paul II regards the 'serious responsibility' of transmitting life through married love that is fully human, exclusive and open to life, as part of the Church's constant teaching. This teaching is constant yet also prophetic, 'always old yet always new', because it sees new life as a 'gift of God' in all circumstances and defends life in the difficult contexts of an anxiety for the future, an anti-life mentality, and a consumer culture. Following some bishops from the developing world, Pope St John Paul II draws attention specifically to activities of governments or public authorities that attempt to limit the freedom of couples in deciding about planning their families, particularly when this is related to aid programmes. At the same time, Pope St John Paul II explains that the Church is aware of the serious problem of population growth and he urges theologians to work on a deeper understanding of the biblical, ethical and personalistic aspects of Church teaching.[54]

Indeed, it is precisely from a personalistic approach that Pope St John Paul II argues against both a distorted confused notion of sexuality and against 'any action that renders procreation impossible.' There is an inseparable connection between the love of the spouses in mutual self-giving and procreation that has been willed by God. Contraception separates these two meanings of the conjugal act and as a result the value of the 'total' self-giving of mutual love has been altered. Pope St John Paul II speaks of contraception as a 'contradictory language...of one not giving oneself totally to the other', a theme that he later develops in his *Theology of the Body*. In contrast to the contraceptive mentality that refuses total gift Pope St John Paul II explains that when couples have recourse to periods of infertility, they respect the connection between love and procreation and act as 'ministers' of God's plan, thus still giving themselves totally. Again, using the analogy of language, natural family planning accepts the cycle of the person and encourages a dialogue of mutual respect, shared responsibility, and self-control. For Pope St John Paul II God, not the Church, is the 'author' of this norm of responsible parenthood. The Church as teacher recognizes and understands the difficulties couples are in, notably also the difficulties people have in understanding the values presented in the teaching. Pope St John Paul II therefore advocates better education and preparation so that people will come to appreciate the full significance of sexuality, and he encourages patience, humility, strength of mind, trust, and prayer, as well as recourse to the sacraments of the Eucharist and Reconciliation.[55]

As lecturer in Lublin before he became pope, Pope St John Paul II was particularly interested in ethics. Having recognized the difficult demands of moral teaching, Pope St John Paul II further explains that the moral order sets out God's plan and therefore it can only be for the benefit and happiness of human beings. The synod had raised the question of gradualism where couples feel unable to obey moral norms taught by the Church due to their 'weakness and objective difficulties.'[56] While the synod did recognize the problem of social sin,[57] Pope St John Paul II explicitly acknowledges that structures of sin hinder the family's full realization of itself and he calls for a conversion of minds and hearts.⁵⁸ As for the personal living out of the moral life, Pope St John Paul II observes that human beings build themselves up through their many free decisions, thus, each person 'knows, loves and accomplishes moral growth by stages of growth.' In terms of marriage, the couple need to be willing to embody the values represented by the law in their concrete decisions. The law is not simply 'an ideal to be achieved in the future.' Quoting his homily at the close of the synod, Pope St John Paul II clarifies that:

> what is known as 'the law of gradualness' or step-by-step advance cannot be identified with 'gradualness of the law', as if there were different degrees or forms of precept in God's law for different individuals and situations. In God's plan, all husbands and wives are called in marriage to holiness, and this lofty vocation is fulfilled to the extent that the human person is able to respond to God's command with serene confidence in God's grace and in his or her own will.⁵⁹

Notably, Pope St John Paul II does not refer to personal weakness, instead he speaks of unfaithfulness to moral norms, and he does make frequent reference to forgiveness and the sacrament of reconciliation.⁶⁰ That Pope St John Paul II stresses the significance of each act in the whole of married life in contributing to personal holiness as a moral principle is significant. To recall, the Majority Report spoke about the importance of the totality of married life, greatly reducing the importance of individual acts, and this moral approach was rejected by Pope St Paul VI in *Humanae Vitae*. Again, significantly Pope St John Paul II notes that conjugal love involves the will of two people, and so additional patience, commitment and also forgiveness is required. Moreover, he sees that the whole Church community is involved in providing support for couples to help them respond to God's plan.

As indicated by the synod, Pope St John Paul II spends considerable time in outlining the importance of the family in the education of children.⁶¹ He explains that it is through the family that children come to know the essential values of human life, the significance of marriage, and the family give children their first experience of the Church. More so perhaps than his predecessors, Pope St John Paul II is especially interested in children in their own rights and not simply as the fruit of marriage. Pope St John Paul II's comments on education and the rights and duties of parents follow the points set out by the Second Vatican Council in *Gaudium et spes* with additional reflection on the role of the state in education. With a further personalistic tone, he adds that the 'most basic element' in education is parental love. Expanding on this, Pope St John Paul II returns to his concept of the family as 'a community of love' where the total self-gift of parents witnesses to love and to the intrinsic dignity of every human being. This inspiring love challenges individualism and selfishness. Moreover, Pope St John Paul II reminds parents to be aware of discernment of God's will in people's lives and to teach the gift of celibacy as 'the supreme form of self-giving.' Self-gift and attention to the virtues also characterize sex education and this has its proper context in moral principles. Pope St John Paul II places sex education clearly in the 'right and duty' of parents following the principle of subsidiarity. Additionally, through the sacrament of marriage and a part of the duty of education, parents bring their children to God and the Church. Pope St John Paul II re-emphasizes the responsibility that parents have because children not only have full human dignity, but they are also children of God, brothers or sisters of Christ, and temples of the Holy Spirit. The family is 'a school of following Christ', where, quoting Pope St Paul VI 'all the members evangelize and are evangelized.' The fruitfulness of families extends to those marriages where there are no children and where there are opportunities to create communities of love for those in need, especially children.[62]

Expanding the family outwards, Pope St John Paul II calls attention to the mission of the family to society and correspondingly, of society at the service to the family. Stressing that the family is 'the first school of the social virtues', Pope St John Paul

II notes that it is in family life that we first experience communion and sharing. By respecting and promoting the dignity of each of its members, by fostering 'authentic and mature communion', the family is 'the place of origin and the most effective means for humanizing and personalizing society.' Faced with societies that dehumanize and depersonalize it is the family that can keep alive the values of humanity and dignity. The family then has a significant social and political role, and society in turn should support the family.[63]

Some of the synod fathers were concerned with the negative way in which some societies treated families and they suggested that Pope St John Paul II present a Charter of Family Rights to the United Nations. Pope St John Paul II outlines these rights from the right to found a family and marry, to rights of education, faith, work, association and security. The rights cover not only economic, social, and healthcare rights but also religious rights. However, Pope St John Paul II follows this list of rights with the social responsibilities that members of the family have to others, especially, the poor and marginalized. The sacrament of marriage gives the couple the power to live out this aspect of their lay vocation.[64] Ambitious for the Christian family as a 'small scale church', Pope St John Paul II calls for the world-wide unity of Christians families like a 'large scale church' to be a sign for the world. This 'spiritual communion' of families is called to foster reconciliation, justice, fraternity, and peace.[65] The world meeting of families has been held in different countries every three years since 1994.

Pope St John Paul II takes the idea of the Christian family as 'Church in miniature', the domestic Church, and inserts it directly into the life and mission of the Church. To do this more securely he identifies 'the many profound bonds' that link the Church and the Christian family following the themes of prophet, priest and king. In its prophetical dimension the Church is Mother and Teacher, guiding the Christian family in the 'service to love.' In turn the Christian family is not only a 'saved community' but is called to be a 'saving community.' Like the Church the

Christian family is encouraged to be a fruitful unity that witnesses to Christ in the world. The Christian family is a 'believing and evangelizing community' that owes an obedience of faith to the plan of God. Preparation for the sacrament of matrimony enables the couple to rediscover and deepen their faith received in baptism. The sacramental celebration of marriage announces the Gospel and so is also a profession of faith throughout its many demands. The Christian family, as a place of joy, love, and hope, is a centre of evangelization as all its members evangelize each other and those with whom they come into contact. Since this is an 'ecclesial service', Pope St John Paul II reminds of the importance of the church community in supporting families especially through difficulties. As 'the primary and most excellent seed-bed of vocations to a life of consecration to the kingdom of God', education for children in proper discernment of God's will is vital. Couples are 'missionaries' in a true sense of the word because they are called to witness to the faith even through struggles and to encourage family members who perhaps do not have faith or are lukewarm.[66]

Continuing the themes of the Christian family's ties with the Church, in its priestly dimension Pope St John Paul II considers each of the sacraments specifically in relation to marriage. He calls this the 'Christian family as a community in dialogue with God.' Following the Second Vatican Council's call to universal holiness, Pope St John Paul II applies the theology of the sacraments as sanctifying, building up the body of Christ, and giving worship to God, specifically to the sacrament of marriage. The family 'draws its nourishment' from the sacrament of marriage, and the sacrament is the 'specific source' of their sanctification. The sacramental grace continues throughout their marriage as Christ abides with them, enabling them to meet the demands of married live. The Eucharist, including its sacrificial aspect, is 'the very source of Christian marriage' and nourish the gift of charity. The sacrament of conversion and reconciliation reflects that mutual forgiveness is a part of daily life and a source of mercy and renewal. Prayer, that is individual, in the family and in public liturgy, as well as education of children in prayer is an 'essential part of Christian life' and a major aspect of that dialogue with God.[67]

In its kingly dimension and inspired by the law of the Holy Spirit, the family is called to exercise a service of love to God and to all human beings. This service is expressed by acknowledging the image of God in every human being who is a brother or sister. From this flows Pope St John Paul II's constant focus on the importance of the family as promoter and defender of dignity and life.[68]

In keeping with his understanding that the focus of the Second Vatican Council was on deepening and explaining Church teaching, Pope St John Paul II uses sixty four of the eighty six paragraphs of *Familiaris Consortio*, bar a brief incursion into the shadows affecting marriage, to set out the theology and anthropology of marriage and family life. In Part Four Pope St John Paul II explores the pastoral care of the family and how the Church is to accompany families. The style of the exhortation is very much that once the rich theology of marriage is understood its pastoral application will become clear. Strengthening and developing pastoral care of the family is 'a matter of urgency' and 'a real matter of priority', and the reason given is not so much because of the shadows in family life but because 'future evangelization depends largely on the domestic Church.' Pope St John Paul II extends the Church's pastoral concern to all families especially those in difficult, irregular, or tragic situations. Moreover, he regards pastoral action as 'progressive', accompanying the family 'step by step.'[69]

Beginning with pastoral accompaniment in preparing for marriage, Pope St John Paul II follows the synod in identifying three main stages of preparation: remote, proximate and immediate.[70] This built on the two stages, remote and proximate, identified by Pope Pius XI.[71] On remote preparation, Pope St John Paul II notes that values, virtues, a sense of responsibility and behaviours need to be formed early on in a child's life and this is where the witness of parents and the support of society and Church are vital. Remote preparation includes spiritual and catechetical formation alongside human formation. Proximate preparation builds on remote preparation and includes not only a religious aspect but also biology and responsible parenthood, and practical aspects such as finance, all in the context of an authentic interpersonal relationship. In this stage solidarity with other families is to be encouraged through supportive family associations.[72] Immediate preparation takes place in the few months before the celebration of marriage so that the sense of the mystery of Christ in the future life of the couple is deepened, the meaning of grace and responsibility of Christian married life is heightened, and so that active and conscious participation in the liturgy is encouraged. These stages of preparation become a true 'journey of faith.' Rather than dwelling on the sacrament of marriage as an exchange of consent before witnesses, Pope St John Paul II inserts preparation for the celebration of the sacrament clearly into the Paschal Mystery and the liturgical activity of the Church community.[73]

The synod expressed concern over the issue of faith in marriage, both in mixed marriages and the faith of Catholic spouses. This question is pressing because sacramental theology presupposes appropriate dispositions, and this raises the question of whether priests can refuse the sacrament. Pope St John Paul II notes that faith is a difficulty in secularized societies, and he explains the reasoning behind admitting to the sacrament of marriage those who are imperfectly disposed. Pope St John Paul II points out that unlike the other sacraments, marital union is rooted in 'the very economy of creation' from the beginning. The decision of a man and woman to commit themselves for their whole lives by their irrevocable consent to this indissoluble and total love and fidelity is to act in accordance with the plan of God even if they are not fully conscious of this. In a real sense through grace, they have already begun 'a journey towards salvation.' Celebration of the sacrament complements and brings this intention to completion even if the intention is also motivated by social and personal reasons. To inquire into the depth or level of faith of couples would be problematic and possibly discriminatory. Nevertheless, when an engaged couple explicitly and formally reject what the Church intends to do in the celebration of marriage, then the couple themselves place an obstacle in the way of the celebration.[74]

Pastoral care should continue after marriage especially for the newly married and young families. This care should involve the whole of the community and other families have a particularly useful role here.[75] Still, Pope St John Paul II says that the person principally responsible for pastoral support of families is the bishop, with the support of priests and deacons in fidelity to the Magisterium. The bishop has been charged with building up his diocesan family as a 'model and source of hope' for the families that belong to it. Given the importance of a family apostolate, Pope St John Paul II adds in the work of the laity, lay specialists, theologians, men and women religious, and responsible media.[76]

When it comes to accompanying people in difficult situations, Pope St John Paul II lists a variety of cases identified at the synod, such as families of migrants, prisoners, addicted people, armed personnel, single-parent families, marginalized persons, people living in poverty and deprivation, the elderly, problem teenagers, widowed and those ideologically divided.[77] He urges real pastoral commitment especially from people who share or understand these situations.[78]

In cases of mixed marriages, along with the synod Pope St John Paul II notes that couples have special needs. He points to three main areas: when it comes to the obligation on the Catholic spouse to have children baptized and brought up in the faith as far as possible; when it involves religious freedom; and procedures for support. He adds that mixed marriages may be good opportunities for ecumenism.[79]

The synod brought up the question of 'extra-marital relations' in the last of its propositions.[80] Similarly, 'pastoral action in certain irregular situations' appears near the end of *Familiaris Consortio*.[81] This may well be because the subject matter of Pope

St John Paul II's exhortation is the role of the Christian family in today's world rather than specific difficulties in families. Nevertheless, families in 'irregular situations', that may be irregular both in religious and civil senses, fall under the Church's pastoral care. First Pope St John Paul II treats of 'trial marriages', presumably involving a couple who live together before marrying to see if they are compatible or if the relationship will work out. According to Pope St John Paul II, trial marriages are unacceptable because they 'experiment' with human beings, thereby compromising human dignity. Human dignity requires 'self-giving love without limitations of time or of any other circumstance.' Having already established that 'the gift of the body in the sexual relationship is a real symbol of the giving of the whole person', and 'a real symbol of the union of Christ and the Church', trial marriages clearly deny both in denying faithfulness and indissolubility: 'between two baptized persons there can exist only an indissoluble marriage.' Pope St John Paul II notes the importance of education in the virtues and values of marriage and recommends further study into the causes of trial marriages, including economic, psychological and social reasons.[82]

Second, Pope St John Paul II looks at 'de facto free unions' where there is no publicly recognized religious or civil bond. Pope St John Paul II notes that there is a variety of reasons for free unions that present different pastoral problems. These range from the problem of harm, economic difficulty, and discrimination, to rejection of society and the family, to the prevalence in certain cultures of accepting stages of relationship, often only marrying once it is shown that the woman can bear children. Pope St John Paul II recognizes that these situations remain serious problems since they involve a loss of religious sense, they deprive couples of the grace of the sacrament, and they weaken the values of the family harming not only the couple and society but also children. These situations are often delicate and need to be addressed case by case in order to enlighten people and society, and to show the true witness of Christian marriage. Moreover, remedying these situations may involve challenging social and cultural structures and public opinion.[83]

Third, Pope St John Paul II addresses the issue of Catholics in civil marriages. He acknowledges that civil marriage may denote a commitment even if divorce has not been excluded from the minds of couples. Nevertheless, pastoral accompaniment is required to help couples understand the need for consistency in their choice of life and the faith they profess. Until they have regularized their situation couples in civil marriages cannot be admitted to the sacraments.[84]

Fourth, in dealing with separated or divorced people who have not remarried, Pope St John Paul II urges forgiveness and reconciliation. Pope St John Paul II recognizes the problems of loneliness and other difficulties especially in cases where separation has been as a last resort or where the spouse is the innocent party. He asks the community to support people with 'respect, understanding, solidarity and practical help' so that people can be helped to remain faithful even in difficult situations. This faithfulness can be a real witness before the world and the Church. The fact of separation or divorce does not preclude a person from receiving the sacraments.[85]

Fifth, in considering people who have divorced and then remarried, Pope St John Paul II notes that this is by no means uncommon and he is clear that the Church cannot 'abandon' these couples to their own devices. It is important to note that the 1917 Code of Canon Law was still in effect at the time of *Familiaris Consortio* and that the Code advocated the general exclusion from Holy Communion of divorced people who had attempted remarriage, speaking of them in terms of the 'publicly unworthy', 'manifestly infamous', 'bigamists.'[86] Pope St John Paul II calls for a careful 'discernment of situations.' He points out that there are significant differences between those who sincerely tried to save their marriages and were abandoned; those who 'through their own grave fault destroyed a canonically valid marriage'; those who entered a second union for the sake of the upbringing of their children; and those who are 'sometimes subjectively certain in conscience that their previous and irreparably destroyed marriage had never been valid.' At the outset, Pope St John Paul II calls on an accompaniment that ensures people do not consider themselves separated from the Church, 'for as baptized persons they can, and indeed must, share in her life.' He encourages listening to the Word of God, attendance at Mass, prayer, charity, bringing up children in the faith, and 'to cultivate the spirit and practice of penance and thus implore, day by day, God's grace.' As a 'merciful Mother' the Church can sustain them in faith and hope. Reaffirming Church practice based on Scripture, Pope St John Paul II gives two reasons why a divorced and remarried person cannot be admitted to the Eucharist: 'the fact that their state and condition of life objectively contradict that union of love between Christ and the Church which is signified and effected by the Eucharist'; and the concern that admittance to the Eucharist would create 'error and confusion' regarding Church teaching on indissolubility. Reconciliation through the sacrament of Penance which would 'open the way to the Eucharist' can only be granted after repentance and a sincere readiness to undertake a way of life that no longer contradicts the indissolubility of marriage. Pope St John Paul II explains what this means in practice: quoting his closing homily to the synod, 'that when, for serious reasons, such as for example the children's upbringing, a man and a woman cannot satisfy the obligation to separate, they "take on themselves the duty to live in complete continence, that is, by abstinence from the acts proper to married couples".' Nor can a pastor perform for a divorced and remarried person any ceremony that would give the impression of a new sacramentally valid marriage.[87]

Pope St John Paul II ends his exhortation with a reflection on the situation of people who do not have a family. He urges everyone to become involved in the remedying of injustice and in offering help and support. Moreover, he says that for people without their own natural family, and notably he himself had no natural family left alive:

the doors of the great family which is the Church ... must be opened even wider. No one is without a family in this world: the Church is a home and family for everyone, especially those who labour and are heavily laden.[88]

Pope St John Paul II finally urges everyone to 'give thought to the fate of the family', for 'the future of humanity passes by way of the family' and he commends the family to the prayers of the Holy Family.[89]

And called to holiness

The topic for the 1987 synod of bishops was the vocation and mission of lay people in the Church and in the world. From the reflections at the 1987 synod, Pope St John Paul II wrote his 1988 apostolic exhortation *Christifideles Laici*. For Pope St John Paul II, the people of God are like the 'labourers in the vineyard' in Matthew's gospel, and the vineyard is the whole world 'which is to be transformed according to the plan of God in view of the final coming of the kingdom of God.'[90] The call to holiness is not just an individual concern. The faithful are asked both to pursue a life of holiness in whatever state of life in which they find themselves, and to be 'leaven' in the world.[91] Pope St John Paul II explains, quoting St Francis de Sales, all the faithful can cultivate a spirit of holiness and live 'according to the Spirit.'[92]

Pope St John Paul II describes the 'inherent social dimension' in human beings as calling a person 'from the innermost depths of self to communion with others and to the giving of self to others.' This 'community of persons' is not simply a social gathering or a social contract or even a way of working together and therefore of getting on peacefully. Rather, for Pope St John Paul II people are called to solidarity with each other, to cultivate a 'spirit of brotherhood', which builds up people as persons, recognizing the dignity of every human being not only as another 'I' but also as a child of God. In this community both the individual person and society benefit, and neither can be set against the other or be in competition with the other. Marriage is crucial to this vision of solidarity because the married couple and the family are 'the first and basic expression of the social dimension of the person.' The first communion of persons is found in Genesis; Jesus restored it to dignity; and St Paul shows the 'deep rapport' between marriage, the mystery of Christ and the Church.[93]

As the 'basic cell' of society, the family 'is the cradle of life and love, the place in which the individual is born and grows.' It is the place of 'humanization', of the development of a culture of life, and where people learn how to participate properly and fully in society. This is why Pope St John Paul II believes that it is so vital to protect and defend the family and its values, especially from anti-life mentalities, situations of poverty and misery, indifference, and from state interventions where what belongs to parental duties, notably education of children, is usurped.[94]

In *Christifideles Laici* Pope St John Paul II calls for the evangelization of culture. He says that service to the individual and society through the development of culture is 'one of the more serious tasks of living together as a human family.' Culture is everything to do with making human life more truly human, and that includes not only promoting human dignity and values that enable people to flourish, but also rediscovering the relationship of human beings to God.[95] Pope St John Paul II insists on the 'crucial significance of the links between the Church and culture.' He repeatedly observes that 'a faith that does not become culture is not fully accepted, not entirely thought out, not faithfully lived.'[96] This is why marriage matters.

Summary

The focus of this chapter has been on the 1980 synod and the exhortation *Familiaris Consortio*. Uniquely perhaps in the teaching of the Magisterium,[97] Pope St John Paul II invited people really to deepen their understanding of marriage and the family from the perspectives of theology, anthropology, morality, and pastoral practice.

Before he was elected pope, Archbishop Karol Wojtyła was so enthused by his experience at the Second Vatican Council that he decided to make the implementation of the Council his major project in his own diocese of Kracow.[98] In his understanding the Council called for a deepening explanation of Church teaching and, as Pope, he sets about this especially in relation to the goods of marriage, of indissolubility, married love and fruitfulness of marriage, because he recognizes the importance of marriage for the Church. This importance is not only in terms of creating a culture of the Christian family that thinks with the mind and heart of the Church. Pope St John Paul II understands that the family is hugely significant for evangelizing society, notably in promoting the dignity of every human being however small and vulnerable, and in creating a community of love and solidarity. Moreover, in perhaps his appraisal of the situation of the Church and with a nod to the whole course of his pontificate, Pope St John Paul II states, 'thus the little domestic Church, like the greater Church, needs to be constantly and intensely evangelized: hence its duty regarding permanent education in the faith.'[99] Many might argue that his great vision of Christian married life and the family does not reflect realities and so is either aspirational or impossible. However, this is to forget that for Pope St John Paul II grace works wonders, and the concept of witness is crucial.

Notably *Familiaris Consortio* is chiefly about the Christian family. Getting the theology and anthropology of the family right is essential because, as Pope St John Paul II observes, 'the future of evangelization depends in great part on the Church of the home.'[100] Pope St John Paul II takes very seriously the scriptural basis for marriage. Love, fidelity and fruitfulness are vital in marriage because marriage is a reflection of the love of God for his people. Married love then is a way for the Church. And Church is a way for marriage as married couples need the grace to become more and more what they are: a community of persons that forms persons. For Pope St John Paul II this concept of a community of love that makes people more truly human is absolutely vital because it is the family that witnesses to human dignity, moral values and virtues, and the joy of self-gift, and it is the family that overcomes tendencies towards individualism and selfishness. However, this sense of the community of persons goes beyond the family as each family forms and influences their society. Moreover, Pope St John Paul II calls for unity in teaching so that the faithful do not 'suffer anxiety of conscience.'[101]

The idea of the Christian family as domestic Church clearly catches Pope St John Paul II's imagination. However, some commentators are concerned with the apparent rigidity of Pope St John Paul II's thinking and they complain that *Familiaris Consortio* is overly saturated with Pope St John Paul II's own personal philosophical and theological position.[102] It is of course up to the reader to decide the extent to which *Familiaris Consortio* can be considered to be the Pope's own personal position. However, undoubtedly the family holds deep significance for the Pope as a human and theological 'reality' that enables human beings to flourish as persons and as community.[103] Moreover, according to Wojtyła, in the Catholic tradition the 'sacrament of matrimony is a sacrament of the laity' and 'to be a lay person means to go out into the world, to have a special relationship to the world.' The lay mission is 'consecration of the world' and this 'finds its primary and basic arena in family life.' Consecration of the world begins with human beings, and human beings begin in families.[104] Family ministry is both of the Church and of the family.

The 1980 synod on the family proposed one further suggestion: the development of a positive theology of sexuality. Pope St John Paul II had begun working on this area while he was still a professor of ethics and during the synod he presented teaching that eventually came to be known as the *Theology of the Body*.

Notes

1. Ac 9:2; 19:9; 19:23; 22:4; 24:14; 24:22.
2. Jn 14:6.
3. Lk 24:13–35.
4. International Theological Commission *Synodality in the Life and Mission of the Church,* 3–4.
5. Pope St Paul VI, Motu proprio *Apostolica sollicitudo* (15 September 1965); International Theological Commission *Synodality* 41.
6. See C. Murphy, 'Collegiality: An Essay Toward Better Understanding' in *Theological Studies* 46 (1985), 38–49.
7. International Theological Commission *Synodality,* 58–61.
8. *Ibid.,* 6–7, 9.
9. International Theological Commission *Sensus Fidei in the Life of the Church,* 122.
10. St J. H. Newman, 'Preface to the Third Edition of the Via Media' in *Roman Catholic Writings on Doctrinal Development by John Henry Newman* (Kansas: Sheed and Ward 1997), p. 86. Newman recognized with profound regret that in earlier lectures he had been highly critical of 'Romanism', pp. 68–69.
11. See J. Heft, 'Tradition, A Catholic Understanding' in *The Idea of Tradition in the Late Modern World* (Oregon: Cascade, 2020), pp. 43–44.
12. St J. H. Newman, *Reply to Mr Gladstone's Pamphlet, To His Grace the Duke of Norfolk* (Toronto: Irving 1875), p. 41; see E. Duffy, *John Henry Newman, A Very Brief Biography* (London: SPCK 2019).
13. International Theological Commission *Synodality* 46.
14. *Ibid.,* 50.
15. *Ibid.,* 8; Pope St John Paul II, *Novo Millennio Ineunte,* 44–45.
16. J. Grootaers and J. Selling, *The 1980 Synod of Bishops 'On the Role of the Family': An Exposition of the Event and an Analysis of the Text* (Leuven: Peeters, 1983), pp. 156, 168–169, 257–258 footnote 129, 294–296
17. E. Pentin, *The Rigging of a Vatican Synod?* (San Francisco: Ignatius Press 2015).
18. International Theological Commission *Synodality* 65–66.
19. *Ibid.,* 68–69.
20. T. Reese, 'Report from the Synod' in *America* (11 October 1980).
21. See R. B. Kaiser, *The Encyclical That Never Was* (London: Sheed and Ward, 1985), p. 283.
22. T. Reese, 'The Close of the Synod' in *America* (8 November 1980).
23. See *The Tablet* (31 January 1981), pp. 116–118; (7 February 1981), pp.

[24] 141–142; *Enchiridion Vaticanum* Il Regno - Documenti 13/81, pp. 386–397.
[24] Propositions 2–4; For the propositions see *The Tablet* (31 January 1981), pp. 116–118; (7 February 1981), pp. 141–142; *Enchiridion Vaticanum* Il Regno - Documenti 13/81, pp. 386–397.
[25] Pope St John Paul II, *Homily*, 17th World Youth Day (28 July 2002) 3.
[26] K. Wojtyła, *Person and Community* (New York: Peter Lang, 2008), p. 359.
[27] Pope St John Paul II, *Familiaris Consortio*, 1, 3.
[28] *Ibid.*, 4.
[29] Propositions 2–6.
[30] Pope St John Paul II, *Familiaris Consortio* 5.
[31] *Ibid.*, 6.
[32] *Ibid.*, 8.
[33] *Ibid.*, 9.
[34] Propositions 8–11.
[35] Pope St John Paul II, *Familiaris Consortio* 11.
[36] Proposition 11.
[37] Pope St John Paul II, *Familiaris Consortio* 16.
[38] *Ibid.*, 11.
[39] *Ibid.*, 12.
[40] Second Vatican Council, *Sacrosanctum Concilium*, 61, 77.
[41] Pope St John Paul II, *Familiaris Consortio* 13.
[42] *Ibid.*, 13.
[43] *Ibid.*, 14.
[44] *Ibid.*, 15.
[45] Propositions 20–34.
[46] Pope St John Paul II, *Familiaris Consortio* 17.
[47] *Ibid.*, 18–20.
[48] *Ibid.*, 21.
[49] Pope St John Paul II, *Address to the Pontifical Academy for Social Sciences* (11 April 2002), 3.
[50] Pope St John Paul II, *Familiaris Consortio* 21.
[51] *Ibid.*, 22–27.
[52] Pope St John Paul II, *Evangelium Vitae*, 6, 11, 59, 88, 92, 94; Pope St John Paul II, *Centesimus annus*, 31.
[53] Pope St John Paul II, *Familiaris Consortio* 28.
[54] *Ibid.*, 29–31; Propositions 22–23.
[55] Pope St John Paul II, *Familiaris Consortio* 32–33.
[56] Proposition 24.
[57] Proposition 7.

58 Pope St John Paul II, *Familiaris Consortio* 9.
59 *Ibid.*, 34.
60 *Ibid.*, 58; 21, 33, 34, 48.
61 Propositions 26–29.
62 Pope St John Paul II, *Familiaris Consortio* 35–40.
63 *Ibid.*, 42–45.
64 *Ibid.*, 46–47.
65 *Ibid.*, 48.
66 *Ibid.*, 49–54.
67 *Ibid.*, 55–62; Propositions 37, 38.
68 Pope St John Paul II, *Familiaris Consortio* 63–64.
69 *Ibid.*, 65.
70 Proposition 35.
71 Pope Pius XI, *Casti connubii* 112.
72 Proposition 39.
73 Pope St John Paul II, *Familiaris Consortio* 66–67.
74 *Ibid.*, 68.
75 *Ibid.*, 69–72.
76 *Ibid.*, 73–76.
77 Propositions 31–33; Pope St John Paul II, *Familiaris Consortio* 77.
78 Pope St John Paul II, *Familiaris Consortio* 77.
79 Proposition 19; Pope St John Paul II, *Familiaris Consortio* 78.
80 Propositions 40, 41 out of 43 propositions in total.
81 Pope St John Paul II, *Familiaris Consortio* 79–84 out of 86 paragraphs.
82 *Ibid.*, 80.
83 *Ibid.*, 81.
84 *Ibid.*, 82.
85 *Ibid.*, 83.
86 P. Travers, 'Reception of the Holy Eucharist by Catholics Attempting Remarriage after Divorce and the 1983 Code of Canon Law' in *Jurist* 55 (1995), p. 190.
87 Pope St John Paul II, *Familiaris Consortio* 84.
88 *Ibid.*, 85.
89 *Ibid.*, 86.
90 Mt 20:1–2; Pope St John Paul II, *Christifideles Laici*, 1.
91 Pope St John Paul II, *Christifideles Laici* 15.
92 *Ibid.*, 56.
93 *Ibid.*, 40.
94 *Ibid.*, 40.

[95] *Ibid.*, 44.
[96] Pope St John Paul II, *Address to the Plenary Assembly of the Pontifical Council for Culture* (18 March 1994), 1.
[97] T. Knieps-Port le Roi, '*Familiaris consortio*—Impasse or Inspiration for a Contemporary Theology of Marriage and the Family?' in *Melita Theologica* (2006), p. 63.
[98] K. Wojtyła *Sources of Renewal* [1975] (London: Fount, 1980).
[99] Pope St John Paul II, *Familiaris Consortio*, 51.
[100] *Ibid.*, 52.
[101] *Ibid.*, 34.
[102] Knieps-Port le Roi, '*Familiaris consortio*' pp. 75–76; p. 63.
[103] Wojtyła, *Person and Community* pp. 342, 350.
[104] *Ibid.*, pp. 354–355.

8 THEOLOGY OF THE BODY

THE SECOND VATICAN Council dogmatic constitution on Divine Revelation, *Dei Verbum* reminds the faithful that Christ commissioned the Apostles to preach the Gospel 'which is the source of all saving truth and moral teaching.' The Apostles handed on to the bishops as their successors 'what they had received from the lips of Christ, from living with him, and from what he did, or what they had learned through the prompting of the Holy Spirit.' This is a 'living tradition' that develops in the Church with the help of the Holy Spirit, 'for there is a growth in the understanding of the realities and the words which have been handed down.'[1] The Council's decree on Priestly Training, *Optatam Totius* asked seminaries to ensure that their students acquire 'a solid and coherent knowledge of man, the world and of God', and attend to the 'necessary connection between philosophy and the true problems of life.' Students were to be formed 'with particular care' in the study of the bible since scripture is the 'soul of all theology.' Moreover, 'special care must be given to the perfecting of moral theology. Its scientific exposition, nourished more on the teaching of the Bible, should shed light on the loftiness of the calling of the faithful in Christ and the obligation that is theirs of bearing fruit in charity for the life of the world.'[2] Above all, priests were to be 'saturated' with the mystery of the Church and of Christ.[3]

The development of moral theology beyond the manual method, and especially the emphasis on scripture and human realities, has been hugely significant for the Church's teaching on marriage and the family. Undoubtedly, the influence of Pope St John Paul II has indelibly marked this teaching, and the Pope's approach raises interesting questions about the place of 'true problems of life', of the call to holiness, and more technically of the use of scripture and the development of tradition. Over his long pontificate, Pope St John Paul II's approach in many of these areas was challenged. Nevertheless, it is perhaps important to remember that this living tradition develops with the help of the Holy Spirit. And Pope St John Paul II's writings show a man who was saturated in the mystery of Christ and his Church.

Archbishop Karol Wojtyła had been thinking about a theology of human love long before he became pope. In 1960 his play *The Jeweller's Shop* appeared under a pseudonym in a Catholic publication. The play is about married love and the difficulties couples encounter when love seems to have died, or when it is dominated by lust, or when love is stifled by resentment or indifference, but especially when human beings cannot accept human inadequacies. Wojtyła asks couples not only to show attentive kindness to each other in small things, but also to put aside feelings of hatred or resentment or alienation by seeing in the other the face of Christ. This is, after all, what all Christians are asked to do.[4] In his academic book *Love and Responsibility*, published in 1960, love as the total gift of the self to the other brings with it responsibility, the responsibility and acceptance of the other which involves loving the other for his or her own sake, not for what I can get out of the relationship.

As a teacher of moral theology with a real interest in the conclusions of the Second Vatican Council it seems that Wojtyła took the call to develop moral theology to heart. By the time he became pope, Wojtyła's theology of human love had crystallized into a series of some one hundred and twenty-nine general audiences running from 5 September 1979 to 28 November 1984, given in preparation for the 1980 synod on the family and ending after publication of *Familiaris Consortio*. Pope St John Paul II's catechesis begins from the words of Jesus, goes back to Genesis, and then forward to the redemption of the body. He toyed with different titles, *Love in the Divine Plan*, *The Redemption of the*

Body, Sacramentality of Marriage and his theology of love is now popularly known as *The Theology of the Body*.⁵

Introduction to the Theology of the Body

The structure of Pope St John Paul II's catechesis is helpfully summarized in his last catechetical audience of the series.⁶ Pope St John Paul II explains that the catechesis can be summed up as *Human love in the divine plan* or more precisely *The Redemption of the Body and the Sacramentality of Marriage*. He divides his teaching into two parts: Part 1 is a study of Christ's words and an analysis of three main collections of texts, first, Matthew 19:8 and Mark 10:6–9 together where Christ refers to 'the beginning' on unity and indissolubility of marriage; second, the Sermon on the Mount in Matthew 5:28 and concupiscence as adultery committed in the heart; third, Matthew 22:30, Mark 12:25, and Luke 20:35 and the resurrection of the body in the other world. Part 2 is an analysis of the sacrament of marriage based on Ephesians 5, and going back to the biblical beginning of marriage expressed in Genesis where the two become one body. The final analysis of Pope St Paul VI's encyclical *Humanae Vitae* which responds to conjugal and family morality and to theological questions is not, says Pope St John Paul II, an 'add on.' Rather the questions it raises permeates the whole of Pope St John Paul II's reflection. Commenting on his method, Pope St John Paul II argues that a search for answers requires a focus on the biblical and personalistic aspects of love and on the development of a theology of the body. However, Pope St John Paul II sees 'theology of the body' as a 'working' term that helps to place the redemption of the body and the sacramentality of marriage on a wider base. He notes that he has not included other aspects of the theology of the body such as suffering and death.

Again, as a matter of method, Pope St John Paul II's reflections on the sacrament of marriage are carried out by considering two dimensions that are essential to sacraments: the dimension of covenant and grace; and the dimension of sign. Both, he says, are linked to words of Christ. Through an analysis of the biblical aspect of love teaching is placed on the sure foundation of revelation. The analysis of personalistic aspects of love ensures that teaching is in line with what is good for human beings and what corresponds to human dignity.

Commenting on his use of scripture, Pope St John Paul II points out that we cannot reach the truth merely by empirical or rational means. Moreover, a merely literal knowledge of scripture is also inadequate. For Pope St John Paul II:

> the scriptures are above all a means to know the power of the living God who reveals himself in them ... to reread the scriptures correctly ... means to know and accept with faith the power of the Giver of life, who is not bound by the law of death which rules man's earthly history.[7]

Thus, the significance of Genesis and 'going back to the beginning' is that this is the 'threshold of the revelation of historical man.'[8] Although Pope St John Paul II shows that he is aware of textural problems in *exegesis*, his method has been seen by some as more *eisegesis*[9] even if he is careful with his texts. Perhaps a clearer account would be to regard Pope St John Paul II's use of scripture not as proof texts for Church teaching but as pastoral reflection.[10]

In addition to scripture as the 'soul' of his theology and anthropology, Pope St John Paul II is very much influenced by the documents of the Second Vatican Council, and most significantly by two paragraphs in *Gaudium et spes*: according to paragraph 22 'the truth is that only in the mystery of the incarnate Word does the mystery of man take on light', that Christ has united himself 'in some fashion' with every human being and therefore our natural human dignity has been raised to a supernatural dignity. The mystery of the human being is linked to the Paschal Mystery and Christ 'blazed a trail' of self-giving love that if we follow it 'life and death are made holy and take on a new meaning.' According to paragraph 24 each human being is made in the image and likeness of God, and this likeness reveals that the human being 'who is the only creature on earth which God willed for itself, cannot fully find himself except through a sincere gift of himself.'

Identifying the main problems

It may be useful at the outset to identify some of the modern problems that provide part of the context for Pope St John Paul II's theological anthropology. Using 'man' in its generic sense, according to Pope St John Paul II, 'modern man' tends towards dualism of the spiritual and physical, and the domination of forces of nature rather than self-mastery. Although modern science has its uses, biological knowledge that separates out what is corporeal in man from what is spiritual results in the body being treated as an object to be manipulated. The human person ceases to identify his or herself subjectively with his or her own body because the body has been 'deprived of the meaning and dignity deriving from the fact that this body is proper to the person.'[11] Pope St John Paul II returns to the old 'Manichaean mentality', where 'in the whole Manichaean myth there is only one hero and only one situation which is always repeated: the fallen soul is imprisoned in matter and is liberated by knowledge' and matter is 'an evil instinct for pleasure.'[12] As a result body and sex have an anti-value.[13] Pope St John Paul II locates these Manichaean habits in the way of thinking of three main influential writers: Freud who interprets humanity in terms of lust of the flesh; Marx in lust of the eyes; and Nietzsche in lust of the pride of life. These interpretations mean that the body becomes the problem rather than the problem being 'lust in the heart.'[14]

As part of this separation of the body and the person Pope St John Paul II critiques those who think that the human being can be reduced to bodily aspects and those who think that the person is only related to consciousness. Those who reduce the person to material aspects claim that natural impulses like the sexual instinct are purely animal characteristics. For Pope St John Paul II this diminishes the person who is always the subject of personal human acts.[15] Pope St John Paul II is implicitly referring to the traditional distinction between *actus humanus*, what a human being does, and *actus hominis*, what happens in a human being. For Pope St John Paul II both the *actus hominis* and *actus humanus* are human acts because they belong to human activity, and the human being is a 'rational animal.' However, unlike the natural reaction of sneezing or coughing which simply happen, masculinity and femininity are 'in the personal dimension of human subjectivity', and the sexual instinct belongs in the 'nuptial meaning of the body,' the gift of self. There is naturalness in the sexual instinct, but there is also 'consciousness of the freedom of the gift.'[16] Unlike those who think that nature is in conflict with the free person, sexuality and the sexual instinct are bound up with rationality and freedom. This is why Pope St John Paul II emphasizes the virtues as ways of integrating reason, emotions, feelings and action.

Pope St John Paul II critiques philosophies of consciousness that reduce the person to the thinking thing, and he includes phenomenology in this critique. Phenomenology is concerned with how things appear to us rather than how things are. Certainly, Pope St John Paul II is interested in subjective reflection, but he is worried that phenomenology's focus on conscious experience and interpretation to discover meaning loses sight of objective truth. In a series of lectures given before he became pope, Wojtyła challenges the a-historicism of philosophies of consciousness which claim to be the first philosophies to discover the human subject.[17] His anthropology has its roots in a philosophy of being, and he thinks that not only does the philosophy of being predate the philosophy of consciousness, it also offers an earlier account of the human person as a subject. Moreover, he thinks that a philosophy of consciousness leads inevitably to 'an annihilation of the subject.'[18] This is because a philosophy of consciousness relies on pure subjectivity and it forgets that the person is a concrete self, a body, it is both a subject and object, for in human experience 'the human being is given to us as someone who exists and acts.'[19] The acting person is more than the actions of the immaterial subjective self. It is all the things going on in the living subject that contribute to his or her being an acting person. And each of these concrete selves is 'in every instance unique and unrepeatable.'[20] One aspect of this uniqueness is that each person experiences his or her own self as existing and acting differently from how they experience others.[21]

Certainly, given the suggestion that theology concerns itself only with things of heaven, Pope St John Paul II emphasizes the body. After all, following the Second Vatican Council 'man is not allowed to despise his bodily life' even if he is more than just a body.[22] Pope St John Paul II explains that theology naturally includes the body because by the Incarnation 'the body entered theology through the main door.'[23] However, Pope St John Paul II's concern with a theology of the body involves the whole person and it is equally a mistake to think that his theology is just about the body as to think that rationality or consciousness is the only thing that matters in the make-up of human beings. So, it is vital for Pope St John Paul II to explain and keep together the exterior and interior of the person. As Pope St John Paul II points out, Christ demands that what seems to belong exclusively to the exterior human being, the body, is also part of the interior, so that the person is a true master of his or her deep impulses. In this way *eros*, which is an interior force of attraction to the good, true, and beautiful meets with the *ethos* of redemption.[24] What matters first is a discernment in the interior sphere, in the heart, and then in the way of being and acting. Thus, the heart is the object of a call, not of an accusation, and the person's consciousness of sinfulness becomes an indispensable condition of the person's aspiration to virtue and to purity of heart.

Pope St John Paul II then considers that the body is proper to the person, not in the sense that the body belongs to the person as any other thing might be possessed. Rather the person is his or her body. And the person is called to imitate Christ in total self-giving love, the 'nuptial' meaning of the body. Pope St John Paul II's task in the *Theology of the Body* is to explain God's plan of love in both the relationship of marriage and celibacy for the Kingdom: both belong to the theology of the body.

Ephesians 5 and Redemption

In the tradition the text of Ephesians 5 has been pivotal for the theology of marriage and the family. In God's plan of salvation Christ loves the Church and gives himself totally up for her. By this self-gift Christ confers a spousal character and meaning on his redemptive love. This great mystery of Christ and the Church is presupposed 'in the beginning', is witnessed in the prophets, and the spousal love of Christ and redemption is rediscovered in the 'great analogy' of Christ and the Church, husband and wife.[25] The words of Ephesians 5 are 'centred on the body', both its 'metaphorical meaning' of the Body of Christ, the Church, and its 'concrete meaning' of the human body as masculine and feminine.[26] Certainly, Pope St John Paul II realizes that the author of Ephesians is not speaking directly of the sacrament of marriage but rather the author treats of the sacramentality of the whole of Christian life; marriage is treated indirectly. Nevertheless, the analogy is significant and, according to Pope St John Paul II it 'operates in two directions':

> on the one hand, it helps us to understand better the essence of the relationship between Christ and the Church. On the other hand, at the same time, it helps us to see more deeply into the essence of marriage to which Christians are called.[27]

Marriage seems to be a way of revelation to show how God so loved the world. This is why it is crucial to ensure we understand marriage. Recalling that the Church carries on the work of Christ in the sacramental economy, according to Pope St John Paul II, marriage is more than a model for the whole sacramental order since marriage was instituted 'in the beginning.' As a 'primordial sacrament' it is 'an essential part of the new heritage, that of the sacrament of redemption, with which the Church is endowed in Christ.' And this new sacramental economy, 'derived from the spousal gracing of the Church on the part of Christ,' differs from the original economy because it is directed not to the first human beings but to human beings after the Fall, 'burdened with the heritage of original sin and with the state of sinfulness.'[28]

From the beginning

The starting point for Pope St John Paul II's *Theology of the Body* are the texts in the gospels of Matthew and Mark and the teaching of Jesus on marriage and divorce.[29] Intriguingly, in both gospels the chapter before deals with the question of who is the greatest. The gospel passages appear to be mid-way between Genesis and Ephesians and so Pope St John Paul II can look backwards and forwards, while starting significantly with Jesus. However, Pope St John Paul II also begins with human experience and the consciousness of the self and the other in the context of sin and grace. For Pope St John Paul II the relationship between Revelation and experience is especially important: human beings, as bodies in the world, are perceived by us mainly by experience therefore experience is an 'indispensable point of reference.' Moreover, our experience is that we wait for the redemption of our bodies. Both these accounts give a reason for trying to understand the body correctly.[30]

Pope St John Paul II directs the questioner in the gospel accounts from Matthew and Mark back to Genesis. Pope St John Paul II regards the story of the creation of human beings in Genesis 2 as part of human experience, but also as anthropology and theology because it is bound up with the 'image of God' in Genesis 1.[31] Moreover the return to Genesis contains not only creation but also the seeds of redemption.[32]

In the creation story God creates the human being as the crown of his good creation.[33] From the beginning there is a clear boundary between the world of animals and human beings created in the image and likeness of God, and, says Pope St John Paul II, humans are well aware of this.[34] This is reflected in the experience of 'original solitude', when 'Adam', generic 'man', comes to name the animals and in doing so realizes that he is aware of himself as a person, a subject, and a being in the world, an object, but different from the visible world: he is 'alone before God.'[35] Human experience is one of self-awareness, that man is aware of himself as a subject on the basis of his own bodily existence, and that he is the author of truly human activity in the task of 'dominion': the body expresses the person; the visible the invisible.[36] Human experience is also of the ethical because his self-knowledge develops with his knowledge of the world and he comes to see that he is a subject of the covenant. As a person he must discern between good and evil, life and death. At the same time, right from the beginning he is in search of the definition of himself. He is alone in the visible world that expresses what he 'is not', and in solitude he discovers his transcendence: that he is not merely a body among bodies, but he is aware of himself as a person, body and soul, who is directed towards relationship, 'communion.'[37]

It is 'not good' for him to be alone so there is a 'second creation': he becomes male and female. In this solitude where he is revealed to himself as a person, he literally, is opened up to a being like himself. Adam's recognition of Eve as 'flesh of my flesh' indicates that the body reveals the human being and the person, a being in the image of God. Thus, the body is not only anthropological but theological. The 'original unity' overcomes solitude leading to both joy and mutual enrichment. Man and woman then are two different ways of the human 'being a body', but this is also a unity since they are both in the image of God.[38] The body does not simply have meaning in the way in which it is perceived externally. Rather, the body 'expresses the person in his ontological and existential concreteness, which is something more than the individual.' The body expresses 'the personal human self' and it acts as an intermediary since it enables man and woman to communicate with each other according to the communion of persons willed by the Creator.[39] Pope St John Paul II notes that the 'image of God' in the human being is not only through his humanity but also through this communion of persons that reaches out in procreation: procreation continues the work of creation.[40] It is important to realize that for Pope St John Paul II this relationship is not simply community. Rather it is a theological concept, 'communion' because it is formed from a 'double solitude.' In their solitude their sex as male or female is a part of their unique identity. Both Adam and Eve are separate from the animal world and each are unique and unrepeatable, but they exist for each other as 'help', that is to say, as person beside person. Human beings are images of God in their solitude but also become images of God who is a communion of persons. This special reciprocity requires self-knowledge and self-determination.[41] It also involves complementarity since they are a 'gift for each other.' They accept and receive each other with 'interior innocence', a purity of heart, that does not see the other as an 'object for me', and so they are not ashamed.[42] In this purity of heart they see each other with pure vision where there is no opposition between the spiritual and the sensible.[43]

In the 'hermeneutics of the gift' God calls creation to existence from nothingness as a gift of love. This is 'a fundamental and 'radical' giving' and 'every creature bears within it the sign of the original and fundamental gift.' Since the concept of giving indicates 'one who gives and the one who receives the gift' there is also the creation of a relationship; specifically, God confers the gift on human beings. Created in the image and likeness of God, 'as the 'image of God', man is capable of understanding the meaning of gift in the call from nothingness to existence. He is capable of answering the Creator with the language of this understanding', and the world also received man as a gift.[44] However, the gift of Adam and Eve to each other has particular meaning because both are images of God and both are an 'I', willed by the Creator for their own sakes.

Pope St John Paul II calls the 'disinterested gift of oneself' the 'nuptial meaning of the body' and it takes place through original innocence. Key for 'gift' in the nuptial meaning is 'alone' and 'helper': the person only realizes his or her essence completely by existing with and for someone in the original truth of masculinity or femininity.[45] The nuptial meaning of the body concerns not only fruitfulness and procreation but also freedom and the total gift of self and the affirmation of the other who is also willed by God for his or her own sake.[46] The person knows the other as a unique, unrepeatable 'self.'[47] In terms of the sacrament where the visible expresses the invisible, the sacramental 'beginning' of the human being and marriage is found in the state of 'original innocence.'[48] Marriage and the state of original innocence, a state before original sin, belongs to the dimension of grace and the mystery of creation.[49]

Pope St John Paul II describes the tree of knowledge in the Garden of Eden as a sign of both the submission and dependence of man, the creature, on his Creator, and his unique relationship with God. The tree of knowledge is thus a symbol of the covenant with God that is broken in man's heart when he disobeys God and eats the fruit, and the symbolical boundary of original innocence and original sin. The state of sin is part of 'historical man', that is every human being,[50] and it refers to the lost grace of the state of original innocence. But Pope St John Paul II explains that this is not simply the 'lost horizon of human existence.' It is also the 'first promise of redemption' with the prophetic sign of the Messiah's triumph over Satan, as he shall crush your head, you shall bruise his heel.[51] This means that historical man participates not only in the history of human sinfulness which is both hereditary and personal, but also in the history of salvation. At the same time human beings are closed to original innocence and open to redemption.[52]

Historical man, that is every human being, is separated from the mystery of original innocence by original sin. Sin has repercussions as it breaks original unity between Adam and Eve, and so marriage loses its supernatural efficacy.[53] However, Pope St John Paul II says that human beings can still approach that mystery by their theological knowledge and their experience of their own sinfulness starting from the experience of shame.[54] The shame experienced by Adam and Eve indicates a 'boundary' experience, a new situation. He says that Adam and Eve move not from 'not knowing' they were naked to 'knowing', but rather there is a radical change that directly concerns the experience of the meaning of the body before the Creator and creatures. Interested in contemporary analysis, Pope St John Paul II is aware of the complexity of shame: 'in the experience of shame the human being experiences fear with regard to his "second self"…this is substantially fear for one's own "self".' In their vulnerability the person needs 'affirmation and acceptance of this "self" according to its rightful value.'[55] Pope St John Paul II explains that the beginning of shame is marked by the person mentally reducing the other person to a mere object.[56] This mental reduction is seeing the other in a limited way, merely with the eyes of the body, resulting in a disturbance in personal intimacy and the peace of the 'interior gaze.'[57] The fruits of breaking the first covenant are concupiscence and three forms of lust: 'lust of the flesh, lust of the eyes, and the pride of life.'[58] The original capacity the first couple had of communicating with each other has been shattered and diversity is now felt as mutual confrontation: it is 'as if sexuality became an obstacle in the personal relationship of man and woman.'[59] Moreover, this disruption is individual as there is now opposition in the heart between the spirit and the body: 'almost a constant danger exists of this way (as possession) of seeing, evaluating, and loving so that the "desire of the body" is more powerful than "the desire of the mind".'[60]

Certainly, after original sin the grace of innocence has been lost and the discovery of the nuptial meaning of the body ceases to be 'a simple reality of revelation and grace.' Pope St John Paul II explains that now 'the heart has become a battlefield between love and lust. The more lust dominates the heart, the less the heart experiences the nuptial meaning of the body. It becomes less sensitive to the gift of the person.'⁶¹ However the nuptial meaning remains 'inscribed in the heart' and 'through the veil of shame, man will continually rediscover himself as the guardian of the mystery of the subject, that is, of the freedom of the gift': he will not reduce the other to 'the position of a mere object.'⁶² Pope St John Paul II believes that the call to rediscover this meaning in the law and written in the heart is addressed to everyone since all have a sense of the meaning of the body. This is shown in the way in which Jesus in the Sermon on the Mount addresses 'historical man', every person in his or her heart.⁶³ Unlike those who make the body the problem, Jesus shifts the point of gravity of sin from 'adultery of the body to the heart.'⁶⁴ Following the tradition that a person acts according to what he is, *operari sequitur esse*, Pope St John Paul II explains that 'a look expresses what is in the heart.'⁶⁵ The look of lust is not an 'accusation of the body' but it is directed at the human heart, calling the person to self-critical examination and a call to overcome lust.⁶⁶ Since marriage as a sacrament is 'an effective sign of God's saving power' God's eternal plan is accomplished in spite of sin and concupiscence. In perhaps an echo to the traditional view that marriage is a remedy for concupiscence, Pope St John Paul II adds that marriage also encourages the domination of concupiscence and the fruits of this dominion are unity, indissolubility and 'a deepened sense of the dignity of woman in the heart of a man, and also the dignity of man in the heart of a woman.'⁶⁷

Since he is trying to bring his reflections 'nearer to the routes taken, in its sphere, by the conscience of contemporary men' and given that contemporary thinking sees a conflict between the erotic and the ethical, thought of principally as norms and prohibitions, Pope St John Paul II turns to an exploration of *eros* and *ethos*. He notes that in the classic philosophy of Plato *eros* 'represents the interior force that drags man toward everything good, true and beautiful.' *Eros* indicates primarily a sensory attraction and is related to the sexual attraction between man and woman. However, unlike lust that indicates 'the subjective intensity of straining toward the object because of its sexual character' and holds dominion over human emotion, Pope St John Paul II thinks that there is room in the concept of *eros* for *ethos*. The attraction of *eros* to the true, good, and beautiful is a call to overcome lust in the '*ethos* of redemption.' *Eros* and *ethos* then 'are not opposed to each other, but are called to meet in the human heart, and in this meeting to bear fruit.' The human spirit has a role 'of an ethical nature' to ensure that 'what is erotic also becomes true, good and beautiful.'[68]

If from the beginning 'man', in the sense of the human being, 'searches for the meaning of his own body', and 'this meaning is at the basis of the theology of the body itself', then part of the mystery of being human is revealed in parenthood. Pope St John Paul II is careful to distance parenthood from 'passive acceptance' of what appears determined by the body and sex. To do this he refers to the biblical term 'know', and in terms of complementarity he explains that the man 'knows' his wife and she is the one who is 'known.' The point Pope St John Paul II makes is not one of activity and passivity. Rather, Pope St John Paul II thinks that the mystery of femininity is revealed by motherhood as is the mystery of masculinity revealed by 'the generative and fatherly meaning of his body.' The construction of the bodies of man and woman is different not only externally but also internally. However, this is not simply a matter of biology. In the consummation of marriage husband and wife come to know the objective aspect of the body as well as the subjective aspect that is 'mutual self-fulfilment in the gift.'[69] There are some who allege a 'misogyny that forms a dark undercurrent to the Catholic theological tradition' and 'a profound fear of female sexuality.'[70] Pope St John Paul II focuses on the 'mystery of woman … revealed in motherhood' in order to give proper honour to women's bodies. Nevertheless, unless it is understood that fatherhood is also revealed, there remains the danger that women are only appreciated for their ability to give children to their husbands or to the Church. The significant point that Pope St John Paul II makes is that the existence of both man and woman is renewed by procreation where they 'know each other reciprocally in the "third", sprung from them both.' 'Knowledge becomes a discovery'; it is a 'revelation of the new man, in whom both of them, man and woman, again recognize themselves, their humanity, their living image',[71] and another image of God. In this 'knowledge-generation cycle' Pope St John Paul II sees the refusal of life to surrender to death as 'man' goes beyond the solitude of his own being and decides again to affirm this being in an 'other.'[72] In contrast to mentalities that reject a total vision of human beings, including those that hold to biological determinism or that fail to acknowledge that people are responsible subjects of their own actions or that regard sexuality as mere information without any context of personal dignity, Pope St John Paul II asks that those who are called to the Christian vocation in marriage be aware of the nuptial self-gift meaning of the body and its procreative meaning.[73]

Redemption

Returning to the words of Jesus and going forwards, Pope St John Paul II points out:

> in the Sermon on the Mount Christ did not invite man to return to the state of original innocence, because humanity has irrevocably left it behind. But he called him to rediscover—on the foundation of the perennial and indestructible meanings of what is human—the living forms of the new man.[74]

Pope St John Paul II has already demonstrated that marriage from the beginning was good and part of the sacrament of creation, with a perfect vision of the other. However, human beings are not destined to return to goodness of creation. Through the Incarnation human nature has been raised up beyond its natural dignity to a 'divine dignity',[75] and this leads us to ask what awaits us in the order of redemption.

Reflecting on the saying of Jesus on the resurrection that 'when they rise from the dead, they neither marry nor are given in marriage',[76] Pope St John Paul II says that marriage and procreation belong to this age, 'marriage and procreation do not constitute...the eschatological future of man. In the resurrection they lose, so to speak, their raison d'etre.'[77] This is not to denigrate marriage. Rather Pope St John Paul II is alluding to the 'new condition of the human body in the resurrection': bodies will keep their masculinity or femininity because this is a part of the person's authentic subjectivity. Nevertheless, 'the sense of being a male or a female in the body will be constituted and understood in that age in a different way from what it had been from the beginning, and then in the whole dimension of earthly existence.' In this promised 'spiritualization of man' the human being who was once subject to death is now restored to 'real life.' Moreover, this is not an angelic restoration; it is a restoration 'in his psychosomatic nature.' Pope St John Paul II adds that this is not a 'disincarnation', but 'a new submission of the body to the spirit.' Spiritualization is not just the spirit dominating the body but fully permeating body. Instead of man being at war with himself, spiritualization is 'the perfect participation of all that is physical in man in what is spiritual in him...the perfect realization of what is personal in man.'[78] This includes the heart.

For Pope St John Paul II the place of the heart is significant because it is 'in a way, the equivalent of personal subjectivity,' where rationality and affectivity meet. He says, 'man is unique and unrepeatable above all because of his heart, which decides his being from within.' The heart is the person's 'inner self.'[79] Certainly, the heart is the place of struggle between love and lust. Pope St John Paul II's appeal to a life of virtues, and especially temperance and purity of heart in relationships is 'reminiscent of the original solitude.'[80] In solitude the person 'is revealed to himself as a person, in order to reveal, at the same time, the communion of persons.' The nuptial significance of being a body is both that this is a sexed body and that as persons human beings are called to 'a life in *communion personarum*.'[81] So, purity of heart is explained 'with regard for the other subject': 'purity is a requirement of love.'[82] In contrast to living an uncontrolled life of earth-bound desires, purity of heart is realized by living a life according to the Spirit.[83] Through the virtue of temperance, 'the capacity for controlling the impulses of sensitive desires', the person knows how to control the body 'in holiness and honour', and so gradually experience his or her own dignity and freedom.[84]

Although marriage is important for Pope St John Paul II, he recognizes that the meaning of the body has significance beyond marriage, and this is confirmed both by the belief that there is no marriage in heaven and by the charism of celibacy. Marriage and procreation 'give a concrete reality' to the meaning of the body in terms of earthly history. However, resurrection of the body indicates 'the end of the historical dimension.' In the resurrection life will 'correspond perfectly' to the fact that human beings are persons created in the image and likeness of God, and that this image 'is realized in the communion of persons.' The meaning of the body will be 'perfectly personal and communitarian at the same time.' The glorification of the body 'will reveal the definitive value of what was to be from the beginning a distinctive sign of the created person in the visible world, as well as a means of mutual communication between persons and a genuine expression of truth and love.' This is new life, not an alien life.[85]

The truth that the meaning of the body is not determined definitively by marriage and procreation is revealed by Jesus in the vocation of the renunciation of marriage for the sake of the Kingdom. As with the vocation to marriage, the vocation to celibacy also highlights the same truth about the person: that there is freedom of the gift of the self to others and that the body 'possesses a full nuptial meaning.'[86] However, to understand the vocation to virginity or celibacy for the Kingdom, as with marriage and procreation, both the beginning and the resurrection must be borne in mind. The choice of virginity or celibacy for the Kingdom is not made from a supposed negative valuing of marriage. Rather, this choice concerns the virtue of continence. Pope St John Paul II points out that in psychology continence has a negative role because continence indicates 'the ability to abstain, that is, mastery over the multiple reactions that are interwoven in the mutual influence of masculinity and femininity.' In addition, he presents a positive role for continence. Continence is 'the capacity to dominate, control and direct drives of a sexual character and their consequences, in the psychosomatic subjectivity of man'; it is a virtue because it is 'a constant disposition of the will';[87] it is 'a self-mastery' that is the capacity to control and guide the person's 'whole sensual and emotive sphere.' In marriage continence keeps in balance the two meanings of the conjugal act: the unity of the couple and responsible parenthood, and so deepens their personal communion.[88] For those who have been gifted with the vocation to celibacy, continence for the Kingdom is 'discovered and welcomed personally as one's own vocation.' By the virtue of continence, a person integrates sexuality into their personality.

Continence expressed in celibacy or virginity for the Kingdom is a personal choice and 'a charismatic orientation towards that eschatological state in which men 'neither marry nor are given in marriage'.'[89] In the Old Testament marriage as a source of fruitfulness was the religiously privileged state for human nature and for the Kingdom of God, and eunuchs were so because of defects. However, in a 'decisive turning point' Jesus roots the vocation to continence 'deep in the reality of earthly life.' Those who freely choose continence for the Kingdom express 'the eschatological virginity of the risen man' united in the communion of saints.[90] According to Pope St John Paul II, earthly continence for the Kingdom is 'a sign that indicates this truth and this reality.' It is a sign that the body is directed to glorification and a witness that anticipates the future resurrection. Moreover, it is an imprint of likeness to Christ. The virginal relationship of the Holy Family demonstrates the 'most perfect fruitfulness of the Holy Spirit.' Christ's own example of celibacy 'for the Kingdom', and Church tradition based on this illustrates that continence for the Kingdom has a particular meaning for the spiritual and supernatural fruitfulness which comes from the Holy Spirit.[91]

As Pope St John Paul II observes in *Familiaris Consortio* 'in spite of having renounced physical fecundity, the celibate person becomes spiritually fruitful, the father and mother of many, cooperating in the realization of the family according to God's plan.'[92] In a different way to marriage and perhaps more so, the person becomes a 'true gift to others.'[93]

On the question of the superiority of virginity over marriage, Pope St John Paul II stresses their complementarity while also affirming the privileged way of continence for the Kingdom.[94] Pope St John Paul II observes that 'marriage and continence are neither opposed to each other, nor do they divide the human (and Christian) community into two camps', the 'perfect' because of continence for the Kingdom and 'less perfect' because of the reality of married life. Instead, the two states explain, complement, and complete each other. Moreover, continence for the Kingdom has 'a special eloquence' for married people.[95] For Pope St John Paul II, marriage helps us understand continence for the kingdom and continence illumines marriage viewed in the mystery of creation and redemption. Marriage that is true to its original institution is 'fully appropriate and of a value that is fundamental, universal and ordinary.' Since this is the case, continence chosen for the Kingdom possesses a 'particular and exceptional value.' Continence for the Kingdom is 'an unquestionable sign of the other world', bearing in itself 'the interior dynamism of the mystery of the redemption of the body.' The choice for continence for the Kingdom is 'proper to a rather exceptional vocation, and not one that is universal and ordinary.' Undoubtedly there is a level of anguish in this decision since it rules out the great good of marriage and children, and it is a choice that has to be renewed continually. Nevertheless, it can be seen as a particular 'solitude for God.'[96] Celibacy is not to be understood as a bachelor life-style or a life only partially given to God,[97] but rather is always directed towards God and the other. Solitude never ceases to be a personal dimension of everyone's dual nature in the call towards a 'new and even fuller form of

Theology of the Body

intersubjective communion with others.' The authentic development of the image and likeness of God is expressed in its Trinitarian meaning of communion.[98] The love expressed in both marriage and continence for the Kingdom is nuptial, that is, is expressed through total gift of self, and this nuptial love has been inscribed in the personal makeup of every man and woman. Love leads to fruitfulness either as 'paternity or maternity in a spiritual sense' in continence for the Kingdom, or in marriage as physical paternity and maternity which, notably is completed by education of children as paternity and maternity in the spirit.[99]

Significantly, Pope St John Paul II argues that the revelation of the nuptial relationship of Christ and the Church in Ephesians 5 is 'equally valid' both for a theology of marriage and for a theology of continence for the Kingdom.[100] Celibacy is, he says, 'a particular response to the love of the Divine Spouse.' In both vocations of marriage and celibacy for the Kingdom God's grace is at work, grace makes the body a temple of the Holy Spirit, and grace helps married couples in their common life.[101] The redemption of the body is not only in the cosmic dimension of resurrection as victory over death. Redemption is also in the words of Jesus to people in their own historical situations. When Jesus calls people in their heart to overcome concupiscence, Jesus gives them hope of victory, 'the hope of every day.' Married and celibate people alike are asked in daily life to draw from the mystery of redemption the inspiration and strength to fulfil their vocations.[102]

The sacramentality of marriage

In reflecting on the sacramentality of marriage, Pope St John Paul II makes use of the traditional Christian saying *lex orandi, lex credendi*, 'the law of prayer is the law of faith.' When the Church celebrates the sacraments, the Church is witnessing to the faith received from the Apostles.[103] The text of Ephesians 5 is seen in the *lex orandi* as an explicit reference to the sacrament of marriage and the text begins with Christ, goes back to Genesis 'in the beginning', then returns to Christ and His Church. According to Pope St John Paul II sacramentality in general 'meets with the body and presupposes the theology of the body.' He explains that a sacrament is a visible sign and 'the body also signifies that which is visible.' Therefore, 'even if in the most general way, the body enters the definition of sacrament, being "a visible sign of an invisible reality", that is, of the spiritual, transcendent, divine reality.' The sacrament is a sign of grace and produces grace. Pope St John Paul II takes *Gaudium et spes* 22 that 'the truth is that only in the mystery of the incarnate Word does the mystery of man take on light', Christ reveals the person to him or herself and makes his or her vocation clear, and he links it to the text of Ephesians. Ephesians too 'reveals man to man' and 'makes him aware of his lofty vocation.'[104] Outlining the structure of the letter to the Ephesians Pope St John Paul II explains that the author presents 'the eternal plan of the salvation of man in Jesus Christ.' Through the revelation of Christ in the Church, sinful humanity is called to a new life in Christ. Ephesians 5 gives a more detailed instruction: the faithful are asked to be imitators of Christ, to walk as children of the light. In the encouragement to engage in the spiritual battle, they are to overcome vices, acquire virtues, and be subject to one another out of reverence.[105]

Perhaps in answer to the modern concern that Ephesians 5 suggests one-sided dominion of husband over wife, and indeed Pope St John Paul II recognizes that 'submission' of wives comes out of the 'mentality of the time',[106] Pope St John Paul II observes that 'reverence for Christ is the basis of the relationship between spouses.' He calls this reverence a 'respect for holiness', '*pietas*', and 'the mutual relations of husband and wife should flow from their common relationship with Christ.' The 'mystery of Christ, penetrating their hearts 'engenders in them that *pietas* towards each other where they are "subject to one another".'[107]

Although Pope St John Paul II accepts that the author of Ephesians is speaking of the sacramentality of the whole of Christian life, and only indirectly about marriage, he says that the analogy of the husband wife relationship to that of Christ and the Church helps to clarify the mystery of the eternal love of God for humanity, and the mystery of Christ and the Church illuminates the marriage relationship of husband and wife. Through this analogy Christian marriage is shown to emerge 'from the mystery of God's eternal love for man and for humanity.' Christ's redemptive love has a spousal character because it is a 'total giving up of himself.' Christ forms the Church as 'his Body and continually builds her up, becoming her head.' Thus, Christ is 'united once and for all with her, as bridegroom with the bride, as husband with his wife.'[108] Christian marriage is also called to be redeeming love. However, Pope St John Paul II points out that the Pauline analogy of the union of head and body is used in 'a more central manner' for the truth about Christ and the Church. This is because in marriage man and woman are 'two distinct personal subjects who knowingly decide on their conjugal union' to become 'one flesh.' There is an 'essential bi-subjectivity which is at the basis of the image of "one single body".' This bi-subjectivity is also manifested in the Christ Church relationship as 'Christ is a subject different from the Church.' The point Pope St John Paul II is making is that individuality is not blurred through the analogy, yet at the same time there is the mystery of union.[109] In marriage this 'uni-subjectivity' is based on 'bi-subjectivity' through the intention that 'the wife's body is not her husband's own body, but it must be loved like his own body.' This is unity not in the ontological sense but in the moral sense, 'unity through love.' This love calls for the recognition of the dignity and sacredness of the body that deserves protection and care.[110]

Pope St John Paul II is aware that the text of Ephesians constantly speaks of the 'great mystery' of Christ and the Church. Sacraments too are 'preached as a mystery' and yet are manifest and accomplish that mystery. This leads him to consider the extent to which analogy can reach the content of the mystery 'more profoundly and with greater exactitude.' He notes that Ephesians is in a certain sense a continuation of the Old Testament presentation of Yahweh's love for his chosen people, and so he turns to the relationship of Christ to the Church as it is connected to the prophetic tradition. He takes first the text from Isaiah where the Holy One calls back his people in the way that a husband remembers his wife. Pope St John Paul II draws attention to the 'love of compassion' and the grace in everlasting love. This analogy is preserved yet also deepened in Ephesians where love consists in Christ giving himself up for the Church in the work of redemption.[111]

Certainly, Pope St John Paul II recognizes the limitations of analogy and he says that the mystery of Christ and the Church remains transcendent. Nevertheless, the analogy to married love gives us a glimpse of Christ's love as 'a total and irrevocable gift of self on the part of God to man in Christ', the living God 'who is Creator and Redeemer.' Like the gift of self in marriage this is a total 'radical' gift and grace. In Ephesians the 'visible sign of marriage "in the beginning"' is linked to 'the visible sign of Christ and the Church' so that the eternal plan of love is transferred into history and is made the foundation of the whole sacramental order.[112]

Having established marriage in the sacramental and ecclesiological order, Pope St John Paul II looks back at marriage in the beginning as the 'sacrament of creation.' Holiness was conferred on humanity in the beginning in the 'sacrament of creation.' The body, as a reality in its masculinity or femininity, makes visible the invisible and so belongs to this sacrament. As an integral part of the sacrament of creation, marriage is the 'primordial sacrament' and it 'expresses the beginning of the fundamental human community' by continuing the work of creation in procreation.[113] Sin deprived marriage, the primordial sacrament, of its supernatural efficacy but marriage still remains 'the platform' for God's plan as the analogy of marriage corresponds to God's love for his people and the mystery of Christ and the Church. The sacrament of redemption, that is 'the fruit of Christ's redemptive love', is a new and super-abounding gracing and a new creation. In this 'great sacrament' of Christ and the Church, the invisible made visible, Christ, the 'second Adam', is 'united with the Church through the sacrament of redemption by an indissoluble bond.' This is 'analogous to the indissoluble covenant of spouses.' Marriage then is an essential part of 'the integral heritage of the covenant with God', from primordial sacrament to the sacramentality of 'the whole heritage of the sacrament of redemption', to Christ and the Church, and to the new sacramental economy.[114]

Noting that the sacrament of marriage is the only sacrament instituted from the beginning and before the Fall, and that the total self-gift in marriage is a reflection of the total self-giving of Christ to the Church, Pope St John Paul II sees marriage as in a sense a 'prototype' of all sacraments. The sacramental order 'draws its origin from the spousal gracing which the Church received from Christ, together with all the benefits of redemption.' Certainly, marriage is also a sacrament of the new covenant because it is directed towards human beings who are burdened with the state of sinfulness. Thus, the analogy of Christ and the Church is not simply a comparison. Rather the analogy is a 'real renewal' or 're-creation' of the primordial sacrament, and this has significance for the understanding of the sacramentality of marriage.[115] By Christ's spousal relationship with the Church the Church itself is 'the great sacrament', the 'new sign of the covenant and of grace.' Developing the Ephesian analogy, Pope St John Paul II explains that the 'roots' of the great sacrament of the Church lie in the sacrament of redemption, 'just as from the depths of the sacrament of creation marriage has emerged.' The primordial sacrament of marriage is 'realized in a new way in the sacrament of Christ and of the Church.' The analogy expresses therefore the mystery of redemption and redemption of the body. Redemption has significance for the two complementary vocations of continence for the Kingdom and of marriage and each witness to hope in redemption and also to the cosmic hope of the redemption of all creation.

As a sign of God's saving power, the joining of man and woman to become one flesh unites them into a 'community of persons' in the likeness of the Trinity. By insisting on the indissolubility of marriage and faithfulness, Pope St John Paul II says that Christ opens up marriage to 'the salvific action of God.' Graces from the redemption of the body help people to overcome the consequences of sin and to come to understand the personal dignity of the human body.[116] Pope St John Paul II affirms that God 'accomplishes his eternal plan even after sin and in spite of the threefold concupiscence [lusts of flesh, the eyes and pride] hidden in the heart of every man, male and female.' Marriage is then 'an exhortation to dominate concupiscence' and unity, indissolubility and an awareness of personal dignity are fruits of this dominion. However, Pope St John Paul II points out that marriage is not merely a remedy for concupiscence. Marriage has a 'special gift' and grace, it 'signifies an ethical order' of 'life according to the Spirit.' Life according to the Spirit is expressed by hope in the daily life of redemption; by the 'enduring and indissoluble communion of persons in a manner worthy of persons'; by their participation in creation and 'the dignity of the spouses themselves as parents'; by their awareness and protection of the sanctity of life. Marriage is 'the basis of hope for the person' in this world and 'the seed of the person's eschatological future', redemption of the body.[117] Pope St John Paul II thinks that the spousal and redemptive dimensions of love have significance and are valid for everyone, married or not. He asks that people seek the meaning of their existence and humanity by reaching out to the mystery of creation through the reality of redemption. There they can find the significance of the body in its masculinity or femininity. The union of Christ and the Church completes the spousal significance with redemptive significance in all areas of life not just in marriage or celibacy.[118]

Language of the Body

Pope St John Paul II takes the rite of marriage as a starting point for the language of the body. In marriage the couple are the ministers, 'the full and real visible sign' of the sacrament. The man and woman administer the sacrament with the priest as witness and presider. The sacramental words 'I take you as my wife/as my husband...' are the sign of the 'coming into being' of the marriage that is only fully constituted by consummation. These words are 'in the order of intention', what they 'both have decided to be from now on' and are part of the 'integral structure' of the sacramental sign. The words necessarily correspond to their human subjectivity as man or woman becoming husband or wife. As spoken words of a vow, the 'language of the body' is given 'an intentional expression on the level of intellect and will, of consciousness and of the heart.' Moreover, these words are in the context of the 'communion of persons' who promise faithfulness in joy, sadness, sickness and health, love, and honour, all the days of their lives. 'The persons—man and woman—become for each other a mutual gift.'[119]

Pope St John Paul II locates the language of the body in the long biblical tradition of a 'prophetism of the body' where from Genesis to the prophets there has been 'the great analogy' of the covenant between God and Israel seen in terms of marriage and whose 'final expression' is the new covenant under the form of a marriage between Christ and the Church. The analogy operates on two levels: first, as the covenantal love between God and Israel, and the covenantal love between husband and wife; second, 'the body itself "speaks"...in the mysterious language of the personal gift' and it speaks both in the language of fidelity and infidelity. Pope St John Paul II notes that the person is not 'the author' of this language, rather 'its author is man as male or female, as husband or wife—man with his everlasting vocation to the communion of persons.'[120] There is subjectivity and an objectivity in this language, 'a true sense ... bringing to light the spousal significance of the body as integrally inscribed in the very structure of the masculinity and femininity of the personal subject.'[121] The language of love, giving, and fidelity refers both to marriage and celibacy for the kingdom. Moreover, for the prophets the language of the body is 'not merely a language of morality, a praise of fidelity and of purity, and a condemnation of adultery.' Instead, in the analogy of Yahweh and Israel 'the body speaks the truth through fidelity and conjugal love. When it commits adultery it speaks lies.' The language of the body is about truth.[122]

The essential 'truth' of the language of the body is confirmed with the words 'I take you as my wife/husband...' and the body speaks this truth 'through conjugal love, fidelity and integrity.' By their consent the couple 'set themselves on the line of the same prophetism of the body', of covenant and grace, 'continually sustained by the power of redemption of the body, offered by Christ to the Church.' The words contain 'the intention, the decision and the choice' and so both parties 'decide to act in conformity with the language of the body, reread in truth.' The sign constituted by their words looks to the future: the marriage bond as 'one and indissoluble', and later blessed by paternity and maternity.[123]

The spouses continue to 'speak' as they carry out 'the conjugal dialogue proper to their vocation and based on the language of the body.' They are continually called to form their life and living together as a communion of persons on the basis of that language. In this way they also participate in the prophetic mission of the Church as witnesses to the grandeur of the sacrament.[124]

Pope St John Paul II's reflection on the sacrament of marriage takes account not only of the origin and prophetic nature of marriage but also of its context in the Sermon on the Mount when Jesus referred to the human heart. Human beings are people of concupiscence, but this is not a condemnation, in the sense that human beings are not completely determined sexual desire. Rather it is a call to overcome concupiscence. According to Pope St John Paul II concupiscence, especially concupiscence of the flesh, 'does not destroy the capacity to reread in truth the language of the body', though concupiscence may cause 'many errors' in this rereading. Conversion and redemption are always possible.[125]

Pope St John Paul II next explores the richness of married love and the language of the body in his reflection on the Song of Songs.

In the poem the language of the body is expressed in terms of 'mutual wonder and admiration', 'an attraction to the other "I"—female or male—which in the interior impulse of the heart generates love.' Love 'unleashes a special experience of the beautiful', of the entire person. In the poem the groom and bride become 'you' for the other's 'I'. Reflecting perhaps the philosophical idea of the I-Thou relationship, Pope St John Paul II explains that 'the term "beloved" indicates what is always essential for love, which puts the second "I" beside one's own "I".' This is not only a sign of deep friendship but an indication of the way in which a person helps the other to identify himself and be open to others in a personal I-Thou relationship. Taking the metaphor of the bride's 'enclosed garden', Pope St John Paul II sees in this a description of the way in which the person is a 'master of her own mystery.' The enclosed garden indicates 'the personal dignity of the woman who as a spiritual subject is in possession and can decide not only on the metaphysical depth but also on the essential truth and authenticity of the gift of herself.' The garden represents the interior inviolability of the person as well as the possibility of entrusting the self to mutual belonging that takes place in the free gift of the self to the other. The language of the body becomes 'a part of the single process of the mutual attraction of the man and woman.' There is search and a discovery of the other that leads to joy. At the same time there is a continual search for something that surpasses the limits of their initial attraction, *eros*. There is a restless search for perfection, purity and self-control because 'this dynamic of love indirectly reveals the near impossibility of one person's being appropriated and mastered by the other.' Human beings are not the subject of possession, domination or objectification. Love that is 'as stern as death' goes beyond *eros* to *agape* and the invitation of communion.[126]

Even when a couple are deeply in love there are always tests and struggles. Pope St John Paul II accepts that the couple in the Song of Songs seem to live in an abstract ideal world. So, he takes up the story in the Book of Tobit and the love between Tobias and Sarah. Tobias and Sarah face the test of death in the confidence that theirs is a love that will stand the test of time. They ask in the words of prayer for mercy and to be allowed to live together to a happy old age. The language of the body becomes 'the language of the liturgy.'[127] The language of the liturgy raises the consent of the man and woman to the mystery of the sacrament and, at the same time, it enables the couple to fulfil their consent through the language of the body. The daily acts and duties and the virtues belonging to marriage form the spirituality of marriage.[128]

Reflections on Humanae Vitae

To complete his reflections on human love in the divine plan Pope St John Paul II looks at their 'concrete application' in marital and family morality and specifically responsible parenthood. Pope St John Paul II uses extensive quotations from *Gaudium et spes* and *Humanae Vitae* showing that Pope St Paul VI's encyclical was very much in keeping with the thinking of the fathers at the Second Vatican Council. Moreover, he says Pope St Paul VI wrote *Humanae Vitae* with 'the authentic Magisterium' having 'before his eyes the authoritative statement' of *Gaudium et spes.*[129] Pope St John Paul II's own thinking has already been set out in the theology of the body and this theology has served to provide the anthropological and theological background. Pope St John Paul II begins by observing that the morality of the marriage act, sexual intercourse, is determined by the nature of the act and the subjects of the act. Pope St John Paul II adds that God has made an inseparable connection between the unitive significance and the procreative significance both of which are inherent in the marriage act. This is written into the actual nature of marital relations and as such belongs to the natural law, is known by reason and so concerns all people. However, it also belongs to the moral order revealed by God and therefore it especially concerns the faithful. He quotes Pope St Paul VI who recognizes the pastoral difficulties in responsible parenthood and that to many the law appears 'not merely difficult but even impossible to observe.' Pope St Paul VI accepts that the law demands 'a resolute purpose and great endurance.' Indeed, Pope St Paul VI adds, 'it cannot be observed unless God comes to their help with that great grace by which the good will of men is sustained and strengthened.' Pope St John Paul II points out that the very nature of divine law is that it is possible to observe, and that the truths of *Humanae Vitae* are confirmed in the biblical background of the theology of the body. In response to those who seek a pastoral approach to the difficulties present 'in concrete life' Pope St John Paul II draws attention to the pastoral concern at the origin of both *Gaudium et spes* and *Humanae Vitae*. According to Pope St John Paul II 'pastoral concern means the search for the true good of man, a promotion of the values engraved in his person by God.' This involves 'the ever clearer discovery of God's plan for human love, in the certitude that the only true good of the human person consists in fulfilling this divine plan.'[130]

Pope St John Paul II addresses the theme of responsible parenthood first from *Gaudium et spes*. The Council stresses that the responsible transmission of life

> does not depend solely on sincere intentions or on an evaluation of motives, but must be determined by objective standards. These, based on the nature of the human person and his acts, preserve the full sense of mutual self-giving and human procreation in the context of true love.[131]

Pope St John Paul II points out that the Council adds 'words of particular importance', that 'the parents themselves and no one else should ultimately make this judgment in the sight of God.' In this judgment parents 'must always be governed according to a conscience dutifully conformed to the divine law itself, and should be submissive toward the Church's teaching office, which authentically interprets that law in the light of the Gospel. That divine law reveals and protects the integral meaning of conjugal love, and impels it toward a truly human fulfilment.' Quoting Pope St Paul VI, responsible parenthood involves 'keeping a right order of priorities', and recognizing duties towards 'God, themselves, their families and human society.' Notably, Pope St John Paul II explains that Pope St Paul VI gives a more complete guidance on responsible parenthood because Pope St Paul VI does not reduce it simply to birth control. Responsible parenthood is not just about biology, it is also about the mastery of reason and will over drives and emotions.[132]

Following the teaching of Pope St Paul VI, Pope St John Paul II outlines the difference between morally licit methods and illicit methods of birth regulation. The 'ethical character' of natural family planning is positive in that the couple rightly use a facility provided to them by nature. The 'ethical character' of contraception is negative because there is a deliberate obstruction of the procreative process. Of course, Pope St John Paul II notes that couple using the natural method may have a contraceptive mentality, though he says this is a separate ethical problem. Pope St John Paul II adds that 'the theology of the body is not merely a theory, but rather a specific, evangelical, Christian pedagogy of the body' that derives from scripture especially the Gospel. Pope St John Paul II observes that, 'as the message of salvation, it reveals man's true good, for the purpose of modelling—according to the measure of this good—man's earthly life in the perspective of the hope of the future world.'[133]

According to Pope St John Paul II, the 'problem consists in maintaining an adequate relationship between what is defined as "domination ... of the forces of nature"[134] and the "mastery of self"[135] which is indispensable for the human person.' He points out that 'modern man shows a tendency to transfer the methods proper to the former to those of the latter.' As he has shown in the theology of the body, 'the mastery of self corresponds to the fundamental constitution of the person; it is indeed a "natural" method.' When a person resorts to artificial means this deprives the person of proper subjectivity and makes the person 'an object

Theology of the Body

of manipulation.' Pope St John Paul II insists that 'the human body is not merely an organism of sexual reactions.' Without excluding sexual reactions, the body is 'at the same time, the means of expressing the entire man, the person, which reveals itself by means of the language of the body.' In order to avoid any reduction, he adds that 'this language has an important interpersonal meaning, especially in reciprocal relationships between men and women.' Following on from his analysis of the language of the body Pope St John Paul II says that the 'language of the body should express ... the truth of the sacrament. Participating in the eternal plan of love the language of the body becomes a kind of prophetism of the body.' For Pope St John Paul II it is essential to realize that human beings are called to witness to God's eternal plan and so to be 'minister of the sacrament.' This is a matter of authentic human freedom that is not mere choice but a freedom that is under the person's self-control. Thus, he repeats:

> this language of the body is something more than mere sexual reaction. As authentic language of the persons, it is subject to the demands of truth, that is, to objective moral norms. Precisely on the level of this language, man and woman reciprocally express themselves in the fullest and most profound way possible to them by the corporeal dimension of masculinity and femininity. Man and woman express themselves in the measure of the whole truth of the human person.[136]

For Pope St John Paul II this mastery of the self is very important because it is precisely because the person is 'master of himself' that he can give himself fully.

As Pope St John Paul II sees it, the conjugal act signifies both love and potential fruitfulness in children. If it is artificially deprived of the fruitful capacity it 'ceases also to be an act of love' because both are activated together. It is a bodily union but

> it does not correspond to the interior truth and to the dignity of personal communion ... if truth is lacking one cannot speak either of the truth of self-mastery, or of the

truth of the reciprocal gift and of the reciprocal acceptance of self on the part of the person.[137]

In contrast to artificial contraception, Pope St John Paul II says that continence in natural family planning is not a matter of technique but is a practice of virtue, 'a definite and permanent moral attitude.' Natural rhythms belong to the objective truth of the language of the body as 'the body speaks not merely with the whole external expression of masculinity and femininity, but also with the internal structures of the organism, of the somatic and psychosomatic reaction.' However, the language of the body is not merely biological. Responsible parenthood is connected to continual effort, commitment and self-denial.[138]

Church tradition, and recently the Second Vatican Council, Pope St Paul VI and Pope St John Paul II recognize the significance of the spiritual life of married couples. In their vocation to the Christian life Christian couples are under the power of the Holy Spirit and grace and these enable the couple to be a witness to Christ before the world. The tradition also acknowledges the difficulties of holding to this witness because 'the power of love is implanted in man lured by concupiscence.' To overcome concupiscence the person needs to be committed to a progressive education in self-control of the will, feelings and emotions, and an education in the virtues.[139] At the centre of the spirituality of marriage is the virtue of chastity. Chastity means 'to love in the order of the heart' and it is connected to the gifts of the Holy Spirit, above all, with respect for the gifts of God and *pietas*. Without the gifts of the Spirit couples cannot bring about a union that becomes the *communio personarum* because it is the gifts of the Spirit, especially the gift of respect, *pietas*, that sustains the couple and opens them up to the sign of the mystery of creation and redemption.[140] This respect is also respect for the work of God who has given an 'interior meaning' to the conjugal act and to married life as a whole that is underscored by 'a profound appreciation of the personal dignity of both the feminine "I" and the masculine "I" in their shared life.'[141]

The Family as Domestic Church?

It is widely recognized that the idea of the family as domestic Church did not have much traction until it resurfaced in the debates of the Second Vatican Council. The idea of the family as the place of religious community is implicit in the Old Testament where the family mirrors the covenant of Yahweh with His people, and the covenant is carried through the generations. It emerges more in the New Testament where whole households are baptised together, and the community gathers in homes for the breaking of bread. The actual term 'domestic church' is found in the writings of St Augustine and St John of Chrysostom. However, as Christianity became the state religion and with the rise of monasticism, the importance of the family receded. Since the Second Vatican Council, and through the theology of Pope St John Paul II, the idea of domestic church has grown 'exponentially.' Nevertheless, as J. Atkinson observes, the term still remains 'relatively rootless.'[142]

The return to the idea of the family as domestic Church was introduced by Bishop P. Fiordelli in the discussions surrounding *Gaudium et spes*. Some years previously, as bishop of Prato, Fiordelli had shown a special concern for the family, the sacramentality of Christian marriage, and the vocation of the family. This concern went beyond the pressing issues of his day, notably divorce and purely civil marriages even for the baptized, to developing a spirituality and theology of marriage, spurred on by the encyclical *Casti connubii* and the writings of Pope Pius XII. As B. Petrà notes, Fiordelli realized that 'if family life, which is the basic cell of society, is de-Christianized, the Church will be mortally wounded.' In 1959, prior to the calling of the Second Vatican Council, Pope St John XXIII had requested that bishops send topics and issues for discussion at a future council. Fiordelli duly obliged with a lengthy list including a question on the holiness of marriage and the place it holds in the Mystical Body of Christ, the Church, following the ecclesiology outlined by Pope Pius XII in 1943 in his encyclical *Mystici Corporis Christi*. As a participant at the Council Fiordelli made a number of interventions on Christian marriage and its role in the Church, on pastoral issues concerning marriage, marriage preparation, the education of children, the evils of abortion, and the principles of responsible parenthood. He supported the proposition that the details of responsible parenthood be tasked to a commission and Pope St Paul VI rather than be debated at the Council. In *Mystici Corporis Christi* Pope Pius XII had highlighted the two sacraments of Orders and Matrimony as ordained by God for the social needs of the Church, the Church being the Mystical Body of Christ. In marriage the spouses help to minister grace to each other and through procreation and education of children they contribute to the growth of the Church. In addition to parishes then, Fiordelli recognized the significance at a 'structural level' of the Christian family: where the priest has the task of 'making his entire parish a family, the family of faith and of love, the family of God' the 'Church becomes a family.' Moreover, the 'family becomes Church' because the parish is subdivided into 'these little cells, holy and fruitful.' Petrà observes that Fiordelli did not use the patristic idea of the family as 'little Church' in his oral intervention in the Council though it is in his written submission because of time constraints and concerns from the Cardinal moderator about relevancy. Notably in his written submission Fiordelli explained that 'the parish can be changed in the course of time' since it belongs in the sphere of ecclesiastical law, but the family can never be changed since it belongs in the sphere of divine law. In subsequent interventions Fiordelli spoke of the family as a community made holy by Christ, 'a little Church with an inherent participation in the mystery of unity or love between Christ and the Church.' The Christian family has been 'consecrated to that sublime mission' by Christ of building up his Mystical Body for the consecration of the world.[143] As Pope St Paul VI says, 'the family has well deserved the beautiful name of "domestic Church"' and it has a particular evangelizing action:

in the family where 'all members evangelize and are evangelized', as evangelizers of other families, and of society.[144]

According to Atkinson, although the term domestic Church appeared in *Lumen Gentium*, it was not theologically grounded in that document. Moreover, the term was used only in an analogous manner. It was Pope St John Paul II who presented a more systematic analysis and theology to the domestic church and eventually, in the *Catechism of the Catholic Church* (1992) the term moved to an ontological relationship with the Church.[145] For Atkinson, this raises a number of problems: first, while Pope St John Paul II asserts that the mystery of Christ as the bridegroom 'lies at the heart of marriage and family', this is rejected by 'modern rationalism'; second, the concept needs more grounding in theology, including the theology of baptism and of creation; third, it risks becoming 'an empty theological tag, used without due regard for its constitutive theological nature' where we can have 'preferences as to its meaning.'[146]

In the *Theology of the Body* and in his Letter to Families, *Gratissimam Sane*[147] Pope St John Paul II gives a theological grounding for the domestic Church. Presumably keeping in mind *Gaudium et Spes* 22, where Christ reveals human beings to themselves, Pope St John Paul II says that husbands and wives 'discover in Christ the point of reference for their spousal love.' This point of reference ensures Jesus is at the heart of the family as he is at the heart of the Church. Pope St John Paul II agrees that the 'great mystery' of the Pauline analogy of the love of husband and wife as the love of Christ for his Church is 'unquestionably a new presentation of the eternal truth about marriage and the family in the light of the New Covenant.' Spousal love of 'one flesh' goes back to Genesis, the very beginning, in creation. However, the bridegroom bride imagery is not an innovation. Pope St John Paul II explains that the text of Ephesians roots the mystery of Christ as bridegroom and Church as bride in the tradition of the Old Testament and the faithful steadfast love of God for his people. This truth about marriage is revealed by

Christ at the wedding at Cana, by Christ's suffering on the Cross, and by the Sacraments.[148] This mystery of eternal love is thus 'already present in creation, revealed in Christ, and entrusted to the Church.' The family itself 'is the great mystery of God.' Pope St John Paul II adds:

> the universal Church, and every particular Church in her, is most immediately revealed as the bride of Christ in the 'domestic church' and in its experience of love: conjugal love, paternal and maternal love, fraternal love, the love of a community of persons and of generations.[149]

The 'great mystery' of Christ and the Church, and of marriage brings with it ethical teaching on love that affirms human dignity. More than that, Pope St John Paul II thinks that the couple can realize the 'radical demands' of love, and love 'to the end', only if they share in the 'great mystery.' 'Modern rationalism' may have moved away from this teaching especially in its dualistic approach to the human being and the contrast between body and spirit. Nevertheless, the response to modern rationalism can be found in the 'Word made flesh. Christ reveals man to himself', and that 'man is a person in the unity of his body and his spirit.' The problem, as Pope St John Paul II sees it, is that despite human progress in psychology and knowledge of the material world, human beings remain 'unknown' to themselves, so the family remains 'an unknown reality', and in many cases we have given up on 'the attempt to be a civilisation of love.' The separation of body and spirit means that human bodies have become just like other bodies in the world, subject to manipulation like raw material, instead of being properly seen as in the image and likeness of God. Similarly, the body spirit separation affects the family and the family faces 'the challenge of a new Manichaeanism' where human beings are treated as objects and human sexuality as something to manipulate and exploit. The profound understanding of masculinity and femininity, and deep wonder at the mystery of the human being has been lost. Pope St John

Paul II laments, 'modern rationalism does not tolerate mystery', nor does it admit that the full truth of human beings has been revealed by Christ: 'for rationalism it is unthinkable that God should be the Redeemer, much less that he should be the "Bridegroom", the primordial and unique source of the human love between spouses.' Finally:

> once man begins to lose sight of a God who loves him, a God who calls man through Christ to live in him and with him, and once the family no longer has the possibility of sharing in the 'great mystery', what is left except the mere temporal dimension of life?'[150]

Summary

Pope St John Paul II's perspective on marriage and the family and on anthropology though his *Theology of the Body* is all encompassing. Through the *Theology of the Body* Pope St John Paul II affirms marriage as the 'primordial sacrament' that says something about the 'sacramentality of the whole heritage of the sacrament of redemption' since marriage refers to the entire work of creation, of redemption, the relationship of Christ and the Church and the new sacramental economy.[151] A theology of marriage and the body is crucial because it sheds light on a theology of Christ and the Church. Certainly the 'great mystery' of Christ and the Church remains 'transcendent' and beyond the reach of analogy. Nevertheless, analogy allows us at least to discern the mystery 'as a love proper to a total and irrevocable gift of self on the part of God to man in Christ.'[152] This is telling us something about the living God who is Creator and Redeemer. And something about marriage that is procreative and redemptive. The procreative aspect of marriage is a participation in the creative activity of God and so is part of God's plan for marriage from the beginning.

For Pope St John Paul II the question of marriage cannot simply be left to the temporal dimension of life. The stakes are too high.

> The Church cannot therefore be understood as the Mystical Body of Christ, as the sign of man's Covenant with God in Christ, or as the universal sacrament of salvation, unless we keep in mind the 'great mystery' involved in the creation of man as male and female and the vocation of both to conjugal love, to fatherhood and to motherhood. The 'great mystery', which is the Church and humanity in Christ, does not exist apart from the 'great mystery' expressed in the 'one flesh' (cf. Gen 2:24; Eph 5:31–32), that is, in the reality of marriage and the family.[153]

In affirming that marriage and the family, and the celibate life for the sake of the Kingdom, are centres for evangelization and conversion, Pope St John Paul II appeals to young people to fulfil the vocation marked out for them:

> it is Jesus in fact that you seek when you dream of happiness; he is waiting for you when nothing else you find satisfies you; he is the beauty to which you are so attracted; it is he who provokes you with that thirst for fullness that will not let you settle for compromise; it is he who urges you to shed the masks of a false life; it is he who reads in your hearts your most genuine choices, the choices that others try to stifle. It is Jesus who stirs in you the desire to do something great with your lives, the will to follow an ideal, the refusal to allow yourselves to be grounded down by mediocrity, the courage to commit yourselves humbly and patiently to improving yourselves and society, making the world more human and more fraternal.[154]

On the one hand Pope St John Paul II's *Theology of the Body* has so caught the popular imagination that there are conferences, workshops, theology of the body for marriage preparation, for teenagers, for beginners, even for pregnancy and childbirth. The Pope's catechesis has also been rewritten for popular consumption with varying success. On the other hand, the *Theology of the Body* has been criticized for being dense, difficult to read, more *eisegesis* than *exegesis*, and 'with no real sense of human love as actually experienced.'[155] Moreover, by focusing on 'male and female in the biblical account' it leaves out 'all the interesting ways in which human sexuality refuses to be contained within those standard gender designations.' J. Granados helpfully organizes the various criticisms under the headings of methodology, anthropological consequences, and 'capacity to explain the whole Christian vision of God, man and the world.' Granados systematically answers each criticism, and he offers areas for further reflection, concluding that 'the development of a Theology of the Body is now a necessity for the Church, as well as an opportunity to present the core of her message, centered on the Incarnation and the Resurrection of the Body.'[156] This leads us on to think of marriage and family life in terms of living the larger life of the Gospel.

Notes

[1] Second Vatican Council, *Dei Verbum*, 7–8.
[2] Second Vatican Council, *Optatam Totius*, 15–16.
[3] *Ibid.*, 9, 14.
[4] Mt 25:40.
[5] The catechetical audiences have been collected in Pope St John Paul II, *The Theology of the Body, Human Love in the Divine Plan* (Boston: Pauline Books, 1997) and are referenced by page number rather than date of the catechesis.
[6] Pope St John Paul II, *The Theology of the Body*, pp. 419–423.
[7] *Ibid.*, p. 236.
[8] *Ibid.*, p. 109.
[9] *Eisegesis* is the interpretation of a biblical text by reading into it one's own ideas.
[10] See W. Kurz, 'The Scriptural Foundations of The Theology of the Body' in *Pope John Paul II on the Body: Human, Eucharistic, Ecclesial* (Philadelphia: St Joseph's University Press 2006), pp. 27–46.
[11] Pope St John Paul II, *Theology of the Body* p. 215.
[12] *Ibid.*, footnote 62, pp. 185–186.
[13] *Ibid.*, p. 164.
[14] *Ibid.*, pp. 165–166.
[15] *Ibid.*, pp. 282–283.
[16] *Ibid.*, pp. 282–283.
[17] K. Wojtyła, 'The Person: Subject and Community' [1976] in *Catholic*

Thought from Lublin Vol. IV Person and Community (New York: Peter Lang, 1993), pp. 219–220.
18. *Ibid.*, p. 220.
19. *Ibid.*, p. 221.
20. *Ibid.*, p. 221.
21. *Ibid.*, p. 221.
22. Second Vatican Council, *Gaudium et spes,* 14.
23. Pope St John Paul II, *Theology of the Body*, p. 88.
24. *Ibid.*, pp. 168–171.
25. *Ibid.*, pp. 336–339.
26. *Ibid.*, pp. 304–314.
27. *Ibid.*, p. 313.
28. *Ibid.*, pp. 339–341.
29. Mt 19:3ff; Mk 10:2ff.
30. Pope John Paul II, *Theology of the Body*, pp. 32–34.
31. *Ibid.*, p. 47.
32. *Ibid.*, p. 33.
33. Gn 1:26–31.
34. Pope John Paul II, *Theology of the Body*, p. 282.
35. *Ibid.*, p. 37.
36. *Ibid.*, pp. 40–41.
37. *Ibid.*, p. 46.
38. *Ibid.*, p. 58.
39. *Ibid.*, p. 56.
40. *Ibid.*, p. 47.
41. *Ibid.*, p. 46.
42. *Ibid.*, pp. 69–7.1
43. *Ibid.*, p. 57.
44. *Ibid.*, p. 59.
45. *Ibid.*, pp. 60–63.
46. *Ibid.*, p. 63.
47. *Ibid.*, p. 79.
48. *Ibid.*, p. 336.
49. *Ibid.*, p. 68.
50. *Ibid.*, p. 106.
51. *Ibid.*, p. 33; p. 93 footnote 7.
52. *Ibid.*, p. 33.
53. *Ibid.*, p. 336.
54. *Ibid.*, p. 68.

55 *Ibid.*, p. 54.
56 *Ibid.*, p. 70.
57 *Ibid.*, p. 58.
58 *Ibid.*, p. 109.
59 *Ibid.*, pp. 118–119.
60 *Ibid.*, pp. 128–130.
61 *Ibid.*, pp. 125–126.
62 *Ibid.*, p. 75.
63 *Ibid.*, p. 106.
64 *Ibid.*, pp. 142–143.
65 *Ibid.*, p. 147.
66 *Ibid.*, pp. 162–165.
67 *Ibid.*, p. 347.
68 *Ibid.*, pp. 168–171.
69 *Ibid.*, pp. 80–81.
70 T. Beattie, *New Catholic Feminism: Theology and Theory* (London: Routledge, 2006), p. 4.
71 Pope St John Paul II, *Theology of the Body*, p. 82.
72 *Ibid.*, pp. 83–86.
73 *Ibid.*, pp. 88–89.
74 *Ibid.*, p. 175.
75 Second Vatican Council, *Gaudium et spes*, 22.
76 Mk 12:25.
77 Pope St John Paul II, *Theology of the Body*, p. 238.
78 *Ibid.*, pp. 239–241.
79 *Ibid.*, p. 177.
80 *Ibid.*
81 *Ibid.*, p. 247.
82 *Ibid.*, p. 177.
83 *Ibid.*, pp. 177–180.
84 *Ibid.*, pp. 200–201.
85 *Ibid.*, pp. 246–24.
86 *Ibid.*, p. 66.
87 *Ibid.*, p. 408.
88 *Ibid.*, pp. 412–415.
89 *Ibid.*, pp. 262–264.
90 *Ibid.*, pp. 264–267.
91 *Ibid.*, pp. 267–270.
92 Pope St John Paul II, *Familiaris Consortio*, 16.

[93] Pope St John Paul II, *Theology of the Body*, pp. 273–274.
[94] *Ibid.*, pp. 276–278.
[95] *Ibid.*, pp. 276–278.
[96] *Ibid.*, pp. 270–272.
[97] *Ibid.*, pp. 292–295.
[98] *Ibid.*, p. 273.
[99] *Ibid.*, pp. 276–278.
[100] *Ibid.*, pp. 280–281.
[101] *Ibid.*, pp. 296–299.
[102] *Ibid.*, pp. 299–302.
[103] *Catechism of the Catholic Church,* 1124 referring to the fifth century theologian Prosper of Aquitaine.
[104] Pope St John Paul II, *Theology of the Body*, pp. 304–306.
[105] *Ibid.*, pp. 306–309.
[106] *Ibid.*, p. 310.
[107] *Ibid.*, pp. 309–311.
[108] *Ibid.*, pp. 312–314.
[109] *Ibid.*, pp. 314–318.
[110] *Ibid.*, pp. 318–321.
[111] *Ibid.*, pp. 321–330.
[112] *Ibid.*, pp. 330–333.
[113] *Ibid.*, pp. 333–336.
[114] *Ibid.*, pp. 336–341.
[115] *Ibid.*, pp. 339–341.
[116] *Ibid.*, pp. 342–347.
[117] *Ibid.*, pp. 347–351.
[118] *Ibid.*, pp. 351–354.
[119] *Ibid.*, pp. 354–357.
[120] *Ibid.*, pp. 357–360.
[121] *Ibid.*, p. 362.
[122] *Ibid.*, pp. 357–360.
[123] *Ibid.*, pp. 360–363.
[124] *Ibid.*, pp. 363–365.
[125] *Ibid.*, pp. 365–368.
[126] *Ibid.*, pp. 368–375.
[127] *Ibid.*, pp. 375–377.
[128] *Ibid.*, pp. 378–380.
[129] *Ibid.*, p. 390.
[130] *Ibid.*, pp. 390–392.

131 Second Vatican Council, *Gaudium et spes* 51.
132 Pope St John Paul II, *Theology of the Body*, pp. 393–394.
133 *Ibid.*, pp. 395–396.
134 Pope St Paul VI, *Humanae Vitae*, 2.
135 *Ibid.*, 21.
136 Pope St John Paul II, *Theology of the Body*, p. 398.
137 *Ibid.*, pp. 396–399.
138 *Ibid.*, pp. 399–403.
139 *Ibid.*, pp. 404–408.
140 *Ibid.*, pp. 408–417.
141 *Ibid.*, pp. 417–419.
142 J. Atkinson, *Biblical and Theological Foundations of the Family* (Washington: Catholic University of America Press, 2014), pp. 1–3.
143 B. Petrà, 'Bishop Petro Fiordelli (1916–2004) at the Council: the Bishop of Prato and the Strange Origin of the Theology of the Family as a "Domestic Church"', in *INTAMS review* 19, 13–33 (2013).
144 Pope St Paul VI, *Evangelii nuntiandi*, 71.
145 J. Atkinson, 'Family as Domestic Church: Developmental Trajectory, Legitimacy, and Problems of Appropriation' in *Theological Studies* 66 (2005), pp. 592–604.
146 *Ibid.*, p. 604.
147 Pope St John Paul II, *Gratissimam Sane*, 19.
148 *Ibid.*
149 *Ibid.*
150 *Ibid.*
151 Pope St John Paul II, *Theology of the Body*, pp. 338–339.
152 *Ibid.*, pp. 330–331.
153 Pope St John Paul II, *Gratissimam Sane*, 19.
154 Pope St John Paul II, *Address, 15th World Youth Day Vigil of Prayer* (19 August 2000), 5.
155 L. J. Johnson, 'A Disembodied 'Theology of the Body" in *Commonweal* (4 June 2004).
156 J. Granados, 'The Theology of the Body in the United States' in *Humanum* (2015) Issue 3. To be recommended is C. Anderson's and J. Granados's accessible book, *Called to Love: Approaching John Paul II's Theology of the Body* (New York: Doubleday, 2009).

9 LIVING THE LARGER LIFE OF THE GOSPEL

For Jesus the place of the heart is significant. Jesus asks us to love God with heart, soul, mind, and strength.[1] Words and action flow from what is stored in people's hearts.[2] The 'pure in heart' are blessed.[3] In his explanation of the parable of the sower, people with 'a noble and generous heart' who hear the Word and 'take it to themselves' yield a large harvest.[4] Jesus asks not for words but for hearts to be close to him,[5] and God knows what is in the heart.[6] The heart is also a place of warning for, as Jesus says, we must be careful not to seek for earthly goods but for true treasures: 'for wherever your treasure is, there will your heart be too.'[7] For love in marriage and family life to be true treasure it must be rooted in not only living the good of human relationships but also in living the larger life of the Gospel.

Heart speaks to heart

When Jesus speaks of the heart it is in the context of Jewish thinking where the heart is the place not only of emotions but also wisdom: Solomon asks Yahweh for 'a heart to understand' and he is given 'a wise heart.'[8] Pope St John Paul II sees the 'category of the heart' as 'in a way, the equivalent of personal subjectivity.' In a real shift from philosophies that put the emphasis of subjectivity in the rational aspect of human beings, the mind or consciousness, Pope St John Paul II makes subjectivity personal by placing it where rationality and affectivity meet. He says, 'man is unique and unrepeatable above all because of his heart, which decides his being from within.' The heart is the person's 'inner self.'[9] Pope St John Paul II may have had in mind here the saying of St Francis de Sales 'try as hard as you like, but in the end only the language of the heart can ever reach another heart'[10] or perhaps St John Henry Newman's motto *cor ad cor loquitur*, heart speaks to heart. Human beings are made for relationships of the heart that are authentic and true.

The depth of the heart is also the place of yearning, including a yearning for the truth.[11] Pope St John Paul II explains that when the young man in Matthew's Gospel comes to Jesus asking what he must do to have eternal life, his question 'from the heart' is 'not so much about rules to be followed, but about the full meaning of life.' It is about drawing nearer to God.[12] Pope St John Paul II recognizes that people cannot imitate the love of Christ in their lives by their own strength. We need first the gift of God's love through the Holy Spirit. He adds,

> Saint Augustine asks: 'Does love bring about the keeping of the commandments, or does the keeping of the commandments bring about love?' And he answers: 'But who can doubt that love comes first? For the one who does not love has no reason for keeping the commandments.'[13]

When people think about Church teaching on marriage, they often start with the perception that this teaching is primarily about a set of commands in the form of 'do nots'. This is to forget, as Pope St John Paul II explains, that 'love and life according to the Gospel cannot be thought of first and foremost as a kind of precept, because what they demand is beyond man's abilities. They are possible only as the result of a gift of God who heals, restores and transforms the human heart by his grace.' After sin, human beings could no longer live up to God's plan for humanity. The law was given through Moses and because of people's 'hardness of heart', Moses allowed divorce. However, 'grace and truth came through Jesus Christ.'[14] Perhaps the real question concerning marriage and family is, what difference does Jesus make?

Mercy, truth and justice

Reflecting on Ephesians 5 Pope Benedict XVI says that 'we learn what marriage is in the light of the communion of Christ and the Church, we learn how Christ is united to us in thinking of the mystery of matrimony.'[15] We also learn that marriage and family life belong in the bigger picture of living the life of the Gospel. And as Pope St John Paul II notes, living the Gospel is difficult for human beings who are beset by their weaknesses. However, it is all too easy to make a weakness into a 'criterion of the truth about a good' in order to feel self-justified and so excuse our failings. Instead, as the story of the Pharisee and the tax collector shows, we depend on God's mercy:

> the tax collector represents a 'repentant' conscience, fully aware of the frailty of its own nature and seeing in its own failings, whatever their subjective justifications, a confirmation of its need for redemption. The Pharisee represents a 'self-satisfied' conscience, under the illusion that it is able to observe the law without the help of grace and convinced that it does not need mercy.[16]

This relationship of mercy and justice figured significantly in the synods leading up to the Apostolic Exhortation of Pope Francis, *Amoris Laetitia*.

The story of marriage and the family so far has demonstrated the richness of the tradition. Reflection on marriage has touched on many significant issues including anthropology, creation and redemption, grace and the call to holiness, challenges to humanity and society, the place of tradition, the role of the Magisterium and "updating" Church teaching. There have also been dangers on the way, of Manichaeism, Gnosticism, Pelagianism, as well as the problem of romanticizing human love or presenting it as the goal, the final reality. Pope Francis draws attention in particular to the two frequent dangers that he thinks are still prevalent: Gnosticism that he interprets as a subjective faith which separates the intellect from the flesh, a faith that is elitist and marked by a cold harsh logic that claims to explain everything; and Pelagianism that puts everything down to human effort and allows human beings to trust only in their own powers.[17]

A strong current has been the analogy first in the Old Testament of the steadfast love of God and human love in marriage, then in the New Testament the love Christ has for the Church as the bridegroom's love for his bride. Certainly, marriage and family life provide a real and concrete example that everyone experiences. But all analogies limp, and after all, 'between Creator and creature no similitude can be expressed without implying an even greater dissimilitude.'[18] Nevertheless, the interconnectedness of marriage with other areas of Church tradition, as well as the significance marriage has in itself, means that the stakes are high and so we cannot ignore its divine institution and treat marriage and family as purely a social institution. This has implications for understanding the actual realities of married life.

Everyday realities remind us of the demands of marriage and family life. Resources for moral thinking on marriage can be found in Scripture, the Tradition of the Church, the Magisterium and through human reason. These resources affirm the three goods of marriage: children, unity of the couple, and fidelity. Throughout the story of marriage and the family the focus has fallen at different times on one of these goods in particular, often in response to a problem or challenge. Perhaps twenty-first century pressing challenges concern the question of the relationship of couples to the Church when marriage has broken down and one or both have entered a new union, and the question of the redefinition of marriage to include same sex couples. The future challenge may relate to the nature of sexuality itself. However, rather than simply asking for practical solutions, these challenges also invite reflection on the broader issues. How these issues are interpreted directly affects the answers to particular challenges.

One issue that came specifically out of responses to the Second Vatican Council concerns the authentic development of Tradition. Interpretations of what authentic development means not only has implications for current problems but also on the direction of the Church itself. Moreover, with the Second Vatican Council's interest in the priestly, prophetic and kingly roles of lay people these questions are set in the context of personal conscience and the search for holiness. How conscience is interpreted equally has bearing on current problems. Notably, what both Pope St John XXIII and Pope St Paul VI have to say about reform and renewal has significant resonance with the approaches of Pope St John Paul II, Pope Benedict XVI and Pope Francis to marriage and the family. And conscience figures in the discussion of indissolubility of marriage especially in the 1990s.

Significantly, one of the themes that has threaded through the story of marriage has been the question of the apparent impossibility of God's demands and the corresponding dependence on God's grace. As Cardinal Ratzinger noted during the 1980 synod on marriage and the family, there is a good deal of difference between saying a couple *are* unable to follow God's commands and *feel* that they are unable to do so. And in some interpretations of the authentic development of Tradition there is a question about what is or is not commanded by God.

God does not command the impossible?

In his first letter to the Corinthians St Paul offers the Corinthian Christians lessons from the history of Israel when God's people failed to trust in God and instead relied on their own strengths and desires. St Paul points out that 'everyone, no matter how firmly he thinks he is standing must be careful he does not fall.' Realizing human dependence on God is key, St Paul adds 'none of the trials which have come upon you is more than a human being can stand. You can trust that God will not let you be put to the test beyond your strength, but with any trial will also provide a way out by enabling you to put up with it.'[19] The idea of test here is not to see whether a person will fall. God already knows what is in the heart. Rather trials reveal a person's very deepest attitudes. In Matthew's gospel, after Jesus laments over the lukewarmness of the people in the lake towns and their failure to repent even though they had seen his miracles, Jesus rejoices that the mysteries of the Kingdom are revealed to 'little children', to those who trust. In clear overtones of the burdens of the law, Jesus says, 'come to me, all you who labour and are overburdened, and I will give you rest. Shoulder my yoke and learn from me, for I am gentle and humble in heart, and you will find rest for your souls. Yes, my yoke is easy and my burden light.'[20]

Further theological thinking on grace and following God's commands emerged from the dispute between St Augustine and the Pelagians. Pelagius wanted to stress human responsibility against those who claimed human beings were too weakened by the Fall and could be excused. So, Pelagius argues that all can by their own will obey the commandments: 'a man is able, if he wishes, to be without sin.' Moreover, according to Pelagius to assert that God continues to offer help through grace is to undermine human responsibility. The just God gives his commandments as a gift to human beings and he gives the will the power to obey them. St Augustine replies that a human being is like a house divided against itself.[21] We are so disabled by sin that we cannot be masters of ourselves without God's grace. By his commands God lets us know that we should do what we can and ask for what we cannot do through the healing of grace.[22] In its decree on Justification the Council of Trent took up St Augustine's teaching. However, the question of grace and its relationship to what is possible resurfaced with Jansenism. The Jansenists claimed that some of God's commands are impossible given the weak powers some people have, and in addition some people lack grace. It appears that Jansen had relied on the work of M. de Bay (Baius), and Baius had mistakenly believed that the view that God does not command the impossible came from Pelagius not St Augustine. St Augustine's teaching was further taken up in pastoral teaching, suggesting that grace is always available, and this is explicitly in Pope Pius XI's *Casti connubii*, and implicitly in Pope St Paul VI's *Humanae Vitae* and Pope St John Paul II's *Familiaris Consortio*.[23]

J. Mahoney points out that the principle that God does not command the impossible suggests that grace is isolated in the will whereby all that is required is developing a 'supercharged will-power' that can overcome every difficulty. This of course results in an 'impoverished' view of grace. Another question is do human beings always know exactly what God's commands are. Mahoney reflects that the principle is about God and not about 'the moral abilities of human beings.' If the principle is located in human abilities then it would seem that God could demand something that a person is unable to do, thus compelling the person to sin. This would suggest that God can be unjust. Moreover, to say that some of God's commands are impossible raises a question over God's goodness. Similarly, to say that at times the best people can do is to choose between two evils suggests that God is limited because he cannot transform circumstances through grace and so people are abandoned to doing what is evil. Yet, we cannot do evil that good may come of it.[24]

For Pope St John Paul II the question 'what shall we do' invites a response of repentance, conversion, and a turning to God in trust. The awareness of God's commands is not merely an accusation, still less condemnation. Rather it is a call to be convinced in the forgiveness of God and in the power of the Holy Spirit acting in the life of the Christian.[25] Quoting *Gaudium et Spes*, Pope St John Paul II explains,

> man, therefore, far from allowing himself to be 'ensnared' in his sinful condition, by relying upon the voice of his own conscience is obliged to wrestle constantly if he is to cling to what is good. Nor can he achieve his own interior integrity without valiant efforts and the help of God's grace. The Council rightly sees sin as a factor of alienation which weighs heavily on man's personal and social life. But at the same time it never tires of reminding us of the possibility of victory.[26]

Pope St John Paul II observes that the 'action of the Spirit' often encounters 'an interior resistance', 'hardness of heart', especially where the sense of sin has been lost. This is why the Church prays for God's grace to save the integrity and sensitivity of people's consciences.[27] Living life under the influence of grace and the Spirit enables people to be free and to discover the 'divine dimension of their being and life.'[28] Pope St John Paul II's approach is clearly not about a super will. It is about trust and dependence on God who supplies what is needed.

Development of tradition and redefining marriage?

The twenty-first century has seen a significant call to recognize the dignity and rights of often marginalized groups, especially those subject to discrimination. Notably, there have been calls for people with same sex attraction to be allowed to marry. The claim is that restricting marriage to one man and one woman is discriminatory and violates the principle of equality. While some might see this call as trivializing marriage, the fact that people want their union to be publicly recognized as not only a civil union but also marriage, and perhaps even blessed, demonstrates the power of the institution of marriage. In Church tradition God is the author of marriage and so it is not in human power to redefine marriage. However, some theologians argue that history tells us that some Church teaching in the past has been wrong and that the time has come to change teaching on sexuality.[29] It is time the Church becomes up to date.

The Second Vatican Council is renowned for *ressourcement*, a return to authoritative sources, and its goal of *aggiornamento*, bringing the Church up to date. Of course, different people have very different views on the highly contested word *aggiornamento*, and consequently on the Council itself, never mind whether the Council's goal has been reached, distorted, thwarted or indeed should have been a goal in the first place. Related to the question of development of tradition, the theme in the story of marriage and family of the relationship of Christians and the world becomes highly significant. In the story of marriage Christian thinking has at times followed the world and at times been a "sign of contradiction".[30] For some the Second Vatican Council set the Church on the path to decentralisation and greater democracy, a real recognition of the role of lay people. Some saw the Council as the opportunity to embrace progress and others as a way of finally "joining" the modern world after centuries of insularity. In the media the Council was characterized as a conflict between discontinuity and continuity, between conservatives and liberals or progressives who advocated accommodation with modernity. As M. Lamb points out, a distinction can be made between the 'virtual Council' seen through various lenses that focus on polarization, and the 'real Council': the real Council cannot be reduced to conflicts or a severing of the council texts from the 'spirit' of the Council.[31]

In his speech opening the Second Vatican Council Pope St John XXIII stressed the importance of dialogue with the world. He disagreed with the 'prophets of doom', people who only see the world in terms of disaster. Pope St John XXIII acknowledged that there were errors and problems but, he said, the world is 'on the threshold of a new era.' Moreover, he was confident that the Church can meet the 'needs of the present day by demonstrating the validity of her teaching rather than condemnation.'[32] Using a phrase that has been taken up by Pope Francis, Pope St John XXIII explained that the Church's 'treasure' is not a museum piece but something to be put to work.[33] Instead then of simply condemning the errors of the world, Pope St John XXIII was convinced that the Church had something to offer the world through her teaching and practices.

Pope St John XXIII recognized that 'the life of the spirit and the life of the body', 'eternal life and temporal life' are two conceptions of human life, both of the individual and of the individual in society. These two conceptions could be distinguished, but they could also be reconciled without excluding one or the other. The Church 'is concerned above all with the spirit' but is also involved with everyday life and looks to sanctify it. Christians are to 'remain on guard' so that they are not distracted from the things of heaven. Interior growth in Christ is after all 'true and definitive progress.' In words that perhaps were not lost on the Archbishop of Kracow, Karol Wojtyła, Pope St John XXIII said that the words of St Paul from Ephesians deserve to appear 'at the entrance of the Ecumenical Council':

> If we live by the truth and in love, we shall grow completely into Christ, who is the head by whom the whole Body is fitted and joined together, every joint adding its own strength, for each individual part to work according to its function. So the body grows until it has built itself up in love.[34]

Thinking about the Church in the world, Pope St Paul VI affirms that 'the Church is deeply rooted in the world.' At the same time the Church is 'being engulfed and shaken by this tidal wave of change' affecting the world. One worry for Pope St Paul VI is that some think that the Church 'should abdicate its proper role, and adopt an entirely new and unprecedented mode of existence.' Pope St Paul VI sees the remedy is to be found in

> an increased self-awareness on the part of the Church. The Church must get a clearer idea of what it really is in the mind of Jesus Christ as recorded and preserved in Sacred Scripture and in Apostolic Tradition, and interpreted and explained by the tradition of the Church under the inspiration and guidance of the Holy Spirit.[35]

Pope St Paul VI draws especial attention to rediscovering a richer understanding of the Church as the Mystical Body of Christ.[36] Pope St Paul VI explains that the mystery of the Church as Body of Christ 'must be lived, so that the faithful may have a kind of intuitive experience of it, even before they come to understand it clearly.' He says that it is part of the ministry of the hierarchy to educate and initiate people into 'the Christian way of life.'[37] For Pope St Paul VI the problem of renewal is how the Church becomes what Christ intended it to be: 'one, holy, and entirely dedicated to the pursuit of that perfection to which Christ called it and for which he qualified it.'[38] Notably, this provides an echo for Pope St John Paul II's later request that the family become what it is intended to be.

Continuing his vision for reform, Pope St Paul VI accepts that the Church adapts to the 'forms of thought' of its 'temporal environment' but without compromising its principles and moral teachings. Indeed, the Church is called to 'correct, ennoble, encourage and sanctify' these forms of thought.[39] Offering some guidance rules, Pope St Paul VI adds that there is 'no question of reforming the essential nature of the Church or its basic and necessary structure...we cannot brand the holy and beloved Church of God with the mark of infidelity.' Indeed, we must 'guard this treasure.' Reform is not change; it is restoring the Church to its 'original image.'[40] Nor is reform adapting to the way of thinking and acting to 'the customs and temper' of the modern secular world. Pope St Paul VI notes the powerful 'fascination of worldly life today' and the suggestion that conformity is inescapable and even a 'wise course.' Pope St Paul VI appeals instead to the message of Christ that 'we must be in the world, but not of it.'[41] To this end Pope St Paul VI urges 'the determination to live in accordance with divine grace, faithfulness to the Gospel of Christ, unity in the ranks of the sacred hierarchy and among Christian communities.'[42] For Pope St Paul VI the 'authorized applications' resulting from the Second Vatican Council 'chart the frame of thought and the safe path to follow.' He adds,

> those who neglect them or want to thwart them, by invoking fidelity to the past, are unfaithful to the mission of the Church today and to its responsibility for tomorrow; those who go beyond them to follow their own inspiration build on the sand a Church without roots. Both undermine the unity and credibility of the Church.[43]

In being in the world Pope St Paul VI suggests the attitude of charity and dialogue 'seeing that the Church's ever-increasing self-awareness and its struggle to model itself on Christ's ideal can only result in its acting and thinking quite differently from the world around it, which it is nevertheless striving to influence.' The 'world' to which he refers consists of those who 'are opposed to the light of faith and gift of grace', those who depend only on themselves, and those who are 'aggressively pessimistic', thinking that 'vices, weaknesses and moral ailments are inevitable.' The Gospel recognizes the existence of these infirmities, understands them and seeks to cure them.[44] This distinction of the Church from the world is not a matter of aloofness or contempt, but a matter of drawing closer to the world with God's mercy. The Church has an attitude of dialogue precisely because the Church has a message to give that the world needs to hear: the 'dialogue of salvation.'[45]

For this dialogue Pope St Paul VI asks for a closer identification with ordinary people and an attitude of friendship. He asks for the avoidance of 'unintelligible language.' Above all, he asks for listening to what people 'have it in their hearts to say', where no one is excluded from the Church's maternal embrace.[46] It seems that these requests have held great resonance for Pope Francis in his approach to marriage and the family.

In terms of same sex unions and redefining marriage, dialogue in charity can and does take place. The Church deplores all unjust discrimination and affirms the dignity of every human being.[47] Justice requires that all cases are treated alike, and different cases differently.

There are already examples where something is reserved only to a particular group of people: it is entirely appropriate and not a matter of discrimination that nursery schools are for infants because it is in that environment that infants can flourish. Marriage is different from other unions because marriage supports two people of the opposite sex to be faithful to each other and to have, bring up and educate their children. As the constant tradition and teaching of the Church demonstrates, marriage is not simply about love between two people. If marriage were only about love, then that would not preclude polygamy or divorce.

Marriage is a spiritual and bodily union of 'one flesh', a total commitment, that results, God willing, in children. Marriage as the union of man and woman requires difference and complementarity. In the often bitter debates about the legalization of same sex unions as marriage, those who believed in the 'traditional' understanding of marriage were frequently branded as bigots. Dialogue does not necessarily mean that people agree on one side or another. Dialogue means that we come to understand the position of the other even if we disagree.

Conscience

The Second Vatican Council's Declaration on Religious Freedom, *Dignitatis humanae* begins by noting that:

> a sense of the dignity of the human person has been impressing itself more and more deeply on the consciousness of contemporary man, and the demand is increasingly made that men should act on their own judgment, enjoying and making use of a responsible freedom, not driven by coercion but motivated by a sense of duty.

Personal dignity involves the personal responsibility that human beings have 'by nature' as rational beings, and by 'moral obligation,' to 'seek the truth', especially religious truth. Once they have found the truth, they should adhere to it. On the matter of conscience,

> in all his activity a man is bound to follow his conscience in order that he may come to God, the end and purpose of life. It follows that he is not to be forced to act in a manner contrary to his conscience. Nor, on the other hand, is he to be restrained from acting in accordance with his conscience, especially in matters religious.[48]

Dignitatis humanae was written with the relationship of government and states to individuals in mind. Referring particularly to the right of parents to educate their children according to the religious beliefs of the parents, the Council observes that the family, 'a society in its own original right, has the right freely to live its own domestic religious life under the guidance of parents.'[49] The Council's specific words on conscience bear repeating in full:

> In the depths of his conscience, man detects a law which he does not impose upon himself, but which holds him to obedience. Always summoning him to love good and avoid evil, the voice of conscience when necessary speaks to his heart: do this, shun that. For man has in his heart a law written by God; to obey it is the very dignity of man; according to it he will be judged. Conscience is the most secret core and sanctuary of a man. There he is alone with God, Whose voice echoes in his depths. In a wonderful manner conscience reveals that law which is fulfilled by love of God and neighbour. In fidelity to conscience, Christians are joined with the rest of men in the search for truth, and for the genuine solution to the numerous problems which arise in the life of individuals from social relationships. Hence the more right conscience holds sway, the more persons and groups turn aside from blind choice and strive to be guided by the objective norms of morality. Conscience frequently errs from invincible ignorance without losing its dignity. The same cannot be said for a man who cares but little for truth and goodness, or for a conscience which by degrees grows practically sightless as a result of habitual sin.[50]

When Pope St Paul VI issued *Humanae Vitae* some responded by saying that the question of responsible parenthood rests on conscience in the sense that a Catholic couple could be permitted to practice contraception if their consciences directed them so to do.[51] Conscience and Church authority became contested notions. On the twenty-fifth anniversary of *Humanae Vitae* Pope St John Paul II published his encyclical *Veritatis splendor*, on the splendour of truth.[52] Pope St John Paul II affirms that conscience is an 'interior dialogue' but he says conscience is also a 'dialogue of man with God, the author of the law.' Conscience has 'binding force' because the commands of conscience come not from human authority but from the authority of God. Conscience has two aspects: it is a 'practical judgement, a judgement which makes known what man must do or not do', or 'it assesses an act already performed by him.' The 'first principle of practical reason', that good should be done and evil avoided, is part of natural law and 'shines in the heart' of every person. Natural law 'discloses the objective and universal demands of the moral good' and conscience 'is the application of the law to a particular case.' Pope St John Paul II states that the dignity and authority of conscience derives from the 'truth about moral good and evil.' As an assessment or verdict on what the person has done, conscience remains 'a pledge of hope and mercy', reminding the person of the need for God's grace and forgiveness. To have a 'good conscience' a person must seek the objective truth, but conscience can make mistakes. This is the case when a person mistakenly subjectively thinks something is true. In the case of error, even if the error cannot be imputable to the person, it remains an evil. When a person is culpably in error because he or she has shown little concern for seeking the good, then the dignity of conscience is compromised. The danger here is that conscience gradually becomes 'blind' by being 'accustomed to sin.' Christians then are called to inform their consciences, to follow continuous conversion to the true and good, and to give 'careful attention' to the teaching of the Magisterium which is a 'great help' in this formation.[53]

Divorce and attempted remarriage

The problem of pastoral accompaniment of people who are divorced and have attempted remarried has long been a matter of discussion. As P. Travers notes, the canons in the 1917 Code of Canon Law spoke of the general exclusion from Holy Communion of divorced people who had attempted remarriage in terms of the 'publicly unworthy', 'manifestly infamous', 'bigamists.'[54] K. Himes and J. Coriden explain that at the turn of the twentieth century there were four possible options to resolve the situation: first, to declare the nullity or dissolution of the first marriage and validate the present union; second, to advise the couple to separate; third, leave the couple in good faith and not to inform them of their canonical status or moral situation; four, permit them to live as brother and sister with no sexual relations.[55] These discussions often involved cases where an earlier marriage seemed invalid but this could not be proved canonically, as well as hardship cases which usually involved an abandoned spouse. At least since the 1960s the legitimacy of general exclusion of the divorced and remarried from the Eucharist has been questioned and various solutions proposed, among them the 'Orthodox' approach where a subsequent 'marriage' is allowed.[56]

One proposed possibility was to apply an 'internal forum solution' on the basis of good faith, where the validity of a previous marriage was doubtful. However, this was generally regarded as a 'new opinion' calling into doubt the Church's traditional teaching on indissolubility.[57] Moreover, the idea of an 'internal forum' in this context causes confusion: in canon law the internal forum and external forum are distinct from the forum of conscience. The forum of conscience refers to the relationship between the person and God; the internal forum and external forum refer to 'different "places" (of the effect) of an act of governance.' The internal forum is characterized by an absence of publicity and so level of secrecy that remains secret. The internal forum is divided into a sacramental forum that refers to matters considered under the sacrament of penance and so protected by the seal of confession, and a non-sacramental forum.[58] Some of these questions on indissolubility were brought to the 1980 synod of bishops and Pope St John Paul II affirmed that divorced and remarried people could not be admitted to Holy Communion unless the matter of the first marriage had been resolved or unless they tried to live as brother and sister.

On 10 July 1993 three German bishops, Archbishop O. Saier, Bishop K. Lehmann, and Bishop W. Kasper issued a pastoral letter calling for better dialogue with people who are divorced and remarried. They also produced a document offering some principles. The German bishops affirmed that people who are divorced and remarried could not be admitted to the Eucharist since their life situation was in objective contradiction to the essence of Christian marriage. They then offered a distinction between 'admitting' the divorced and remarried to communion which, as a public act, would contradict Church teaching, and the divorced and remarried 'approaching' communion after pastoral discernment. They recommended prayerful accompaniment with a priest and a personal review of conscience to discern if in their situation they could approach the Eucharist. The priest, Church and the congregation should respect the person's individual judgment of conscience.[59] Although not at issue in the letter, in theory, respect for the person's individual judgment of conscience could equally apply to people in faithful same sex unions.

The pastoral letter generated much publicity and the theologians G. Grisez, J. Finnis and W. E. May wrote an open letter to the German bishops. Grisez, Finnis and May point out that the proposal by the German bishops is not about whether a person, in good or bad faith, decides unilaterally whether he or she can take communion. Rather the proposal establishes a way in which the person and others can regard reception of communion as legitimate, even though the German bishops agree that 'there can be no general, formal, official admission because the church's position on the indissolubility of marriage would thereby be obscured.'[60] For the authors the German bishops allow that a decision of conscience authorizes admission to the sacraments.

In 1993 the Congregation for the Doctrine of the Faith wrote to the German bishops and they met to discuss the issue. There was no full agreement. On 14 September 1994 the CDF presented a response to 'different pastoral solutions', solutions that suggested that:

> a general admission of divorced and remarried to Eucharistic communion would not be possible, but the divorced

and remarried members of the faithful could approach Holy Communion in specific cases when they consider themselves authorized according to a judgement of conscience to do so.

Where a priest is consulted, he would have to respect their eventual decision to approach Holy Communion.[61] The CDF rejected these solutions and reaffirmed the teaching in *Familiaris Consortio* that the divorced and remarried cannot receive Holy Communion so long as they find themselves in a situation that objectively contravenes God's law. However, the CDF added that the Church does 'take to heart' the situation of the faithful, and accompanies them, inviting them to 'share in the life of the Church in the measure that is compatible with the dispositions of divine law, from which the Church has no power to dispense.' Indeed, 'spiritual communion' seems to be included in this participation.[62] The CDF notes that marriage and the reception of Holy Communion are public realities and not based purely on personal convictions.[63]

The CDF's letter was met with severe criticism in Germany and Pope St John Paul II was branded authoritarian, doctrinally rigid, lacking in any pastoral sensitivity, and, by one journalist, limited by his own culture and nation, and 'a Pole with old world (if not pre-Christian) ideas.'[64] Some attempted to mitigate the message of the CDF's letter. Travers interprets the CDF letter as locating exclusion from the sacraments 'on the objective grave sinfulness of a Catholic's attempt to remarry after divorce, rather than on the question whether such a person is subjectively guilty or conscious of grave sin.' He observes that under Canon 912 'any baptized person who is not prohibited by law can and must be admitted to Holy Communion.' Under Canon 915 'those who are excommunicated or interdicted after the imposition or declaration of the penalty and others who obstinately persist in manifest grave sin are not to be admitted to Holy Communion.' After a painstaking account of the relevant canons in the 1983 Code of Canon Law, he concludes that not every divorced and remarried person 'has the full awareness of the grave sinfulness of his or her act of attempted remarriage that would be necessary for it to constitute a mortal sin.' In some cases the person may have repented of the attempted marriage but the circumstances now limit his or her freedom not to continue to participate in it, yet it cannot be said the person has an attitude of obstinacy, obduracy or stubbornness.[65]

The CDF's letter was affirmed by Pope St John Paul II in his 1997 *Address to the Pontifical Council for the Family*. Pope St John Paul II acknowledges that the situation of divorced people who have been attempted remarriage is 'painful' and 'distressing'; they cannot be abandoned by the Church. Pope St John Paul II sees that it is vital that:

> these men and women know that the Church loves them, that she is not far from them and suffers because of their situation. The divorced and remarried are and remain her members, because they have received Baptism and retain their Christian faith.[66]

Pope St John Paul II reaffirms the teaching in *Familiaris Consortio* 84 as by the 'very authority of the Lord', 'the divorced and remarried cannot be admitted to Eucharistic Communion since "their state and condition of life objectively contradict that union of love between Christ and the Church which is signified and effected by the Eucharist".' He adds that this also refers to the Sacrament of Penance which requires conversion and repentance.[67] However, he offers a practical response to people in this situation, noting especially the Church's concern for their children. He calls for a 'pastoral plan of preparation and of timely support for couples at the moment of crisis.' Priests must 'guide and support' the divorced and remarried with an 'open heart' so that they do not despair and so that they can 'approach the divine mercy by other ways.' People in 'irregular situations' should be welcomed with 'charity and kindness,' and helped to 'clarify their concrete status by means of enlightened and enlightening pastoral care.'

'Fraternal and evangelical welcome' is 'the first step required to integrate them into Christian practice.' The 'human and Christian formation' of their children and the supportive assistance of family members contributes to preparing the hearts of the parents 'to receive the strength and necessary clarity to overcome the real difficulties on their path.' Pope St John Paul II writes in the hope that 'even those who are living in a situation that does not conform to the Lord's will may obtain salvation from God, if they are able to persevere in prayer, penance and true love.'[68]

Travers revised his opinion in the light of Pope St John Paul II's 1997 *Address to the Pontifical Council for the Family* given that, in the opinion of Travers, the Pope had clarified interpretation of the relevant canons.[69] However, M. Lawler thinks that the argument still stands: 'the civil remarriage of the divorced Catholic without annulment may constitute grave matter in the eyes of the Church; it may even, on occasion, constitute grave sin. But it constitutes *grave* sin only when there is full awareness and full, free consent.' A person not guilty of grave sin must be admitted to Holy Communion.[70]

Given that the CDF's letter was met with 'a very lively response' and some criticism, Cardinal Ratzinger, the Prefect of the Congregation, organised a study of some of the objections to Church teaching and practice, and the proposed solutions. He summarized these objections and offered a response.[71] One area the study looked at was the Orthodox Church's approach of tolerance of a second union through *oikonomia* and the principle of *epikeia*.

Eastern Orthodox tradition of oikonomia *and* epikeia

In the Orthodox tradition *akribia*, strictness in the application of the law, and *oikonomia*, mercy, flexibility and leniency, exist side by side.[72] *Oikonomia* however defies precise definition, indeed L. Orsy point out that there is a plurality of interpretations.[73] In one interpretation *oikonomia* means 'the ability of the church to extend mercy when the reality of a person's life does

Living the Larger Life of the Gospel

not conform to ideal norms.'[74] In another interpretation *oikonomia* is related to the divine economy of God's mercy towards human weakness and the 'power of the keys' whereby Christ hands down this authority to his Apostles thus allowing them to dispense his mercy.[75] Again, *oikonomia* is related to stewardship of household goods and so it concerns the welfare of the Church and the good of the individual. *Oikonomia* allows bishops, as stewards of God's household, and prompted by an extraordinary situation, to 'heal the social body', by relaxing the law in a specific situation as a condescension to human weakness. *Oikonomia* has limits: 'it cannot go against dogma. It must not include the use of wrong means, not even for a holy purpose. Nor should it be a source of scandal for the community.' The bishop cannot do anything against revealed truth. Intervention 'should always serve a positive aim.' Moreover, 'since every need for *oikonomia* arises out of an individual situation, each use of it is unique. It cannot and must not serve as a precedent for future actions.' *Oikonomia* is not the same as a dispensation nor is it equivalent to *epikeia*. Both dispensation and *epikeia* are juridical notions; *oikonomia* is theological, while *epikeia* constitutes a larger more merciful interpretation of law in instances not provided by the letter of the law. It presupposes sincerity in wanting to observe the law, and interprets the mind of the lawgiver in supplying his presumed intent to include a situation that is not covered by the law. It favors the liberty of the interpreter without contradicting the express will of the lawgiver. Orsy points out that *oikonomia*, as understood by the Orthodox Church, does not exist in the Latin Church. *Oikonomia* belongs in the 'world of mysteries' not the world of the law. According to Orsy, *oikonomia* can be used in the case of a divorced and remarried person.

Epikeia differs from *oikonomia* in that *epikeia* is a juridic principle, *oikonomia* is a theological principle and can apply not only to church law but also to divine and moral law. Its practice is not codified, and it does not follow precedence. *Epikeia* is a virtue belonging to justice that allows for the setting aside of the letter of the law. It is interpreted in terms of the intention of the legislator in cases where the circumstances are different from those for which the law was conceived: 'if he (the legislator) had known about this situation he would not expect the law to apply.'[76] *Epikeia* allows for looking beyond a literal interpretation of the law but it still keeps the intention of the law in mind. St Thomas Aquinas explains that as an aspect of justice, *epikeia* only applies to cases where the application of the law, presumably human law, would frustrate justice and be contrary to the common good. For instance, generally a person should return deposits but if a madman wants his sword back so that he can kill someone then it would be better to set aside the letter of the law for the common good.[77] Thus, *epikeia* is not an exception to the law nor does it allow an injustice, nor does it allow the law to be set aside on the grounds of the law's apparent severity or inconvenience. Rather it is an instance of excellent decision-making where the law serves the common good and justice.

As part of the conversation on divorce and remarriage the Orthodox theologian J. Meyendorff offers an outline of Orthodox theology that resists a simple contrast to the Catholic approach. Meyendorff's initial question is, 'is it right to say simply that "the Orthodox Church admits divorce"?.'[78] Meyendorff explains that the Orthodox approach starts from 'different presuppositions': first, the sacrament of marriage is conferred upon the spouses through the blessing of the priest. As a sacrament, marriage creates an eternal bond because it relates to eternal life in the Kingdom and as such it cannot be dissolved by the death of one of the partners. The mystery of the sacrament of marriage puts it in the realm of a spiritual mystical union.[79] Recall, that from the Catholic perspective marriage is a contract or covenant that is indissoluble, but since marriage concerns only earthly life it is dissolved on the death of one of the partners. Second, as a sacrament marriage is a gift of grace and the Orthodox Church is able to accept that grace was not received, for instance if the couple were not ready to receive the grace when they married, or they were unable to make the grace fruitful. In such cases the Orthodox Church 'may admit the fact that the grace was not "received", tolerate separation and allow remarriage.' Meyendorff adds that the Orthodox Church does not encourage remarriage because of 'the eternal character of the marriage bond.' Nevertheless, remarriage is tolerated 'when, in concrete cases, it appears as the best solution for a given individual.'

From an Orthodox analysis of scripture Meyendorff acknowledges the 'repeated condemnation of divorce by Christ.' However, the possibility of divorce on the grounds of 'unchastity' in Matthew 19, and St Paul's admission that a wife can separate from her husband indicate that 'ultimately, sin can destroy marriage.' Thus, the Orthodox can allow separation but they discourage any form of remarriage either after widowhood or after divorce. According to K. Schembri, Christ says that the marriage bond should not be broken, not that it cannot be broken and so in the Orthodox view no separation is a 'moral ideal' rather than an ontological truth.[80] Meyendorff continues, since no Church father denounced imperial laws of divorce and remarriage enacted in the early centuries of the Christian empire, and instead viewed these laws as simply inevitable, this gives ground for Church toleration of later unions while remaining faithful to the norm set by New Testament revelation that 'only the first and unique marriage was blessed in Church during the Eucharist.' Meyendorff adds that in the early centuries second and third marriages took place as civil ceremonies only. There followed a period of penance of about seven years, during which the couple were excommunicated and admitted by stages of repentance to 'weepers', 'hearers' and 'prostrators', until they were again considered full members of the Church. The Orthodox Church issued divorces only when obliged to once the Church had the 'legal monopoly' of registering and validating all marriages. Notably, Meyendorff suggests that the Orthodox Church should stop 'giving' divorces and allow this through the civil authorities, and give 'permission' to remarry if reconciliation is impossible and there has been a period of penance.

Schembri notes that although practice varies from one Orthodox Church to another, in general it is accepted that the end of the marital relationship is denoted by death, adultery, or iniquity. Divorce is not granted on the basis of mutual agreement of the spouses. However, he also observes that in some areas divorce has become frequent.[81] Schembri explains that remarriage is tolerated through *oikonomia* only in certain conditions: before a new marriage there has to be the death of the spouse or an ecclesiastical divorce affirming that the previous marriage has died. An innocent spouse must demonstrate that he or she tried to save the previous marriage and that he or she cannot live a celibate life without harm. For some Orthodox Churches, a spouse guilty of breaking a marriage cannot remarry so long as the other spouse is alive; if marriage was broken as a result of adultery the spouse cannot marry the adulterous partner even after the death of the other spouse. Orthodox clergy and their wives cannot remarry and remarriage bars ordination. Remarriage is non-sacramental and has a penitential tone since it acknowledges not only the death of a marriage but also the inability to follow the call to lifelong celibacy. The remarried couple are also excluded for one or two years from the Eucharist for a period of repentance and mourning.[82]

The option to remarry is presented by the Orthodox tradition neither as a tolerated ill, nor as a minor evil. From the pastoral point of view, for people whose previous marriage is irrevocably dead and who are incapable of remaining single, second marriage is indeed a good; it is the closest possible realization of the ideal in their context. Despite their penitential tone, the prayers confer a blessing onto the entire rite through which the Orthodox Churches acknowledge the second marriage. The fact that the crowning rite, with its profound liturgical significance, has been re-introduced to the subsequent marriage ceremony by the Eastern Churches, points to the recognition of the second marriage as real, though partial and imperfect. Since the second marriage does not entirely correspond to the ideal of the unity between Christ and Church, it lacks the fullness of a sacramental value, but rather in an imperfect manner, it still constitutes a sacrament.[83]

Ratzinger's response

Cardinal Ratzinger's succinct summary of the 'objections' to Church teaching and the conclusions reached after further study on the pastoral care of the divorced and remarried was published in 1998 and a part of his text appears under the title *Concerning some objections to the Church's teaching on the Reception of Holy Communion by Divorced and Remarried Members of the Faithful*.[84]

The first objection concerned the use of scriptural texts. It was argued that Matthew 5:32, 19:9 and 1 Corinthians 7:12–16 allowed for a flexible rather than a strictly legal interpretation of the law. Ratzinger points out that there is no consensus on the meaning of the term *porneia*, and that the Pauline privilege in Corinthians refers to the dissolution of a non-sacramental marriage for the good of the faith. The teaching of the Church on the indissolubility of marriage 'is faithful to the words of Jesus.'

The second objection took the form of an appeal to the Orthodox practice of *oikonomia* as more equitable in difficult situations. In an article published in 1972 Ratzinger asserted that the traditions of both East and West agreed on the total impossibility of separation of Christian spouses that could lead to remarriage during the lifetime of the spouses. However, he thought that there was patristic evidence of a more 'elastic' practice and that there could be an appeal to *oikonomia* in exceptional circumstances since some of the Church fathers seemed to allow leniency.[85] Ratzinger referred to Origen who had observed that some bishops had made a concession for remarriage even though it contradicted Scripture,[86] Ambrosiaster who had a 'highly individual interpretation' of 1 Corinthians 7:11, and some comments made by St Basil of Caesarea. St Basil seemed to have allowed second or even third marriages but further research has indicated that this probably referred to the remarriage of widows or widowers. St Basil further suggested that a remarried man had to do seven years penance following the steps of penance for reconciliation[87] and the Orthodox approach interpreted this as allowing the man to remain in the second marriage but St Basil does not make this clear. Canon 8 of the Council of Nicaea allowed for admitting those in second marriages to communion, but this referred to schismatics who were refusing to admit to communion widows who had remarried. After this further research had thrown doubt on these exceptions, and especially after *Familiaris Consortio*, Ratzinger decided that the appeal to *oikonomia* was no longer an option.[88] In response to the second objection Ratzinger explains that there is a 'clear consensus' among the fathers on the indissolubility of marriage: 'since it derives from the will of the Lord, the Church has no authority over it.' Moreover, for this very reason 'from the outset' Christian marriage was different from marriage in Roman society and the fathers 'clearly excluded divorce and remarriage, precisely out of faithful obedience to the New Testament.' According to Ratzinger, divorced and remarried faithful were 'never officially admitted' to Holy Communion after penance, though 'in certain territories' the Church did not revoke 'concessions.' Although this point is not made by Ratzinger, it should be noted that there is insufficient evidence to say whether or not after a period of penance remarried spouses actually continued in their marriage or whether they led a future life of celibacy. Ratzinger accepts that as a result of historical differences there is different practice more influenced by civil law in Eastern Churches, but in the West there was a return to the fathers at the Council of Trent, reaffirmed at the Second Vatican Council.

The third objection was the proposition that since some issues could not be dealt with in the external forum, the Church should respect and tolerate individual conscience and in particular appeal could be made to the principle of *epikeia*. Ratzinger distinguishes three different 'areas of inquiry': first, *epikeia* applies to human and ecclesiastical norms not to 'norms over which the Church has no discretionary authority' and indissolubility is a norm of divine law; second, the Church does have authority to 'clarify' conditions that must be fulfilled for a marriage to be considered indissoluble, hence the nullity procedures, and this allows for the principle of *oikonomia* 'without touching the indissolubility of marriage.' Moreover, since marriage has 'a fundamental public ecclesial character' the principle that 'no one is a judge in his own case' applies and so a case has to be brought before the relevant tribunal; third, the possibility that mistakes may occur in marriage cases or where there is not a developed tribunal system mean that there may be some 'questionable decisions.' In these situations, 'the application of *epikeia* in the internal forum is not automatically excluded from the outset.' Ratzinger adds that this demands further study and clarification.

The fourth objection argued that the Magisterium of Pope St John Paul II had reversed the doctrinal development of the Second Vatican Council which was more personalistic. Moreover, the objection questions whether the marriage is dead if the 'personal bond of love between the spouses' no longer exists. Ratzinger points out that 'the Council did not break with the traditional concept of marriage, but on the contrary developed it further', and within the covenant aspect there remains the contractual aspect. The very term 'sacrament' takes marriage out of a purely juridical realm. Suggesting that a marriage is dead when the couple no longer love each other is to sanction divorce. Ratzinger raises for 'further study' the question of whether non-believing Christians can truly enter into a sacramental marriage: 'faith belongs to the essence of the sacrament; what remains to be clarified is the juridical question of what evidence of the "absence of faith" would have as a consequence that the sacrament does not come into being.'

The fifth objection charges Church teaching with being overly legalistic and not pastoral. This includes the charge that people today do not understand the language used. Ratzinger accepts the inadequacy at times of language and urges preachers and catechists to make the content accessible without compromising the truth.

Kasper and Ratzinger: On the Church

The 1993 letter on Holy Communion for the divorced and remarried from the three German bishops was a symptom of a much deeper issue: the question of the relationship of the universal Church to local churches. A dispute that at times became personal began to surface through a number of articles and publications between the German Cardinals Kasper and Ratzinger. In response to a lecture given by Ratzinger which in turn had responded to an essay by Kasper, Kasper wrote an article titled 'On the Church' that was published in America *The Jesuit Review*.[89]

According to Kasper the 'pressing pastoral problem' is the 'gap' between norms promulgated in Rome for the universal Church and the 'needs and practices' of 'our' local church. Kasper explains that people and priests cannot understand the reasons behind 'regulations coming from the center' and tend therefore to ignore them. He observes that the question of Holy Communion for the divorced and remarried is a good example of this. This gap places the bishop in a dilemma: he is pulled between protecting the unity of the Church or taking pastoral care of his flock. However, Kasper sees a simple solution: 'the bishop must be granted enough vital space to make responsible decisions in the matter of implementing universal laws.' This solution does not permit a local bishop to make concessions in matters of faith. But it does take advantage of the flexibility in 'special circumstances' that Kasper says has always been in the tradition that 'permitted exceptions to general norms, imposed justice tempered by mercy, gave scope to equity and created an extensive system of dispensation.' Moreover, Kasper says the tradition allowed a local bishop to suspend a new law temporarily 'if he judged it harmful in his territory.'

Notably, Kasper puts the problem of the relationship of universal church to local churches down to a failure to implement the Second Vatican Council's view of ecclesiology. Kasper argues that the Second Vatican Council advocated decentralization, but the opposite happened. For various reasons, including the failure of bishops to take on their responsibilities, Kasper claims that 'the right balance between the universal church and particular churches has been destroyed', and he says that this is the view of many bishops. In particular, he says that Cardinal Ratzinger takes a 'purely abstract and theoretical point of view' on the relationship of the universal and local churches. Kasper especially takes exception to Ratzinger's assertion that 'the universal church is a reality ontologically and temporally prior to every individual church.' In essence, Kasper suggests that this leads to 'an undeclared assumption identifying (*de facto*) universal Church and the pope and curia.'[90] Although Kasper and Ratzinger engage with each other through mainly historical argument of ecclesiology, Kasper claims that 'the conflict is between theological opinions and philosophical assumptions': Kasper says that Ratzinger's side 'proceeds by Plato's method; its starting point is the primacy of an idea that is a universal concept.' Kasper's own side 'follows Aristotle's approach and sees the universal as existing in a concrete reality.' As far as Kasper is concerned, this diversity of opinion has been accepted before and so should be accepted today. Resolution of the relationship between the universal church and local churches is not only highly relevant for pastoral situations but it is also crucial for relationships with other Christian 'churches.'

In his response to Kasper, Ratzinger[91] regards any attempt to misuse 'theology or any interpretation of the faith by the magisterium' to gain power or reverse a council as a serious matter, and he outrightly rejects the suggestion that the CDF's letter identified the reality of the universal church with the pope and Curia. As far as Ratzinger is concerned, 'the inner priority of unity' of the one bride, the Church, who may be wearing multi-coloured garments, is 'plainly evident.' He adds, 'the church of

Rome is a local church and not the universal church a local church with a peculiar, universal responsibility, but still a local church.' Addressing Kasper's suggestion that Ratzinger has simply presented his own 'Platonic' theological opinion, Ratzinger points out that the universal Church is a practical reality, not an abstraction, as indicated when speaking of the sacraments. Patently, the sacrament of baptism does not merely socialize someone into the local church: 'in baptism the door to the one church is opened to us.'

Certainly, the debate between Kasper and Ratzinger raises interesting questions that have yet to be worked out. Indeed, Kasper was a significant figure at the 2015 synod on the family leading up to *Amoris Laetitia* where the proposal of the three German bishops resurfaced alongside the issue of decentralisation. Nevertheless, the question of sacramental theology brings other issues that are significant for marriage: the faith of the parties, and the need for evangelization.

Pope Benedict XVI

As Pope Benedict XVI, Ratzinger suggested that there may not be a valid sacramental marriage where faith is lacking, though he chose not to pronounce on the matter and left it open for further study.[92] However, Pope Benedict XVI frequently notes that marriage, 'this fundamental human reality is subjected to a multitude of problems and threats' and is especially in need of evangelization and practical support. This is particularly pressing since, he notes, the mission of marriage and the family is to form the person, transmit the faith, and act as 'Christian leaven' in the world. Repeating *Familiaris Consortio* and the long held tradition that marriage is not a social construct, Pope Benedict XVI says that the 'right relationship' between man and woman is 'rooted in the essential core of the human being'; marriage cannot be separated from fundamental human questions, 'who am I?' 'what is a human being?', and thus to questions about God. The biblical answer is that human beings are made in the image of God, and God is love. 'It is therefore the vocation to love that makes the human person an authentic image of God: man and woman come to resemble God to the extent that they become loving people.' The body has a 'theological character', and what is biological 'is the expression and fulfilment of our humanity' precisely because there is an 'indissoluble connection' between soul, body, and spirit in human beings, and this includes sexuality. In the 'totality' of the human person, the person's 'yes' in marriage is 'a step beyond the present moment', signifying 'always' and 'a space for faithfulness.' Simultaneously, 'yes' is 'an assent to the gift of a new life.' Pope Benedict XVI's concern is that 'various forms of the erosion of marriage' such as free unions, trial marriages, or same sex unions, make the body into a 'secondary thing' that can be manipulated or 'used as one likes.' Pope Benedict XVI points out that the 'truth about marriage and the family' is 'deeply rooted' in the truth about human beings and this truth is actuated in salvation history, the history of God's covenant with humanity. Indeed, following scripture, the union of man and woman in the covenant of marriage is 'a symbol of salvation history.' For Pope Benedict XVI love in marriage and God's love is so closely connected that:

> the debasement of human love, the suppression of the authentic capacity for loving, is turning out in our time to be the most suitable and effective weapon to drive God away from men and women, to distance God from the human gaze and heart.[93]

In in his 2007 post synodal exhortation on the Eucharist, *Sacramentum caritatis* Pope Benedict XVI observes that the Eucharist, as sacrament of the Bridegroom and Bride, and 'as the sacrament of charity, has a particular relationship with the love of man and woman united in marriage.' He notes that the Eucharist 'strengthens the indissolubility and love of every Christian marriage.' The family as domestic Church and 'a community of life and love' has a eucharistic dimension as a sign of Christ's love for his Church, 'a love culminating in the Cross.' Pope Benedict XVI confirms that 'the indissoluble, exclusive and faithful bond uniting Christ and the Church, which finds sacramental expression in the Eucharist, corresponds to the basic anthropological fact that man is meant to be definitively united to one woman and vice versa.' The 'irrevocable nature of God's love in Christ for his Church' implies indissolubility. Pope Benedict XVI recognizes the painful situation that some married people find themselves in and, referring to *Familiaris Consortio*, he says that 'the Church's pastors, out of love for the truth, are obliged to discern different situations carefully, in order to be able to offer appropriate spiritual guidance to the faithful involved.' Although he reiterates that divorced and remarried faithful cannot be admitted to the Eucharist, they still belong to the Church and the Church continues to accompany them. Any doubt regarding the validity of a previous marriage has to go through the relevant tribunal in 'full respect for canon law.' Pope Benedict XVI repeats that pastoral care should not be understood as if it is in conflict with the law: 'the fundamental point of encounter between the law and pastoral care is love for the truth.' Remarried faithful who cannot separate should live as brother and sister. Pope Benedict XVI re-emphasizes the importance of proper preparation and discernment to avoid 'impulsive decisions or superficial reasons' that lead people to take on 'responsibilities that they are then incapable of honouring.'[94]

In his address to the US bishops on their *ad limina* visit in 2012 Pope Benedict XVI notes their concern about the crisis over marriage, the family and sexuality. He mentions especially the 'powerful political and cultural currents seeking to alter the legal definition of marriage.' He regards the defence of marriage as 'a social reality' to be question of justice. Pope Benedict XVI also acknowledges that the rich tradition of Christian marriage has suffered from 'deficiencies' in catechesis, and that there is a general failure to understand the sinfulness of cohabitation or to appreciate the virtue of chastity.[95] However, according to Pope

Benedict XVI 'just as the eclipse of God and the crisis of the family are linked, so the new evangelization is inseparable from the Christian family.'[96] In what he calls a 'reductive vision', the family is seen 'merely as the object of pastoral action.' Instead, Pope Benedict XVI recalls the need to remind people that both the vocation to priesthood and marriage

> share the same root in the love of Christ who gives himself for humanity's salvation. They are called to a common mission: to witness to and make present this love at the service of the community in order to build up the People of God.

He accepts that 'in these difficult times' families require 'special attention.' Nevertheless, he does not think that this need diminishes the identity of the family. He adds, 'no vocation is a private matter, and even less so is the vocation to marriage, because its horizon is the entire Church.'[97]

Interestingly, Kasper's eightieth birthday was a few days after the resignation of Pope Benedict XVI, and so Kasper was still eligible to vote in the 2013 papal conclave.

Pope Francis: evangelization and the family

In his homily at the opening of Fifth General Conference of the Council of Bishops of Latin America and the Carribean (CELAM) Pope Benedict XVI declared that the Church grows 'by attraction.'[98] The CELAM conference document, known as the *Aparecida* document is influential not least because its chief editor was the Archbishop of Buenos Aires, Cardinal Bergoglio, now Pope Francis. Many see in *Aparecida* the blueprint for the Pope's emphasis on mission and evangelization, care of the family, the option for the poor and marginalized, and Pope Francis's insistence that the joy of the encounter with Christ should reach all wounded people.[99] Indeed, 'new evangelization' is addressed not only to those who do not know the Gospel, but also to the faithful who express the faith in 'different ways' but do not take part in worship, and the baptized whose lives do not reflect the demands of baptism.[100] The implication here is that the faithful who live in situations that are not in accord with Church teaching may also be in need of evangelization.

In what becomes significant for his teaching on marriage and the family in *Amoris Laetitia,* Pope Francis asks that priests and the faithful who walk with people 'on a journey of openness to God' do so in the recognition that responsibility may be diminished or even nullified by ignorance. Referencing *Familiaris Consortio,* Pope Francis reminds them 'to accompany with mercy and patience the eventual stages of personal growth as these progressively occur.' Moreover, he says that the confessional is not a 'torture chamber but rather an encounter with the Lord's mercy that spurs us on to do our best.' Indicating perhaps the power of grace, he adds 'everyone needs to be touched by the comfort and attraction of God's saving love, which is mysteriously at work in each person above and beyond their faults and failings.'[101]

Indeed, in challenging times, Pope Francis advises

> let the grace of your baptism bear fruit in a path of holiness. Let everything be open to God; turn to him in every situation. Do not be dismayed, for the power of the Holy Spirit enables you to do this, and holiness, in the end, is the fruit of the Holy Spirit in your life. When you feel the temptation to dwell on your own weakness, raise your eyes to Christ crucified and say: "Lord, I am a poor sinner, but you can work the miracle of making me a little bit better." In the Church, holy yet made up of sinners, you will find everything you need to grow towards holiness.[102]

Notably, Pope Francis affirms, 'we are capable of loving with the Lord's unconditional love, because the risen Lord shares his powerful life with our fragile lives.'[103] God, he says, is always present in people's lives even when that life appears to be wrecked.[104] Significantly, Pope Francis observes the Pelagian or Semi-pelagian tendency to see grace in terms of the idea that all things are possible by the efforts of the human will: 'grace, precisely because it builds on nature, does not make us superhuman all at once. That kind of thinking would show too much confidence in our own abilities.' Instead, he notes:

> unless we can acknowledge our concrete and limited situation, we will not be able to see the real and possible steps that the Lord demands of us at every moment, once we are attracted and empowered by his gift. Grace acts in history; ordinarily it takes hold of us and transforms us progressively.[105]

Pope Francis recognizes that the family is 'experiencing a profound cultural crisis' and that relationships are in need of healing.[106] His general approach is to see the Church as a 'field hospital' where the first task is to 'heal the wounds.'[107] He also thinks that 'time is greater than space', that we need to learn how to wait because God lets us see things slowly: in much the same way as the statue of Our Lady, the Immaculate Conception slowly emerged from the river at Aparecida, God's message emerges. Moreover, an intellectual approach risks losing people and so the Church needs to think about language and about ensuring that the Church does not appear to be distant. Notably, he affirms that the Church speaks to grown-ups: 'ours is not an age of change but a change of age.' In speaking to people 'from the heart', the Church should take as its model for accompaniment the story of the road to Emmaus because without accompaniment the road leads to a sense of disappointment and abandonment. His question to the Church is, 'are we a Church capable of warming hearts?'[108]

For Pope Francis, debate and discussion are no bad things, after all, he says, 'in the Church there legitimately coexist different ways of interpreting many aspects of doctrine and Christian life', in their variety, they 'help to express more clearly the immense riches of God's word.' He takes seriously the situations people find themselves in, for

> the questions of our people, their suffering, their struggles, their dreams, their trials and their worries, all possess an

interpretational value that we cannot ignore if we want to take the principle of the incarnation seriously. Their wondering helps us to wonder, their questions question us.[109]

Leading up to Amoris Laetitia

In February 2014 Pope Francis called a special consistory for the family as a preparation for an extraordinary synod of bishops in October of the same year. Some one hundred and eighty-five cardinals gathered for closed-door sessions and Pope Francis urged them to speak openly on all matters concerning marriage and family life including contraception, cohabitation, divorce, and same sex relationships. For some commentators the fact that Kasper was invited to give a speech to the consistory was an indication that change was in the air. Kasper's speech was later published as *The Gospel of the Family*. Pope Francis responded to a journalist's question on the division between synod fathers:

> Cardinal Kasper made a beautiful and profound presentation that will soon be published in German, and he examined five points; the fifth was that of second marriages. I would have been concerned if in the consistory there wasn't an intense discussion. It wouldn't have served for anything. The cardinals knew that they could say what they wanted, and they presented many different points of view that are enriching. The fraternal and open comparisons make theological and pastoral thought grow. I am not afraid of this, actually I seek it.[110]

The first synod of bishops called by Pope Francis in 2013 to take place in 2014 was an 'extraordinary' one because it did not take place in the regular cycle of synods and was designed to feed into the ordinary synod of 2015. The working title was *The Pastoral Challenges of the Family in the Context of Evangelization*. With the prospect of local churches making decisions about significant aspects of Church teaching such as whether people who are divorced and have attempted remarriage can receive Holy Communion, the question of marriage and its challenges, especially given the importance of marriage and the family for evangelization, seems to be pressing. Notably, the day after he announced the coming synod Pope Francis described the Church as

> like a great orchestra in which there is great variety. We are not all the same and we do not all have to be the same. We are all different, varied, each of us with his own special qualities. And this is the beauty of the Church: everyone brings his own gift, which God has given him, for the sake of enriching others. And between the various components there is diversity; however, it is a diversity that does not enter into conflict and opposition. It is a variety that allows the Holy Spirit to blend it into harmony.[111]

Certainly, Pope Francis thinks that 'it is not advisable for the Pope to take the place of local Bishops in the discernment of every issue which arises in their territory. In this sense, I am conscious of the need to promote a sound "decentralization".'[112]

As with previous synods there were preparatory documents to gather testimony and proposals and a consultation questionnaire. In his speech at the opening of the 2014 synod Pope Francis explains that the participants

> bring the voice of the Particular Churches, assembled at the level of local Churches through the Bishops' Conferences. The Universal Church and the Particular Churches are divine institutions; the local Churches are thus understood as human institutions. You will give voice in *synodality*. It is a great responsibility: to bring the realities and problems of the Churches, in order to help them to walk on that path that is the Gospel of the family.

Pope Francis urged the participants to speak with honesty, *parrhesia* or apostolic zeal, and listen with humility so that the synod could 'unfold *cum Petro et sub Petro*', with and under Peter.[113]

In his speech at the conclusion of the 2014 synod Pope Francis describes the synod journey as at times 'running fast', at times 'moments of fatigue', consolations and desolations. He notes in particular certain temptations: the temptation of so-called intellectuals and traditionalists 'to hostile inflexibility' and not allowing to be 'surprised by God'; the temptation of so-called do-gooders, progressives and liberals 'to a destructive tendency to goodness, that in the name of a deceptive mercy binds the wounds without first curing them and treating them'; the temptation to 'transform stones into bread to break the long, heavy, and painful fast and also to transform the bread into a stone and cast it against the sinners, the weak, and the sick, that is, to transform it into unbearable burdens'; the temptation to 'come down off the Cross, to please the people, and not stay there, in order to fulfil the will of the Father; to bow down to a worldly spirit instead of purifying it and bending it to the Spirit of God'; the temptation to 'neglect the *depositum fidei*, not thinking of themselves as guardians but as owners or masters [of it]; or, on the other hand, the temptation to neglect reality, making use of meticulous language and a language of smoothing to say so many things and to say nothing!'. Nevertheless, Pope Francis appreciates these temptations and 'animated discussions' as opportunities to speak frankly. This 'movement of the spirits' keeps in sight the good of the Church, of families, the 'supreme law' and the 'good of souls', 'without ever putting into question the fundamental truths of the Sacrament of marriage: the indissolubility, the unity, the faithfulness, the fruitfulness, that openness to life.' The Church is 'the caring Teacher, who is not afraid to roll up her sleeves to pour oil and wine on people's wound.' Pope Francis observes that 'many commentators' see 'a disputatious Church, where one part is against the other, doubting even the Holy Spirit, the true promoter and guarantor of the unity and harmony of the Church.' Instead, the synod is *cum Petro* and *sub Petro*, and it is the duty of the pope to guarantee the unity of the Church, remind the faithful of their duty to follow faithfully the Gospel of Christ, to remind pastors of their first duty to nourish their flock and seek the lost sheep. The conclusion of the extraordinary synod left one year to present a summary of what was discussed at the synod and to prepare the guidelines for the ordinary synod in 2015.[114]

Notes

1. Mk 12:29–30.
2. Lk 6:45.
3. Mt 5:8.
4. Lk 8:15.
5. Mt 15:8; Mk 7:6.
6. Lk 16:15; Ac 15:9.
7. Mt 6:19–21.
8. 1 K 3:9–12.
9. Pope St John Paul II, *Theology of the Body, Human Love in the Divine Plan* (Boston: Pauline Books, 1997) p. 177.
10. St Francis de Sales, *St Francis de Sales: Selected Letters* (New York: DeSales Resource Centre 2011), p. 22.
11. Pope St John Paul II, *Veritatis splendor*, 1.
12. Mt 19:16–21; Pope St John Paul II, *Veritatis splendor*, 7, 8.
13. Pope St John Paul II, *Veritatis splendor*, 22.
14. Pope St John Paul II, *Veritatis splendor*, 22, 23; St Augustine, *On John's Gospel*, 82, 3; Jn 1:17.
15. Pope Benedict XVI, *General Audience* (14 January 2009).
16. Pope St John Paul II, *Veritatis splendor*, 104; Lk 18:9–14.
17. Pope Francis, *Gaudete et Exsultate*, 36–40, 47–48.
18. Lateran Council IV, 6.
19. 1 Co 10:1–13; see *New Jerusalem Bible* footnote f, p. 1903.
20. Mt 11:27–30.
21. St Augustine, *Retractions*, 3, 18, 52.
22. St Augustine, *On Nature and Grace*, 43, 50.
23. J. Mahoney, *The Making of Moral Theology* (Oxford: Clarendon Press, 1987), pp. 48–54.
24. *Ibid.*, pp. 54–57.
25. Pope St John Paul II, *Dominum et Vivificantem*, 31.
26. *Ibid.*, 44.
27. Second Vatican Council, *Gaudium et spes* 37; Pope St John Paul II, *Dominum et Vivificantem*, 44, 45.
28. Pope St John Paul II, *Dominum et Vivificantem*, 60.
29. 'Interview: T. Fox with C. Curran, 'Curran: Papacy should admit some of its teachings are wrong' in *National Catholic Reporter* (21 November 2014) https://www.ncronline.org/news/accountability/curran-papacy-should-admit-some-its-teachings-are-wrong#.VG9ZYXbh9ho.facebook

30 Lk 2:34.
31 M. Lamb, 'Vatican II After Fifty Years: The Virtual Council Versus the Real Council' in *The Second Vatican Council Celebrating Its Achievements and the Future* (London: Bloomsbury 2013), p. 11.
32 Pope St John XXIII, *Address on the Solemn Opening of the Council* (11 October 1962), 4, 7.
33 Ibid., 6.
34 Pope St John XXIII, *Address on the Celebration of the Second Vatican Ecumenical Council* (5 June 1960).
35 Pope St Paul VI, *Ecclesiam suam*, 26.
36 Ibid., 30–31, 35.
37 Ibid., 37.
38 Ibid., 41–42.
39 Ibid., 42.
40 Ibid., 46–47.
41 Ibid., 48–49.
42 Ibid., 51.
43 Pope St Paul VI, *Address to the Swiss Bishops Ad Limina Visit* (1 December 1977).
44 Pope St Paul VI, *Ecclesiam suam*, 58–59.
45 Ibid., 63–65, 70.
46 Ibid., 87, 94.
47 *Catechism of the Catholic Church*, 2358.
48 Second Vatican Council, *Dignitatis Humanae*, 1–3.
49 Ibid., 5.
50 *Gaudium et spes*, 16.
51 See J. Smith, *Humanae Vitae a Generation Later* (Washington: Catholic University of America Press, 1991), pp. 148–155.
52 See A. Fisher, *Catholic Bioethics for a New Millenium* (Cambridge: Cambridge University Press, 2012), pp. 56–68.
53 Pope St John Paul, *Veritatis Splendor*, 58–64.
54 P. Travers, 'Reception of the Holy Eucharist by Catholics Attempting Remarriage after Divorce and the 1983 Code of Canon Law' in *Jurist* 55 (1995), p.190.
55 K. Himes and J. Coriden 'Pastoral Care of the Divorced and Remarried' in *Theological Studies* 57 (1996) pp. 97–123.
56 Travers, 'Reception of the Holy Eucharist by Catholics Attempting Remarriage after Divorce and the 1983 Code of Canon Law', p. 209.
57 Himes and Coriden 'Pastoral Care of the Divorced and Remarried', pp. 98–101.

58 *New Commentary of the Code of Canon Law* J. Beal, J. Coriden, T. Green (eds.), (New York: Paulist Press 2000), p. 186.
59 O. Saier, K. Lehmann, W. Kasper 'Pastoral Ministry: The Divorced and Remarried' in *Origins* 23:38 (10 March 1994) pp. 670–676.
60 G. Grisez, J. Finnis and W. E. May, 'Indissolubility, Divorce and Holy Communion' in *New Blackfriars* Vol.75 No.883 June (1994), pp. 321–330.
61 CDF, *Concerning the Reception of Holy Communion by the Divorced and Remarried Members of the Faithful* (14 September 1994), 3.
62 *Ibid.*, 6.
63 *Ibid.*, 7–8.
64 R. B. Kaiser, *The Politics of Sex and Religion* (Indiana: Leaven Press, 1985), pp. 10, 231.
65 Travers, 'Reception of the Holy Eucharist by Catholics Attempting Remarriage after Divorce and the 1983 Code of Canon Law', pp. 187–217.
66 Pope St John Paul II, *Address to the Pontifical Council for the Family* (24 January 1997), 2.
67 *Ibid.*, 3.
68 *Ibid.*, 3, 4.
69 P. Travers, 'Holy Communion and Catholics Who Have Attempted Remarriage After Divorce: A Revisitation', in *Jurist* 57 (1997) pp. 517–540.
70 M. Lawler, *Marriage and the Catholic Church: Disputed Questions* (Collegeville Minnesota: Liturgical Press, 2002), pp. 106–107.
71 Cardinal J. Ratzinger, *Concerning some objections to the Church's teaching on the Reception of Holy Communion by Divorced and Remarried Members of the Faithful* (CDF:1998).
72 K. Schembri, 'The Orthodox Tradition on Divorced and Remarried Faithful: What Can the Catholic Church Learn?' in *Melita Theologica* 65/1 (2015), pp. 127–128
73 L. Orsy, 'In Search of the Meaning of Oikonomia: Report on a Convention' in *Theological Studies* 43/2 (1982) pp. 312–319. Orsy offers a summary from papers presented at the Fifth International Congress, Society of the law of the Eastern Churches held from September 22–27, 1981.
74 S. Kanniyakonil, 'The Indissolubility of Marriage in the Syro-Malabar Church' in *Marriage, Families and Spirituality* 24, (2018), p.106.
75 Schembri, 'The Orthodox Tradition on Divorced and Remarried Faithful: What Can the Catholic Church Learn?' p. 128.
76 B. Killeen, 'Theology, Law and Christian Life' in *Keeping Faith in Practice: Aspects of Catholic Pastoral Theology* (London: SCM Press, 2010), 227–240 p.23.
77 Aquinas *Summa Theologiae* II-II, q.120; A. R. Luño 'Can Epikeia Be Used in The Pastoral Care of the Divorced and Remarried Faithful?' in

L'Osservatore Romano 26-XI (1997)
78 J. Meyendorff, *Marriage: An Orthodox Perspective* (New York: St Vladimir's Seminary Press 2000), pp. 54–58.
79 Schembri, 'The Orthodox Tradition on Divorced and Remarried Faithful: What Can the Catholic Church Learn?', pp. 126–127.
80 *Ibid.*, p. 130.
81 *Ibid.*, pp. 130–131.
82 *Ibid.*, pp. 131–133.
83 See M. Hnyp, 'Re-examining Second Marriage in Catholic Moral and Pastoral Theology: In Search of an Alternative Avenue through the Eastern Practice of *Oikonomia*' in *INTAMS review* 17 (2011), p. 34.
84 Ratzinger, *Concerning some objections to the Church's teaching on the Reception of Holy Communion by Divorced and Remarried Members of the Faithful* (CDF:1998).
85 J. Ratzinger, *On the Question of the Indissolubility of Marriage* (1972)
86 Origen, *Commentary on Matthew*, 14, 23.
87 St Basil, *Letter 217*.
88 See N. Healy, 'The Merciful Gift of Indissolubility and the Question of Pastoral Care for Civilly Divorced and Remarried Catholics' in *Communio* 41 Summer (2014), pp. 312–313.
89 W. Kasper, 'On the Church' in *America The Jesuit Review* 23 April (2001).
90 K. McDonnell, 'The Ratzinger/Kasper Debate: The Universal Church and Local Churches' in *Theological Studies* 63 (2002), pp. 231, 236.
91 J. Ratzinger, 'The Local Churches and the Universal Church' in *America The Jesuit Review* 19 November (2001)
92 See Ratzinger, *Concerning some objections to the Church's teaching on the Reception of Holy Communion by Divorced and Remarried Members of the Faithful* (CDF:1998), note 4.
93 Pope Benedict XVI, *Address to the Participants in the Ecclesial Diocesan Convention of Rome* (6 June 2005).
94 Pope Benedict XVI, *Sacramentum Caritatis*, 27–29.
95 Pope Benedict XVI, *Address to the Bishops of the United States of America from Region VIII on their Ad Limina Visit* (9 March 2012).
96 Pope Benedict XVI, *Address to the Participants at the Plenary Assembly of the Pontifical Council for the Family* (1 December 2011).
97 Pope Benedict XVI *Address, Pastoral Visit to Ancona Meeting with Families and Priests* (11 September 2011).
98 Pope Benedict XVI, *Homily* (13 May 2007).
99 CELAM, *Aparecida*, 29.
100 Pope Francis, *Evangelii Gaudium*, 14.

[101] *Ibid.*, 44.
[102] Pope Francis, *Gaudete et exsultate*, 15.
[103] *Ibid.*, 18.
[104] *Ibid.*, 42.
[105] *Ibid.*, 49–50.
[106] Pope Francis, *Evangelii Gaudium*, 66–67.
[107] Pope Francis, 'A Big Heart Open To God: An Interview with Pope Francis' in *America The Jesuit Review* 30 September (2013).
[108] Pope Francis, *Meeting with the Bishops of Brazil, Address* (28 July 2013).
[109] Pope Francis, *Gaudete et exsultate*, 43, 44.
[110] Catholic News Agency, Transcript of interview with Pope Francis with *Corriere della Sera* (5 March 2014).
[111] Pope Francis, *General Audience* (9 October 2013), 3.
[112] Pope Francis, *Evangelii Gaudium*, 16.
[113] Pope Francis, *Greeting to the Synod Fathers During the First General Congregation of the Third Extraordinary General Assembly of the Synod of Bishops* (6 October 2014).
[114] Pope Francis, *Address for the Conclusion of the Third Extraordinary General Assembly of the Synod of Bishops* (18 October 2014).

10 *AMORIS LAETITIA* AND 'DANCING TOWARDS THE FUTURE WITH IMMENSE HOPE'.

WRITING TO THE first Christians, St Peter, fisherman, and 'apostle of Jesus Christ', offers down to earth advice to new Christians: 'rid yourselves, then, of all spite, deceit, hypocrisy, envy and carping criticism.'[1] St Peter add, 'love each other intensely from the heart', 'be sympathetic', 'have compassion', come to agreement and 'never repay one wrong with another ... instead repay with a blessing,' 'have respect for everyone,' 'welcome each other into your houses without grumbling,' and be at the service of others.[2] When it comes to marriage St Peter astutely realizes that people, and here he is thinking particularly of pagan husbands, can be won over by 'the interior disposition of the heart, consisting in the imperishable quality of a gentle and peaceful spirit.'[3] Whatever happens, St Peter says 'simply proclaim the Lord Christ holy in your hearts, and always have your answer ready for people who ask you the reason for the hope you have. But give it with courtesy and respect and with a clear conscience.'[4]

St Peter's letter to Christians speaks of the 'great joy' that faith in Christ brings, even if there are trials.[5] The leaders of the Church are to 'give a shepherd's care to the flock' and not 'lord it over' them. The faithful should stay alert and be 'strong in faith', in the knowledge that they can unload their burdens on to God because he is concerned about them.[6] With Christ as the 'living stone, rejected by human beings', St Peter encourages his readers and listeners to 'set yourselves close to him so that you, too, may be living stones making a spiritual house,' and to 'sing the praises of God who called you out of darkness into his wonderful light.'[7] *Amoris Laetitia*, with its focus on practical wisdom, dialogue, and joy, seeks to present Church teaching as a 'beacon of a lighthouse in a port'[8] for the boat of marriage.

A synod experience

The beginning of June 2015, at my computer in St Mary's University, Twickenham and coming to the end of term, I was expecting a few emails to tie up loose ends. An email popped up. I did not recognize the name, but the address was one standardly used by the clergy of the diocese. I clicked on the email: a name, and would I please ring this number. I rang the number and a relieved voice on the other end of the telephone said he was glad I had rung—he was concerned in case I thought it was a joke. At that point my thoughts instantly turned to the seminarians I had taught who were now completely finished for the academic year and were kicking their heels waiting for their pastoral placements to start.

I was invited to meet the Papal Nuncio who explained that Pope Francis had appointed me an expert, *adiutrix*, to the forthcoming synod on the family in October. If I were willing, this would involve three weeks working in Rome. So began a unique experience of participating in the universal Church at work.

Leading up to the synod, and no longer simply an observer, I began to study some of the expectations that were being floated in the media. There seemed to be acute polarization: on the one hand indignation at the suggestion that Pope Francis might depart from teaching; on the other hand a sense of victory at the possibility of real change to teaching. Anger, excitement, were at times palpable from press and religious commentators alike; vilification and adulation alike, though from different quarters, for Pope Francis and for Pope St John Paul II. The was much criticism of the preparatory documents and of the questionnaires. Charges of manipulation of the bishops were rife.[9] On reflection, it was very much like the media frenzy that accompanied the 1980 synod on the family and there are many parallels. The very fact that Holy Communion for the divorced and remarried was on the agenda must therefore mean that Pope Francis planned to change Church teaching dramatically; the very fact that the bishops at the 2014 extraordinary synod had mentioned homosexuality must therefore mean an approval of same sex unions. People were taking sides and the media were identifying 'hot topics' that would mark Pope Francis out as a radical, a reformer, a destroyer, a progressive, a conservative, depending on who was speaking at the time. Pope Francis himself noted that some of the very public and divisive debates 'range from an immoderate desire for total change without sufficient reflection or grounding, to an attitude that would solve everything by applying general rules or deriving undue conclusions from particular theological considerations.'[10]

Of course, if attention had been paid to the rationale of synods in general, and Pope Francis's call for a real dialogue on all matters that the bishops and the faithful raised as relevant, and in particular his request for honesty and openness, then it would not come as a surprise that there were many things on the table. Moreover, as Pope Francis reminded participants in his opening remarks 'the Synod is neither a convention, nor a "parlour", a parliament nor senate, where people make deals and reach a consensus.' The synod is a 'protected space in which the Church experiences the action of the Holy Spirit.'[11] As it turned out, although the bishops at the 2014 extraordinary synod had mentioned homosexuality, it was decided at the 2015 synod that this was not really within the remit of a synod on marriage and family, especially given all the other topics to be considered. There was some sifting and sorting of topics, again to take into account the consultation that had taken place after the 2014 extraordinary synod, and considerable admiration is due to those who collated all the information from around the world into a workable document. The major concern I had with the working document, the *instrumentum laboris*, entitled

The vocation and mission of the family in the Church and in the contemporary world, was that the 'shadows' of family life seemed to outweigh the brightness, making discernment of the vocation and mission of the family difficult. As part of 'listening', the document began with an account of the sociological and cultural context and challenges of the family, mostly dwelling on the weaknesses of the family. Problems from inclusion to affective fragility and immaturity and the pastoral challenges gave way to a consideration of discerning the family vocation but this, and the section on the mission of the family, were interspersed with more worries over indissolubility and declining births, people's fear of marriage and commitment, differences, inadequate preparation for marriage, and caring for 'wounded families.' It seemed to be a huge task ahead.

Arriving at the synod on a rather overcast Roman October I found a group of cardinals, archbishops, bishops, and priests who were concerned with one thing: to discern what was good for the people of God. There were many other participants from people working in family planning, marriage preparation and catechesis, to bioethicists, married couples and even a synod baby who was regularly wheeled round to meet various prelates. I am sure that some had certain agendas and set ways of thinking. Indeed, Pope Francis himself observed, 'in the course of this Synod, the different opinions which were freely expressed—and at times, unfortunately, not in entirely well-meaning ways—certainly led to a rich and lively dialogue.'[12] Nevertheless, my experience of the whole three weeks was of a concerted effort to do what was right, good, and true.

Setting the framework for the task ahead, according to Pope Francis, the Church carries out her mission 'in fidelity, truth and love':

> *To carry out her mission in fidelity* to her Master as a voice crying out in the desert, in defending faithful love and encouraging the many families which live married life as an experience which reveals of God's love; in defending

the sacredness of life, of every life; in defending the unity and indissolubility of the conjugal bond as a sign of God's grace and of the human person's ability to love seriously ... *The Church is called to carry out her mission in truth*, which is not changed by passing fads or popular opinions. The truth which protects individuals and humanity as a whole from the temptation of self-centredness and from turning fruitful love into sterile selfishness, faithful union into temporary bonds. 'Without truth, charity degenerates into sentimentality. Love becomes an empty shell, to be filled in an arbitrary way. In a culture without truth, this is the fatal risk facing love' ... *And the Church is called to carry out her mission in charity*, not pointing a finger in judgment of others, but—faithful to her nature as a mother—conscious of her duty to seek out and care for hurting couples with the balm of acceptance and mercy; to be a 'field hospital' with doors wide open to whoever knocks in search of help and support; even more, to reach out to others with true love, to walk with our fellow men and women who suffer, to include them and guide them to the wellspring of salvation.[13]

One question that became pressing early on was what precisely was the aim of the synod? It became clear that the aim was not simply to repeat the teaching of *Familiaris Consortio*. However, there was a danger in seeming to present a 'pastoral' document, pastoral in a somewhat negative sense, since in some eyes 'pastoral solutions', especially connected to marriage and the family, were viewed with suspicion as somehow compromising Church teaching. Other questions presented themselves: what was the starting point? The working document presented to the bishops began with a rather despairing account of the state of marriage today, its problems and its crises. If it were recognized that the Church saw all situations as opportunities for pastoral care, and that people made 'little steps', to what extent could it be said that there were 'seeds' in certain relationships, and could these be seeds of goodness? Was the real issue not rejection of

Church teaching but rather inadequate catechesis and a failure to know never mind understand the teaching? Was this in part due to a difficulty with language? To what extent is Church teaching merely aspirational? These questions were worked out in the *aula*, the hall of the synod, in the *circoli minores*, the small discussion groups, in the many moments of relaxed conversations, all supported by people praying for the success of the synod. Ultimately, these questions were dealt with in the long post synodal exhortation presented by Pope Francis on 'love in the family': *Amoris Laetitia*.

Amoris Laetitia, *The Joy of Love*

'Families are not a problem; they are first and foremost an opportunity.'[14] Without shying away from the challenges in marriage and the family, and in order fully to love and cherish family life, Pope Francis calls his exhortation *The Joy of Love*. In terms of the evangelizing role of the family, Pope Francis may be echoing here the *Aparecida* document on the joy of being disciples of Christ, joy that 'serves as remedy for a world fearful of the future.'[15] Citing St Thomas Aquinas, Pope Francis explains that joy 'refers to an expansion of the heart.' Unlike happiness or pleasure, joy can coexist with sorrow, difficulties and struggles.[16] Joy presupposes love, delights and rests in the good, and draws people together because it is something shared. In contrast to an unrealistic conception of a ready-made idyllic perfect love, joy accepts the realities of a shared marriage life that inevitably goes through stages including growing old together, suffering and eventually death. To take joy as the characteristic of marriage and family life is not to ignore problems, rather it is to integrate them into a bigger picture. The problem with starting from an account of sociological, cultural and pastoral difficulties is that people rapidly become overwhelmed or the discussion stalls as it is entangled in particulars. Certainly, Pope Francis is acutely aware of the need for the Church to listen to people's actual experience in order to be 'grounded in reality', and that listening exercise also took place over the two synods leading up to *Amoris Laetitia*. However, Pope Francis begins his exhortation with a chapter 'inspired by Scriptures, to set a proper tone.'[17]

At the synod some of fathers observed that the challenges of life, the 'signs of the times', need to be read through the eyes of faith. Following *Aparecida* the see, judge, act method is not purely a sociological analysis. Instead 'see' is journeying together to understand reality with the eyes of faith and heart of God; 'judge' is according to Jesus Christ, Way, Truth, Life; 'act' is from the Church in spreading the Kingdom.[18] The advantage of the method is that it operates in both the historical horizontal and transcendent vertical dimensions, it gives space to stop and reflect, and it results in not only words but also discernment and action. In beginning from scripture Pope Francis sets the tone for interpreting love, marriage, and the family within the signs of the times but from the perspective of faith.

Pope Francis invites us to follow the many stories in the bible of marriage and family life and to 'cross the threshold' of the home to find the couple 'in its deepest reality', though he leaves further reflection on the home life of Jesus until chapter three. In the home the couple 'that loves and begets life' is a true icon of the Creator God. Fruitful love 'becomes a symbol of God's inner life.'[19] He adds that this 'Trinitarian dimension' finds expression in St Paul who 'relates the couple to the "mystery" of the union of Christ and the Church' in Ephesians 5.[20] Making implicit use of the philosophical I-Thou concept, and of Pope St John Paul II's solitude, Pope Francis explains that the notion of 'helper' in Genesis 2 suggests a 'direct encounter, face to face.' Given his interest in both dialogue and in the significance of small gestures, Pope Francis calls this encounter 'a kind of silent dialogue', reflecting also perhaps Pope St John Paul's language of the body. This encounter gives rise to self-gift and the founding of a new family. The two become 'one flesh' physically, 'in the union of their hearts and lives', and with children, spiritually.[21]

Children, like 'living stones' build up the family and society, and with this image from the psalms in mind Pope Francis links the family to the domestic church, and a home 'filled with the presence of God' where children are educated and brought up in the faith.[22] Notably, Pope Francis conveys a real sense of the significance of the child in his or her own right, not as the property of a family, but with their own life to lead.[23]

Pope Francis moves from the 'idyllic' picture to 'a bitter truth' also found in scripture and the 'pain, evil and violence' that break up the family communion.[24] He notes the simplicity of the family of Jesus, the encounters of Jesus as he enters the homes of real people with their own specific problems, and the way in which Jesus used homely yet also realistic images of family life in his parables. These realities demonstrate that 'God is a source of comfort and companionship for every family that experiences difficulties or suffering.'[25] Pope Francis draws attention to the importance of work for family life, both for men and women, the scourge of unemployment, and the danger of exploitation and social or economic imbalances.[26] Love, the 'virtue' of tenderness and closeness are central to the experience of the Christian family.[27] And to face daily challenges, Pope Francis advises looking to the icon of the Holy Family who suffered violence and displacement; all the while Mary trusted in God.[28]

The call to imitate Mary in facing challenges with 'courage and serenity' leads Pope Francis onto the next chapter on 'the experiences and challenges of families.' To focus on 'concrete realities' Pope Francis takes up some of the situations presented in the *Relatio Finalis*, the final document of the 2015 synod, and the *Relatio Synodali*, the findings of the 2014 synod, as well as examples from his own experience. Additionally, there is a loud echo of CELAM's final document, *Aparecida*. The chapter encompasses a wide range of issues that do not fall easily into neat categories, and while Pope Francis echoes *Aparecida* in setting 'lights and shadows' alongside each other,[29] there do seem to be more shadows. Looking at both 'lights and shadows' there appears to be more freedom for family members, yet less support. These contrasts can also be seen in 'extreme individualism', identified also at *Aparecida*, that has weakened family bonds and reduced the individual to 'an isolated unit', coupled with a stressful and fast pace of life.[30] The demands of authenticity both foster spontaneity and the use of personal talents, but also arrogance, fear of commitment and self-centredness. Free choice enables people to plan and make the most of themselves, yet easily 'degenerates into an inability to give oneself generously to others.' Applying these factors to family life, family can 'come to be seen as a way station, helpful when convenient', where relationships are 'left to the changing winds of personal desire and circumstances.' Pope Francis perceptively observes that without the guidance of truths or values everything becomes permissible, and the fear of loneliness and desire for stability exists side by side with the fear of entrapment in relationships.[31] Pope Francis sees that it is unrealistic merely to decry current evils, and notes that it is unhelpful to try and impose rules by 'sheer authority.' Instead, he calls for a 'more responsible and generous effort to present the reasons and motivations for choosing marriage and the family.' However, this is not purely for the sake of the institution of marriage. Rather it is so that people can be helped 'better to respond to the grace God offers them.'[32]

Asking for a 'healthy dose of self-criticism', with perhaps a nod towards *Aparecida*, Pope Francis further reflects on Church responses that have contributed to current problems.[33] Responses include at times the overemphasis on procreation to the detriment of the unitive meaning of marriage; the lack of provision of 'solid guidance' to young couples and neglect of their concerns. In addition, the times when the Church has proposed 'a far too abstract and almost artificial theological ideal of marriage, far removed from the concrete situations and practical possibilities of real families.' The Church must be 'humble and realistic.'[34] Continuing with his critique, Pope Francis does not think that the focus of the past on doctrine, bioethics, and moral issues, has given sufficient support, and he says that 'we', the Church, find it 'difficult to present marriage more as a dynamic path to personal development and fulfilment', instead of a 'life-long burden.' Moreover, Pope Francis says that 'we find it hard to make room for the consciences of the faithful, who very often respond as best they can to the Gospel amid their limitations, and are capable of carrying out their own discernment in complex situations.' However, this does not entail a purely subjective view of conscience as he adds 'we have been called to form consciences, not replace them.'[35]

Although he appreciates the witness given by married people whose relationships have been lasting, fruitful and faithful, and he acknowledges the good guidance and counselling that has taken place through the Church, Pope Francis is concerned that 'we have often been on the defensive, wasting pastoral energy on denouncing a decadent world without being proactive in proposing ways of finding true happiness.' At the same time, he does accept that there is a place for 'warning against cultural decline', especially when relationships are seen as ephemeral in our current consumer culture.[36] Certainly, the critique Pope Francis offers suggests that new strategies are needed. Perhaps a good point of departure is to stress the positive aspects in the Church's tradition on marriage and family life that does present marriage in a more dynamic way, and this is clearly present as previous chapters of this book have shown.

The problems that characterize contemporary culture are legion[37] and include fear of commitment, many options yet no real future, fear of failure, affective immaturity, narcissism, an attitude that 'everything is disposable', commercialization of the body and pornography, weakened social bonds, an anti-child mentality as opposed to responsible parenting, forced state interventions in birth control, loneliness, and the tendency to see very young and old lives as burdens. Added to this list are lack of state support, poverty and lack of suitable housing, failure of society to protect the family or to put in place supportive strategies, sexual abuse and exploitation of children, and the migrant crisis.[38] In an echo of *Aparecida* Pope Francis sees the dangers of the distraction and speed of the mass media that presents so many competing meanings, invading the home itself, and further leading to a compartmentalization of family life.[39] Pope Francis also notes the problems of addiction to drugs, lack of tolerance towards those who are doing their best in difficult circumstances, the effects of marriage breakdown on children, and domestic violence.[40] But according to Pope Francis,

> we need to find the right language, arguments and forms of witness that can help us reach the hearts of young people, appealing to their capacity for generosity, commitment, love and even heroism, and in this way inviting them to take up the challenge of marriage with enthusiasm and courage.[41]

In the midst of these problems Pope Francis draws particular attention to what many would regard as an additional problem, that of a child with disabilities. In contrast to seeing people with disabilities as problems, Pope Francis points to the 'invaluable witness' to the gift of life of families who welcome and care for life in all its frailty. He includes in this witness those who care for elderly people, and he notes the 'serious threats' of euthanasia and assisted suicide.[42]

At the level of society Pope Francis decries the lack of regard and support for marriage and the 'legal deconstruction' of the family. He points out that the weakening of the family 'as that natural society founded on marriage…poses a threat to the mature growth of individuals, the cultivation of community values and the moral progress of cities and countries.' He acknowledges 'the great variety of family situations that can offer a certain stability', though he steps short of suggesting these are good situations, and he states that de facto or same sex unions 'may not simply be equated with marriage.' Pope Francis is clear that 'only the exclusive and indissoluble union between a man and a woman has a plenary role to play in society as a stable commitment that bears fruit in new life.'[43]

On the situations of women, men, and gender issues Pope Francis notes the gains that have been made in terms of the recognition of women's rights and their participation in public life. However, he categorically states that 'unacceptable customs still need to be eliminated.'[44] He lists shameful ill-treatment, domestic violence, enslavement even within marriage, genital mutilation, lack of access to work and roles of decision-making. Pope Francis also considers surrogacy to be a form of exploitation of women. He distances certain 'inadequate' forms of feminism from the proper emancipation of women and the recognition of their dignity and rights. Pope Francis adds that men have an important role in family life, not least because families need fathers to be not only physically present, but also emotionally, psychologically and spiritually present.[45] Pope Francis deals with the relatively new phenomena of 'various forms of gender ideology', also the subject of concern at *Aparecida*.[46] He refers here specifically to an ideology and not to gender dysphoria. Quoting the 2015 synod, he explains that he has in mind an ideology that 'denies the difference and reciprocity in nature of a man and a woman and envisages a society without sexual differences, thereby eliminating the anthropological basis of the family.' He is especially concerned with gender ideology that results in education programmes and legislation that 'promote a personal identity and emotional intimacy radically separated from the biological difference between male and female', where personal identity becomes pure choice that can change over time. Pope Francis notes that ideologies do 'seek to respond to what are at times understandable aspiration', though he does not clarify this in relation to gender ideology. However, there is a real problem when ideologies become 'absolute and unquestionable, even dictating how children should be raised.' At the same time, he speaks of technologies that 'manipulate the reproductive act, making it independent of the sexual relationship between a man and a woman.' He links these technologies to ideologies 'that attempt to sunder what are inseparable aspects of reality', and he calls on people to accept and respect the gift of creation.[47]

Although there are more shadows than light, Pope Francis does not think that this exploration of the challenges facing marriage and the family should be a cause for simply 'doleful laments.' Instead, Pope Francis views these as challenges to 'seek new forms of missionary creativity' especially given that 'there is no stereo-type of the ideal family, but rather a challenging mosaic made up of many different realities, with all their joys, hopes and problems.' Nevertheless, this is not to say that there is no longer value in the traditional family. Pope Francis agrees with the synod and Bishops of Columbia that the Church does have a prophetic message of hope since 'the great values of marriage and the Christian family correspond to a yearning that is part and parcel of human existence.'[48]

Having established that the challenges of the family are opportunities for evangelization, Pope Francis next turns to Jesus, Church teaching and the vocation of the family. Again, in an echo perhaps of *Aparecida's* call, 'we must all start again from Christ',[49] Pope Francis begins with Jesus. He observes that Church teaching must be inspired and transformed by the *kerygma* 'and its message of love and tenderness' warning that 'otherwise it becomes nothing more than the defence of a dry and lifeless doctrine.' In this chapter Pope Francis links the 'gaze of Jesus' and his encounter with people characterized by love, mercy, tenderness, patience, and truth, with the teaching of the Church on marriage. Quoting at length from the 2014 and 2015 final synodal documents, marriage is a divine gift with indissolubility a part of that gift, and Jesus 'restores and fulfils God's plan.' Referring to Ephesians 5, 'marriage and the family have been redeemed by Christ and restored in the image of the Holy Trinity.' The 'spousal covenant, originating in creation and revealed in the history of salvation, takes on its full meaning in Christ and his Church.' Through the Church, Christ gives the graces necessary for marriage and family life. The 2015 *Relatio* speaks of the interaction of Jesus with people in everyday circumstances, and notably his encounters with the Samaritan woman and the woman caught in adultery. For the synod and for Pope Francis this accompaniment in mercy, where consciousness of sin is awakened through love, is the paradigm for the Church.[50]

Pope Francis puts together the experience of the generations when he speaks of the joy of the family. He talks of the hidden life of Jesus in Mary's womb, the birth of Jesus and the joy of the shepherds and the Magi, joy in spite of exile and persecution. There is joy in the expectation of Zechariah for his son John, and joy in the anticipation of Simeon and Anna. There is joy and peace in the hidden home life of Jesus before he begins his public ministry. Quoting Pope St Paul VI, the love lived by the Holy Family at Nazareth teaches the meaning of family life and shows how 'every family, despite its weakness, can become a light in the darkness of the world.'[51]

Turning to Church documents, Pope Francis refers to *Gaudium et spes*, and selected highlights of the teaching of Pope St Paul VI, Pope St John Paul II and Pope Benedict XVI giving each a short paragraph. Pope Francis allows the documents of the Church to speak for themselves as he selects and quotes extensively without his own comment or he cites from the synod. Perhaps in a reflection on the synod's understanding that it was not there simply to repeat the teaching of Pope St John Paul II, this section is particularly brief and rather cursory. Pope Francis notes that *Gaudium et spes* promotes the dignity of marriage, as a 'community of life and love', of mutual self-giving, grounded in Christ. Citing the 2015 synod, Pope Francis explains that spouses are given a special grace by Christ through the Holy Spirit to live a life of love and to 'build up the Body of Christ and form a domestic church.' Notably Pope Francis includes the comment from the synod that 'the Church, in order fully to understand her mystery, looks to the Christian family, which manifests her in a real way.' He draws attention to the teaching of Pope St Paul VI in *Humanae*

Vitae on responsible parenthood and 'a right order of priorities', and in *Evangelii Nuntiandi* on the relationship between the family and the Church. Pope Francis notes the catechesis of Pope St John Paul II, and *Familiaris Consortio* with its 'general vision of the vocation of men and women to love', and the 'basic guidelines for the pastoral care of the family and for the role of the family in society.' He refers to Pope Benedict XVI's reflections on the love of men and women under the sign of the Cross and the way in which married love is an image of God's love for his people just as God's love for his people is a sign for married love.[52]

Pope Francis next devotes some paragraphs to the Sacrament of Matrimony, and he quotes extensively and at length from the 2015 *Relatio Finalis,* less so from the 2014 *Relatio Synodali,* interspersed with quotes from *Familiaris Consortio* and *Gaudium et spes.* Quoting the 2015 synod first Pope Francis embeds the sacrament in scripture and the revelation of the Trinity. The family, he says, is 'an image of God, who is a communion of persons.' Christ returns marriage and the family to their 'original form' and raises marriage 'to the sacramental sign of his love for the Church.' Pope Francis reiterates that 'the sacrament of marriage is not a social convention, an empty ritual or merely the outward sign of a commitment.' Stressing traditional teaching, 'the sacrament is a gift given for the sanctification and salvation of the spouses.' Quoting *Familiaris Consortio,* marriage is a 'real representation' through the sacramental sign, of the relationship between Christ and the Church, and the spouses are 'a reminder' of what took place on the Cross. Notably, Pope Francis places marriage within vocational discernment. However, he also adds that conjugal love is 'an imperfect sign of the love between Christ and the Church', presumably indicating the nature of analogy.[53] He does not explore the issue of the closeness of that analogy at this stage.

Quoting the 2014 synod, the elements that constitute marriage are 'total self-giving, faithfulness and openness to new life.' These are divine gifts and faith makes it possible for the couple to 'assume the goods of marriage as commitments that can be better kept through the help of the grace of the sacrament.' The 2014 synod's language on grace does not consider whether or not with grace all things are possible. However, Pope Francis adds that the sacrament sanctifies their sexual union which becomes 'a path of growth in the life of grace for the couple.' Noting the reach of grace, he says that 'the common life of husband and wife, the entire network of relations that they build with their children and the world around them, will be steeped in and strengthen by the grace of the sacrament.' Both husband and wife face challenges together and 'both are called to respond to God's gift with commitment, creativity, perseverance and daily effort.' Moreover, they can call on the Holy Spirit for assistance, 'so that his grace may be felt in every new situation that they encounter.'[54]

Following the Latin tradition, the man and woman are 'ministers' of the sacrament; by manifesting their consent and expressing it physically they receive this great gift. Pope Francis notes that when two non-Christian spouses are baptized, so long as they do not reject their vows, their union becomes sacramental. Pope Francis follows Canon Law in that in some cases there can be a valid marriage without the presence of an ordained minister, and that marriages between the baptized are sacramental. In these paragraphs Pope Francis follows the tradition of the Catechism and does not allude to some of the questions that had arisen at the synod such as the faith of the spouses.[55]

Still in the chapter on Church teaching, Pope Francis tackles the subject of 'seeds of the Word and imperfect situations.' In *Casti connubii* Pope Pius XI had said that since grace requires co-operation, the 'seeds' of grace in sacramental marriage may remain latent until the couple cultivate them.[56] However, the provenance for the idea of 'seeds' being present in imperfect situations, goes back to early Christianity and St Justin Martyr who saw the possibility of dialogue with Judaism and pagan philosophies. St Justin declared that 'there seem to be seeds of truth among all men.'[57] The notion of these 'seeds' specifically in other cultures can also be found in the CELAM conferences.

Reflecting on the evangelization of South America the Bishops of the Americas acknowledged that indigenous peoples already had the 'seeds of the Word' present in their cultures, as suggested by the Second Vatican Council's decree *Ad Gentes* 11. These seeds made it easier for the people to 'find in the Gospel life-giving responses to their deepest aspirations.'[58] One concern at the 2015 synod was that talk of 'seeds' in 'imperfect situations' might suggest that these were seeds of goodness and that therefore the 'imperfect' situation might be regarded as good in itself. Quoting the 2014 synod, Pope Francis explains that the Gospel of the family 'nourishes seeds that are still waiting to grow', as well as caring for plants that are wilting. He then quotes from *Familiaris Consortio* that 'building on the gift of Christ in the sacrament, married couples "may be led patiently further on in order to achieve a deeper grasp and a fuller integration of this mystery in their lives".' Taking from the 2015 synod, Pope Francis points out that as the order of redemption 'illuminates and fulfils' that of creation, natural marriage is 'fully understood in the light of its fulfilment in the sacrament of Matrimony.' Moreover, 'only in contemplating Christ does a person come to know the deepest truth about human relationships.' Pope Francis follows the 2015 synod in thinking that the 'discernment of the presence of "seeds of the Word" in other cultures', as expressed in *Ad Gentes*, 'can also apply to the reality of marriage and the family.' In a way this seems to mirror the extension of evangelization to the 'new evangelization', evangelization of the faithful who have become lukewarm. Quoting the 2015 synod, 'positive elements' exist in 'true natural marriage' and in forms of marriage in other religious traditions. Pope Francis argues that 'seeing things with the eyes of Christ' should inspire pastoral care for the faithful who are living together, only civilly married, or divorced and remarried. Pope Francis then quotes the 2015 synod and outlines how beginning from the example of Christ, the Church 'turns with love to those who participate in her life in an imperfect manner'; the Church seeks the grace of conversion for them; encourages them to do good, take loving care of each other and serve the community.[59]

It is interesting to note that encounter with Jesus, conversion, discipleship, living in loving community, and then missionary service are the stages in the process of forming missionary disciples in *Aparecida*.[60] With the 2015 synod, Pope Francis thinks that in the case of a couple in a stable and publicly recognized but 'irregular union', with deep affection and responsibility for children, and able to weather trials, it may be opportune to lead them to the sacrament of marriage. He then quotes from the 2015 synod which itself referred to *Familiaris Consortio*, for the need for a careful discernment in situations of 'wounded families', noting that degrees of responsibility may not be equal and 'factors may exist which limit the ability to make a decision.' Supporting the synod's pastoral approach, 'therefore, while clearly stating the Church's teaching, pastors are to avoid judgements that do not take into account the complexity of various situations, and they are to be attentive, by necessity, to how people experience and endure distress because of their condition.'[61]

On the 'transmission of life and the rearing of children', Pope Francis refers to *Gaudium et spes*, the *Catechism*, and *Humanae Vitae*. Pope Francis begins with the definition of marriage as an 'intimate partnership of life and love' which is good for the spouses; sexuality is 'ordered' to the conjugal love of man and woman. He then points out that where a marriage has not been blest with children it is still a fully human and Christian union. He notes that the conjugal union is 'by its very nature' ordered to procreation. However, he says that children do not 'appear at the end of a process' but rather they are 'present from the beginning of love as an essential feature.' Since this feature 'cannot be denied without disfiguring that love itself' love is open to fruitfulness, 'hence no genital act of husband and wife can refuse this meaning.' Focusing on new life as gift and with reference to the CDF's instruction on the gift of life, *Donum Vitae*, Pope Francis says that 'a child deserves to be born of that love and not by any other means.'

Quoting the 2015 synod, this is because 'according to the order of creation, conjugal love between a man and a woman, and the transmission of life are ordered to each other.' To help couples, Pope Francis calls for a return to the message of *Humanae Vitae* 'which highlights the need to respect the dignity of the person in morally assessing methods of regulating births.' Recalling that the family is 'the sanctuary of life', that 'protects human life in all its stages including its last', Pope Francis denounces termination, euthanasia and also the death penalty.[62] On the theme of bringing up children, Pope Francis reiterates Church teaching that presents education as an 'essential and inalienable right' of parents. He adds, 'schools do not replace parents, but complement them.' However, he notes that a 'rift' has opened up between family and society, family and school, where the primacy of parental responsibility has been eroded. He sees a role for the Church here in helping parents be up to the task of educating their children properly.[63]

Moving to the relationship of the family and the Church, Pope Francis offers thanks for the witness of faithful families. He observes that it is through the family as 'domestic church' that people experience a community of persons and learn endurance, love and forgiveness, worship to God and self-gift. Pope Francis calls the Church 'a family of families, constantly enriched by the lives of all those domestic churches.' Quoting the 2015 synod, 'the Church is good for the family, and the family is good for the Church.' Therefore, safeguarding the sacrament of marriage is the concern of the whole Christian community. Indeed, Pope Francis calls the love in families a 'perennial source of strength for the life of the Church' and the 'fruits' of love such as care, forgiveness, support and endurance in good and bad times, make the vocation of the family for the Church and society 'unique and irreplaceable.'[64]

Pope Francis's chapter four on love in marriage is more typical of his own style and would serve as an insightful resource for marriage preparation. Pope Francis offers a pastoral meditation based on St Paul's First Letter to the Corinthians 13:4–7 on some of the features of true love. Pope Francis sees that these features of love are relevant in daily situations and can be applied to family life. Although Pope Francis does not use the language of virtue in this section, he clearly thinks of some of these features as rooted dispositions. Love through patience is not simply a matter of endurance. Patience involves self-control and it enables a person to accept other people even if they act differently to the way the person would like them to act. However, patience is not a completely passive attitude because it is always ready to be of assistance to others. Significantly, love is more than a mere feeling; it bears fruit in the form of self-gift and service. Love is not envious; 'it recognizes that everyone has different gifts and a unique path in life'; it holds everyone in esteem and accepts that everyone has their own right to happiness; it also rejects injustice. Love is not arrogant or self-important but is focused on others. Pope Francis notes especially the emptiness of people who revel in their own knowledge of the faith and look down on those who know less, or those who seek dominion and competition in family life; he reminds people of the danger of pride and the need for humility, so that they can sincerely understand, forgive, and serve others. Love is gentle and thoughtful; love listens and attends to others with 'a kind look.' Kindness builds up the bonds of relationships and instead of words that demean, anger, or sadden, love uses words of 'comfort, strength, consolation and encouragement.' Love is generous; it looks to the good of others and seeks to love more than be loved. Love is not resentful and does not foster interior irritation; instead, love always seeks to make peace even by simple small gestures. Love involves true forgiveness 'which is rooted in a positive attitude that seeks to understand other people's weaknesses and to excuse them.' At times love and forgiveness require 'a great spirit of sacrifice' but it is also a 'liberating experience.' Pope Francis recognizes that love involves a level of maturity and personal integration as he observes that 'we need to learn to pray over our past history, to accept ourselves, to learn how to live with our limitations, and even to forgive ourselves, in order to have this same attitude to others.' Moreover, he says that love assumes that we have been loved and forgiven first by God:

> we have known a love that is prior to any of our own efforts, a love that constantly opens doors, promotes and encourages. If we accept that God's love is unconditional, that the Father's love cannot be bought or sold, then we will become capable of showing boundless love and forgiving others even if they have wronged us.[65]

Love rejoices at the good and happiness of others; love celebrates with others. Love endures all things and does not speak evil against others. Love speaks well of others and sees any weakness in a wider context: 'all of us are a complex mixture of lights and shadows. The other person is much more than the sum of the little things that annoy me.' Pope Francis understands that 'love does not have to be perfect for us to value it.' Love trusts, 'it sets free, it does not try to control, possess and dominate everything.' Love hopes, and ultimately hopes in everlasting life where we will be transformed and 'the person's true being will shine forth in all its goodness and beauty.' Love has a positive attitude and never gives up 'even in the darkest hour.'[66]

Specifically, in terms of the growth of love between husband and wife, Pope Francis describes married love as 'spiritual and sacrificial', combining friendship and erotic passion, that 'endures long after emotion and passion subside.' 'Infused by the Holy Spirit, this powerful love is a reflection of the unbroken covenant between Christ and humanity that culminated in his self-sacrifice on the cross.' Pope Francis explains that 'marriage is the icon of God's love for us' and that God is 'as it were, "mirrored"' in the couple when they celebrate the sacrament of matrimony. God is a communion of Persons, and in the 'mystery of marriage' God makes of the two spouses 'one single existence.' This, he says, has 'daily consequences': 'starting with the simple ordinary things of life they can make visible the love with which Christ loves his Church.' Nevertheless, and using *Familiaris Consortio* 9 to support his thinking, Pope Francis significantly adds 'we should not however confuse different levels: there is no need to lay upon two limited persons the tremendous burden of having to reproduce perfectly the union existing between Christ and his Church, for marriage as a sign entails "a dynamic process..., one which advances gradually with the progressive integration of the gifts of God".' Notably, *Familiaris Consortio* 9 is talking generally about a 'continuous, permanent conversion' in the personal and social lives of people, brought about 'in steps which lead us ever forward' to 'a richer understanding and fuller integration' of the mystery of Christ in our lives, rather than about marriage specifically. Presumably, Pope Francis makes this distinction to address those who think that the analogy of married love and Christ's love for the Church is either not subject to the limitations of all analogies or is purely aspirational and in the realms of idealism and so cannot support indissolubility.[67]

Turning to the lifelong sharing of marriage, Pope Francis speaks of the characteristics of good friendship that marriage joins with 'an indissoluble exclusivity expressed in the stable commitment to share and shape together the whole of life.' He observes that everyone expects and wants their marriages to last and this desire is not simply expressed in a formula or vow but is 'rooted in the natural inclinations of the human person.' He adds, 'for believers, it is also a covenant before God that calls for fidelity.' He notes that weak love that cannot accept challenges 'cannot sustain a great commitment.' Nevertheless, he thinks that 'promising love for ever is possible' if we go beyond our own limited ideas and plans and have the gift of grace. Passion has a place in married love as 'directed towards an ever more stable and intense union', because marriage was not instituted only for procreation, but also for mutual love. As an 'all-encompassing' friendship, marriage is 'exclusive, faithful and open to new life.'[68] Pope Francis understands that 'joy' has more depth than pleasure or happiness and it can bear sorrow as well; he affirms that 'in marriage, the joy of love needs to be cultivated.' The 'love of friendship' sees 'beauty' in the other person, the 'great worth' and 'sacredness' of the other, that resists the feeling of the need to possess the other. Tenderness is a sign of this love, and this love and sense of beauty endures even if the person is no longer physically appealing, indeed even if they are annoying. Using very practical examples, Pope Francis reminds people of the importance of a tender look and kind words that can build up relationships and the hurt caused when there is no longer such a look or when simple words like 'please' and 'thank you', 'sorry' are lacking: 'love opens up our eyes and enables us to see, beyond all else, the great worth of a human being.' In cultivating joy in marriage Pope Francis observes that delighting in the good of the other and finding joy in others is a foretaste of heaven. Moreover, joy can grow through pain and sorrow as people share in their struggles together. Addressing young people in particular, Pope Francis speaks of the added depth to love in taking responsibility for another in marriage and building strong ties. This is 'much more meaningful than a mere spontaneous association for mutual gratification, which would turn marriage into a purely private affair.' Pope Francis emphasizes the 'enduring importance' of marriage in its social and public character, for 'as a social institution, marriage protects and shapes a shared commitment to deeper growth in love and commitment to one another, for the good of society as a whole.' The love in marriage is 'so serious and generous that it is ready to face any risk.' He agrees that commitment does involve some risk but a refusal to commit 'fails to recognize the rights of another person and to present him or her to society as someone worthy of unconditional love.' In affirming the enduring nature of the marriage contract Pope Francis adds, 'this "yes" tells them that they can always trust one another, and that they will never be abandoned when difficulties arise or new attractions or selfish interests present themselves.'[69]

    For Pope Francis it is important to realize that people grow into ever deepening love, often through little steps, simple words, and gestures. Pope Francis thinks that 'marital love is not defended primarily by presenting indissolubility as a duty, or by repeating doctrine, but by helping it to grow ever stronger under the impulse of grace.' This is not to accuse previous strategies but to move the conversation on. Pope Francis speaks of grace not in terms of the heroic but in the everyday: 'growth can only occur if we respond to God's grace through constant acts of love, acts of kindness that become ever more frequent, intense, generous, tender and cheerful.' He reminds people of the dangers of thinking that there is an 'idyllic and perfect love' that does not require growth, does not accept sickness, sorrow, or death.[70]

The next section on dialogue is an insightful analysis of the need for proper communication in marriage, a skill that should form a key part of marriage preparation. Pope Francis recognizes that dialogue is essential for fostering love in marriage and family life. Moreover, it is a skill that requires 'a long and demanding apprenticeship.' Indeed, Pope Francis presents the skill of listening and dialogue very much as a practice of virtue. Pope Francis notes that people communicate differently, and that communication is more than the use of words: it includes tone, gestures, and attitudes. Dialogue demands time given appropriately not only in terms of hours spent but also an appreciation of the time to listen, the time to respond and the time to talk. To overcome the tendency to rush in with opinion before listening, Pope Francis encourages the cultivation of 'inner silence' and a measured pace. As he rightly points out, rather than being presented with ready solutions, often people simply want to be heard. Proper dialogue involves developing 'the habit of giving real importance to the other person', taking them and their concerns seriously, remembering that everyone has something to contribute. He asks people to put themselves into the shoes of the other and 'try to peer into their hearts to perceive their deepest concerns' and take those concerns as the starting point of dialogue. Pope Francis recommends keeping 'an open mind' that respects differences of opinion, dealing sensitively when hard feelings begin to emerge, and being careful to avoid hurtful words but rather choosing words that build up the person. Showing love for the other person helps to better understand what they are saying. Finally, worthwhile dialogue is the fruit of 'interior richness nourished by reading, personal reflection, prayer, and openness to the world around us.'[71]

Returning to the theme of love, Pope Francis speaks of passion and he observes that the mystics affirmed married love as a symbol for the union of the human heart with God. Emotions also have a part to play, and Pope Francis notes that Jesus was not afraid to show his emotions. Pope Francis explains that emotions are not good or evil in themselves, what is morally good or evil is how we allow those emotions to influence us. Thus, attraction is not automatically good if it leads to domination and the desire to possess the other person. In contrast, an integrated emotional life benefits the whole family. Following Pope Benedict XVI who responds to the Nietzschean charge that Christianity's 'commandments and prohibitions' have poisoned love as *eros*, desire, Pope Francis takes on Pope Benedict XVI's reply that Christianity only rejects a distorted and destructive *eros*. According to Pope Francis, and once again emphasizing the need for growth and learning, people need to be trained in limiting and integrating their emotions and instinct so that they know how to channel them properly in ways that enrich personal relationships. While emotion, pleasure and joy certainly are aspects of being human, sexuality also is a part of being human. However, and following Pope St John Paul II, a mature sexuality requires discipline and self-control: 'sexuality is not a means of gratification or entertainment; it is an interpersonal language, wherein the other is taken seriously in his or her sacred and inviolable dignity.' Passion and the erotic dimension of love are gifts from God that enrich the relationship of the spouses and affirm the dignity of the other.[72]

In contrast to the 'healthy realism' of an integrated sexuality, Pope Francis draws attention to sexuality that has been depersonalized and so is unhealthy. In particular he warns of sexuality poisoned by a 'use and discard' mentality where the body of the other becomes an object useful only for as long as it gives satisfaction, or the dignity of the other and the vocation to love 'end up being less important than an obscure need to "find oneself".' Moreover, Pope Francis recognizes that exploitation, domination, and manipulation can take place within marriage and he rejects interpretations of submission that demean women or makes wives into servants. He warns that 'our human equilibrium is fragile; there is a part of us that resists real human growth.'[73]

Quoting the 2015 synod, Pope Francis commends the many people who remain unmarried yet are very supportive of their families. He regards virginity as 'a form of love' and a sign of the coming Kingdom. He speaks of the complementarity of both the married and virginal states of life and notes there is no basis to play one off against the other in terms of inferiority or superiority. Virginity is an 'eschatological sign of the risen Christ', marriage is a 'historical sign for us living in this world, a sign of the earthly Christ who chose to become one with us and gave himself up for us.' Each symbolize different values and are 'different ways of loving.' Pope Francis warns of the dangers of celibacy becoming 'a comfortable single life' of freedom. He speaks of the witness and values marriage holds for celibacy noting generosity, faithfulness, and care for the other even in sickness, loving service even when children prove to be troublesome.[74] Pope Francis further observes that with longer life-spans couples are expected to stay together for longer and this requires a renewal of the initial decision. The answer to success is to see the other as 'a companion on life's journey', to have a 'shared and lasting life project.' The pledge of love then is 'greater than any emotion, feeling or state of mind, although it may include all of these. It is a deeper love, a lifelong decision of the heart.' In spite of ageing or physical changes, 'the marriage bond finds new forms of expression and constantly seeks new ways to grow in strength', all of which is possible with the help of grace.[75]

After his reflection on married love, Pope Francis turns to love made fruitful: 'love always gives life.' It is in the family that new life is born and is welcomed as a gift. However, Pope Francis is all too aware of the many instances when this is not the case and children are rejected, abandoned and 'robbed of their childhood.' In the case of children who appear unwanted he urges extended families to make sacrifices and assume responsibility for the child. While agreeing that large families are 'a joy' for the Church, quoting Pope St John Paul II, Pope Francis adds that responsible parenthood 'does not mean "unlimited procreation or lack of awareness of what is involved in rearing children, but rather the empowerment of couples to use their inviolable liberty wisely and responsibly, taking into account social and demographic realities as well as their own situation and legitimate desires".' Missing from *Amoris Laetitia*, Pope St John Paul II's quote ends with 'in the light of objective moral criteria.'[76]

Pope Francis goes on to speak of the joys of pregnancy, sharing in the mystery of creation, where every child from an embryo is a part of the eternal loving plan of God. He observes that science can tell a lot about the growing embryo but only God fully knows the child. In circumstances where presumably the parents did not plan the pregnancy, he encourages parents to pray for strength because 'it is important for that child to feel wanted.' A child, he says, 'is not an accessory or a solution to some personal need.' Children are unique and irreplaceable gifts regardless of parental expectations, desires or plans. Pope Francis sees that in the family the love bestowed on the child is 'a spark of God's love' and he says that children have a right to receive love from both father and mother. Affirming the child's need and natural right for a father and mother is respecting the child's dignity. Parents 'show their children the paternal and maternal face of the Lord.' Pope Francis is especially concerned that motherhood remains valued as a mission that is of benefit not only to children but also to society. Taking first the role of mothers, Pope Francis explains their significance in countering self-centred individualism, in helping children grow as persons, in communicating the faith, and in enabling children to grow in confidence, self-esteem and empathy. Then turning to fathers, he notes that fathers open children to the challenges and limits of life, as well as having affection and concern for his wife. Pope Francis is concerned with both an overly authoritarian view of fatherhood and with the acceptance of absent fathers. He asks fathers to share with their wives in the upbringing of children in all its joys and sorrows, so that fathers are 'present' but not controlling. Pope Francis is also aware of the 'real suffering' of infertility and the generosity of families who adopt or foster children. Fruitfulness in families with and without children has many expressions, including solidarity with others and social action, and a readiness to play a Christian role in society. A married couple who experience love know that 'love is called to bind the wounds of the outcast, to foster a culture of encounter and to fight for justice.' The family has the job of 'domesticating' the world and 'helping each person to see fellow human beings as brothers and sisters.' By their witness, families pass on the love of Jesus and the message of the Gospel. As Church, and as people invited to the Eucharist families should help to heal divisions and avoid scandalous distinctions between people, especially those who are poor or suffering.[77]

To counteract individualism where others are seen as 'bothersome or a threat', Pope Francis situates the nuclear family within its broader network of relationships, notably family members who need assistance or companionship and consolation. He reminds sons and daughters of the commandment to honour parents who after all gave them the gift of life, and he notes that this commandment 'has to do with something sacred' coming as it does after the commandments dealing with God. Pope Francis thinks that the success of society rests on this intergenerational solidarity: 'the virtuous bond between generations is the guarantee of the future, and is the guarantee of a truly humane society.' Nevertheless, he is also aware of the problem of not truly leaving behind parents in forming a new unit in marriage. Marriage, he says, 'challenges husbands and wives to find new ways of being sons and daughters.' He asks families to be especially attentive to the needs and contributions of elderly people particularly in cultures where they are not valued or where they are regarded as burdens or redundant. The family is also the place where brothers and sisters learn about solidarity and a true sense of fraternity and care for others. Not only relations but also friends and other families form the larger family, and this larger family can provide significant support for families who face specific challenges including single parent families, elderly people with no family support of their own, and 'those who have made a shipwreck of their lives.'[78]

In chapter six, 'some pastoral perspectives', Pope Francis says he does not offer a 'pastoral plan', but he does want to reflect on pastoral challenges since the synod 'raised the need for new pastoral methods.' The 2014 synod emphasized that people need to experience the Gospel of the family 'as a joy' and 'we are called to help sow seeds; the rest is God's work.' At the same time the Church's teaching on the family is a 'sign of contradiction.' Pastoral planning has both to enable families in their evangelizing role and reach out to families to help them overcome obstacles they face. Nor can the message be 'merely theoretical' without connection to people's problems. Quoting the 2014 synod, the Gospel of the family 'responds to the deepest expectations of the human person', and so presents not simply 'a set of rules' but also proposes clearly needed values, as well as denouncing factors that prevent authentic family life or that lead to discrimination. Since the parish makes a significant contribution to pastoral care, Pope Francis agrees with the 2015 synod that priests, deacons, catechists, and pastoral workers need more adequate formation and training to deal with family problems. Pope Francis recommends making use of married clergy in this regard. Seminarians should be better prepared and families and lay women should be a part of the seminary process to 'keep them well grounded in reality.' Better use should also be made of professional expertise.[79]

One real area of concern and pastoral development is the preparation of engaged couples for marriage and the need for this was recognized by many of his predecessors. Above all, Pope Francis says, 'we need to help young people discover the dignity and beauty of marriage.' This involves showing the attraction of marriage and its 'social dimension of existence', the deep meaning of sexuality, and the benefits of marriage for children. Preparation should engage with the virtues, notably chastity, and with the witness of married couples. The connection between baptism, marriage and the other sacraments should also be brought out and participation in the life of the Church should be encouraged. Indeed, engaged couples can be a valuable resource for the Church and their friendship can be contagious, fostering friendship and fraternity in the Christian community. In terms of actual programmes, Pope Francis leaves these to each local church, but he suggests not overwhelming couples by too much information. 'Marriage preparation should be a kind of "initiation" to the sacrament of matrimony, providing couples with the help they need to receive the sacrament worthily and to make a solid beginning of life as a family.' Pope Francis goes back to the basics for good preparation with an eye to the practical and to what couples realistically need. Remote preparation, that is general preparation for young people, can take the form of example, discussion groups and topics of real interest. Individual meetings with a couple remain essential because 'the primary objective is to help each to learn how to love this very real person' with whom life will be shared. Significantly, Pope Francis points out that 'learning to love someone does not happen automatically, nor can it be taught in a workshop just prior to the celebration of marriage.' Preparation begins from birth via the example of Christian parents so pastoral initiatives aimed at helping married couples also helps their children. Preparation of engaged couples should assist them to recognize problems and risks so that they can acknowledge any potential problems rather than glossing over them and even gain the wisdom to call off the relationship if necessary. Discussion about personal expectations, hopes, interpretations of love and the kind of life they wish to build are essential. Indeed, 'the decision to marry should never be encouraged unless the couple has discerned deeper reasons that will ensure a genuine and stable commitment.' Preparation entails coming to know people's weak points, encouraging realistic trust in developing good points, and forming a willingness to face problems and sacrifices with a firm resolve. In effect, good preparation enables them to come to know who the other person truly is.

Clearly good preparation does not see the wedding ceremony as the end of the process. Instead, it should be centred on an understanding of the marriage bond, a deepening of love, and assistance in overcoming problems. This pastoral care helps them to accept the Church's teaching, have recourse to the Church's valuable resources, and offers 'practical programmes, sound advice, proven strategies and psychological guidance.' Where married couples can go to for advice in the future is an additional essential resource. Pope Francis recommends the sacrament of reconciliation as a part of the preparation process so that the couple can bring their relationship and any past mistakes before God and receive his merciful forgiveness and healing strength. As for the celebration itself, Pope Francis urges couples to 'have the courage to be different', and not be overwhelmed by the consumer aspects of the wedding. He encourages them to make the liturgical celebration 'a profound personal experience', to appreciate 'the meaning of each of its signs' of covenantal love, to pray together and reflect on the readings. Addressing the situation of couples who do not grasp the 'theological and spiritual import' of the words of consent, it must be stressed that the words do not merely refer to the present, but they 'involve a totality that includes the future: "until death do us part".'[80]

Given that the sacrament is a reality that permeates the whole of the couple's life together, it is important that accompaniment continues after the ceremony especially in the early years of married life. Pope Francis is realistic enough to realize that many couples marry purely on the basis of an initial attraction and once this wanes the marriage becomes vulnerable. Sometimes even the process that should have taken place during their engagement needs to be completed in the early years of marriage. Pope Francis notes another challenge: the realization that marriage is a lifelong project that requires the couple's creative and active attention. A spouse cannot expect the other to be perfect. Rather 'each must set aside all illusions and accept the other as he or she actually is: an unfinished product, needing to grow, a work in progress.' For Pope Francis the important thing is for the couple to be realistic about each other, accepting of each other as they are, but also to be prepared to grow together. And he presents this growth dynamically: 'young love needs to keep dancing towards the future with immense hope.' Pope Francis calls hope the 'leaven' in a relationship that helps people overcome obstacles and frames life as 'hope also bids us live fully in the present, giving our all to the life of the family, for the best way to prepare a solid future is to live well in the present.' As a part of communication, Pope Francis points out that 'as love matures, it also learns how to "negotiate".' However, for Pope Francis negotiation and renegotiation are not matters of calculation but are 'an interplay of give and take', 'so that there will be no winners and losers, but rather two winners.'[81]

Accepting the reality of the other person is, for Pope Francis, a way of avoiding 'unduly high expectations' that are often the cause of marriage breakdown. Nevertheless, Pope Francis does think that people can change and grow. Implicitly referring to St Paul, Pope Francis thinks that 'each spouse is God's means of helping the other to mature.' Indeed, Pope Francis says, 'each marriage is a kind of "salvation history", which from fragile beginnings—thanks to God's gift and a creative and generous response on our part—grows over time into something precious and enduring.' Pope Francis adds that 'the greatest mission of two people in love' is to help the other grow and shape their identity. Even in difficult moments they can surprise each other and 'new doors' can be opened up in the relationship. 'At every new stage, they can keep "forming" one another.'[82]

The couple's generosity regarding new life is also a part of dialogue. Pope Francis speaks of responsible parenthood in the context of the formation of conscience. The paragraph on conscience from the 2014 synod had been the subject of considerable critique because it presented conscience in subjective terms.[83] Significantly, it was revised in the 2015 synod. Pope Francis quotes *Gaudium et spes* on conscience as 'the most secret core and sanctuary' of the person. There each one is 'alone with God, whose voice echoes in the depth of his heart.' The important aspect here is that people are called to attend to the voice of God, not their own voices. Pope Francis then quotes the 2015 synod, 'the more the couple tries to listen in conscience to God and his commandments, and is accompanied spiritually, the more their decision will be profoundly free of subjective caprice and accommodation to prevailing social mores.' Without any further comment, Pope Francis thinks that the couple should make the decision reflecting on their own situation, taking guidance from others and the Church. He also thinks that natural methods of regulating births should be promoted, and young couples should be encouraged 'to be essentially open' to the great gift of children.[84]

For Pope Francis the idea that patience and time are necessary to everyday living comes out clearly in how he regards growth in the married relationship. He encourages couples and families to spend quality time together, to share moments and to be present to each other rather than constantly looking to the future, to celebrate important occasions, to pray together and for each other. He also thinks that common ground can still be found if one of the couple is not a believer since 'love is always a gift of God.'[85]

Certainly, Pope Francis recognizes the importance of the parish and of married lay people in marriage preparation and support, especially in times of crisis. He also realizes that many couples once married 'drop out' of the Christian community. Pope Francis says that baptisms, First Holy Communions, funerals, and weddings can all give opportunities for reminding couples of the 'beautiful ideal' of Christian marriage, and of the support the parish can offer.[86]

Pope Francis likens marriages that have been faithful over time to 'fine wine' that begins to 'breathe' with time, where love is stored deep in the heart. He acknowledges that struggle and crises are realities in every marriage. However, he does not think that crisis inevitably weakens marriage. Instead, each crisis can 'become an apprenticeship in growing closer together or learning a little more about what it means to be married.' A crisis can be an opportunity if we listen to what it teaches 'with the ear of the heart.' In practical terms Pope Francis reminds couples that a crisis needs to be faced together and it is important for the couple to 'create opportunities for speaking heart to heart.' Moreover, they should not be afraid or reluctant to seek help or support, especially when the crisis is one that many other couples have already successfully faced. In particular, it is vital that couples learn how to seek forgiveness and forgive. Pope Francis also observes that marriages often break down because a person does not feel fulfilled, or things have not turned out as they planned, or they were not sufficiently prepared for inevitable changes in the other person and in the relationship. Pope Francis once again asks for a renewed 'yes' to the marriage relationship and for the couple to work to strengthen the marriage bond. Nevertheless, he is well aware that frequently this does not happen, and, with the 2015 synod, he agrees that there is an urgent need for a 'ministry of care' for those whose marriages have broken down.[87]

There are many factors involved in marital breakdown. Pope Francis notes especially the problem of emotional immaturity and poor childhood experiences. 'Coming to grips' with personal history requires the recognition of the need for healing, prayer for the grace to forgive and be forgiven, willingness to accept help, and persistence. Conflict resolution involves facing up to one's own faults and admitting the need for change, not merely identifying faults in the other person.[88] However, Pope Francis does accept that at times separation is inevitable, especially where there is grave injustice, violence, or excessive demands or when personal dignity is at stake, though it should be a last resort. For those who have separated, whatever the reason, Pope Francis asks that pastoral support begins with proper discernment and respect. He notes that for people who have been abandoned or who have unjustly suffered separation or divorce, forgiveness is not easy, 'but grace makes this journey possible.' He encourages people who are divorced but have not remarried to find strength in the eucharist, and he urges practical community support to avoid loneliness or financial struggle.[89] People who are divorced but have entered a new union 'should be made to feel part of the Church', and they remain part of the community. As a matter of Christian charity, there should be no discrimination and they should be encouraged to participate in the life of the community. Quoting the 2014 synod, Pope Francis notes that 'these situations "require careful discernment and respectful accompaniment".' He draws attention to the simplifications he had made to the process of annulment that make it more streamlined.[90] Of course, often those who suffer most in marital breakdown are children and Pope Francis urges parents to take careful responsibility to lessen the burden on children, especially by refraining from disparaging the other spouse in front of the children. Parishes should also do their part to ease the burden on children by supporting families, including children of a new union. Pope Francis is very clear that 'divorce is an evil' and the increase in divorces is 'troubling.' Therefore, he thinks that one of the most important pastoral tasks is to prevent the spread of divorce by supporting families and healing wounds in the first place.[91]

Under the heading 'certain complex situations', Pope Francis discusses marriages where only one party is Catholic. Pope Francis notes that mixed marriages, that is marriages between Catholics and other baptized persons, can be a valuable resource for ecumenism. He repeats the teaching that sharing the eucharist can only be in exceptional circumstances and according to stated norms. Marriages where there is 'disparity of cult' can be places of religious dialogue, but they also carry additional difficulties notably in countries where freedom of religion does not exist. Special discernment is required when a person who has been married now wishes to be baptized.[92] Still under complex situations, Pope Francis brings up the issue of families where one of its members experiences same-sex attraction. The 2015 synod had already discerned that the question of same-sex unions in themselves did not specifically belong to a synod on the vocation of marriage. Pope Francis states clearly that same-sex unions cannot be considered similar or even analogous to God's plan for marriage and the family. However, since people who are attracted to another person of the same sex live in families Pope Francis points out that the dignity of every person should be respected and there should be no unjust discrimination. Families should be given respectful pastoral guidance so that 'those who manifest a homosexual orientation can receive the assistance they need to understand and fully carry out God's will in their lives.'[93] Pope Francis further urges proper and appropriate support, and pastoral outreach, including practical support, for single-parent families.[94]

The final pastoral perspective is on bereavement. Once again, the community should be on hand to accompany the bereaved person and grieving family with prayer for those who have died, not forgetting our own preparation for death. Those who accompany the family should be aware of the stages in the grieving process and be prepared to give time to answer questions, so that the bereaved person can begin to come to terms with their new reality.[95]

Since a significant aspect of marriage and family life is the education of children, Pope Francis turns to this theme in chapter seven. Undoubtedly, parents have an 'essential role' in the education of their children, especially in helping them develop in the areas of maturity, prudence, good judgement, and common sense. Pope Francis urges parents to consider carefully what they want their children to be exposed to especially given the prevalence of electronic devices in the home. However, rather than being a controlling presence, Pope Francis asks parents to give time to their children and he encourages being present through conversation and listening. As he explains, 'what is most important is the ability lovingly to help them grow in freedom, maturity, overall discipline and real autonomy.' Making a neat distinction between where children are physically and 'existentially', Pope Francis calls parents to seek to understand where their children 'really are in their journey.' He thinks it 'a good thing' that children frequently surprise and challenge their parents. According to Pope Francis, 'education includes encouraging the responsible use of freedom to face issues with good sense and intelligence. It involves forming persons who readily understand that their own lives, and the life of the community, are in their hands, and that freedom is itself a great gift.'[96]

On the question of ethical formation, Pope Francis expects partnership with schools, however, he thinks that parents cannot simply delegate the moral formation of their children to others. Parents after all shape their children. It is interesting to note what Pope Francis says about freedom, moral formation and teaching since this may implicitly say something about his general methodological approach beyond the parent and child relationship. Pope Francis thinks that 'deep hurt' can be caused if children feel that they are no longer important, or their parents no longer care for them. He thinks that moral formation takes place through sensitive dialogue and using language the child can understand. Formation 'should also take place inductively, so that children can learn for themselves the importance of certain values, principles and norms, rather than by imposing these as absolute and unquestionable truths.'[97] Pope Francis comments on formation of conscience and notes that more is required than simply either judging what seems best or knowing what to do. Using the language of virtue, he sets this in the context of cultivating a 'profound affective inclination, a thirst for the good that outweighs other attractions.' Notably, this inclination 'helps us to realize that what we consider objectively good is also good "for us" here and now.'

In one of his constant refrains, Pope Francis encourages the development of good habits from childhood, repetitions of good behaviour to root moral conduct, and these habits include the simple 'please', 'thank-you' and 'sorry' of everyday life. Moral education also concerns freedom and 'the virtuous life thus builds, strengthens and shapes freedom.' Moreover, quoting *Gaudium et spes*, human dignity demands action from conscious and free choice 'as moved and drawn in a personal way from within.'[98] For children, understanding that they have hurt someone and that their behaviour has consequences plus loving correction that lead to progress is important for moral growth.[99] Pope Francis recommends 'patient realism' that appreciates small steps of improvement, good experiences, the witness of role models, taking into account the child's age and maturity to develop true freedom and not merely free choice.[100] Noting that some behaviours and ways of thinking are deeply rooted in the family experience, Pope Francis explains that it is the family, 'the first school of human values', that provides 'an education in hope' of critical awareness, patience, self-control, responsibility, sensitivity to the suffering of others, and the ability to live respectfully alongside others. Echoing the concerns of Pope Pius XI and Pope Pius XII on the power of the media, Pope Francis says that parents need to have a critical appreciation of new methods of communication and the media since these have a disproportionate influence on their children.[101] Catholic schools play a significant part in the development of children, and Pope Francis reminds parents and schools that there is a right of conscientious objection to certain educational programme. This ties into the issue of adequate sex education especially in 'an age when sexuality tends to be trivialized and impoverished.' Adequate sex education should be seen 'within the broader framework of an education for love, mutual self-giving.' Sex education should provide information appropriate to the age of the child, helping them to develop a critical attitude to information, especially given the prevalence of pornography, and information that is not beneficial or indeed harmful. Sex education that fosters a 'healthy sense of modesty' is vital. Pope Francis observes that sex education that concentrates on 'protection' through 'safe sex' offers a negative account of sexuality that turns the possibility of future children into enemies and that encourages young people to use others for their own pleasure. Instead, he encourages the development of programmes that help young people grow in maturity so that they can channel their desires with a view to committed and 'authentic self-giving.' Sex education should also help young people to accept differences and to accept themselves and their bodies as gifts. Without going deeply into the question of sex and gender, Pope Francis explains that a gender rigidity of roles in marriage is not always helpful and that men as well as women can care for children and undertake domestic tasks without losing a sense of their masculinity.[102]

Pope Francis points out that the home is the first place where children discover the faith and the need to serve our neighbour. Although faith is 'God's gift', 'parents are the means that God uses for it to grow and develop.' This task presumes that parents trust God, seek him, and recognize their need for him, and Pope Francis endorses a family catechesis where parents are evangelizers of their own family. To bring out the beauty of faith, Pope Francis suggests creativity, action, symbols, stories and above all good witness, especially the witness of their own parents who pray with them. Handing on the faith in families has repercussions outside the family as children also become evangelizers to others. In promoting faith with the help of God, Pope Francis says that families can come to weather storms, and 'in all families the Good News needs to resound, in good times and in bad, as a source of light along the way.' Through this evangelizing experience the Church's pastoral care for families enables them to be 'domestic churches' and 'leaven' in the world.[103]

Of the whole of the exhortation, chapter eight caused the most interest and was either highly criticized or highly praised. Titled 'accompanying, discerning and integrating weakness', this chapter dealt with what some regarded as the hot topics of the synod. In the virtual synod of the media, commentators were looking for a reforming pope who would radically change Catholic teaching. In the real synod, these hot topics were real enough, but risked derailing the synod by taking away focus from other important areas. In chapter eight Pope Francis begins by reflecting on the frailty of people in the context of the Church's call for a 'fuller response' to God. Quoting the 2015 synod, the Church 'must accompany with attention' those who are weak or wounded, and restore in them 'hope and confidence, like the beacon of a lighthouse in a port or a torch carried among the people to enlighten those who have lost their way or who are in the midst of a storm.' Using an analogy now firmly associated with Pope Francis, he says the Church's task is often like that of a 'field hospital.' Pope Francis gives a concise and traditional presentation of the main characteristics of Christian marriage:

> Christian marriage, as a reflection of the union between Christ and his Church, is fully realized in the union between a man and a woman who give themselves to each other in a free, faithful and exclusive love, who belong to each other until death and are open to the transmission of life, and are consecrated by the sacrament, which grants them the grace to become a domestic church and a leaven of new life for society.[104]

Pope Francis notes that some unions 'radically contradict this ideal, while others realize it in at least a partial and analogous way.' Avoiding language that might suggest these situations are good, Pope Francis recognizes 'constructive elements' in some of these unions.[105]

Whereas *Familiaris Consortio* spoke of moral progress in terms of the law of gradualness, Pope Francis discusses these constructive elements in the context of 'gradualness in pastoral care.' Quoting the 2015 synod, Pope Francis agrees that where a civil union or even a simple cohabitation is stable, legally recognized, has appropriate affection, responsibility for children, and ability to overcome trials, then pastoral care can eventually bring the couple to celebrate the sacrament of marriage. Pastoral care involves promoting marriage especially to those who distrust marriage and put off making a commitment, and discernment for those situations which no longer live out the reality of marriage. 'Pastoral dialogue' is needed so couples can distinguish 'elements in their lives that can lead to a greater openness to the Gospel of marriage in its fullness.' Pope Francis lists some of the varied reasons why couples do not enter a sacramental marriage, noting that often this is due to economic or cultural factors. Turning to the law of gradualness, Pope Francis quotes *Familiaris Consortio* that the human being 'knows, loves and accomplishes moral good by different [sic] stages of growth.' For Pope St John Paul II the person 'builds himself up through his many free decisions';[106] for Pope Francis, these stages are realized by free acts of people 'who are not in a position to understand, appreciate, or fully carry out the objective demands of the law.' According to Pope St John Paul II married people cannot 'look on the law as merely an ideal to be achieved in the future: they must consider it as a command of Christ the Lord to overcome difficulties with constancy.' Certainly, Pope Francis thinks that the law is 'a gift for everyone without exception; it can be followed with the help of grace.'[107]

In the discernment concerning 'irregular situations' or 'situations of weakness or imperfection', Pope Francis observes that in the history of the Church there have been two ways of thinking: 'casting off and reinstating.' He explains that 'the way of Jesus' has always been 'the way of mercy and reinstatement ... the way of the Church is not to condemn anyone for ever; it is to pour out the balm of God's mercy on all those who ask for it with a sincere heart.' Thus, account must be taken of the complexity of situations and be attentive to how people experience distress because of their condition. The imperative is to reach out and help people find their proper way of participating in the church community so that they can experience 'unmerited, unconditional and gratuitous' mercy, and this applies to everyone not just people who are divorced and remarried. Pope Francis accepts that there are clear cases where a person 'flaunts an objective sin as if it were part of the Christian ideal, or wants to impose something other than what the Church teaches' then this is a matter of separation from the community: 'such a person needs to listen once more to the Gospel message and its call to conversion.' However, Pope Francis does not exclude the person and he says that the person can still take part in the life of the community through social service and prayer meetings or other initiatives with discernment with the parish priest. He adds that the Church has the responsibility of helping all those in irregular situations to understand the work of grace in their lives, and to offer them assistance so that they can reach the fullness of God's plan for them.[108]

Equally, pastoral discernment is necessary for those who are divorced and who have entered a new union. He notes that this is not a rigid category and presents a series of different scenarios. One scenario may be 'a second union consolidated over time, with new children, proven fidelity, generous self-giving, Christian commitment, a consciousness of its irregularity and of the great difficulty of going back without feeling in conscience that one would fall into new sins', and quoting *Familiaris Consortio*, for serious reasons, such as the upbringing of children, the couple cannot satisfy the obligation to separate. In *Amoris Laetitia* the footnote to *Familiaris Consortio* 84 explains, 'in such situations, many people, knowing and accepting the possibility of living "as brothers and sisters" which the Church offers them point out that if certain expressions of intimacy are lacking, "it often happens that faithfulness is endangered and the good of the children suffers",' referring to *Gaudium et spes* 51. Of note, the context for *Gaudium et spes* 51 is where, as a result of 'certain modern conditions' the couple do not want to increase the size of their family, and a more accurate rendition from the translation on the Vatican website is 'where the intimacy of married love is broken off, its faithfulness can sometimes be imperilled and its quality of fruitfulness ruined, for then the upbringing of the children and the courage to accept new ones are both endangered.' A second scenario is where a person tried to save their marriage yet was unjustly abandoned. In the third scenario a divorced person enters a second union for the sake of the children's upbringing and is 'subjectively certain in conscience' that their previous and irreparably broken marriage had never been valid. The fourth scenario is a new union after a recent divorce 'with all the suffering and confusion which this entails for children and entire families.' The fifth scenario concerns 'someone who has consistently failed in his obligations to the family.' The aim of presenting these scenarios is to demonstrate that no 'easy recipes' exist, and different situations require distinguishing from others with careful discernment.[109] With many of the 2015 synod fathers, Pope Francis sees that integration of people who are divorced and remarried is 'key' to their pastoral care, 'while avoiding any occasion of scandal.' Integration is not simply the realization that they 'belong to the Church as the body of Christ', but they also 'know that they can have a joyful and fruitful experience in it.' Participation can be expressed in different ways through careful discernment of which 'various forms of exclusion' can be surmounted, for instance a person may read or may take up the collection, and integration must take account of the upbringing of their children. Given the very different circumstances in which people find themselves, Pope Francis does not propose to give a blanket set of rules, but he does want to give encouragement 'to undertake a responsible and personal discernment of particular cases.' He adds, quoting the 2015 synod, 'since "the degree of responsibility is not equal in all cases", the consequences or effects of a rule need not always necessarily be the same.' In the footnote Pope Francis says that this applies not only to discernment in ways in which people can participate in the life of the community but also 'with regard to sacramental discipline, since discernment can recognize that in a particular situation no grave fault exists.'

Significantly, at the 2015 synod many of the fathers said that in their experience the faithful were simply not coming to their priests for advice and help in sorting out their situations. Instead, they were making their own decisions when it came to receiving the eucharist, and in many cases priests were unaware of people's true situations. Perhaps to address this, and to get people to face and understand their situation, Pope Francis quotes extensively from the 2015 synod, saying that 'priests have the duty to accompany [the divorced and remarried] in helping them to understand their situation according to the teaching of the Church and the guidelines of the bishop.' He explains that 'an examination of conscience through moments of reflection and repentance' may be a useful part of the process. A process of accompaniment and discernment

> guides the faithful to an awareness of their situation before God. Conversation with the priest, in the internal forum, contributes to the formation of a correct judgement on what hinders the possibility of a fuller participation in the life of the Church and on what steps can foster it and make it grow.[110]

Pope Francis understands this to be a part of the small steps that people make on the way to moral progress. This process requires 'humility, discretion and love for the Church and her teaching, in a sincere search for God's will and a desire to make a more perfect response to it.' These attitudes help to ensure there are no misunderstandings or double standards, for instance thinking that a priest can grant exceptions.[111] This process described by Pope Francis is one that actively encourages the person to come to the priest.

In this process of accompaniment Pope Francis explains that the Church possesses 'a solid body of reflection concerning mitigating factors and situations.' Pope Francis refers to *Familiaris Consortio* 33 that a person may 'know full well the rule, yet have great difficulty in understanding its "inherent values".' Moreover, some people may 'be in a concrete situation which does not allow him or her to act differently and decide otherwise without further sin'; factors may exist which limit the ability to make a decision. Quoting the Catechism 1735 and 2352, responsibility can be diminished or even nullified by factors such as ignorance, inadvertence, habit, immaturity, and psychological and social factors. As Pope Francis points out, 'a negative judgement about an objective situation does not imply a judgement about the imputability or culpability of the person involved.' As the Catechism 1857 shows, it is not new to argue that a person may be in an objectively sinful situation, a situation of grave matter, yet not be fully culpable and not be in a state of mortal sin because the other criteria of sin—full knowledge and freedom of will, are lacking. Nevertheless, the Church is there to help the person. Thus, the process of pastoral discernment must take account of levels of responsibility and the person's 'properly formed' conscience. Pope Francis asks that 'every effort should be made to encourage the development of an enlightened conscience', and he adds that informing conscience is not merely about recognizing that a situation does not 'correspond objectively to the overall demands of the Gospel.' Conscience also recognizes 'with sincerity and honesty what for now is the most generous response which can be given to God.' Quoting St Thomas Aquinas on the movement of general rules to their application in particular situations, Pope Francis states that 'a pastor cannot feel that it is enough simply to apply moral laws to those living in "irregular situations", as if they were stones to throw at people's lives.' Pope Francis repeats his previous points more explicitly:

> because of forms of conditioning and mitigating factors, it is possible that in an objective situation of sin—which may not be subjectively culpable, or fully such—a person can be living in God's grace, can love and can also grow in the life of grace and charity, while receiving the Church's help to this end.[112]

This distinction between the objective and subjective allows it to be said that certain situations are wrong, and they remain wrong, they do not become good situations, even if the person involved is not fully culpable. There are some morally wrong living situations that are situations of grave sin, but the state of a person's soul cannot be judged simply by that person's living arrangements. In a footnote Pope Francis suggests that the 'Church's help' can include 'the help of the sacraments.' However, he does not specify which sacraments, nor does he explicitly say that people can receive sacraments for which they are ineligible. However, he does take the opportunity to reminds priests that the confessional is 'not a torture chamber, but rather an encounter with the Lord's mercy.' Moreover, he says the Eucharist 'is not a prize for the perfect, but a powerful medicine and nourishment for the weak.' For Pope Francis, the reality is that small steps are in themselves pleasing to God and perhaps more so when there have been struggles and he calls for 'fraternal charity.'[113]

One notable issue discussed at the 2015 synod was the relationship of truth and mercy. In explaining the 'logic of pastoral mercy' Pope Francis categorically states

> in order to avoid all misunderstanding, I would point out that in no way must the Church desist from proposing the full ideal of marriage, God's plan in all its grandeur ... a lukewarm attitude, any kind of relativism, or an undue reticence in proposing that ideal, would be a lack of fidelity to the Gospel and also of love on the part of the Church for young people themselves. To show understanding in the face of exceptional situations never implies dimming the light of the fuller ideal, or proposing less than what Jesus offers to the human being.[114]

At the same time, quoting the 2014 synod, 'there is a need to accompany with mercy and patience the eventual stages of personal growth as these progressively appear.' Addressing those who would prefer 'a more rigorous pastoral care which leaves no room for confusion', he continues,

> I sincerely believe that Jesus wants a Church attentive to the goodness which the Holy Spirit sows in the midst of human weakness, a Mother who, while clearly expressing her objective teaching, "always does what good she can, even if in the process, her shoes get soiled by the mud of the street".[115]

In entering the realities and complexities of people's lives, and knowing the power of tenderness, the Church patterns herself on Jesus who 'is the shepherd of the hundred, not just of the ninety-nine. He loves them all.' 'Mercy is the very foundation of the Church's life.' Certainly, Pope Francis believes that 'concern must be shown for the integrity of the Church's moral teaching', but 'special care should always be shown to emphasize and encourage the highest and most central values of the Gospel, particularly the primacy of charity as a response to the completely gratuitous offer of God's love.' He adds, 'the worst way of watering down the Gospel' is to put so many conditions on mercy that it loses its meaning and real significance. On the relationship of truth and mercy, Pope Francis says that 'mercy does not exclude justice and truth, but first and foremost we have to say that mercy is the fullness of justice and the most radiant manifestation of God's truth.' The 'mindset' Pope Francis encourages is 'a pastoral discernment filled with merciful love, which is ever ready to understand, forgive, accompany, hope, and above all, integrate.' Tellingly, and in a way that distances the discernment process proposed by Pope Francis from that of the internal forum solution proposed by the German bishops, where the personal review of conscience would lead to the priest, Church and the congregation respecting the person's individual judgment of conscience,[116] Pope Francis encourages people to speak with their priest or other committed lay people: 'they may not always encounter in them a confirmation of their own ideas or desires, but they will surely receive some light to help them better understand their situation and discover a path to personal growth.'[117]

In the final chapter of *Amoris Laetitia* Pope Francis reflects on the spirituality of marriage and the family, and this chapter is in some sense a summing up of much of the exhortation. Pope Francis implicitly roots the goods of marriage, the union of the couple, faithfulness, and fruitfulness in God and in spirituality. Pope Francis begins by pointing to the Second Vatican Council's decree on the laity, *Apostolicam Actuositatem* where lay spirituality is said to takes its character from married life, and 'family cares' should not be 'foreign' to that spirituality. The Trinity is present 'in the temple of marital communion', and 'God dwells deep within the marital love that gives him glory.' In keeping with his down-to-earth approach, Pope Francis explains that God is present in 'real and concrete families', with their joys and struggles. Following his theme of the small signs of love, Pope Francis adds that 'the spirituality of family love is made up of thousands of small but real gestures.' His emphasis on the importance of early family experiences in the development of the person comes to the fore as he says, 'a positive experience of family communion is a true path to daily sanctification and mystical growth, a means for deeper union with God.' The 'demands' of family life help people grow 'in openness of heart and thus to an ever fuller encounter with the Lord.' The family does not detract from spirituality. Rather, because people have 'an inherent social dimension', spirituality 'becomes incarnate in the communion of the family' where socialization first begins.[118]

Pope Francis urges families to be rooted in Christ so that Christ can illumine all their experiences, positive and negative, and the grace of the Holy Spirit can transform difficulties into 'an offering of love.' All moments of married life, including sexuality, 'can be experienced as a sharing in the full life of the resurrection.' Family prayer, acts of piety, sharing in the Eucharist, are all treasured moments of spirituality. Indeed, 'the food of the Eucharist offers the spouses the strength and incentive needed to live the marriage covenant each day as a domestic church.' In terms of faithfulness, Pope Francis says that spouses reflect God's own faithfulness as they follow the 'firm decision' to live and grow old together. This faithfulness is not 'following the law with obedient resignation.' Rather 'it is a matter of the heart, into which God alone sees.' Pope Francis avoids any sense that the couple can be enough for each other. He explains that love 'at the height of its freedom' happens 'when each spouse realizes that the other is not his or her own, but has a much more important master, the one Lord.' Only God can be 'the ultimate centre' of a person's life, and it is healthy realism, and a measure of disillusionment, to stop expecting from the other person what is proper to the love of God alone. Since the family is called to care for life, Pope Francis says that the family 'has always been the nearest hospital.' This hospital fosters family spirituality: 'life as a couple is a daily sharing in God's creative work, and each person is for the other a constant challenge from the Holy Spirit', a turn of phrase that many couples may want to dwell on. Family life is also 'a shepherding in mercy.' Pope Francis observes that 'each of us, by our love and care, leaves a mark on the life of others', and each of us is a 'fisher of men.' Fruitfulness in marriage then is helping others, and this is 'a way to worship God.'[119]

For Pope Francis spirituality in the family is rooted in Christ: 'it is a profound spiritual experience to contemplate our loved ones with the eyes of God and to see Christ in them.' This contemplation opens people up to the dignity of the other person and to a being present with the other person where the self is forgotten. On a practical level, following the model of Jesus's own encounters with other people, the loved one 'merits our complete attention', because that person 'possesses infinite dignity as an object of the Father's immense love.' And as with Jesus, 'no one is overlooked.' An experience of loving attention gives rise to a tenderness which can 'stir in the other the joy of being loved', and this tenderness includes loving care 'in treating the limitations of the other.' Openness, caring for others and 'spreading happiness', especially through hospitality, are additional signs of fruitfulness. This reaching out to others, notably to the poor and neglected, is a sign of and participation in 'the Church's motherhood.'[120] For Pope Francis,

> social love, as a reflection of the Trinity, is what truly unifies the spiritual meaning of the family and its mission to others, for it makes present the kerygma in all its communal imperatives. The family lives its spirituality precisely by being at one and the same time a domestic church and a vital cell for transforming the world.[121]

Concluding his exhortation Pope Francis observes that the teaching of Jesus in Matthew 22:30 where there is no marriage in heaven, and St Paul in 1 Corinthians 7:29–31 where things of the world are passing away, set marriage in the eschatological dimension, 'in the context of the ultimate and definitive dimension of our human existence.' He adds, 'we urgently need to rediscover the richness of this teaching. By heeding it, married couples will come to see the deeper meaning of their journey through life.' Pope Francis then sums up his central message:

> no family drops down from heaven perfectly formed; families need constantly to grow and mature in the ability to love. This is a never-ending vocation born of the full communion of the Trinity, the profound unity between Christ and his Church, the loving community which is the Holy Family of Nazareth, and the pure fraternity existing among the saints of heaven.[122]

By approaching marriage from the eschatological perspective, Pope Francis thinks we will have a better understanding of the 'historical journey' and 'stop demanding of our interpersonal relationships a perfection, a purity of intentions and a consistency which we will only encounter in the Kingdom to come. It also keeps us from judging harshly those who live in situations of frailty.' Nevertheless, this is not a reason to remain where we are. Pope Francis adds 'all of us are called to keep striving towards something greater than ourselves...what we have been promised is greater than we imagine.' 'Let us keep walking together.'[123]

And the aftermath

Reactions to *Amoris Laetitia* were and remain varied. Some commentators claim the exhortation changes nothing, others claim it changes everything.[124] Cardinal R. Burke argues that a post-synodal apostolic exhortation, 'by its very nature, does not propose new doctrine and discipline, but applies the perennial doctrine and discipline to the situation of the world at the time.' He says that the 'only key to the correct interpretation of *Amoris Laetitia* is the constant teaching of the Church and her discipline that safeguards and fosters this teaching.'[125] According to Cardinal Kasper the exhortation 'doesn't change anything of church doctrine or of canon law—but it changes everything' by giving 'room for Christian freedom of conscience.'[126] Notably, *Amoris Laetitia* 300 allows for bishops to formulate 'guidelines' for interpreting the exhortation.

In September 2016 a set of *dubia*, formal questions, formulated by Cardinals R. Burke, C. Caffarra, W. Brandmüller, and J. Meisner were brought to the Pope and the CDF asking for clarifications. The 'dubia' were published in an open letter in November 2017 after the Cardinals had not had a response from Rome.[127] The four cardinals were concerned that there could be different interpretations of chapter eight and so they specifically asked if footnote 351 allowed couples 'in certain cases' to receive absolution and then communion without fulfilling the requirements of *Familiaris Consortio* 84; if it remained the case that moral norms prohibiting intrinsically evil acts that are binding without exceptions and cannot be changed by circumstances or intentions; if living in adultery is an objective situation of grave habitual sin; if the exhortation presented a creative interpretation of conscience whereby conscience could be in opposition to God's law. Earlier in September 2016 Pope Francis received a copy of a document produced by the bishops of Buenos Aires to aid the priests of their diocese in implementing chapter eight of *Amoris Laetitia*. The bishops note that Pope Francis 'has opened several doors in pastoral care for families.' In their 'minimal criteria' the bishops stress that 'it is not right to speak of giving 'permission' for access to the sacraments', rather it is about pastoral discernment. The journey of discernment is 'to foster or renew a personal encounter with the living Christ.' Accompaniment by the priest is an exercise of 'pastoral charity.' The bishops note that 'the path does not necessarily end with receiving the sacraments, but may lead to other ways of achieving further integration into the life of the Church.' The bishops suggest that in limited and very specific cases and when a decree of nullity has not been obtained, and the couple cannot fulfil the requirements of living in continence, *Amoris Laetitia* does offer the possibility of access to the sacraments of reconciliation and the eucharist.[128] In his reply to the bishops Pope Francis noted that the bishops had produced 'a true example of accompaniment for priests' adding 'the writing is very good and fully explains the meaning of chapter VIII of *Amoris Laetitia*. There are no other interpretations.'

In relation to these two very different reactions to *Amoris Laetitia*, the *dubia* and the document from the bishops of Buenos Aires, the nature of *dubia* is that they invite a 'yes' 'no' answer. In *Amoris Laetitia* Pope Francis made it clear that 'not all discussions of doctrinal, moral or pastoral issues need to be settled by interventions of the magisterium. Unity of teaching and practice is certainly necessary in the Church, but this does not preclude various ways of interpreting some aspects of that teaching or drawing certain consequences from it.'[129] Indeed, the significant legacy of *Amoris Laetitia* may be the way in which Pope Francis encourages bishops to be guided by the Spirit.

Summary

At his address on the conclusion of the 2015 synod and buried in a footnote, Pope Francis set out an acrostic on *famiglia*, the Italian word for family that helps to summarize the Church's mission as the task of:

- Forming new generations to experience love seriously as fruitful, lasting, faithful and open to others, lived according to God's will, in defence of life and to enhance marriage preparation to convey the deeper meaning of Christian marriage;
- Approaching others, since a Church closed in on herself is a dead Church;
- Manifesting and bringing God's mercy to families in need' and 'to all those hurting in soul and body;
- Illuminating consciences;
- Gaining and humbly rebuilding trust in the Church;
- Labouring intensely to sustain and encourage those many strong and faithful families which, in the midst of their daily struggles, continue to give a great witness of fidelity to the Church's teachings and the Lord's commandments;
- Inventing renewed programmes of pastoral care for the family based on the Gospel and respectful of cultural differences', 'pastoral care which is capable of communicating the Good News in an attractive and positive manner;
- Aiming to love unconditionally all families, particularly those experiencing difficulties, since no family should feel alone or excluded from the Church's loving embrace.[130]

Pope Francis offers a different approach to his predecessors, as did Pope St John Paul II to his predecessors. This is not so much a question of different strategies or policies. Rather, it is different people, and Pope Francis's strength lies in the way in which he uses home-spun wisdom and a practical approach with a focus on the small steps people can make. Moreover, he makes great use of the Jesuit focus on accompaniment and discernment. In his homily at the opening of the 2015 synod Pope Francis recalls Pope St John Paul II had said 'error and evil must always be condemned and opposed; but the man who falls or who errs must be understood and loved ... we must love our time and help the man of our time.'[131] The idea of hating the sin but loving the sinner does not produce an opposition between doctrine and pastoral practice. The ideal of marriage, presented throughout the tradition, is the norm; the individual marriage is the realization or partial realization of that norm.

Pope Francis thinks that discernment is necessary whenever we have problems to resolve or need to make important decisions. Pope Francis explains discernment in Jesuit terms:

> it is a means of spiritual combat for helping us to follow the Lord more faithfully. We need it at all times, to help us recognize God's timetable, lest we fail to heed the promptings of his grace and disregard his invitation to grow. It involves striving untrammelled for all that is great, better and more beautiful, while at the same time being concerned for the little things, for each day's responsibilities and commitments.[132]

Notably, discernment is an objective process since 'discernment also enables us to recognize the concrete means that the Lord provides in his mysterious and loving plan, to make us move beyond mere good intentions.' Pope Francis does think that discernment is 'a supernatural gift' and 'a grace.' Discernment goes beyond the 'Church's sound norms' in the sense that:

> even though it includes reason and prudence, it goes beyond them, for it seeks a glimpse of that unique and mysterious plan that God has for each of us, which takes shape amid so many varied situations and limitations. It involves more than my temporal well-being, my satisfaction at having accomplished something useful, or even my desire for peace of mind. It has to do with the meaning of my life before the

Father who knows and loves me, with the real purpose of my life, which nobody knows better than he.[133]

Indeed, 'ours is not an age of change but a change of age.'[134]

Notes

[1] 1 P 2:1.
[2] 1 P 4:7–10.
[3] 1 P 3:4–5.
[4] 1 P 3:15–16.
[5] 1 P 1:6.
[6] 1 P 5:2–3; 6–9.
[7] 1 P 2:4–5; 9.
[8] Pope Francis, *Amoris Laetitia*, 291.
[9] M. Colonna, *The Dictator Pope: The Inside Story of the Francis Papacy* (New Jersey: Regnery, 2017).
[10] Pope Francis, *Amoris Laetitia*, 2.
[11] Pope Francis, *Synod for the Family, Introductory Remarks* (5 October 2015).
[12] Pope Francis, *Conclusion of the Synod of Bishops, Address* (24 October 2015).
[13] Pope Francis, *Homily, Mass for the Opening of the XIV General Assembly of the Synod of Bishops* (4 October 2015). See also Pope Benedict XVI, *Caritas in Veritate*, 3.
[14] Pope Francis, *Amoris Laetitia*, 7.
[15] CELAM *Aparecida*, 28–29.
[16] Pope Francis, *Amoris Laetitia*, 126.
[17] Ibid., 6.
[18] CELAM, *Aparecida*, 19.
[19] Pope Francis, *Amoris Laetitia*, 10–11.
[20] Ibid., 11.
[21] Ibid., 12–13.
[22] Ibid., 15–17.
[23] Ibid., 18.
[24] Ibid., 19–20.
[25] Ibid., 21–22.
[26] Ibid., 23–26.
[27] Ibid., 27–28.
[28] Ibid., 30.

[29] CELAM *Aparecida*, 5.
[30] *Ibid.*, 44.
[31] Pope Francis, *Amoris Laetitia*, 31–34.
[32] *Ibid.*, 35.
[33] CELAM *Aparecida*, 100.
[34] Pope Francis, *Amoris Laetitia*, 36.
[35] *Ibid.*, 37.
[36] *Ibid.*, 38–39.
[37] See also CELAM *Aparecida*, 51.
[38] Pope Francis, *Amoris Laetitia*, 39–46.
[39] CELAM *Aparecida*, 39.
[40] Pope Francis, *Amoris Laetitia*, 39–46.
[41] *Ibid.*, 40.
[42] *Ibid.*, 47–48.
[43] *Ibid.*, 52–53.
[44] See also CELAM *Aparecida*, 48–49.
[45] Pope Francis, *Amoris Laetitia*, 54–55.
[46] CELAM *Aparecida*, 40.
[47] Pope Francis, *Amoris Laetitia*, 56.
[48] *Ibid.*, 57.
[49] CELAM *Aparecida*, 12.
[50] Pope Francis, *Amoris Laetitia*, 58–64.
[51] *Ibid.*, 65–66.
[52] *Ibid.*, 67–70.
[53] *Ibid.*, 71–73.
[54] *Ibid.*, 74.
[55] *Ibid.*, 75.
[56] Pope Pius XI, *Casti connubii*, 39–41.
[57] St Justin, *First Apology*, 44.
[58] CELAM *Aparecida*, 4.
[59] Pope Francis, *Amoris Laetitia*, 76–78.
[60] CELAM *Aparecida*, 278.
[61] Pope Francis, *Amoris Laetitia*, 78–79.
[62] *Ibid.*, 80–83.
[63] *Ibid.*, 84–85.
[64] *Ibid.*, 86–88.
[65] *Ibid.*, 108.
[66] *Ibid.*, 89–119.
[67] *Ibid.*, 120–122.

68 *Ibid.*, 123–125.
69 *Ibid.*, 126–134.
70 *Ibid.*, 135.
71 *Ibid.*, 136–141.
72 *Ibid.*, 142–152.
73 *Ibid.*, 153–157.
74 *Ibid.*, 158–162.
75 *Ibid.*, 163–164.
76 *Ibid.*, 165–167.
77 *Ibid.*, 168–186.
78 *Ibid.*, 187–198.
79 *Ibid.*, 199–205.
80 *Ibid.*, 206–216.
81 *Ibid.*, 217–220.
82 *Ibid.*, 221.
83 See T. Berg, 'Conscience, Freedom, and the 'Law of Graduality' at the Synod of the Family' in *Homiletic & Pastoral Review* (14 September 2015).
84 Pope Francis, *Amoris Laetitia*, 222–223.
85 *Ibid.*, 224–225.
86 *Ibid.*, 226–230.
87 *Ibid.*, 231–238.
88 *Ibid.*, 239–240.
89 *Ibid.*, 241–242.
90 *Ibid.*, 243–244.
91 *Ibid.*, 245–246.
92 *Ibid.*, 247–249.
93 *Ibid.*, 250–251.
94 *Ibid.*, 252.
95 *Ibid.*, 253–258.
96 *Ibid.*, 259–262.
97 *Ibid.*, 263–264.
98 *Ibid.*, 265–267.
99 *Ibid.*, 268–270.
100 *Ibid.*, 271–273.
101 *Ibid.*, 274–278.
102 *Ibid.*, 279–286.
103 *Ibid.*, 287–290.
104 *Ibid.*, 292.
105 *Ibid.*, 291–292.

106. Pope St John Paul II, *Familiaris Consortio*, 34.
107. Pope Francis, *Amoris Laetitia*, 293–295.
108. Ibid., 296–297.
109. Ibid., 298.
110. Ibid., 300.
111. Ibid., 299–300.
112. Ibid., 305.
113. Ibid., 301–305.
114. Ibid., 307.
115. Ibid., 308.
116. O. Saier, K. Lehmann, W. Kasper, 'Pastoral Ministry: The Divorced and Remarried' in *Origins* 23:38 10 March (1994), pp. 670–676.
117. Pope Francis, *Amoris Laetitia*, 306–312.
118. Ibid., 313–316.
119. Ibid., 317–322.
120. Ibid., 323–324.
121. Ibid., 324.
122. Ibid., 325.
123. Ibid., 325.
124. See C. Lamb, 'Compassion is this pastor's watchword' in *The Tablet* 14 April (2016).
125. Cardinal R. Burke, 'Amoris Laetitia and the Constant Teaching and Practice of the Church' in *National Catholic Register* (12 April 2016).
126. C. Lamb, 'Cardinal Walter Kasper: Amoris Laetitia 'changes everything'' in *The Tablet* (14 April 2016).
127. E. Pentin, Full Text and Explanatory Notes of Cardinals' Questions on 'Amoris Laetitia' in *National Catholic Register* (14 November 2016).
128. Bishops of Buenos Aires, *Basic criteria for the implementation of chapter viii of Amoris Laetitia* https://cvcomment.org/2016/09/18/buenos-aires-bishops-guidelines-on-amoris-laetitia-full-text/
129. Pope Francis, *Amoris Laetitia*, 3.
130. Pope Francis, *Conclusion of the Synod of Bishops, Address* (24 October 2015), footnote 8.
131. Pope Francis, *Homily, Mass for the Opening of the XIV General Assembly of the Synod of Bishops*; Pope St John Paul II, *Address to the Members of Italian Catholic Action* (30 December 1978).
132. Pope Francis, *Gaudete et exsultate*, 169.
133. Pope Francis, *Gaudete et exsultate*, 170.
134. Pope Francis, *Meeting with the Bishops of Brazil, Address* (28 July 2013).

11 CONCLUDING REFLECTIONS

'LOVE ONE ANOTHER as I have loved you.'[1] We know that we can never approximate the love that Jesus has for each one of us. But as Christians we try. To love others as Jesus loves us is not merely an aspiration, or purely an ideal that sounds good, or something I know I will never be able to do. If it were, people would be tempted to despair, or give up, or remain content with the mediocre. Jesus explains 'I have loved you just as the Father has loved me. Remain in my love.'[2] Loving as Jesus loves has its source in God and grace, not in our own devices or power, and it roots love in something deeper than human relationships.[3] Moreover, the call to love others says something significant about giving of self, about our own dignity as loved by Jesus, and about the other person's dignity who is also loved by Jesus and worthy of our love. It says something about solidarity, being in this together. If we apply this saying of Jesus to love in marriage, then maybe things would be clearer. Marriage would then be a real sign of evangelization for, 'it is by your love for one another, that everyone will recognize you as my disciples.'[4]

Jesus then says that a sign of remaining in his love is keeping God's commandments.[5] According to St Augustine, St John the Evangelist 'said many things, and nearly everything was about charity', love.[6] Christians do not follow the commandments for the sake of the law but out of love for God who gifted his commandments out of love for us. For St John, the beloved disciple, 'our love is not to be just words or mere talk, but something real and active.' We are asked to be 'children of the truth' and our conscience helps us to discern if we are living 'the kind of life that he wants.' God 'knows everything', and if our conscience is at peace, 'we need not be afraid in God's presence, and whatever we ask him, we shall receive.'[7]

In his exhortation after the 2018 synod on young people, Pope Francis observes that if young people grow up in 'a world in ashes', or 'in a desert devoid of meaning', or with an experience of 'uprootedness' due to feelings of being betrayed by previous generations in terms of injustice, violence, selfishness, and lack of concern for others, then they will also develop 'a deep sense of orphanhood.' Pope Francis says that the response to this is to create 'a home', 'a family' to 'learn to feel connected to others.' Home is a place of forgiveness, trust, patience, belonging.[8] Here Pope Francis is thinking of church which should be modelled on this sense of belonging. However, he also says that 'the family should be the first place of accompaniment.'[9] Even when young people have had poor experience in their families, it is still worthwhile to invest in family life and so not be 'robbed of a great love.'[10] With the findings of the 2018 synod Pope Francis notes that young people are still enthused about marriage, 'young people intensely feel the call to love; they dream of meeting the right person with whom they can form a family and build a life together.'[11] In spite of 'a culture of relativism and the ephemeral' that thinks it is not worth making life-long commitments, Pope Francis urges young people to 'be revolutionaries', 'to swim against the tide' and 'to opt for marriage.'[12]

The story of marriage so far has shown that there are some practicalities concerning marriage, and Pope Francis lists some of these for young people: marriage requires preparation from the earliest moments of life, growing in self-knowledge and in the virtues, openness to dialogue and helping others. But God gives the grace to achieve the ideal of married life.[13] What is vital is discernment in finding the purpose God has for a person's life and formation of conscience 'which allows discernment to grow in depth and in fidelity to God.' In this process of formation of conscience we let ourselves be 'transformed by Christ.'[14] Discernment and formation of conscience requires prayer, silence, time, questioning not just of what we want but us in relation to others and God, conversation with Jesus as our friend, and accepting the listening and accompaniment of others.[15]

Pope Francis also gives practical advice to those who are accompanying young people, and this advice is highly relevant for marriage preparation as well as accompaniment in general. Pope Francis speaks of 'listening' that 'calls for three distinct and complementary kinds of sensitivity': sensitivity to the actual person by giving time and taking the person's concerns seriously without being shocked or bored, 'listening unconditionally'; sensitivity that is marked by discernment, grasping 'exactly where grace or temptation is present', working out what the person is really trying to say about what is happening in their life, listening to the spirit; sensitivity to what is driving the person, the direction in which the person truly wants to move and not merely their superficial desires, a 'deeper kind of listening' that hears the intention of the heart. Discernment here 'becomes a genuine means of spiritual combat, helping us to follow the Lord more faithfully.' Accompanying in discernment asks the accompanying person to 'disappear' so the person can follow the path they have discovered; it asks the accompanying person not to impose their own 'roadmaps.'[16] In many ways perhaps, Pope Francis is bringing the charism of the confessional into everyday dealings with people.

Becoming a community of persons

Pope Francis says that 'it takes courage to form a family.' However, he adds that the assurance that God blesses marriage and the family through the sacrament of matrimony can help people overcome even the most difficult trials. Pope Francis notes the modern pressures to married life, pressures that the 2015 synod also identified: the focus on the individual rather than community, that relationships last until there are difficulties or only as long as feelings of love last. The 'culture of the temporary' makes everything provisional. Marriage, he says, 'is risky' precisely because egoism threatens it, and 'selfishness always returns and does not know how to open up to others.'[17]

As people enter into serious relationships they face a perhaps unexpected time of loss: loss of individual independence as the ego is sacrificed for the sake of the relationship. For people who are used to a highly individualised life-style where carving out 'me time' and focusing on what fulfils 'me' are paramount, a sense of the loss of individuality and independence can seem troubling. Moreover, in a culture where everything seems transient, many people are afraid to commit because they are also afraid of failure. However, remembering that each human being is an image of God, and God is Three Persons, an analogy may help even if the analogy is necessarily limited: just as God is one and three, in the one-in-flesh of married life, the one does not lose individuality. This is something that the early church fathers often pointed out—there are still two individuals in a joint married life. Moreover, the gains of married life are significant: the family is a safe place where there is someone to listen to me, to accept me, love me for who I am.

Fear is much more difficult to deal with. In the past young people may have feared (and respected) authority of perhaps parents, teachers, priests, the state. Now people can find out by judicious use of the Internet just what teachers know; they are all too well aware of the shortcomings of parents; social media encourages distrust of the state; the paedophile scandals have done away with respect for clergy. Young people no longer fear authority, and many feel that they can no longer rely upon state, religion or parents. Each person can only rely on him or herself, hence the refuge into a compartmentalized life, or in virtual reality where I can be who I want to be, or in gang culture where I gain a sense of belonging, or in a constant redefinition or re-invention of the self. Or finally settling into a not-botheredness that is in fact a step beyond despair. Many young people are no longer afraid of authority, but not because all authority has failed. Instead they fear their own failure, especially the biggest fear that they will not find love. Lack of self-esteem, lack of confidence, fear that they will never afford a home of their own or have job security, even fear that they are not "liked" enough on social media, are rife, and this does not touch upon the even greater fears of young people who are migrants, or live in war zones, or in abject poverty or in cycles of addiction and violence, or in broken homes or in the crisis of pandemic.

Yet at the same time there is a yearning for spirituality, for belonging, for home, for lasting relationships. Fear is one reason why the promotion and defence of marriage is a part of a bigger project of social justice, solidarity, and care, where the vocation and mission of the family is vital. Yearning is one reason why the stability, faithfulness, unity, and fruitfulness of marriage is vital. Love does make us vulnerable because it exposes the cry in all human beings to be appreciated, accepted, held, and seen as uniquely valuable, to have our fears assuaged and to be comforted.

To say 'I hurt' has two meanings: I feel hurt, and I hurt others. Both of these hurts exist in close relationships. But the stability of marriage as a commitment to the other for better or worse allows for growing into a greater openness and compassion. There is always going to be warfare in our hearts because we are tempted towards pride as well as humility, hatred as well as love. Nevertheless, as Jesus himself shows on the cross, the vulnerable heart is wounded but also the place where God is. Pain, suffering and wounds need not remain as problems, rather they can be areas of discovery and redemption. The point is to walk on in hope and trust. It is important for people to realize that married life is not about being a perfect couple or perfect people. In order to avoid living an illusion, couples need to discover and accept who each one of them is, with their dark and light: if a person sees only the gifts and the light then there is a temptation to idolize the other; if the person sees only the wounds then there is a temptation simply to do for the other. The task is to see and love the person that God has set beside us, because the community in marriage, the family, is a theological phenomenon. The community of the family grows by *hesed*, fidelity and tenderness, and gentle concern. Nevertheless, the family is not a community as an end in itself because the family in turn sends its growing children out to found new communities of love. And of course, learning to love takes a lifetime because it depends on the Holy Spirit to reach into all areas of my life.

Friendship in married love is not simply a friendship of equals for as long as the friends remain friends, or where the superior is owed more love than the inferior. Married love is a form of *pietas*,[18] a deep respectful love that has something of the sacred about it. Friendship mirrors the love of God who loved us first and gave himself to us; where each person wants the good of the other as if it were their own good. It is a love characterized by total self-gift. And as St Augustine explains, the laws of love are not heavy to the one who loves. Marriage has always been about more than just the historical issue. Marriage is about how to live as a Christian in the world but not of it; how to be leaven; how to cherish earthly realities yet not hold onto them. The story of marriage is also the story of God's people loved with God's steadfast love, the story of his Church established and loved with the ultimate self-giving love of Christ. It is also the story of Church history, moral theology and the story of ecclesiology, the relationship of the faithful to the Church and of relationships within the wider Church. It is a story of evangelization. Throughout the whole story of marriage and family life there have been threads of real pastoral concern, true appreciation of the joys and anxieties that marriage brings, and a genuine sense of the significance of marriage as a vocation and path to holiness not only for its individual members but for the world. All of these stories have one end in sight and this is reflected in the fact that marriage and family are great, good, beautiful and true but they are only a foretaste of the communion to come, the eternal marriage, the 'marriage of the Lamb'.[19] Marriage and family life belong in the bigger context of life in Christ, and eternal life. There are no sacraments, including the sacrament of marriage, in heaven because sacraments prepare us for heaven and find their fulfilment there in the eternal banquet, where every tear is wiped away. With Jesus everything changes.

Notes

1. Jn 15:12.
2. Jn 15:9.
3. See St Augustine, *On the Gospel of John*, Tractate 65, 1; 82, 2.
4. Jn 13:35.
5. Jn 15:10.
6. St Augustine, *Homilies on the First Epistle of St John*, Prologue, 19.
7. 1 Jn 3:18–24.
8. Pope Francis, *Christus Vivit*, 216–217.
9. *Ibid.*, 242.
10. *Ibid.*, 263.
11. *Ibid.*, 259–262.
12. *Ibid.*, 264.
13. *Ibid.*, 265–266.
14. *Ibid.*, 279–282.
15. *Ibid.*, 283–291.
16. *Ibid.*, 291–298.
17. Pope Francis, *Address to the Young People of Umbria* (4 October 2013).
18. Pope St John Paul II, *The Theology of the Body, Human Love in the Divine Plan* (Boston: Pauline Books, 1997), pp. 309–311.
19. Rev 19:7.

BIBLIOGRAPHY

Magisterium

Popes

Siricius, Pope St Letter to Bishop Himerius of Tarragona (385).

Innocent I, Pope St *Letter to Victricius* (404).

—— *Letter to Exsuperius* (405).

—— *Letter to a Certain Probus* (date unknown).

Leo I, Pope, St *Letters* (442–460).

Gregory I, Pope St *Pastoral Rule* (c.590–591).

—— *The Books of the Morals, An Exposition on the Book of Job* (c.591–596).

Gregory II, Pope. *Replies to Questions Put By Boniface* (22 November, 726).

Zacharias, Pope St *Epistola VII ad Pipinum Majorem Domus itemque ad episcopos, abates et proceres Francorum* (c.746).

Nicholas I, Pope. Letter to Answer the Bulgarians' Questions (866).

Council of Trent. *Session XXIV* (1563).

Catechism of the Council of Trent, The Roman Catechism (1556).

Leo XIII, Pope. *Aeterni Patris* (1879).

Leo XIII, Pope. *Arcanum Divinae* (1880).

Pius XII, Pope. *To the Court of the Sacred Roman Rota* (3 October 1941).

—— *Christmas Radio Message* (24 December 1941).

—— *To the Medical-Biological Union San Luca* (12 November 1944).

—— *At the Court of the Holy Roman Rota* (6 October 1946).

—— *To the Members of the Pontifical Academy of Science* (8 February 1948).

Pius XII, Pope. *To the Catholic Doctors Convened in Rome for their Fourth International Congress* (29 September 1949).

—— *To the Participants in the Congress of the Italian Catholic Union of Obstetrics* (29 October 1951).

—— *Radio Message on the Occasion of the Family Day* (23 March 1952).

—— *To Participants in the First International Symposium on Genetic Medicine* (7 September 1953).

—— *Christmas Radio Message* (24 December 1953).

——*To Participants in the VIII Congress of the World Medical Association* (30 September 1954).

—— *To the Participants in the Second World Congress on Fertility and Sterility* (19 May 1956).

John XXIII, Pope St *Address on the Celebration of the Second Vatican Ecumenical Council* (5 June 1960).

—— *To the Members of the Court of the Sacred Roman Rota* (13 December 1961).

—— *To Participants in the First European Meeting of Youth* (2 September 1962).

—— *Address on the Solemn Opening of the Council* (11 October 1962).

Vatican II. *Sacrosanctum Concilium* (1963).

Paul VI, Pope St *Ecclesiam suam* (1964).

Vatican II. *Lumen gentium* (1964).

—— *Dei Verbum* (1965).

—— *Optatam Totius* (1965).

——*Gravissimum Educationis* (1965).

—— *Apostolicam Actuositatem* (1965).

—— *Dignitatis Humanae* (1965).

—— *Gaudium et spes* (1965).

Paul VI, Pope St Motu proprio *Apostolica sollicitudo* (15 September 1965).

—— *Humanae Vitae* (1968).

—— *Evangelii nuntiandi* (1975).

—— *Address to the Swiss Bishops Ad Limina Visit* (1 December 1977).

John Paul II, Pope St *Address to the Members of Italian Catholic Action* (30 December 1978).

—— *Familiaris Consortio* (1981).

—— Apostolic Constitution *Sacrae Disciplinae Leges* (25 January 1983).

—— *Charter of the Rights of the Family* (1983).

—— *Dominum et Vivificantem* (1986).

—— *Christifideles Laici* (1988).

—— *Redemptoris Missio* (1990).

——*Centesimus annus* (1991).

—— *Veritatis splendor* (1993).

—— *Gratissimam Sane Letter to Families* (2 February 1994).

—— *Address to the Plenary Assembly of the Pontifical Council for Culture* (18 March 1994).

—— *Catechism of the Catholic Church,* 1994.

—— *Evangelium vitae* (1995).

—— *Message to Participants in the Seventh International Meeting of the Catholic Fraternity of Covenant Communities and Fellowships* (9 November 1996).

—— *Address to the Pontifical Council for the Family* (24 January 1997).

—— *The Theology of the Body, Human Love in the Divine Plan.* Boston: Pauline Books, 1997.

—— *Fides et Ratio* (1998).
—— *Address, 15th World Youth Day Vigil of Prayer* (19 August 2000).
—— *Novo millennio ineunte* (2001).
—— *Address to the Pontifical Academy for Social Sciences* (11 April 2002).
—— *Message for the 42nd World Day of Prayer for Vocations* (17 April 2005).

Benedict XVI, Pope. *Address to the Participants in the Ecclesial Diocesan Convention of Rome* (6 June 2005).
—— *Homily* (13 May 2007).
—— *Sacramentum Caritatis* (2007).
—— *General Audience* (14 January 2009).
—— *Letter concerning the remission of the excommunication of the four bishops consecrated by Archbishop Lefebvre* (10 March 2009).
—— *Address, Pastoral Visit to Ancona Meeting with Families and Priests* (11 September 2011).
—— *Address to the Participants at the Plenary Assembly of the Pontifical Council for the Family* (1 December 2011).
—— *Address to the Bishops of the United States of America from Region VIII on their Ad Limina Visit* (9 March 2012).

Francis, Pope. *Evangelii Gaudium* (2013).
—— *Meeting with the Bishops of Brazil, Address* (28 July 2013).
—— 'A Big Heart Open To God: An Interview with Pope Francis'. In: *America The Jesuit Review* (30 September 2013).
—— *General Audience* (9 October 2013).
—— *Greeting to the Synod Fathers During the First General Congregation of the Third Extraordinary General Assembly of the Synod of Bishops* (6 October 2014).

—— *Address for the Conclusion of the Third Extraordinary General Assembly of the Synod of Bishops* (18 October 2014).

—— *Homily Closing Mass of the 8th World Meeting of Families* (27 September 2015).

—— *Homily, Mass for the Opening of the XIV General Assembly of the Synod of Bishops* (4 October 2015).

—— *Synod for the Family, Introductory Remarks* (5 October 2015).

—— *General Audience* (7 October 2015).

—— *Conclusion of the Synod of Bishops, Address* (24 October 2015).

—— *Amoris Laetitia* (2016).

—— *Gaudete et Exsultate* (2018).

—— *Angelus* (27 December 2020).

Roman Curia

Congregation for the Doctrine of the Faith. *Concerning the Reception of Holy Communion by the Divorced and Remarried Members of the Faithful* (14 September 1994).

—— *Concerning Some Objections to the Church's Teaching on the Reception of Holy Communion by the Divorced and Remarried Members of the Faithful* (1998).

Pontifical Council for Justice and Peace. *Compendium of the Social Doctrine of the Church*. Washington DC: Libreria Editrice Vaticana, 2004.

International Theological Commission. *In Search of a Universal Ethics: A New Look at the Natural Law*.

—— *Sensus Fidei in the Life of the Church* (2014).

—— *Synodality in the Life and Mission of the Church* (2 March 2018).

Bishops

CELAM. *The Aparecida Document.* 2007.

Bishops of Buenos Aires, *Basic criteria for the implementation of chapter viii of Amoris Laetitia*. 5 September, 2016.

Books

Aelred, St *Spiritual Friendship*.

—— *The Liturgical Sermons*.

—— *The Mirror of Charity*.

Alamichel, M. *Widows in Anglo-Saxon and Medieval Britain*. Oxford: Peter Lang, 2008.

Alphonsus Liguori, St *The History of Heresies, and Their Refutation: or the Triumph of the Cross*.

—— *Guide for Confessors*.

Ambrose, St *Exposition on the Christian Faith*.

—— *On the Duties of the Clergy*.

Anderson, C., and Granados, J. *Called to Love: Approaching John Paul II's Theology of the Body*. New York: Doubleday, 2009.

Apostolic Constitutions.

Aquinas, Thomas, St *Explanation of the Ten Commandments*.

—— *Summa contra Gentiles*.

—— *Summa Theologiae*.

Aristotle. *Nicomachean Ethics*.

Atkinson, J. *Biblical and Theological Foundations of the Family*. Washington DC: Catholic University of America Press, 2014.

Augustine, St *Answer to the Pelagians*.

——*Confessions*.

——*Contra Faustum*.

——*Expositions of the Psalms*.

——*Letters*.

——*On the Catechising of the Uninstructed*.

Bibliography

—— *On Continence.*
—— *The Excellence of Marriage.*
—— *On the Good of Widowhood.*
—— *On Holy Virginity.*
—— *On John's Gospel.*
—— *On the Morals of the Manichaeans.*
—— *On Marriage and Concupiscence.*
—— *On the Sermon on the Mount.*
—— *Sermons.*
—— *The Enchiridion on Faith, Hope, and Charity.*
—— *The Trinity.*
—— *On Nature and Grace.*
—— *Retractions.*
—— *Questions on the Heptateuch Ex.73.*
Basil of Caesarea, St *Letters.*
Beal, J., Coriden, J., and Green, T. (eds.), *New Commentary on the Code of Canon Law.* New York: Paulist Press, 2000.
Beale, G. K., and Carson, D. A. (eds.). *Commentary on the New Testament Use of the Old Testament.* Grand Rapids Michigan: Baker Academic, 2007.
Beattie, T. *New Catholic Feminism: Theology and Theory.* London: Routledge, 2006.
Bellarmine, R, St *Doctrina Christiana.*
—— *The Art of Dying Well.*
Boethius. *Against Eutyches and Nestorius.*
Borkowski, A. *Textbook on Roman Law.* London: Blackstone, 1997.
Borromeo, C, St *Selected Orations, Homilies and Writings.*
Brown, P. *The Body and Society.* New York: Columbia University Press, 2008.

—— *The Rise of Western Christendom Triumph and Diversity, AD 200–1000*. Oxford: Wiley-Blackwell, 2013.

Brown, R. *An Introduction to the New Testament*. New York: Doubleday, 1997.

Brugger, E. C. *The Indissolubility of Marriage and the Council of Trent*. Washington DC: Catholic University of America Press, 2017.

Bulman, R. *From Trent to Vatican II: Historical and Theological Investigations*. Oxford: Oxford University Press, 2006.

Buxbaum, Y. *The Life and Teachings of Hillel*. New York: Rowman and Littlefield, 1994.

Chapp, L. *The God of Covenant and Creation: Scientific Naturalism and its Challenge to the Christian Faith*. London: T&T Clark, 2011.

Clement of Alexandria, St *Stromata*.

—— *Christ the Educator*.

Clement of Rome, St Letter to the Corinthians.

Cohen, A. *Matthew and the Mishnah*. Tubingen: Mohr Siebeck, 2016.

Colish, M. *Studies in Scholasticism*. Aldershot: Ashgate, 2006.

Collins, R. *First Corinthians* Sacra Pagina Series. Collegeville Minnesota: Liturgical Press, 1999.

Colonna, M. *The Dictator Pope: The Inside Story of the Francis Papacy*. New Jersey: Regnery, 2017.

Connell, S. *Aristotle on Female Animals*. Cambridge: Cambridge University Press, 2016.

Costen, M. *The Cathars and the Albigensian Crusade*. Manchester: Manchester University Press, 1997.

Coyle, J. K. *Manichaeism and Its Legacy*. Leiden: Brill, 2009.

Doms, H. *The Meaning of Marriage*. New York: Sheed and Ward, 1939.

Evans, C. *The Social Gospel in American Religion: A History*. New York: New York University, Press 2017.

Fishbane, S. *Deviancy in Early Rabbinic Literature*. Leiden: Brill, 2007.

Fisher, A. *Catholic Bioethics for a New Millenium*. Cambridge: Cambridge University Press, 2012.

Fitzmyer, J. *Essays on the Semitic Background of the New Testament Vol.1*. Grand Rapids, Michigan: William Eerdmans, 1997.

Fletcher, J. *Morals and Medicine*. Princeton: Princeton University Press 1954.

—— *Situation Ethics: The New Morality*. Louisville: Westminster John Knox Press, 1966.

Ford, J. Memorandum (4 July 1966) http://www.twotlj.org/F-G-4-Ott-1.pdf

Foucault, M. *Discourse and Truth and Parrēsia* [1983] Chicago: University of Chicago Press, 2019.

France, R. T. *The Gospel According to Matthew: An Introduction and Commentary*. Grand Rapids Michigan: Eerdmans, 1985.

Francis de Sales, St *Treatise on the Love of God*.

—— *Letters*.

—— *Philothea or an Introduction to the Devout Life*.

Francisco de Vitoria. *On the American Indians (De Indis)*.

Franklin-Brown, M. *Reading the World: Encyclopedic Writing in the Scholastic Age* Chicago: University of Chicago Press, 2012.

Frier B. and McGinn, T. *A Casebook on Roman Family Law*. Oxford: Oxford University Press, 2004.

Garland, R. *Daily Life of the Ancient Greeks*. London: Greenwood Press, 2009.

Gillespie, M. A. *The Theological Origins of Modernity*. Chicago: University of Chicago Press, 2008.

Gregory of Nazianzus, St *Letters.*

—— *Orations.*

Grootaers, J., and Selling, J. *The 1980 Synod of Bishops 'On the Role of the Family': An Exposition of the Event and an Analysis of the Text.* Leuven: Peeters, 1983.

Hall, E. *The Arnolfini Betrothal: Medieval Marriage and the Enigma of Van Eyck's Double Portrait.* Berkeley: University of California Press, 1994.

Harrington, D. *The Gospel of Matthew Sacra Pagina Series.* Collegeville Minnesota: Liturgical Press, 1991.

Harrington, J. *Reordering Marriage and Society in Reformation Germany.* Cambridge: Cambridge University Press, 1995.

Helmholz, R. H. *The Oxford History of the Laws of England Vol.1 The Canon Law and Ecclesiastical Jurisdiction from 597 to the 1640s.* Oxford: Oxford University Press, 2004.

Herlihy, D. *Medieval Households.* Cambridge Massachusetts: Harvard University Press, 1985.

Hess, H. *The Early Development of Canon Law and the Council of Serdica.* Oxford: Oxford University Press, 2002.

Hildebrand, D. von. *Marriage: The Mystery of Faithful Love* [1929]. Manchester New Hampshire: Sophia Institute, 1984.

—— *In Defense of Purity: An Analysis of the Catholic Ideals of Purity and Virginity.* Eugene Oregon: Wipf and Stock, 1962.

Hooker, M. *The Gospel According to St Mark.* London: A & C Black, 1991.

Hoose, B. *Proportionalism.* Georgetown: Georgetown University Press, 1987.

Hugenberger, G. *Marriage as a Covenant: Biblical Law and Ethics as Developed from Malachi.* Eugene, Oregon: Wipf and Stock, 1994.

Hugh of St Victor. *Sacraments of the Christian Faith.*

Hunt, E. *Christianity in the Second Century: the Case of Tatian.* New York: Routledge, 2003.

Hunter, D. *Marriage and Sexuality in Early Christianity.* Minneapolis: Fortress Press, 2018.

Ignatius of Antioch, St *Letters.*

Ignatius of Loyola, St *The Spiritual Exercises.*

Instone-Brewer, D. *Divorce and Remarriage in the Bible.* Grand Rapids: Eerdmans, 2002.

Irenaeus, St *Against Heresies.*

Isidore of Seville, St *De ecclesiasticis officiis.*

—— *The Etymologies.*

Jerome, St *Against Jovinian.*

—— *Commentary on Isaiah.*

—— *Letters.*

—— *The Perpetual Virginity of Blessed Mary, Against Helvidius.*

Jewish Study Bible. A. Berlin and M. Brettler (eds.), Oxford: Oxford University Press, 2004.

John Chrysostom, St *Baptismal Instructions.*

—— *Homilies.*

—— *How to choose a wife.*

Jolowicz, H. F. and B. Nicholas. *Historical Introduction to the Study of Roman Law.* Cambridge: Cambridge University Press, 1972.

Jurasinski, S. *The Old English Penitentials and Anglo-Saxon Law.* Cambridge: Cambridge University Press, 2015.

Jurgens, W. *The Faith of the Early Fathers Vols.1, 2, 3.* Collegeville, Minnesota: Liturgical Press, 1970.

Justin Martyr, St *Dialogue with Trypho*

—— *Apology 1.*

Kaiser, R. B. *The Encyclical That Never Was, The Story of the Pontifical Commission on Population, Family and Birth, 1964–1966.* London: Sheed and Ward 1985.

—— *The Politics of Sex and Religion.* Indiana: Leaven Press, 1985.

Kamas, J. *The Separation of the Spouses with the Bond Remaining: Historical and Canonical Study with Pastoral Implications.* Rome: Editrice Pontificia Universita Gregoriana, 1997.

Kasher, A. *Jews, Idumaeans and Ancient Arabs.* Tubingen: J.C.B. Mohr, 1988.

Kasper, W. *Theology of Christian Marriage.* New York: Seabury Press, 1980.

Kelly, W. *Pope Gregory II On Divorce and Remarriage.* Rome: Universita Gregoriana Editrice 1976.

King, J. C. *Origen on the Song of Songs as the Spirit of Scripture.* Oxford: Oxford University Press, 2005.

Lactantius. *Divine Institutes.*

Lambeth Conference Resolutions Archive From 1930.

Lampe, P. *Christians at Rome in the First Two Centuries: From Paul to Valentinus.* Minneapolis: Fortress Press, 2003.

Lansing, C. *Power and Purity: Cathar Heresy in Medieval History.* Oxford: Oxford University Press, 1998.

Lawler, M. *Marriage and Sacrament: A Theology of Christian Marriage.* Collegeville Minnesota: Liturgical Press, 1993.

—— *Marriage and the Catholic Church: Disputed Questions.* Collegeville Minnesota: Liturgical Press, 2002.

Levine, É. *Marital Relations in Ancient Judaism.* Wiesbaden: Harrassowitz Verlag, 2009.

Lewis, C. S. *Miracles.* London: Centenary Press, 1947.

Lind, G. *Common Law Marriage.* Oxford: Oxford University Press, 2008.

Locke, J. *Two Treatises of Government.* [1689]. London: Routledge 1987.

Lombard, P. *The Sentences.*

Lovano, M. *The World of Ancient Greece Vol.1.* California: Greenwood, 2020.

MacDonald, M. *Colossians, Ephesians* Sacra Pagina Series. Collegeville Minnesota: Liturgical Press, 2000.

Mahoney, J. *The Making of Moral Theology.* Oxford: Clarendon Press, 1987.

Marcus Minucius Felix. *Octavius.*

Marenbon, J. *The Philosophy of Peter Abelard.* Cambridge: Cambridge University Press, 1997.

Martos, J. *Doors to the Sacred: A Historical Introduction to Sacraments in the Catholic Church.* Missouri: Liguori, 2001.

Matthews, P. *Discerning Persons: Profound Disability, the Early Church Fathers and the Concept of the Person in Bioethics.* Steubenville OH: Franciscan Press, 2020.

McCarthy, C. *Marriage in Medieval England: Law, Literature and Practice.* Woodbridge: Boydell, 2004.

Meyendorff, J. *Marriage: An Orthodox Perspective.* New York: St Vladimir's Seminary Press, 2000.

Moloney, F. *'A Hard Saying' The Gospel and Culture.* Collegeville Minnesota: Liturgical Press, 2001.

Mounier, E. *Existentialist Philosophies, An Introduction.* London: Rockliff, 1948.

—— *Personalism* [1949]. Notre Dame: Notre Dame University Press, 1970.

Murphy-O'Connor, J. *1 Corinthians.* Dublin: Veritas, 1980.

Myths from Mesopotamia: Creation, the Flood, Gilgamesh and Others. Oxford: Oxford University Press, 2000.

Nauert, C. *Humanism and the Culture of Renaissance Europe* Cambridge: Cambridge University Press, 2006.

Neusner, J. *The Rabbinic Traditions About the Pharisees Before 70 Part II: The Houses.* Oregon: Wipf & Stock, 1971.

Neusner, J. *The Rabbinic Traditions About the Pharisees Before 70 Part II*, 38; *The Literature of the Sages First Part.* Netherlands: Brill, 1987.

Newman, J. H., St *Reply to Mr Gladstone's Pamphlet, To His Grace the Duke of Norfolk.*

—— *Roman Catholic Writings on Doctrinal Development by John Henry Newman.* Kansas: Sheed and Ward 1997.

Noonan, J. *Contraception: A History of its Treatment by the Catholic Theologians and Canonists.* Cambridge Massachusetts: Harvard University Press, 1986.

Oberman, H. A. *Luther: Man Between God and the Devil.* New Haven: Yale University Press, 1989.

Origen. *Against Celsus.*

—— *Commentary on Matthew.*

—— *Commentary on 1 Corinthians.*

—— *De Principiis.*

—— *Homilies.*

Pasnau, R. *Metaphysical Themes, 1274–1671.* Oxford: Oxford University Press, 2011.

Passion of the Holy Martyrs Perpetua and Felicity.

Pentin, E. *The Rigging of a Vatican Synod?* San Francisco: Ignatius Press, 2015.

Pinckaers, S. *The Sources of Christian Ethics.* Edinburgh: T&T Clark, 2001.

Pinon, S. *The Ivory Tower and the Sword: Francisco Vitoria Confronts the Emperor.* Eugene Oregon: Pickwick, 2016.

Probert, R. *Marriage Law and Practice in the Long Eighteenth Century: A Reassessment.* Cambridge: Cambridge University Press, 2009.

Ratzinger, J. *On the Question of the Indissolubility of Marriage.* 1972.

Ravier, A. *Francis de Sales: Sage and Saint.* New York: DeSales Resource Centre, 2007.

Rees, B. R. *Pelagius: Life and Letters, (Vol. II, The Letters of Pelagius and his Followers).* Woodbridge: Boydell, 1998.

Reynolds, P. *Marriage in the Western Church: The Christianization of Marriage During the Patristic and Early Medieval Periods.* Leiden: Brill 2007.

Rosen, C. *Preaching Eugenics: Religious Leaders and the American Eugenics Movement.* Oxford: Oxford University Press, 2004.

Rummel, E. *Biblical Humanism and Scholasticism in the Age of Erasmus.* Leiden Netherlands: Brill, 2008.

Sanger, M. *The Pivot of Civilisation In Historical Perspective.* Seatle: Inkling Books 2001.

—— *Birth Control Advances: A Reply to the Pope.* (1931)

Satlow, M. *Jewish Marriage in Antiquity.* Princeton: Princeton University Press, 2001.

Schafer, S. *Marriage, Sex and Procreation: Contemporary Revisions to Augustine's Theology of Marriage.* Eugene, Oregon: Pickwick, 2019.

Schemenauer, K. *Conjugal Love and Procreation: Dietrich von Hildebrand's Superabundant Integration.* Maryland: Lexington, 2011.

Schillebeeckx, E. *Marriage: Human Reality and Saving Mystery.* London: Sheed and Ward, 1965.

Selin, G. *Priestly Celibacy: Theological Foundations.* Washington: Catholic University of America Press, 2016.

Sheehan, M. *Marriage, Family and Law in Medieval Europe.* Toronto: University of Toronto Press, 1996.

Sheldon, C. *In His Steps. What Would Jesus Do?* Grand Rapids: Revell 1984.

Slater, T. *A Manual of Moral Theology:* Vol.1. St Pius X Press, 2012.

Smith, J. *Humanae Vitae a Generation Later*. Washington: Catholic University of America Press, 1991.

Stol, M. *Women in the Ancient Near East*. Berlin: De Gruyter, 2016.

Stone, R. *Morality and Masculinity in the Carolingian Empire*. Cambridge: Cambridge University Press, 2012.

Sumption, J. *The Albigensian Crusade*. London: Faber, 1978.

Tertullian. *Against Marcion*.

—— *Exhortation to Chastity*.

—— *On Fasting*.

—— *On Monogamy*.

—— *To His Wife*.

Thatcher, A. *God, Sex and Gender*. Oxford: Wiley-Blackwell, 2011.

Tutino, S. *Uncertainty in Post-Reformation Catholicism: A History of Probabilism*. Oxford: Oxford University Press, 2018.

Vine, W. E., Unger, M., White Jr, W. *Vine's Complete Expository Dictionary of Old and New Testament Words*. Nashville: Thomas Nelson, 1996.

Vorgimler, H. *Sacramental Theology*. Collegeville Minnesota: Liturgical Press, 1992.

Wilken, R. L. *The First Thousand Years: A Global History of Christianity*. New Haven: Yale University Press, 2012.

Witte, J. *Church, State and Family: Reconciling Traditional Teachings and Modern Liberties*. Cambridge: Cambridge University Press, 2019.

Wojtyła, K., *Sources of Renewal* [1975]. London: Fount, 1980.

—— *Catholic Thought from Lublin* Vol. IV *Person and Community*. New York: Peter Lang, 1993.

Articles and chapters in books

Atkinson, J. 'Family as Domestic Church: Developmental Trajectory, Legitimacy, and Problems of Appropriation'. In: *Theological Studies* 66 (2005), pp. 592–604.

Barr, B. A. 'Three's A Crowd: Wives, Husbands, and Priests in the Late Medieval Confessional'. In: *A Companion to Pastoral Care in the Late Middle Ages (1200–1500)*. Leiden: Brill, 2010, pp. 213–234.

Berg, T. 'Conscience, Freedom, and the 'Law of Graduality' at the Synod of the Family'. In: *Homiletic & Pastoral Review* 14 September, 2015.

Bevilacqua, A. 'The History of the Indissolubility of Marriage'. In: *Proceedings of the Catholic Theological Society of America* 22 (2012).

Black, R. 'Humanism'. In: *Renaissance Thought: A Reader*. London: Routledge, 2001, pp. 68–94.

Blenkinsopp, J. 'Deuteronomy'. In: R. Brown, J. Fitzmyer, R. Murphy (eds.), *The New Jerome Biblical Commentary*. London: Geoffrey Chapman, 1990.

Burke, R. 'Amoris Laetitia and the Constant Teaching and Practice of the Church'. In: *National Catholic Register* 12 April 2016.

Chilton, B. 'Mamzerut and Jesus'. In: *Jesus From Judaism to Christianity*. New York: T&T Clark, Continuum, 2007.

Clark, E. 'The Celibate Bridegroom and His Virginal Brides: Metaphor and the Marriage of Jesus in Early Christian Ascetic Exegesis'. In: *Church History* 77:1, (March 2008), pp. 1–25.

Duby, G. 'The Knight, the Lady and the Priest: the Making of Modern Marriage in Medieval France' In: *Contesting Christendom: Readings in Medieval Religion and Culture*. New York: Rowman & Littlefield, 2008, pp. 91–98.

Finn, T. 'Sex and Marriage in the Sentences of Peter Lombard'. In: *Theological Studies* 72 (2011), pp. 41–69.

Fletcher, J. 'Technical Devices in Medical Care' [1970]. In: *On Moral Medicine: Theological Perspectives in Medical Ethics*. Grand Rapids: Eerdmans, 1998.

Gane, R. 'Old Testament Principles Relating To Divorce and Remarriage'. In: *Journal of the Adventist Theological Society* 12/12 (Autumn 2001), pp. 35–61.

Gasparri, P. 'Preface to the 1917 Code'. In: *The 1917 or Pio-Benedictine Code of Canon Law*. Edward Peters San Francisco: Ignatius Press, 2001.

Granados, J. 'The Theology of the Body in the United States'. In: *Humanum* (2015) Issue 3.

Grisez, G., Finnis, J., and May, W. E. 'Indissolubility, Divorce and Holy Communion'. In: *New Blackfriars*. Vol.75 No.883 June (1994), pp. 321–330.

Grubbs, J. E. 'Pagan and Christian Marriage: the State of the Question'. In: *Journal of Early Christian Studies* 2/4 (1994), pp. 361–412.

Grubbs, J. E. 'Emperor Constantine'. In: *Christianity and Family Law: An Introduction*. Cambridge: Cambridge University Press, 2017.

Gundry-Volf, J. M. 'The Least and the Greatest: Children in the New Testament'. In: *The Child in Christian Thought*. Grand Rapids, Michigan: Eerdmans, 2001.

Haar, C. 'Tomás Sánchez and Late Scholastic Thought on Marriage and Political Virtue'. In: *The Concept of Law (Lex) in the Moral and Political Thought of the 'School of Salamanca'*, Leiden, the Netherlands: Brill, 2016, pp. 81–105.

Harrington, D. 'The Gospel According to Mark'. In: R. Brown, J. Fitzmyer, R. Murphy (eds.), *New Jerome Biblical Commentary*. London: Geoffrey Chapman, 1993.

Healy, N. 'The Merciful Gift of Indissolubility and the Question of Pastoral Care for Civilly Divorced and Remarried Catholics'. In: *Communio* 41 Summer (2014), pp. 306–330.

Heft, J. 'Tradition, A Catholic Understanding'. In: *The Idea of Tradition in the Late Modern World.* Oregon: Cascade, 2020, pp. 33–55.

Hendrix, S. 'Luther on Marriage'. In: *Lutheran Quarterly XIV* (2000), pp. 335–350.

Himes, K., and Coriden, J. 'Pastoral Care of the Divorced and Remarried'. In: *Theological Studies* 57 (1996) pp. 97–123.

Hittinger, R. 'Popes Leo XIII and Pius XI'. In: *Christianity and Family Law: An Introduction.* Cambridge: Cambridge University Press, 2017.

Hoeflich, M., Grabher, J. 'Normative Legal Texts'. In: *The History of Medieval Canon Law in the Classical Period.* Washington: Catholic University of America Press 2008.

Holland, G. 'Celibacy in the Early Christian Church'. In: *Celibacy and Religious Traditions.* Oxford: Oxford University Press, 2008.

Horrell, D. and Adams, E. 'The Scholarly Quest for Paul's Church at Corinth: A Critical Survey'. In: *Christianity at Corinth: The Quest for the Pauline Church.* Louisville: Westminster John Knox Press, 2004, pp. 1–43.

Hunter, D. 'Helvidius, Jovinian, and the Virginity of Mary in Late Fourth Century Rome'. In: *Journal of Early Christian Studies* 1/1 (1993), pp. 47–71.

Johnson, L. J. 'A Disembodied "Theology of the Body"'. In: *Commonweal* 4 June 2004.

Kaiser, W. 'Justinian and the Corpus Iuris Civilis'. In: *The Cambridge Companion to Roman Law.* Cambridge: Cambridge University Press, 2015.

Kanniyakonil, S. 'The Indissolubility of Marriage in the Syro-Malabar Church'. In: *Marriage, Families and Spirituality* 24, 2018, pp. 106–120.

Kasper, W. 'On the Church'. In: *America The Jesuit Review* 23 April (2001).

Keenan, J. 'Moral Theology'. In: *From Trent to Vatican II: Historical and Theological Investigations.* Oxford: Oxford University Press 2006, pp. 161–178.

Killeen, B. 'Theology, Law and Christian Life'. In: *Keeping Faith in Practice: Aspects of Catholic Pastoral Theology.* London: SCM Press, 2010, pp. 227–240.

Knieps-Port le Roi, T. *'Familiaris consortio*—Impasse or Inspiration for a Contemporary Theology of Marriage and the Family?' In: *Melita Theologica* (2006), 57/2 pp. 63–78.

Kuefler, M. 'The Marriage Revolution in Late Antiquity: The Theodosian Code and Later Roman Marriage Law'. In: *Journal of Family History* 32/4 (2007) pp. 343–370.

Kurz, W. 'The Scriptural Foundations of The Theology of the Body'. In: *Pope John Paul II on the Body: Human, Eucharistic, Ecclesial.* Philadelphia: St Joseph's University Press 2006.

Lamb, C. 'Compassion is this pastor's watchword'. In: *The Tablet* 14 April (2016).

Lamb, C. 'Cardinal Walter Kasper: Amoris Laetitia "changes everything"'. In: *The Tablet* 14 April (2016).

Lamb, M. 'Vatican II After Fifty Years: The Virtual Council Versus the Real Council'. In: *The Second Vatican Council Celebrating Its Achievements and the Future.* London: Bloomsbury 2013, pp. 7–18.

Lambert, W. G. 'Mesopotamian Creation Stories'. In: *Imagining Creation.* Leiden: Brill, 2008, pp. 15–60.

Laney, C. J. 'No Divorce and No Remarriage'. In: *Divorce and Remarriage: Four Christian Views.* Illinois: Intervarsity Press, 1990.

Levine, P., Bashford, A. 'Introduction: Eugenics and the Modern World'. In: *The Oxford Handbook of the History of Eugenics*. Oxford: Oxford University Press, 2010, pp. 3–24.

Lövestam, E. 'Divorce and Remarriage in the New Testament'. In: *The Jewish Law Annual* Volume 4. Leiden: Brill, 1981.

Luño, A. R. 'Can Epikeia Be Used in The Pastoral Care of the Divorced and Remarried Faithful?' In: *L'Osservatore Romano* 26-XI (1997).

Mayeski, A. M. 'Like a boat is marriage: Aelred on marriage as a Christian way of life'. In: *Theological Studies* 70 (2009), pp. 92–108.

McDonnell, K. 'The Ratzinger/Kasper Debate: The Universal Church and Local Churches'. In: *Theological Studies* 63 (2002), pp. 227–250.

McDougall, S. 'The Making of Marriage in Medieval France'. In: *Journal of Family History* 38/2 (2013) pp. 103–121.

Murphy, C. 'Collegiality: An Essay Toward Better Understanding'. In: *Theological Studies* 46 (1985), pp. 38–49.

Murray, J. 'Thinking About Gender: The Diversity of Medieval Perspectives'. In: *Power of the Weak: Studies on Medieval Women*. Chicago: University of Illinois Press, 1995, pp. 1–26.

Novembri, V. 'Philosophia and Christian Culture: An Antidote for Female Weakness in Jerome's Letters'. In: *Papers Presented at the Fifteenth International Conference on Patristic Studies, 2007 Studia Patristica XLIV*. Leuven: Peeters, 2010.

Olson, C. 'Celibacy and the Human Body: An Introduction'. In: *Celibacy and Religious Traditions*. Oxford: Oxford University Press, 2008.

Orsy, L. 'In Search of the Meaning of Oikonomia: Report on a Convention'. In: *Theological Studies* 43/2 (1982), pp. 312–319.

Petrà, B. 'Bishop Petro Fiordelli (1916–2004) at the Council: the Bishop of Prato and the Strange Origin of the Theology of the Family as a "Domestic Church"'. In: *INTAMS review* 19, (2013) pp.13–33.

Quesnell, Q. 'Made Themselves Eunuchs for the Kingdom of Heaven'. In: *Catholic Biblical Quarterly* 30/3 (1968), pp. 335–338.

Rabaneda, P. U. 'Leander of Seville and His Influence on Isidore of Seville'. In: *A Companion to Isidore of Seville*, Leiden: Brill 2020, pp. 101–134.

Ratzinger, J. 'The Local Churches and the Universal Church'. In: *America The Jesuit Review* 19 November (2001).

Reese, T. 'Report from the Synod'. In: *America* 11 October (1980).

Reese, T. 'The Close of the Synod'. In: *America* 8 November (1980).

Roberts, W. 'Christian Marriage'. In: *From Trent to Vatican II: Historical and Theological Investigations.* Oxford: Oxford University Press 2006, pp. 209–226.

Saier, O., Lehmann, K., and Kasper, W. 'Pastoral Ministry: The Divorced and Remarried'. In: *Origins* 23:38 10 March (1994) pp. 670–676.

Salvi, S. 'Towards a New Era of Modernity? Late Scholastic Speculation on Bigamy and Polygamy'. In: *Family Law and Society in Europe from the Middle Ages to the Contemporary Era.* Switzerland: Springer 2016, pp. 155–186.

Schembri, K. 'The Orthodox Tradition on Divorced and Remarried Faithful: What Can the Catholic Church Learn?' In: *Melita Theologica* 65/1 (2015), pp. 121–141.

Spadaro, A. 'Interview with Pope Francis, A Big Heart Open to God'. In: *America* 30 September (2013), pp. 15–38.

Tine, R. J. Van. 'Castration for the Kingdom and Avoiding the αἰτία of Adultery (Matthew 19:10–12)'. In: *Journal of Biblical Literature* 137/2 (2018), pp. 399–418.

Travers, P. 'Reception of the Holy Eucharist by Catholics Attempting Remarriage after Divorce and the 1983 Code of Canon Law'. In: *Jurist* 55 (1995) pp. 187–217.

Travers, P. 'Holy Communion and Catholics Who Have Attempted Remarriage After Divorce: A Revisitation'. In: *Jurist* 57 (1997) pp. 517–540.

Treggiari, S. 'Marriage and the Family in Roman Society'. In: *Marriage and Family in the Biblical World*. Illinois: Intervarsity Press, 2003, pp. 132–182.

Veronese, F. 'Jonas of Orleans'. In *Great Christian Jurists and Legal Collections in the First Millenium*. Cambridge: Cambridge University Press, 2019, pp. 413–428.

Viviano, B. 'The Gospel According to Matthew'. In: R. Brown, J. Fitzmyer, R. Murphy (eds.), *The New Jerome Biblical Commentary*. London: Geoffrey Chapman, 2000, pp. 642–643.

Widok, N. 'Christian Family as Domestic Church in the Writings of St John Chrysostom'. In: *Studia Ceranea* 3 (2013), pp. 167–175.

Witte, J. 'The Reformation of Marriage Law in Luther's Germany: Its Significance Then and Now'. In: *Journal of Law and Religion* 4/2 (1986), pp. 293–351.

Witte, J. 'Grotius and the Natural Law of Marriage'. In: *Studies in Canon Law and Common Law in Honor of R.H. Helmholz*. Berkeley: The Robbins Collection 2015, pp. 231–249.

INDEX OF NAMES AND THEMES

Abelard, P. 154
Abortion 208, 212, 216, 229, 236, 238, 258, 318
Abuse 149
Accompaniment 2, 4, 251, 269–270, 271, 273–274, 345, 346, 360, 362, 363, 386, 390, 403–404, 405, 408, 412, 416, 424, 426, 432–433
   small steps 269, 363, 377, 394, 395, 410, 416–417, 418, 419, 426
Adam and Eve 24, 25, 87, 88, 95, 96, 97, 103, 104, 105, 107, 110, 113, 139, 292, 293, 294, 295, 307,
Adelphoi, brethren 53, 57, 101
Adultery 11, 27, 30–32, 41, 42, 43, 44–45, 46, 47, 50, 66, 69, 87, 93, 94, 105, 106, 109, 110, 115, 133, 148, 150, 186, 212, 285, 296, 309–310, 352, 386, 423
   moicheia 44–45
Aelred, St 2, 139–141, 153
Albigensians, Bogomils and Cathars 146–147
Alcuin 12, 138
Alexander III, Pope 143
Alexander VIII, Pope 192
Alphonsus Liguori, St 191–193
Ambrose, St 47, 99, 102
Ambrosiaster 47, 353

Analogy 17, 34, 37, 38, 50, 52, 64, 92, 113, 128, 171, 175, 178, 181, 264, 304–306, 307, 309–310, 319, 321, 387, 412, 434
   Christ and Church, husband and wife 3–4, 6, 52, 64, 91, 98, 109, 112, 113, 144, 147, 175, 177, 197, 200, 212, 231, 237, 260, 261, 272, 274, 290, 304–306, 307, 309, 319, 321, 332, 387, 394, 322, 332, 360, 379, 385, 387, 394, 422
   Christology, husband and wife 92, 196, 260
      with language 264, 309–310
      limitations of, 17, 306, 322, 387, 394, 434
      marriage and baptism 64, 98–99
      parents and bishops, family as flock 2, 116, 138
      sin and sickness 128, 135, 193
      Trinity 113, 180, 261, 307–308, 379, 385, 387, 393, 422, 434
Church as beacon of a lighthouse 374, 412
Church as 'field hospital' 363, 377, 412
Annulment 132, 348, 355, 407
Anselm, Archbishop of Canterbury, St 141
Anthony of Egypt, St 86

Aparecida, CELAM Conference 2007 361–362, 378, 379, 380–381, 383, 384, 385, 388–389, 390

Apollinarians 101

Apostolic Constitutions 127

Aquinas, Thomas St 39, 148–153, 160, 180, 186, 191, 192, 195, 211, 350, 378, 417
Arians 100, 101
Aristotle 29, 38–39, 153, 154, 357
Ascetics, asceticism 59, 60, 62, 86, 87, 91, 96, 100, 102, 104, 137, 161
   extreme forms, encraticism 64, 65, 86, 88, 94–95, 102, 206
Atkinson, J. 319
Augustine of Hippo, St 6, 11, 12, 17, 22, 39, 95, 106–113, 116, 136, 137, 138, 144, 146, 148, 159, 175, 179, 190, 191, 211, 330, 334, 431, 436
Augustine of Canterbury, St 129, 132–133
Augustus, Emperor 68–69, 114

Basil of Caesarea, St 11, 105–106, 128, 353–354
Beal, J. 243–244
Bede, St 133–134, 137
Bellarmine, Robert, St 174–175
Bevilacqua, A. 133–134
Benedict XIV, Pope 218
   Magnae nobis 1748 194
Benedict XV, Pope

Providentissima Mater Ecclesia 1917 199

Benedict XVI, Pope 8, 331, 386, 387, 397
Ratzinger, J. 256, 257, 333, 348, 353–356, 356–358, 358–361
   Concerning some objections to the Church's teaching on the Reception of Holy Communion by the Divorced and Remarried Members of the Faithful 1998 353–356
   Sacramentum caritatis 2007 359
Bereavement 408
Biologism, biological materialism 221
Boethius 153, 219–220
Boniface, St 134
Borromeo, Charles, St 174
Brandmüller, W. Cardinal 423–424
Brown, P. 86
Buber, M. 222
Buenos Aires Bishops, *Basic criteria for the implementation of ch.viii of Amoris Laetitia* 424
Burke, R. Cardinal 423–424

Caffarra, C. Cardinal 423–424
Calvin, Calvinists 159, 185, 191–192
Canon law 126–128, 129, 189, 200, 218, 346–347, 388
   early canons 94, 106, 125, 126, 127, 128, 129, 134, 138, 156,

Index of Names and Themes 465

1917 Pio-Benedictine Code of Canon Law 171, 197–199, 200, 207, 212, 241, 242, 273, 343
1983 Code of Canon Law 241–244, 346

Carterius 12, 100–101
Catechisms, catechetical teaching 173–174, 231, 270, 360, 378, 388
  Catechism of the Council of Trent, the *Roman Catechism* 173–174, 213, 221
  Catechism (1992) 35, 319, 388, 390, 417
    family catechesis 411
    formation 401–402, 432
    pastoral teaching 135–139, 173–175, 257, 269–270, 360, 373–374
    gradualness in pastoral care 412–413
    pastoral dialogue 413
Celibacy 7, 11, 46–47, 52, 59, 60, 61, 69, 89, 90, 91, 93, 94, 96–104, 106, 112, 115, 117, 156, 158, 176, 225, 227, 258–259, 266, 290, 300–302, 309–310, 322, 398
Children, procreation 2, 9, 24, 34, 37, 63, 65, 88, 89, 93, 97, 98, 109, 110, 136, 138, 175, 176, 178, 185, 190, 197, 200, 214, 223–224, 225, 226, 229–231, 231, 233, 235, 236, 260, 266, 298–299, 312, 379–380, 381–382, 390–391, 399

children as gifts 9, 212, 216, 233, 235, 260, 263, 293, 359, 390, 399–400, 405
children seen as burdens 11, 146–147, 207, 209, 216
and divorce 407
education, parents as educators 37, 116, 138, 148, 199, 232, 236, 266, 276, 341, 391, 408–411
population growth, see also contraception 207, 237–241, 263
procreation as co-operation with God 89, 185, 212, 232, 235, 237, 260, 263, 293
procreation seen as evil 11, 86, 88, 96, 97, 117, 146–147
responsible parenthood 237–241, 312–316, 318, 386, 399, 405
sex education 266, 410–411
See technology, reproduction
Church 242, 252, 267–268, 277–278, 386–387
and Christian relationship with the world 2, 5, 7–9, 11, 14, 18, 59, 62–65, 70–71, 83–87, 125, 160, 179, 193–195, 206–207, 210, 227–228, 232–233, 237, 241–242, 244, 253, 257, 263, 267, 268, 273, 275–276, 278, 283, 292, 300, 302, 308, 316, 318, 320, 322, 337–339, 364–365, 382, 436
as family 261, 271, 274–275, 318, 391, 432
decentralisation 337, 356–358, 364–365, 423–424

domestic, little church, see Marriage
ecclesiology 240, 245, 317–318, 436
house church 56, 57
Mystical Body of Christ 197, 317–318, 322, 338
order 63, 126, 135, 136, 137, 242
'sign of contradiction' 7, 241, 253, 337, 401
see *sensus fidei*
see Synod, synodality
Clement of Alexandria, St 87, 88, 89–90
Clement of Rome, St 85
Co-habitation, see Unions, non-marital
Collins, R. 57–58
Colossae, Colossians 62–63
Common good 140, 187, 227, 350
Communio, community 16, 24, 25, 33, 39, 40, 43, 55, 56, 57, 58, 59, 60–61, 64, 65, 127, 141, 179, 184, 187, 222, 225, 233, 244, 254, 257, 260, 261, 262, 265, 266, 268, 270, 271, 275–276, 277, 278, 293, 302, 306, 307–308, 317, 318, 320, 359, 361, 383, 386, 390, 391, 402, 405, 407, 408, 409, 413, 414, 415, 422, 433–437
see Theology of the Body
Complementarity 25, 44, 139, 150, 183, 261

inequality, equality 61–62, 63, 64, 89, 90, 92, 97, 104–105, 149–150, 160, 177, 197, 213–214, 222–223, 236–237, 262, 292, 293, 297, 304, 341, 384, 398
celibacy and marriage 259, 302–303, 307, 398
Concupiscence 108, 109, 110, 145, 146, 148, 152, 153, 175, 180, 191–192, 199, 217, 227, 285, 295, 296, 303, 308, 310, 316, 308
Congregation for the Doctrine of the Faith 344–345
Congregation of the Holy Office 225–227
Conscience 188–189, 193, 206, 217, 229, 235, 237, 238–239, 240, 252–253, 278, 313–314, 331, 333, 336, 341–343, 345, 346, 354–355, 382, 405, 409–410, 414, 415, 416, 417, 419–420, 423, 431–432
Consent 12, 29, 66, 67, 69, 70, 85, 111, 114, 115, 129, 131, 134–135, 136, 141, 142–143, 145, 148, 150, 160, 174, 184, 190, 200, 211, 218, 222–223, 226, 243, 244, 270, 308–309, 310, 388
Constantine, Emperor 114
Consummation 12, 130, 134, 142, 143, 223, 297, 309, 142–143, 223, 309, 388
Continence 87, 88, 99, 100, 108, 111, 112, 128, 157, 174, 216,

Index of Names and Themes 467

274, 300–301, 302, 303, 307, 316, 424
see Virtues
Regulation of birth 391
    contraception 13, 208, 209–210, 212, 216, 235–236, 237–241, 255, 264, 342
    contraception compared to natural times of infertility 229, 241, 264, 314
    contraception as intrinsic evil 239, 255
    contraceptive mentality 314
    natural family planning 314
    responsible parenthood 237–241, 238–240, 312–316, 318, 386, 399, 405
Contract 8, 13, 26, 27, 35, 37, 39, 68, 98, 117, 125–126, 131, 141, 144, 150, 159, 160, 172, 174, 193, 194, 195, 200, 218, 222, 231, 244, 350
    marriage as civil contract 70, 85, 128, 133, 157, 158, 174, 194, 195–196, 200, 215
Corinth, Corinthians 56–62
Councils 127–128
    Council of Carthage VII 256 127
    Council of Elvira 305–314 94
    Council of Carthage XI 419 134
    Council of Arles 524 131
    Council of London 1102 141
    Council of Westminster 1200 141
    Fourth Lateran Council 1215 138, 153
    Second Council of Lyons 1274
    The Profession of Faith of Michael Palaeologus 147
    Council of Florence 1439 147

    Council of Trent 1545–1643 157–159, 172–173, 175, 188–189, 190, 196, 211, 217, 334, 354
    First Vatican Council 1869 198
    Second Vatican Council 1962–1965 231–237, 241, 251–252, 259, 269, 277, 285–286, 289, 332–333, 336–338, 339, 354, 355, 357
    Lumen Gentium 1964 231–232, 262, 319
    Dei Verbum 1965 283
    Ad Gentes 1965 389
    Apostolicam Actuositatem 1965 232, 262, 420
    Dignitatis humanae 1965 15, 341–342
    Optatam Totius 1965 283
    Gaudium et spes 1965 5, 15, 232–237, 239, 242, 244, 260, 262, 266, 286, 304, 312, 313, 317, 335, 342, 386, 387, 390, 405, 410, 414–415
Covenant 11, 17, 23, 31, 32, 33–35, 38, 39–40, 115, 117, 156, 160, 233, 236, 237, 241–244, 258, 259–260, 286, 292, 295, 307, 309, 310, 317, 322, 350, 355, 359, 385, 393, 394, 403, 421
Creation 11, 23–25, 96–97, 270, 293, 298, 306, 308
    pagan creation myths 10–11, 22–23.
Culture, consumer, of the temporary 258, 263, 382, 398, 403, 433, 434

Didache 126
Didascalia Apostolorum 127
Diocletian, Emperor 92, 94
Dionysius Exiguus 128
Discernment 18, 100, 174, 181, 257, 258, 266, 268, 273, 289, 345, 360, 365, 376, 379, 382, 387, 389, 390, 407, 408, 413, 414, 415–416, 417, 419, 424, 426, 432, 433, 382, 387, 390, 407, 424, 426–427, 432–433
  of the heart, see *Theology of the Body*
  of situations 273–274, 360, 407, 413–416, 417, 419–420
  sensitive listening 433
Divorce 11, 15, 16, 21–22, 27–28, 29, 30, 31–32, 40–43, 45–47, 48, 60–61, 66, 68, 69, 91, 94, 109, 114–115, 117, 130, 131, 133, 134, 150, 157, 186, 194–195, 196, 207, 215, 233, 255, 258, 273, 274, 317, 330, 340, 364, 407
  see remarriage
Docetists 100–101
Doms, H. 225
Domestic, little church, see Marriage
  see Theology of the Body
Domitian, Emperor 84–85
Dowry 26, 27, 28–29, 32, 65, 66, 98, 130, 131, 135, 142

Ebionites 100
Ethelred, Archbishop of Canterbury 134

Eugenics 207–210, 216, 228, 229
Eugenius IV, Pope
  Bull of Union with the Armenians 147–148
Evangelization 1–2, 10, 57, 64, 260, 268, 276, 277, 318–319, 322, 358, 361–362, 378, 385, 389, 411, 431, 436
Existentialism 205, 219
Exsuperius, bishop of Toulouse 133

Family 266, 379–380, 386, 421, 434
  bright spots and shadows 2–3, 233, 234, 257–258, 376, 380–381
  community of persons 260–262, 266, 277–278, 307–308, 432–434
  elderly people, people with disabilities 263, 383, 401
  first natural society, school of human virtue 229, 232, 236, 262, 266–267
  joy 386, 394–395, 401
  role in the world 237, 244, 261, 266–267, 278, 399–400, 421–422
  sanctuary of life 10, 263, 269, 308, 391
  single-parent families 271, 401, 408
  wounded families 390, 401, 412
  Holy Family, see Mary
Fidelity 37, 38, 109, 110, 111–112, 175, 177, 212, 233, 259, 261, 262, 270, 277, 309, 310, 332, 339, 394, 414, 425, 432, 436

Index of Names and Themes 469

Finn, T. 144
Fiordelli, P. Bishop 317–318
Fletcher, J. 229–230
Ford, J. 240
Forum, internal and external 344, 354, 355
  internal forum as discernment with the priest 416
France, R. 47, 48
Francis, Pope xv, xvi, 1, 2, 4, 9, 16, 18, 177, 237, 245, 253, 254, 331, 333, 337, 340, 361–366, 374–375, 376, 378–427, 432–434, 245, 340
  Jorge Bergoglio, CELAM Conference see Aparecida
  Amoris Laetitia xvi, 9, 15, 177, 331, 362, 374, 378–423
  dubia 423–424
  Famiglia 425
Francis de Sales, St 175–178, 275, 329–330
Francisco de Vitoria 183–184, 186
Fuchs, J. 240

Gaius, *Institutes* 69, 113
Galton, F. 208
Gane, R. 31
Gender ideology 384
  gender 322–323
  gender roles 184, 411
German Bishops, Saier, O., Lehmann, K., Kasper, W. 344–346, 356, 419–420
Gillespie, M. A. 182
Gnosticism 57, 331–332
God's faithful love, *hesed* 17, 34, 36, 37, 40, 42, 51, 53, 55, 70, 117, 258, 319, 421, 436, 259, 305–306, 387, 393, 421, 431, 436
  mercy 3, 18, 37, 52, 193, 413, 419
  God's plan for humanity 6, 9, 10, 22–26, 39, 43, 65, 83, 93, 136, 290, 296, 313
  author of marriage 22, 145, 174, 196, 197, 210–211, 233, 336
  Divine law of marriage 210, 233, 236, 240, 264, 265, 313–314, 318, 408
  friendship with God 138, 156, 161, 171, 172, 180
  fruitfulness 24, see Children
  possibility, impossibility of God's commands 158–159, 171–172, 190–192, 217, 256, 260, 313, 333–336, 388, 413
Grace 6, 9, 12, 13, 36, 37, 46, 91, 102, 103, 107, 108, 111, 113, 126, 135–139, 141, 145–148, 153, 155, 158–161, 172, 175, 176, 180, 185, 188, 190–191, 195, 197, 206, 213–215, 217, 224, 232, 234, 240, 242, 259, 260, 262, 265, 268, 270, 272, 274, 277, 286, 291, 294–295, 303–304, 306, 307, 310, 313, 316, 318, 330, 331, 333, 334–336, 339–340, 343, 350–351, 362–363, 377, 381, 385, 386, 388, 389, 394, 396, 398, 406, 407, 412, 413, 414, 417, 420, 426, 431, 432, 433
  seeds of grace 215, 377, 388–389, 401
Granados, J. 323
Gratian 129, 142
Orthodox 45

Gregory I, Pope St 132–133, 135–136, 149
  Libellus responsionum 132
  Regula Pastoralis 135–136
Gregory II, Pope, St 134
Gregory of Nazianzus, St 5, 105
Grisez, G. 238
Grisez, G., Finnis, J., May W.E. 345
Grootaers, J. 254
Grotius, Hugo 185–186

Happiness 150–151, 155, 160–161, 197
Haar, C. 184
Harrington, D. 49
Heart xv, 1, 5–6, 18, 36, 37, 39, 140, 176, 177, 179, 181, 213, 214, 222, 259, 262, 265, 277, 289, 295–296, 299, 310, 329–330, 333, 363, 373, 378, 406, 433, 435
Helmholz, R. H. 129–130, 132
Helvidius 100–102, 117
Hildebrand, von D. 221–225, 227
Hillel and Shammai, rabbinic schools 21–22, 40–41, 45
Himerius, Bishop of Tarragona 133
Himes, K., Coriden, J. 343–344
Hobbes, T. 186–187
Holiness 1–2, 7, 9, 10, 13, 14, 42, 43, 54–55, 61, 83, 86, 87, 89, 104, 112, 116, 117, 126, 135–139, 146, 158, 160–161, 173, 174, 176, 178, 184, 196, 197, 213, 215, 218, 231–232, 233, 236, 263, 265, 268, 275–276, 284, 300, 304, 306, 317, 331, 333, 362, 387, 436
Homosexuality 255, 375, 408

Hooker, M. 42, 43
Hospitality, charitable acts 10, 85, 90–91, 105, 141, 145, 421–422
Households, household codes 62–65, 97, 116
Hugh of St Victor 145–146
Human being, 182–183, 232–233
  acts, truly human 177, 234, 236, 240, 278, 288
  as an other, helper 25, 39, 276, 293, 379, 404–405, 421
  as gift 9, 212, 216, 233, 235, 260, 263, 293–294 359, 390, 399–400, 405
  as image of God 24, 258, 269, 291–292, 293, 298, 300, 359
  as a kind 25, 181–182
  body, material aspect 58–59, 65, 103, 146, 241, 258, 287–288, 289, 292, 295, 296, 304, 315, 359, 411
  dignity 1, 7, 10, 18, 55, 139, 160, 181, 196, 214, 220, 221, 232, 234, 236, 237, 242, 257, 262, 266, 267, 269, 272, 275, 276, 278, 286, 287, 296, 298, 308, 316, 336, 391, 397, 408, 410, 422, 431
  dualism 287–288
  flourishing 13, 18, 151, 153, 155, 178, 181, 185, 187, 195
  individualism 186, 266, 278, 381, 399, 400, 433–434
  rights, responsibilities 182–183, 184, 242, 256, 262, 267
  sexuality 255, 259, 263–264, 278, 300, 322–323, 332, 359, 397–398, 402, 420
  social, communio 24, 25, 39, 258, 275–276, 292, 293

Index of Names and Themes 471

unique, unrepeatable 24, 39, 289, 293, 294, 299, 329
value, personal 258
see Theology of the Body
Humanism 154–155
  new humanism 258
  culture of life 276
Hume, B. Archbishop of Westminster 255, 258
Hunt, E. 88
Hunter, D. 100

Ignatius of Antioch, St 83, 85
Ignatius of Loyola, St 18, 174
Indissolubility 9, 109, 114, 133, 143, 144, 148, 149, 150, 175, 180, 199, 200, 211, 212, 214, 232, 235, 243, 255, 260, 261–262, 272, 274, 277, 285, 296, 308, 333, 344, 345, 353–355, 359–360, 366, 376, 377, 385, 394, 396
Infanticide 236
Infertility, childless marriage 110, 223–224, 230, 235, 260, 266, 390, 400
Innocent I, Pope 133
Innocent III, Pope 129
Instone-Brewer, D. 44–45, 47
International Theological Commission 253
Irenaeus, St 83, 88
Isidore of Seville, St 136–137
Jansenism 190–192, 217, 256, 334
Jesus 8, 9, 10–11, 55, 55–56, 57, 59, 63, 70–71, 83, 84, 87, 91, 105, 117, 125, 141, 171, 195, 205, 304, 334, 338, 353, 379, 385, 386, 400, 413, 418, 419, 421, 433
  bridegroom 11, 21, 51–52, 55, 70, 96, 98, 113, 258, 305, 319–320, 321, 332, 360
  brothers, *adelphoi* 53, 57, 100, 101
  calling disciples, vocation 1–2, 251, 322, 330, 373, 385, 390
  and celibacy 46–47, 46–48
  and family life, children 21, 49–51, 380, 386
  genealogy 40
  heart 329, 397, 435
  love 431
  marriage 21–22, 31, 32, 40–46, 54, 210, 260, 262, 276, 284, 291, 296, 298, 300–301, 303, 304, 310, 319, 422
  parentage 40, 47–48
  wedding feasts 52–53
Jerome, St. 12, 47, 99–100, 101–104, 106, 111
John the Baptist 51, 52
John the Evangelist, St 431
John of the Cross, St 171
John VIII, Pope 134
John XXIII, St Pope 231, 237, 241, 337–338
John Chrysostom, St 2, 96–99, 116, 251
John Paul II, St Pope 1, 2, 3, 4, 7, 14, 15, 25, 184, 206, 234, 237, 241, 244–245, 283–284, 335, 339, 344, 346, 355, 386, 387, 399, 425, 426
  Wojtyła, K. 220, 257, 277, 284, 288, 338
  The Jeweller's Shop 1960 284

Love and Responsibility 1960 284
Familiaris Consortio 1981 14, 257–275, 302, 335, 346, 347, 354, 358, 360, 362, 377, 387, 389, 390, 393, 394, 412, 413, 414, 416, 423
Christifideles laici 1988 14, 275–276
Veritatis splendor 1993 15, 342–343
Evangelium vitae 1995 263
Address to the Pontifical Council for the Family 1997 347–348
see *Theology of the Body* 14, 264, 278
John Scholasticus 128
Jonas, bishop of Orleans 137
Jovinian 102–103, 107, 117
Justin Martyr, St 88, 388

Kantian ethics 187
Kasper, W. 125, 356–358, 361, 364
see German Bishops
King, J. C. 92
Krempel, B. 225

Lambeth Conference 1930, Church of England 209–210
Laney, J.C. 45
Lactantius 92–94
Law of gradualness, see Moral Theology
Lawler, M. 348
Leo I, Pope St 133
Leo VI, Emperor 135
Leo XIII, Pope 2, 195–197, 211
Arcanum Divinae 1880 13, 196–197
Levine, É. 34

Levirate law 33
Lewis, C. S. 54
Locke, J. 186
Lombard, Peter 142–143, 145–146, 147, 150
Lövestam, E. 44, 45
Love, unity 6, 36–37, 39, 63, 65, 97, 149, 171, 175, 177, 197, 199, 212–213, 222–223, 234, 238–239, 244, 305, 312, 380, 391–394, 398, 431
affectio maritalis 69, 70, 114
agape 311
ahab 36
eros 289, 296–297, 311, 397
hesed 17, 36, 37, 40, 42, 117, 436
friendship 38–39, 108, 139–141, 149–150, 171, 218, 234, 240, 394, 436
kindness 9, 14, 37, 98, 193, 196, 284, 347, 392, 396
pietas 304, 316, 436
pleasure 6, 38, 39, 54, 89, 93, 96, 99, 108, 109, 117, 136, 152, 153, 175, 178, 187, 190, 287, 378, 394, 397, 411
same-sex attraction, unions 227, 243–244, 332, 336, 340, 341, 345, 359, 364, 375, 383, 408
self-control 89–90, 109, 117, 136, 137, 264, 299–300, 301, 314–316, 397
self-gift 5, 6, 39, 222, 224, 233, 234, 259, 261–262, 264, 266, 278, 286–287, 288, 290, 293–294, 296, 309, 316, 379, 436

Index of Names and Themes 473

witness to God's love 262, 277–278, 436
see Heart
Lust, inordinate desire, objectifying the other 6, 14, 27, 36, 89, 93, 95, 105, 107–108, 110, 111, 138, 149, 153, 157, 174, 178, 188, 284, 287, 295–297, 299, 308
Luther, Martin 156–157, 191–192
Protestant reformers 153, 172–173, 185, 193–194

Mahoney, J. 335
Malthus, T. 207
Mamzer 32, 47–48
Manichaeanism 88, 94–96, 97, 99, 102, 107, 117, 146, 147, 206, 287
Manuals 188–189, 190, 193
pastoral manuals 135–139
Marcus Minucius Felix 84
Marriage
banns 141–142, 143, 158, 194
as blessing 21, 33–35, 97, 211, 213, 433
baptized unbelievers 243
as covenant 11, 17, 23, 31, 32, 33–35, 38, 39–40, 115, 117, 160, 233, 236, 237, 241–244, 258, 259–260, 286, 292, 295, 307, 309, 310, 317, 322, 350, 355, 359, 385, 393, 394, 403, 421
clandestine, *tametsi* decree 131, 132, 141–142, 158, 183, 194
clergy, marriage 99, 115, 156–157
dialogue 396–397, 406, 432

domestic, little church 2, 7, 115–116, 231, 232, 262, 267, 269, 277, 278, 317–321, 359–360, 380, 386, 391, 411, 421, 422
ends, primary and secondary 199, 211, 217, 218, 221–225, 225–227, 230–231, 236–237, 238–239, 242, 243, 390–391
fellowship, partnership 12, 14, 89, 97, 98, 138, 139, 183, 233, 386, 390, 435
goods of marriage 5, 8, 9, 37–38, 109, 117, 136–137, 138, 145, 148, 174, 175, 177, 211, 215, 233, 237, 243, 260, 322, 387, 435
in God's plan 6, 9, 10, 17, 22–26, 65, 222, 223, 230, 231, 233, 258, 261, 270, 306, 313
faith of spouses 2, 3, 141, 194, 232, 242–243, 268, 270–271, 355, 358, 388, 394
fear of failure 3, 376, 381, 382, 434–435
forgiveness 6, 10, 262, 265, 268, 273, 335, 343, 391, 392, 403, 406, 407, 432
fruitfulness 24, 34, 303, 315, 379, 390–391, 399
marriage debt, conjugal rights 29, 60, 111–112, 139, 178, 188, 193, 213
marriage in heaven 54, 149, 422
Marriages Act 1753 (English law) 194
mixed marriages 61, 194, 255, 270, 271, 407–408

order of creation 22, 157, 180, 241, 391
Paschal Mystery, Christ's passion 150, 158, 237, 259–260, 270, 387, 393
preparation, remote, proximate, immediate 217, 231, 264, 269–270, 396, 402–404, 432
prohibited degrees 32, 43, 44, 58, 68, 130, 131, 132, 141, 157
reflecting God's love, see Analogy
Sacrament of marriage 4, 5, 9, 10, 54, 144–148, 150, 195, 196–197, 199, 200, 214, 231, 243, 259–260, 270, 290–291, 294, 296, 303–308, 312, 355, 358, 387
society, a good for xvi, 8, 10, 17, 18, 65, 86, 87, 93, 109, 117, 125, 140, 157, 160, 176, 184, 185, 193, 195, 197, 214, 232, 233, 236, 391, 395, 400, 422
spiritual marriages 61, 88
spirituality in marriage 12, 35, 53, 61, 92, 116, 126, 139–141, 150, 153, 160, 173–178, 181, 221–225, 270, 312, 316, 379, 393, 403, 420–422
unitive, procreative, inseparable connection 241, 312, 381, 390–391
wounded families 390, 406
seeds of grace, see Grace
see also Family, Children
see also Practice and Laws
MacDonald, M. 63, 64–65
Mahoney, J. 335
Malthus, T. 207
Marcion 86, 88, 102
Martos, J. 144–145, 146

Mary at the Cross 53
at the wedding of Cana 52–53
ever virgin 100, 101
Holy Family 386, 422
marriage to St Joseph 100, 110, 142–143, 145
model for Christians 100, 380
McDougall, S. 131–132
Media 14, 215, 271, 337, 374–375, 383, 410, 412, 434, 435
Meisner, J. Cardinal 423–424
Mercy and truth 331–333, 343, 348–349, 362, 376–377, 413–414, 418–419
Meyendorff, J. 350–352
Modernity 184, 195–197
Moloney, F. 46
Moral theology 8, 153–156, 160, 171–172, 178, 184–188, 200, 229, 238–239, 240, 245, 264–265, 283–284, 312, 330, 381–382, 436
casuistry 189
equiprobabilism 192
ethos 289, 296, 297
formation 409–410
human acts and morality 177, 188–189, 234, 236, 240, 278, 288, 413, 417
intrinsically evil acts 217, 239, 255, 423
Jansenism 190–192
law of gradualness, opposed to gradualness of the law 256, 264–265, 412, 413
laxism 190, 193
legalism 13, 18, 43, 189, 193, 200, 218, 355–356

Index of Names and Themes 475

morality of flourishing, love 13, 18, 151, 153, 155, 178, 181, 185, 187, 421, 431
morality of obligation 155–156, 178, 184, 229, 330
objective situation, subjective responsibility 15, 240, 242, 256, 264–265, 274, 313, 315, 342, 343, 345–346, 347, 413, 414, 417–418
probabilism 189, 192
probabiliorism 192
proportionalism 240
scripture, place of 283
rigorism 190, 192, 193
tolerating the lesser evil, opposed to doing evil 241
totality argument 241
Mounier, E. 219
Murphy-O'Connor, J. 58, 59, 60, 61
Natural law 171, 172, 178–188, 200, 240, 312, 343
Newman, J. H. St 252–253, 330
Nicholas I, Pope, St 134–135
  To the Bulgars (Letter 99) 134–135
Nominalism 155–156, 159, 160, 172, 182, 184, 186, 189
Novembri, V. 104
Origen 47, 91–92, 353
Orsy, L. 348–349
Orthodox Approach 344
  Akribia 348
  Oikonomia 348–353, 354, 355
  Epikeia 348–353, 354–355
Parousia 55–56, 58, 61, 62, 85–86
Parrhesia xv, 365

Passions 149–153, 155, 187, 192, 394, 397
  concupiscible, irascible 152
Pastoral teaching, concern 135–139, 173–174, 313, 347–348
  see catechesis, catechetical teaching
  see manuals
Paul, St 2, 4, 5, 11, 41, 56–65, 83, 84, 86, 88, 89, 98, 99, 103, 105, 106–107, 109, 111, 112, 116, 126, 135, 136, 137, 148, 152, 180, 181, 192, 276, 333, 338, 351, 379, 391–392, 404, 422
Paul III, Pope 182–183
Paul VI, St Pope 14, 234, 251, 316, 338–390, 386
  Commission on population, 'Majority' and 'Minority' reports 237–241, 265
  Ecclesiam suam 1964 15
  Humanae vitae 1968 14, 240–241, 255, 285, 312–316, 335, 342, 386–387, 390, 391
  Evangelii Nuntiandi 1975 387
Pelagius, Pelagians 102, 107, 110, 159, 190, 206, 332, 334, 362–363
  semi-pelagians 191, 362–363
Penance, confession 94, 106, 128, 134, 138–139, 143, 145, 193, 274, 344, 347, 348, 351–352, 354
  Forgiveness 6, 108, 111, 117, 181, 262
  Penitential books 128–129, 138–139
  see Sacraments
Pepin, king of the Franks 134

Perpetua, St and Felicity, St 87
Personalism 205–206, 219–220, 230
Personalistic understanding of marriage 139, 200, 214, 218, 234, 236–237, 243–244, 263–264
Peter, St 1, 2, 373
Phenomenology 220, 221, 288
Pius IX, Pope 218
   Acerbissimum vobiscum 1852 194–195
Pius X, Pope, St
   Arduum sane munus 1904 199
Pius XI, Pope 218, 221, 238, 239, 269, 410
   Casti connubii 1930 13, 207, 209–210, 210–218, 222, 229, 238, 317, 334, 388
Pius XII 221, 226, 227–231, 238, 239, 317, 410
Polygamy, polygany 30, 93, 130, 149, 183, 186, 212, 255, 261
Porneia 44–45, 353
   ervat daoebaoer 31
   indecency 31, 41
Practices and laws: marriage, divorce, adultery ancient Near East 26–28
   Bulgars 134–135
   Old Testament 28–33
   Ancient Greece 65–66
   Ancient Rome 67–69
   Rome and early Christianity 69, 113–115, 128, 129, 134–135
   Roman law 43, 58, 69, 114, 115, 129, 130, 134–135, 142
   Irish and Celtic 130–132
   North European 130–132, 142

   Theodosian Code 113–115
   Rites 85, 135, 136, 141, 143, 145, 146, 147, 308
Pride 6, 105, 108, 111, 117, 145, 149, 207, 252, 287, 294, 308, 392, 435
Promethean freedom, mentality 182, 184, 229–230

Remarriage 21, 31, 32, 91, 133, 134, 273–274, 343–356, 360, 364, 375, 389, 407, 414–418
   after death of spouse 91, 98, 103, 106, 115, 117, 135, 354
   after divorce 15, 16, 31, 32, 40–47, 103, 106, 110, 133–134, 148, 157, 273, 343–348, 353, 407, 415
   see Eucharist, Sacrament
   see Orthodox Approach
Resurrection of the body 87, 149, 259, 285, 298–299, 300, 301, 303, 420
Reynolds, P. 137
Roberts, W. 158

Sacraments 54, 144–148, 156–157, 157–158, 172, 174, 175, 176, 180, 259–260, 268–269, 285–286, 402, 436–437
   admission to sacraments 273, 274, 418, 424
   Eucharist 56, 57, 94, 106, 133, 134, 135, 264, 268, 274, 359–360, 407–408, 418, 420–421, 424
   of marriage, see Marriage

Reconciliation 264, 265, 268–269, 274, 351, 354, 362, 403, 406, 418, 424
Sacramentum 109, 144
Spiritual communion 346
Saier, O., Lehmann, K., Kasper, W. (Bishops)
see German Bishops
Salvation 3, 10, 17, 22, 35, 39, 40, 42, 65, 83, 89, 102, 104, 112, 138, 148, 149, 171, 179, 185, 191–193, 244, 258, 260, 270, 290, 294, 304, 314, 322, 340, 348, 359, 361, 377, 385, 387, 404.
Sánchez, Tomás 189–190
Sanger, M. 209–210
Satlow, M. 21, 49, 54
Schembri, K. 351, 352
Schemenauer, K. 224
Schillebeeckx, E. 144, 237
Scholasticism 12, 154
Secularism 13, 195–197
Selling, J. 254
Seminaries 283, 401
Sensus fidei 14, 252–253, 256, 257–258
Separation 32, 45, 61, 67, 109, 134, 148, 157, 158, 175, 212, 273, 407
Sexuality 24, 54, 57, 86, 87, 92, 100, 200, 239, 255, 259, 264, 278, 288, 295, 297, 298, 301, 320, 322, 332, 336, 359, 360, 390, 397, 402, 410–411, 420
Shame 25, 110, 149, 152, 293, 295
Sheldon, C. M. 205–207
Signs of the times 241–242, 254, 257, 379

Sin, sinfulness 6, 15, 31, 58–59, 61, 86, 87, 88, 89, 96, 98, 102, 103, 105, 108, 110–111, 112, 113, 128, 138, 139, 140, 141, 147, 149, 150, 152, 153, 157, 159, 175, 176, 178, 180, 185, 188, 190, 191, 192, 193, 212, 216, 217, 264, 289, 296, 304, 308, 334, 335, 336, 342, 343, 346–347, 348, 351, 360, 362, 366, 386, 414, 417–418, 423, 426
 Original sin 25, 107–108, 110, 145, 291, 294–295, 306, 307, 330
 structures of sin, social sin 264–265
Siricius, Pope St 102, 133
Situation ethics 206
Slater, T. 188
Social Gospel Movement 207
Social justice 206, 435
Solidarity 257, 261, 262, 275, 277, 400, 401, 431, 435
Sterilization 208, 209, 216–217, 229, 258
Stol, M 26–28
Subsidiarity 266
Synod, synodality 15, 126–127, 251–254, 364–365, 375
 5th General Synod (1980) 14, 251, 254, 254–256
 3rd Extraordinary Synod (2014) 14, 364–366, 384, 385, 387, 388–389, 401, 405, 407, 418

14th Ordinary Synod (2015) 14, 254, 385, 386, 387, 389, 390, 391, 398, 401, 405, 406, 408, 412, 415, 416, 418, 425, 426, 433
15th Ordinary Synod (2018), young people 432

Tatian the Syrian 88–89, 102
Technology, science 200, 207–208, 217, 227–231, 238–239, 258, 399
  artificial fertilization 228, 229
  Donum Vitae 1987 390–391
  reproduction 208, 384–385, 390–391
Tertullian 85, 86–87, 88, 90–91, 127
Thatcher, A. 43, 46
Theodore of Canterbury, St 128–129
Theology of the Body 14, 264, 278
  Adam and Eve 292–293
  body, material aspect of the person 289, 292, 295, 304
  celibacy 290
  communio 292, 293, 299, 300, 307–308, 309, 310
  complementarity 293, 297–298
  concupiscence 295, 296, 308, 310, 316
  consciousness 288–289
  critique of Freud, Marx, Nietzsche 287
  domestic Church 317–321
  double solitude 293
  Ephesians 5, 'great analogy' 290–291, 304–305, 306–307, 322
  Eros, ethos 289, 296–297, 310
  experience 291
  Fall 291, 295
  Gaudium et spes 286
  Genesis 291–292
  God's plan of love 290, 296
  heart, place of discernment 289, 295–296, 299, 310
  historical man 286, 294, 296
  Incarnation 286, 289
  interior innocence, purity of heart 293
  language of the body 308–312, 315–316, 379
  marriage, primordial sacrament 290–291, 307
  methodology 285–286
  'modern man', anthropological problem 287–288
  masculinity, femininity, male, female 288, 292, 293, 294, 295, 296, 297–298, 299, 306, 309, 310, 316
  nature and person 287–288
  nuptial meaning of the body, gift, self gift 288, 290, 293–294, 296, 299, 300, 309
  original innocence 294
  original sin 294–295
  original solitude 292, 299, 379
  original unity 292, 293, 294
  person as help to be truly a person 293, 294
  person, truly human 287–288, 289, 292
  phenomenology 220, 288
  philosophies of consciousness 288–289
  philosophy of being 288–289
  pietas 304, 316

procreation, children, parenthood 293, 294, 297, 313–314
redemption 289, 290–291, 294, 298–303, 305, 306–307, 308
resurrection of the body 300
sacrament, sacramentality 294, 303–308, 309, 312
self-mastery 314–315
shame 293, 295, 296
spirituality of marriage 312, 316
structure 285
tree of knowledge 294
use of scripture 284, 286
unique, unrepeatable 289, 293, 294, 299
virtues 288, 299–300, 312
see Children, Human Being
Traditio Apostolica 127
Tradition, development of 8, 238–239, 283–284, 332–333, 336–341, 423
Travers, P. 343, 346–347, 348
Trinity 219–220
Truth and mercy 331–333, 343, 376–377, 431

Unions, non-marital, 'irregular situations' 216, 227, 271–272, 347, 359, 383, 389–390, 412, 413–420
civil marriages 273
co-habitation 44, 67, 68, 69, 106, 114, 272, 389, 360, 412–413
'free', with no public recognition 272–273
redefining marriage 336–341
same-sex union 115, 227, 243–244, 336, 340–341, 345
wounded families 390, 406, 412

Utilitarianism 187

Van Tine, R. J. 47
Victricius, bishop of Rouen 133
Virginity 11, 12, 57, 61, 89, 96, 99, 100–104, 105–106, 111–112, 137, 140, 158, 174, 176, 300, 301, 398
Virtues 87, 93, 98, 128, 150–153, 156, 161, 172, 173, 179, 184, 188, 206, 217, 234, 262, 266, 269, 272, 278, 288 299–300, 301, 304, 380, 392, 396, 402, 409, 432
   cardinal, intellectual, moral, theological 151
   chastity 87, 91, 101, 110, 138, 140, 212, 213, 236, 316, 360
   continence as a virtue 300–302
Viviano, B. 45
Vocation 1, 2, 13, 24, 39, 42, 112, 137, 171, 173, 176, 218, 234, 244, 258–259, 268, 303, 316, 322, 361, 387
   leaven in the world xvi, 2, 9, 18, 160, 275, 358, 404, 411, 412, 436
Voluntarism 184–185

William of Ockham 156
Widows, widowhood 31, 32, 33, 50, 90, 91, 94, 98, 101, 102, 106, 112, 117, 137, 140, 141, 271, 351, 354
Wilken, R.L. 126

Zacharias, Pope, St 134

SCRIPTURAL INDEX

Genesis 158, 174, 214, 285, 286, 291–292, 303–304
   1:22 34
   1:26–31 23–24, 44, 97
   2–3 23–24, 44, 59, 65, 104, 379
   3:16 104
   4:1–16 51
   7:9 44
   9:1 34
   12:2–3 34
   21:8–14 50
   22:2 36
   24 28–29
   24:67 36
   25:27–34 50
   27:1–40 30, 35, 50
   37:1–4 50

Exodus
   21:10–11, 22 29

Deuteronomy
   6:1–9 33, 38, 115
   7:3–4 32
   11:18–21 33
   20:7 29
   21:1–4 31
   22:13–29 30–31, 32

Leviticus
   18:6–17 32
   19:20 31
   21:7 32, 42

2 Samuel
   16:20–22 30

Ezra
   10 32

Book of Tobit 36, 128, 311–312

Psalms
   110 101
   128 37
   136 37
   139 24

Song of Songs 36, 310–311

Isaiah 52, 306
   54:5–8 34
   62:4–5 34

Jeremiah 52
   3:8–14 32

Ezekiel
   16:6–14 34
   44:22 32, 42

Hosea 37, 52
   2:4 32
   2:16 34
   2:18 29
   6:6 52
   16:2–20 34

Malachi
  1:10–16 31
  2:10, 14 34
  2:16 42

Matthew 174, 291
  1:1–17 39
  1:25 100–101
  4:18–19 2
  5:28–32 43, 98, 285, 353
  7:7–11 50
  9:14–25 10, 50, 51
  11:25 50
  12:46–50 53
  15:4–6 50
  15:19 45
  15:21–28 50
  17:14–18 50
  18:1–5 50
  19:3–15 21–22, 43–44, 45, 46–
    48, 49, 158, 285, 351, 353
  19:16–19 50
  21:15 50
  21:28–32 50
  22:1–14 10, 52
  22:30 149, 285, 422
  24:40–41 112
  25:1–13 10, 52

Mark 291
  2:18–22 10, 51
  3:13–19 2
  5:22–43 50
  7:9–13 50
  7:24–30 50
  9:2–8 42
  9:17–27 50
  9:25–48 42, 50
  10:6–9 22, 158, 285
  10:17–19 50

  12:13–17 7
  12:25 285

Luke
  1:46–55 53
  2:52 53
  3:23–38 40
  5:4 1
  5:8–11 1, 2
  5:33–39 10, 51
  7:11–15 50
  8:41–56 50
  9:38–48 50
  11:9–13 50
  14:25–27 54
  15:11–32 50
  16:17–18 32, 41–42
  17:34–35 112
  18:19–20 50
  20:35 285

John
  1:32–34 52
  1:41–42 2
  2:1–12 52–53
  3:29 52
  4:46–52 50
  15:12 6
  17:16–18 63
  19:26 53

Acts
  10:47–48 2
  15:20 44
  16:15 2
  16:33–34 2
  17:16–34 83

Scriptural Index

Romans
    2:14–15 181
    7 107

1 Corinthians
    1:1–2 57
    1:7 47
    1:11–13 57
    1:16 2
    3:23 57
    5:1–13 58
    6:12–20 58
    7 88, 99
    7:3–7 60
    7:7, 8 59
    7:12–17 2, 60, 61, 353
    7:25–35 58, 61, 422
    9:19–23 55
    11:1 58
    11:2–16 61, 62, 105
    13:4–7 391–392
    16:21 57

2 Corinthians
    2:4 57
    5:19–20 64

Ephesians 62, 64–65, 109
    4:17 64
    5 85, 91, 97, 148, 175, 176, 231, 262, 285, 290–291, 303–304, 331, 338, 379, 385
    5:9 64
    5:21 64
    5:25 4, 6, 158
    5:28 65
    6:1 65

Philippians
    2:5–8 5
    3:1–13 56

Colossians
    1:15–20 64
    3:18–21 63–64

Galatians
    3:28 56

1 Thessalonians
    4–5 55, 56

1 Peter
    3:1 2

1 John
    4:10

Hebrews
    13:4 136

Revelation
    19:7 70

www.ingramcontent.com/pod-product-compliance
Lightning Source LLC
Chambersburg PA
CBHW030330240426
43661CB00052B/1581